THE

St. Louis Baseball

READER

Sports and American Culture Series

Bruce Clayton, Editor

THE

St. Louis Baseball

READER

Edited by
RICHARD PETERSON

University of Missouri Press
Columbia and London

Copyright © 2006 by
The Curators of the University of Missouri
University of Missouri Press, Columbia, Missouri 65201
Printed and bound in the United States of America
All rights reserved
5   4   3   2   1   10   09   08   07   06

Library of Congress Cataloging-in-Publication Data

The St. Louis baseball reader / [edited by] Richard Peterson.
       p. cm. — (Sports and American culture series)
   ISBN-13: 978-0-8262-1687-8 (hard cover : alk. paper)
   ISBN-10: 0-8262-1687-0 (hard cover : alk. paper)
   1. Baseball—Missouri—Saint Louis—History—20th century.   2. St. Louis Browns
(Baseball team)—History.   3. St. Louis Cardinals (Baseball team)—History.
I. Peterson, Richard F.   II. Title: Saint Louis baseball reader.   III. Series.
   GV863.M82S7 2006
   796.357'640977866—dc22

2006012904

∞™ This paper meets the requirements of the
American National Standard for Permanence of Paper
for Printed Library Materials, Z39.48, 1984.

Text designer: Jennifer Cropp
Jacket design: The DesignWorks Group, Inc.
Typesetter: Crane Composition, Inc.
Printer and binder: Thomson-Shore, Inc.
Typefaces: Minion, Ballpark Script, and Full Block

Contents

● The Gas House Gang

● The House That Busch Built

THE

St. Louis Baseball

READER

Introduction

The Road to St. Louis

It was a St. Louis baseball team that first broke my heart, but another St. Louis team gave me comfort during the dark early years of my life as a baseball fan.

I saw my first major-league game on May 9, 1948. My hometown Pittsburgh Pirates came through in grand style that day by beating the Cincinnati Reds and All-Star pitcher Ewell Blackwell, 6–4. It was a perfect day for a nine-year-old beginning a lifelong love affair with baseball. While my father stuffed me with hot dogs and peanuts, but no Cracker Jack (I loved the prizes, but hated eating that sticky stuff), slugger Ralph Kiner, my boyhood hero, hit two home runs off the side-winding Blackwell.

After watching Kiner's home runs sail through Pittsburgh's polluted air and into Greenberg Gardens, I decided that there was nothing better in life than going out to Forbes Field and watching the Pirates. As long as I was at the game, the Pirates were bound to win, and Kiner would surely hit at least two home runs.

My youthful dream of an endless stream of Pirate victories and Kiner home runs came to a shocking and sorrowful end a week later when the St. Louis Cardinals came to town. My father wanted me to see the Cardinals because their best player, Stan Musial, grew up in nearby Donora and should have been in a Pirate uniform. That afternoon the Cardinals, with local hero Musial and his teammates Country Slaughter and Red Schoendienst leading the way, shellacked my beloved Pirates and taught me my first lesson about the pain of being a baseball fan.

I didn't know it at the time, but there was plenty of pain in store for me as a Pirate fan. In the 1950s the Pirates became one of the worst teams in baseball, thanks in large part to former Cardinal mastermind Branch Rickey. When

Rickey was with the Cardinals in the 1920s and 1930s, he created a baseball dynasty by building the first minor-league farm system in baseball history. When he moved on to the Brooklyn Dodgers in the early 1940s, he revolutionized baseball and built another championship team by integrating the national pastime. In the 1950s, when Rickey came to Pittsburgh, he decided, rather oddly, that the best way of creating yet another championship team was by signing All-American athletes from other sports. We had great basketball players like Johnny and Eddie O'Brien, but they discovered, years before Michael Jordan, that dribbling a basketball is no guarantee that you can hit a curveball. We even had a Heisman trophy winner in Ohio State's Vic Janowicz, but, while a triple-threat football player, he just couldn't play baseball. Janowicz was such a terrible catcher for the Pirates that once as he circled behind home plate in a desperate effort to catch a pop fly, one frustrated fan cried out, "Why don't you signal for a fair catch?"

Stuck with one of the worst teams in baseball history, a desperate Rickey turned to other teams for help, especially the Cardinals. He made several deals for players who were on the Cardinal championship teams of the 1940s, but unfortunately for Rickey and the Pirates, most of them were now over the hill. At one time in the 1950s, the Pirate pitching staff had Murry Dickson and Howie Pollet, starting pitchers for the Cardinals in the 1946 World Series, and Ted Wilks, the Cardinals' winning pitcher in the final game of the 1944 World Series. Rickey acquired an aging Erv Dusak, who played on the 1942 Cardinal championship team, and an ancient Walker Cooper, the catcher for the Cardinals during their three consecutive pennant years from 1942 to 1944.

Not all the former Cardinals were grizzled graybeards, but they played for the Pirates as if they were already washed up. Utility infielder Dick Cole was only twenty-five when he joined the Pirates, but he was so erratic on ground balls that he should have worn his glove on his shin. Joe Garagiola, who starred for the Cardinals in the 1946 World Series when he was only twenty years old, bounced around with St. Louis for five years before he was traded to the Pirates in 1951. Playing on a 1952 team that lost 112 games, Garagiola discovered in Pittsburgh that baseball is a funny game and parlayed his experiences with the Pirates into a stellar career in broadcasting.

Garagiola wasn't the only former St. Louis player to turn his ballplaying experiences with the Pirates into an outstanding career in another field. Johnny Berardino, the regular second baseman with the St. Louis Browns in the early 1940s, was acquired by the Pirates in 1950 after being placed on waivers by the Cleveland Indians. After spending a part of the 1951 season with the Browns, Berardino returned to the Indians, where he was traded back to the

Pirates, along with former Cardinal Ted Wilks, during the 1952 season. Berardino may not have thought that playing with the infamous 1952 Pirates was all that funny, but he did finish out his career with Pittsburgh's minor-league affiliate Hollywood Stars and eventually went on to a lucrative acting career on television as a regular on *General Hospital.*

Johnny Berardino was only one of several former Brownies who found their way into Pirate uniforms. Rickey may have been searching for the best young athletes or the oldest Cardinals available, but when it came to the Browns and the Pirates, he had to settle for has-beens with colorful ethnic names, including Fritz Ostermueller, Eddie Pellagrini, John Hetki, and Walt Judnich. The most colorful name of all, however, belonged to Bob Dillinger, who seemed to have the perfect moniker for a player who led the American League in stolen bases for three consecutive years. But when Dillinger came to the Pirates in 1950, he'd lost the knack for pilfering and was shipped to the White Sox in 1951 after playing in only twelve games.

Home-run king Ralph Kiner was the idol of Pittsburgh fans desperate for a hero during the dark years of the early 1950s, but my favorite Pirate was former Cardinal Murry Dickson. I was a small, slight Little League pitcher, and Dickson, without much of a physique or fastball, somehow, at the age of thirty-five, managed to win twenty games in 1951 for a seventh-place ball club. Unfortunately, he lost twenty-one games the following year and nineteen the year after for a last place ball club. Rickey then traded him to the Phillies, where he lost twenty games in 1954. Dickson's feat in 1951 also made me aware of the Browns' ace pitcher, Ned Garver, who in the same year won twenty games for the last-place Browns. Like Dickson, Garver was on his way to a twenty-game-loss season the following year until the Browns traded him to Detroit.

Besides the Pirates, the teams I followed most closely when I was growing up were the Cubs and the Browns, because they lost games as consistently as my inept home team. While my Pirates set a franchise record with nine consecutive losing seasons, they had to battle the Cubs for last place in each of those years. From 1947 to 1956, the Pirates with six last-place finishes and the Cubs with four reigned unchallenged over the lower depths of the National League. In 1957, as if to honor their mutual futility, they tied for last place. There were several bad teams in the American League during that period, including the Washington Senators and the Philadelphia Athletics, but the Browns were consistently awful. After winning their only pennant in 1944 and finishing third in 1945, the Browns celebrated the postwar period by finishing with a losing record for eight consecutive years before they moved to Baltimore after the 1953 season. Once the franchise moved to Baltimore, I lost interest in the old Browns, but that didn't prevent them from having three more losing seasons before they finally finished at .500 in 1957.

I didn't pay much attention to the Cardinals during the 1950s. With the exception of Stan Musial, who was winning batting titles on his way to becoming the player of the decade, the team played in the shadow of the Dodgers, Giants, and Yankees. After winning world championships in the 1920s, 1930s, and 1940s, the Cardinals managed one second-place finish in the 1950s and ended the decade with a mediocre .504 overall percentage. But they still played a major role in the fate of my Pirates, who were finally emerging out of their losing ways in the late 1950s on their way to a miraculous season in 1960 and their first World Series victory in thirty-five years.

After a long string of disastrous trades with St. Louis, the Pirates finally began to turn things around in 1956 when they acquired National League Rookie of the Year Bill Virdon from the Cardinals for local product Bobby Del Greco, who had the dubious distinction in 1952 of playing for the Pirates right out of a Pittsburgh high school. The Pirates also parted with left-handed pitcher Dick Littlefield, who had been a member of the St. Louis Browns team that moved to Baltimore before becoming a Pirate. Virdon was one of several key acquisitions made by the Pirates in the late 1950s that turned them into a contender, but when they appeared to be one starting pitcher short of winning a pennant in 1960, they turned to the Cardinals again and acquired left-hander Vinegar Bend Mizell for a couple of minor-leaguers.

As I was dancing in the streets of downtown Pittsburgh after Bill Mazeroski's dramatic home run defeated the Yankees in the 1960 World Series, I had no idea that second baseman Julian Javier, one of the minor-leaguers that the Pirates traded away for Mizell, would become one of the stalwarts of the Cardinals championship teams in the 1960s. By the 1963 season, after a shocking three-way trade between the Cardinals, Pirates, and Cubs, Javier was joined by Dick Groat, the National League's Most Valuable Player in 1960 and one of the few Rickey All-Americans who could actually play baseball. In 1964 the Cardinals corrected their foolishness in trading away Bill Virdon with their own steal of the century, acquiring Lou Brock from the Cubs. They went on to win their first world championship in nearly twenty years.

In the 1960s, while the Cardinals were winning three National League pennants and two World Series titles, I made a decision that would eventually send me on the road to St. Louis or, more accurately, to a university town one hundred miles south of St. Louis, but a hotbed for Cardinal baseball. In the 1960s I completed my undergraduate degree at a state college not too far from Pittsburgh and went on to graduate school at nearby Kent State. In 1969

I completed my Ph.D. in English and accepted a teaching position at Southern Illinois University. I was thrilled with the teaching opportunity, but the baseball fan in me was unhappy with the idea of living 650 miles from Pittsburgh and my Pirates.

My frustration increased once I moved to southern Illinois because my Pirates, helped along by former Cardinals Nellie Briles and Dave Giusti, started winning division titles. They also won pennants and World Series titles in 1971 and 1979. I was able to ease my pain by watching the Pirates on WGN out of Chicago, WTBS out of Atlanta, and KPLR out of St. Louis, or by listening to radio broadcasts out of Pittsburgh at night on a crackling and fading signal from KDKA. I also went up to Busch Stadium from time to time with a carload of my new colleagues, but only when the Pirates were in St. Louis. When one of my colleagues, an amateur photographer, gave me copies of the shots that he took of Roberto Clemente and Willie Stargell during batting practice, I framed them and still have them hanging in my study.

The Cardinals, after matching their 1930s and 1940s successes in the 1960s, struggled in the 1970s and finished the decade with their first overall losing record since the 1910s. There were a number of good things that happened in the 1970s for Cardinal fans, including MVP awards for Joe Torre and Keith Hernandez and a record-shattering season and career stolen-base records for Lou Brock, but it was also the decade that saw the retirement of the great Bob Gibson and the firing of popular Red Schoendienst after a record twelve consecutive seasons as the Cardinals' manager.

The Cardinals didn't regain their championship ways until they hired Whitey Herzog in 1980. Playing Whitey Ball, they turned the baseball hat trick for the fourth decade in franchise history by winning three pennants in the 1980s. In 1982 they won their ninth and final World Series title of the twentieth century, and with their aggressive, hit-and-run style of play, made baseball interesting at a time when I badly needed a distraction. In 1985, just as the Cardinals were finishing their season with 101 wins and their fourth consecutive year with an attendance figure of more than two million fans, an article appeared in *The Sporting News* detailing the collapse, both on and off the field, of my Pittsburgh Pirates. There were even rumors that the Pirate franchise would be moving to another city.

While I grimly contemplated the possibility of my home team becoming the New Orleans Pirates, I found some relief in following the Cardinals. I admired Whitey Herzog's boldness in trading hotshot and hothead Gary Templeton for Padres shortstop Ozzie Smith. At a time when former Cardinal George Hendricks was being derided in Pittsburgh as "Joggin' George" because he wouldn't run out ground balls, I had fun watching Vince Coleman steal his way to Rookie of the Year honors. While Pirates were being traded for calling their general manager a bozo and even the team mascot was implicated in a drug scandal, I watched Willie McGee bat and field his way to the National League MVP Award, Tommy Herr become one of the best clutch hitters in baseball, and John Tudor, after being acquired in a trade with the Pirates for the jogging Hendricks, win twenty-one games.

The Pirates managed to survive their decade from hell and, under Jim Leyland, won three straight division titles from 1990 to 1992. They also prevented Joe Torre from having the success Whitey Herzog enjoyed in the 1980s. In 1995, in the midst of his second losing season, Torre was fired by new general manager Walt Jocketty. By 1995 my Pirates were also floundering and were once again on the verge of moving to another city. The Pirates were saved by new ownership and the promise of a new ballpark, but even with PNC Park to attract fans, the Pirates went on a binge of consecutive losing seasons that continued well into the new century.

As for the Cardinals, under the leadership of new manager Tony La Russa, they surged back into contention, eventually won several division titles, and played their way back into the World Series in 2004. In 1997 they acquired Mark McGwire from Oakland, and the following year they became America's team when McGwire shattered Roger Maris's single-season home run record. With record-shattering attendance to match McGwire's heroics, the Cardinal fans, regarded as the most loyal and knowledgeable in baseball, became known as the Cardinal Nation.

The St. Louis Baseball Reader is a tribute to the Cardinal Nation and to those loyal fans who loved and remember the old St. Louis Browns. It is also a celebration of the many legendary stars and colorful characters who wore St. Louis uniforms and the wonderful storytellers who wrote about them. The collection includes the works of Hall of Fame writers who covered St. Louis baseball during their careers. We have Bob Broeg's insightful pieces on the diverse personalities of the great Dizzy Dean and Stan Musial, J. Roy Stockton's famous essay on the Gas House Gang, and Red Smith's study of the quiet dignity of Jesse "Pop" Haines. There are also essays by nationally prominent writers in praise of Cardinal athletes, like Roger Angell's on Bob Gibson, George Will's on Curt Flood, and Jim Murray's on Ozzie Smith.

The storytelling begins with a section on the voices of fans, broadcasters, and writers that includes novelist John Grisham, who grew up a Cardinal fan in Mississippi, and Jack Buck, the most identifiable voice in Cardinal history. After that, *The St. Louis Reader* goes back to the beginnings of St. Louis baseball, from its founding father to "Der Poss Bresident," Browns' owner Chris Von der Ahe, then weaves its way through a rich tapestry of baseball immortals, including George Sisler and Rogers Hornsby, and the championship ball clubs that turned the Cardinals into a dynasty. There are also a number of oral history pieces and personal accounts of significant events and characters in St. Louis baseball history, ranging from Grover Cleveland Alexander's version of the climactic moment in the 1926 World Series and Bill Veeck's delightful story of his wild ride as the last owner of the Browns to Whitey Herzog's recollection and regrets about the play that cost the Cardinals the 1985 World Series.

The history of St. Louis baseball is a tale of two teams. The St. Louis Browns, after a promising beginning in the American League, became the city's lovable losers until the franchise flew away to Baltimore after the 1953 season. The St. Louis Cardinals, after struggling for decades, became a dynasty in the 1920s, 1930s, and 1940s. By the end of the twentieth century the Cardinals had become the National League's most successful and respected franchise and, by the first decade of the twenty-first century, had moved into a new baseball palace befitting its lofty position in baseball history. St. Louis fans, no doubt, will have much to celebrate in the future, but *The St. Louis Baseball Reader* is a reminder of the city's extraordinary baseball past, told by those who were either eyewitnesses or participants in the glory.

Fans, Broadcasters, and Writers

Often, when a player signs a free agent contract to play for the Cardinals, he will tell the press that the loyalty of St. Louis baseball fans was an important part of his decision. Celebrated novelist John Grisham and broadcaster Bob Costas are but two of the legion of baseball fans who either grew up with St. Louis baseball or became converts later in life. In their short essays, they eloquently express the appeal of the great Cardinal tradition and the passion, civility, and knowledge of the St. Louis baseball fan.

Growing Up with the Game
John Grisham ——————————————————————————————

My first memory of throwing and catching a baseball goes back to the age of five, or maybe six—those years are not that clear. It was not a leisurely game of catch with my father, nor was it a pickup game in the neighborhood. It was beside an old barn, at the edge of a cotton field in rural Arkansas, with a man I would never see again. But I would always remember him.

I was throwing with Juan, a migrant Mexican worker on our farm. I had a ball and glove that I'd found under the Christmas tree months earlier. Juan had neither. His hands were like leather, and he could throw a baseball from our house to our barn, which seemed like a mile. We worked on my fastball and my curve, and I have often suspected that Juan was the first of many to realize the severe limits of my talent. But he was patient, and after a long day of picking cotton, I could always coax him into another game of catch. We would throw until dark, then I would walk to the front porch and listen to a game on the radio. Juan would go to sleep.

We were Cardinals fans, and the highlight of every day was the sound of Harry Caray's voice coming to us all the way from St. Louis. My grandfather had followed Dizzy Dean and the Gas House Gang. My father worshipped Stan Musial. My Cardinals were Bob Gibson and Lou Brock. Baseball links generations like no other sport and few other traditions. Our church and family were the most important institutions. Baseball was a very close third.

After we left the farm, we moved each summer to a different town around the Deep South. My brothers and I could instantly judge the quality of life in every new place by a quick inspection of the local ball fields. We usually arrived too late to register for the youth leagues, and so we spent hours each day playing pickup games with the neighborhood kids.

I was ten before I wore my first uniform. I wore it badly and played even worse, but when I dressed for a game, I felt like a Cardinal. The coach wisely kept me on the bench, but because he was a good coach, he taught me my first lessons from baseball. If you want to play more, then practice more.

The second lesson quickly followed the first. We lost every game but two. Winning is easy, but losing with grace takes guts. Our coach made us smile after each loss. Baseball is a game of failure, he said. Get three hits at ten at bats, and they'll put you in the Hall of Fame.

My career peaked when I was twelve. I had some nice stats. I made the all-star team and realized that the major leagues would indeed be just a few years away. This brought about the third lesson. The game will humble you. Get cocky, believe it when others say you're good, and a slump will arrive overnight and last two weeks.

In the spring and the summer, our lives revolved around the ballparks in those small towns. We would play all day on the fields, then run home, clean up, put on our uniforms, and hustle back, lay the chalk, rake around the bases, cut the grass, fill the water coolers, warm up, and get ready for the real games.

Since there was little else to do in town, everyone came to the ballpark. The fathers and the old men brought their lawn chairs and sat behind home plate where they corrected the umpires and yelled instructions to those of us on the field. Between innings they relived their youths with tales of home runs hit over trees and sliders that would buckle knees. The mothers and the grandmothers would gather near the bleachers where they would watch the toddlers, and maybe the game, and plan church socials and weddings and talk about the urgent social matters of the town. The older teenagers would hang together behind a dugout. Some would hold hands and sneak away; others would actually hide in bushes and smoke. There was always a crying baby or two because everybody came to the games.

I remember all sorts of activities taking place during our games. Peas were shelled, quilts knitted, checkers played, votes solicited and promised, fights started and settled, romances carried out in the shadows behind the bleachers. And through it all you could hear Harry Caray somewhere in the background, in his colorful, scratchy voice, describing every play of our beloved Cardinals.

The languid and sporadic pace of baseball allows folks to visit, to engage, to catch up on important matters. No other sport is less rushed.

My fondest childhood memories are of those long, hot summer nights at the ballparks with everyone I knew gathered close by, watching us boys play our games. I can still feel the heavy air, and the dust from the infield, and the sweat of the action, and I can still hear the sound of the game—the chatter from the infield, the shouts from the coaches, the calls from the umpires, the idle laughter of the old men behind the backstop, the cheers from the mothers, and the encouragements from the fathers, the babies, the Cardinals on the radio.

As children we were not allowed to play baseball every day; we were expected to. It made us laugh and cry, win and lose; it broke our hearts and made us feel like champions. And it brought everyone together.

Baseball was life in those wonderful days.

Bob Costas Will Never Be as Young as He Looks Today
Bob Costas ——————————————————————————

During the McGwire-Sosa home run chase in 1998, the national press descended upon St. Louis for that momentous weekend in September when the Cubs were here. One writer, from *Newsday* in New York, said that the combination of passion and civility among St. Louis baseball fans is what makes it the best baseball town in America, and I agree with that. Cardinal fans have tremendous passion for the game, they are extremely knowledgeable. The Cardinals have a rich history which the fans very much appreciate, but they also show appreciation for opposing players. You see very little of the kind of ugliness and mean-spiritedness that you see in other stadiums and arenas. It's that combination of passion and civility that distinguishes St. Louis fans.

I think it's also important in recent years that the new ownership went out of its way to make the ballpark reflect Cardinal history to disguise the fact as much as possible that it was one of the "cookie cutter" stadiums from the late '60s and '70s. All of the other ones, Three Rivers, Riverfront, Veteran's Stadium, they were all just soulless bowls. They managed to make Busch Stadium into a place that felt like a ballpark and had little touches that were not only pleasing to the eye, but acknowledged Cardinal history. That is a big part of it, too. Even though the game has changed a lot, and it's more reliant now on power, Cardinal fans have grown up with teams that have won in subtle ways. The real old timers remember the Gas House Gang, or the teams of the '40s. Middle-aged fans remember the teams of the '60s. People in their thirties remember the teams of the '80s and taking the extra base, laying down a bunt, playing hit and run, the smart subtle plays that make a difference in close, well-pitched games. Cardinal fans have a tremendous appreciation of that. That, in general, is what sets them apart.

I'm going to give you one memory now, because the other people are going to give you Musial, Brock, Gibson, Flood and Boyer, Mark McGwire and Ozzie Smith. So I am going to go down a different path. I am going to talk about one specific night in 1979. The Cardinals played an extra-inning game against the Astros at Busch Stadium, and the Cardinals had a part-time out-fielder named Roger Freed. Freed was the quintessential "everyman." He looked like a guy from a weekend softball league, and was a very clumsy out-fielder, but he had some power. Vern Rapp had been his manager in the minor leagues and he helped pave the way for Freed to come to the Cardinals. He didn't cut a dashing figure, he didn't have much finesse in the outfield, but he was a fan favorite, and one year he hit close to .400 as a pinch hitter.

The Cardinals are losing 6–3 going into the bottom of the eleventh. The Cardinals load the bases with two outs in the bottom of the inning against Joe Sambito, who was then the best left-handed reliever in the National League. Freed comes off the bench to pinch hit. Not many fans were even in the ball-park at that point. The paid attendance was only 6,349. It was during a kind of lull in the Cardinals' fortunes; they weren't really a contender, and it was before Herzog got there. There might have been 900 people in the park, or even fewer, still around by the time Freed comes to bat. In this sort of impos-sible everyman's "Casey at the Bat" situation, he lines a home run over the left centerfield fence . . . a two-out, pinch-hit grand slam that turns a three-run deficit into a 7–6 win and is clearly the single greatest moment of Roger Freed's life, or at least his baseball life. Stuff like that may happen to Barry Bonds with regularity, but it didn't happen to Roger Freed that often. Roger Freed actually passed away a few years ago. I'm sure he replayed that night in his head every day of his life thereafter. It was just so classic and so unex-pected. The fans just loved this guy so much because he was so unassuming and just happy to be in the big leagues. Freed cut such an unlikely figure on the field, and Sambito was pretty close to untouchable at that point. I can still see him rounding the bases and the combination of excitement and surprise on the faces of the fans. Even some people in the press box were kind of high-fiving over the kind of joy of it all. That's a memory that sticks out for me, that I think a lot of people are not likely to mention.

Growing up on Commack Island, Long Island, I knew of the Cardinals and their history. I often listened to KMOX on my father's car radio through the crackle and the static. KMOX would come in sometimes very clearly. I heard Harry Caray and Jack Buck and I knew there was a certain romance about the team. I got here in 1974. The Cardinals had just concluded a regular season in which Lou Brock stole 118 bases. It was a particularly exciting baseball season in St. Louis. People were still buzzing about it in the off-season. I noticed how KMOX's programming became very baseball heavy starting around early

February. Even in December and January, if you were doing a sports talk show, at least half the questions would be about baseball. The football Cardinals had a good team then under Don Coryell, but still half the questions would be about baseball. On January 10, you would still get more questions about baseball than about basketball or hockey, so you could tell it was a baseball town.

From France Laux to Mike Shannon, St. Louis fans have listened on the radio to some of the most colorful broadcasters in baseball history. Two of those broadcasters, covering a span of fifty years of Cardinal baseball, made their own baseball history when they received the Hall of Fame's Ford C. Frick award "for major contributions to the game of baseball." Jack Buck, inducted in 1987, preceded Harry Caray into the broadcaster's wing of the Hall of Fame by two years, though Caray began his Cardinal broadcasting in 1944, ten years before Buck joined him in the booth. Caray left after the 1969 season, eventually to become the voice of the Cubs, but Jack Buck continued his illustrious career as the voice of the Cardinals until his death in 2002.

Hall of Fame Acceptance Speech
Jack Buck

Ralph Kiner's Introduction:

"Jack Buck, sports director of radio station KMOX in St. Louis, has been broadcasting St. Louis Cardinal baseball for thirty-three years.

"A graduate of Ohio State University, he got his baptism behind the microphone during his collegiate days by doing OSU basketball and football. After which he became the baseball announcer for Columbus in 1950 and 1951, and Rochester in 1953, both Cardinal farm clubs. Rochester general manager Bing Devine was so impressed that he recommended Buck to the big club in 1954 as color man, sharing the booth with Harry Caray. Buck became the principal broadcaster in 1970 upon Caray's departure and he has been the voice of the Red Birds ever since.

"A versatile announcer, Buck has broadcast two All-Star games, four World Series, and eight Super Bowls. His goodness of tongue adds a refreshing enthusiasm to his broadcasts, which are enlivened by his wit and humor.

"His reputation for fairness has made him a popular figure among the players. Not as well known are his generous efforts on behalf of the St. Louis Cystic Fibrosis Foundation. He joins his contemporaries, Mel Allen, Red Barber, Bob Elson, Russ Hodges, Ernie Harwell, Vince Scully, Jack Brickhouse, Curt Gowdy, Herb Carneal, and Bob Prince, all previous recipients of the award. May I present to you, Jack Buck." (applause)

Jack Buck:

"Thank you, Ralph. And good afternoon, ladies and gentlemen, Commissioner Ueberroth and folks of the baseball world. What a lovely day. What a great weekend and what a terrific honor. You'll be happy to know that I'm feeling fine, and my pulse is at 169 and holding steady, and I fully expect to get through this time period in good shape.

"In the back here, in the library, is a plaque which says, Jack Buck 1924, which is my year of birth, dash, then a blank. It's very difficult for me to look at that plaque. When I go home I am going to send to the Hall of Fame, to Ed Stack, the figures 2020 and they can put it up there, 1924–2020, so that when I die they can say that loud mouth finally went, and now the Cardinals can hire a nice young announcer to do the work. I'll be 95 at that time.

"Congratulations to Jack Lang, to Jim Hunter, to Ray Dandridge, to Billy Williams. I had the pleasure of knowing these gentleman who are going into the Hall of Fame. Billy Williams batted in the ninth inning of every game the Cardinals and the Cubs played and the pitcher was Bob Gibson. They had a unique arrangement. He was some hitter. Sweet swinger from Whistler, Alabama, and I feel so happy for him. And for Jim Hunter whom I don't know as well. And when I was broadcasting in Columbus, Minneapolis had two, more than two, but two very fine baseball players, Willie Mays and Ray Dandridge. So I'm not unacquainted with another of your new inductees to the Hall of Fame.

"I was here twice previously. When Stan Musial was inducted, when Bob Gibson was inducted. And I had the pleasure of knowing the late Ford Frick. I shared a glorious moment with him one day in St. Louis when Mr. Frick dedicated the statue of Stan 'The Man' Musial outside our Busch Stadium. And so because I knew Ford Frick this award has even more meaning. So here stands a dirty-necked kid from Holyoke, Massachusetts, wondering how in the heck he got here.

"I want to spend the first half-hour of my talk. (laugh) I want to spend a little while giving thanks to people because I'm the sort of guy who, when you do a favor for him, the debt is never repaid. My eight kids are here. They're all boys except five. (laugh) And now you know why you couldn't get rooms in Cooperstown for this weekend.

"In 1950, the late Alan Bannister took a chance on an announcer who had never done a baseball game in his life and I've loved him ever since. And then Bing Devine in 1953 in Rochester, New York. And then the folks in St. Louis in 1954, and primarily Gussie Busch, a wonderful gentleman. Eighty-eight years old as of today, still going very strongly, and a wonderful friend of mine, along with his wife, Margaret. And August Busch now who runs Anheuser Busch and the ball club. . . . Fred Kuhlmann, Lou Sussman, and Mike Roarty, America's favorite Irishman and the best marketing man in the country. . . .

"Making the trip over here today is a fella that's always dangerous to say he's your best friend, but I kinda think that Bob Hyland, who runs KMOX, the number one radio station in the country, is my best friend. And he made the trip over here today. And Dick Brescia who hired me . . . for CBS. And the late Frank Miller, Neil Pilson, Bob Kipperman, and Frank Murphy. And my good friends at CBS-TV, and Hank Stram and Joe Theisman. I want them to know that I'm thinking about them. And Harry Caray, from whom I learned so much, both good and bad. (applause) What to say and what not to say. I hope some day Harry has the thrill of this moment. And the people I work with now, Mike Shannon and Jay Randolph. Ken Wilson and the others.

"I have eight healthy and wonderful kids and I wish they would stand, if I can remember their names. Beverly, Jack, Chris, Bonnie, Dan, and Betsy. Down there in front. There's six of them. (applause) And, I'd like to acknowledge their mother, Alice. And down in front, Joe and Alice. And Joe wants to be a broadcaster. And my wife, Carol, who holds all of this together for me. (applause) . . . .

"I have the number one job in baseball. Not the number one job in broadcasting, but the number one job in baseball. I don't want to be belligerent about it, but I kind of think, Mr. Steinbrenner and others, that St. Louis is not only the heartland of America, but the best baseball city in the United States. (applause) Boo me if you want, go ahead, that's what baseball is all about. We have a network of 110 stations, and I have the job every night of walking into the best seat in the ballpark and describing Cardinal baseball for the folks in Missouri and Illinois, and Kentucky and Tennessee, and Indiana and Oklahoma, and Arkansas, Louisiana, Mississippi, Iowa, and Minnesota.

"The thing that happened when they told me about this Ford Frick Award. All of my family, all of my friends, and the Cardinal fans told me that they were proud of me. And that made me so proud to have done what I was able to do, lucky as I have been.

"This job transcends play-by-play. I have taken advantage of it to do some good things for Cystic Fibrosis, for the police department, for Boys Town of Missouri, the Veterans Hospital and other hospitals, and kids that need a helping hand—Mike Fry, Lance Holeshowers, and a kid back in St. Louis who's as gutsy a person as I've ever met, John O'Leary. I've tried to help. I've tried to be a part of it.

"I have a couple of brothers here. Earl and Frank and another brother, Bob, and three sisters, Kathleen, Mary, and Barbara.

"I've had the pleasure of broadcasting Cardinal baseball. The first year I was there, '54, one Sunday afternoon in May, Stan Musial hit five home runs. I said, 'My God, does he do this every Sunday?' He did something every Sunday. He didn't hit five home runs every Sunday. But imagine the people I've had the fun of describing: Boyer, McCarver, and Maris, and Cepeda, and

Cunningham, and Javier and Groat, and, currently, Ozzie Smith and Jack Clark, and Willie McGee and Bob Forsch. And the best manager who ever managed, Whitey Herzog.

Most of all, most of all (I'm coming to the end of my half hour), the biggest kick I get is to communicate with those exiled from the game in hospitals, homes, and prisons. Those who have seldom seen a game. Some who can't travel to the game. Those who are blind. And after all of those years, I realize that my energy comes from the people at the other end.

Tuesday night we go home. . . . We play the Mets in St. Louis, and if you've never been there, if you've never been there, there's no way to tell you what you're missing. Such a beautiful sport with no politics involved. No color, no class. Only as a youngster can you play and as a pro can you win. The game has kept me young, involved, excited. And to be up here with the gems of baseball, and this is like, for you people, I'm sure, looking at some diamonds in the front window of a jewelry store. For me to be standing up here is a thrill and a joy I'll never forget.

Even though I've been doing it for so long, you know what I miss? I miss being with my ballclub. . . . So when I'm able to digest what has transpired here this weekend, and Tuesday night walk up into the booth, have the best seat in the house, and broadcast for a team that has a pretty fair chance of winning this year, I want the Cardinal fans to know, when they hear me, that I'm humble, happy, and very grateful. Thank you. (applause)

Hall of Fame Acceptance Speech
Harry Caray ─────────────────────────────────────

Ralph Kiner's Introduction:
"It's a pleasure for me to be able to be in this position to present the Ford C. Frick Award to a person that I've known since 1946 when he was broadcasting the St. Louis Cardinals games in my rookie year. For close to forty-five years this man Caray, with a brilliant colorful style, personified baseball in the Midwest before television blanketed the country and before back yards and front yards were covered with satellite dishes. Caray's outspoken, opinionated, sometimes outrageous approach was the public's pipeline from the Great Plains to the Eastern seaboard. His classic rendition of "Take Me Out to the Ball Game" during the seventh-inning stretch has been cheered by fans and ballparks throughout the United States. (applause)

"Caray began his major-league career behind the mike with the St. Louis Cardinals in 1944. After twenty-five years in St. Louis he migrated to California where he spent the 1970 season broadcasting the games of Charlie Finley's Oakland A's. He then moved on to Chicago where he announced for the White Sox for eleven years after which he went cross-town to Wrigley Field. For forty-three years, almost seven thousand games, he never missed an at bat until he was felled by a stroke in February of 1987. His ensuing comeback has been remarkable to say the least. Caray relishes his reputation as a fearless and outspoken critic. But no one has been a better salesman for baseball for close to half a century. I introduce Harry in the immortal words of Harry Caray, 'How can a guy from Mexico lose the ball in the sun?' (laughter) Harry Caray." (applause)

Harry Caray:

"I don't know. Thanks, I think, Ralph. Yeh, yeh, all right. We'll do all that. Well, here I am. (applause) You know, I've wondered. I really have wondered what I should say today. I've been told by others, some of whom are up here on the platform, how greatly I'd be affected by the emotion of the moment, and I am. You cannot possibly stand here and not feel the presence of the legendary figures who have been here before, and the more I think of all the history that surrounds me, the more inadequate I feel.

"What a thrill it is to be here today with such super great baseball stars as Johnny Bench, Carl Yastrzemski (applause) and Red Schoendienst (applause). Not forgetting the other great people who I've known through the years. By the way, Red Schoendienst and I broke in at the same time and with the same team, the St. Louis Cardinals. Red as a player and I as a broadcaster, and it's very probable that umpiring that day was the great Al Barlick, who's here, too. (applause)

"As I reflect on what I'm doing up here in such outstanding company, past and present, I look back on forty-five years of broadcasting. The thrills of the wonderful game of baseball which we all love so passionately. And then I think of the fan, and perhaps that's who I represent today. You, the fan. (applause) We are all fans of the world's greatest game, baseball, and I know that it is the fans who are responsible for my being here. I've always tried in each and every broadcast to serve the fans to the best of my ability. In my mind, they are the unsung heroes of our great game. (applause)

"The baseball players come and go, but the game goes on forever. The players, the writers, the broadcasters, no matter how great, are temporary actors on the stage. It's the game. It's baseball. Reaching new heights all the time. Generation after generation. I'm very proud of being some part of this important piece of Americana.

"And, speaking of pride, if you don't mind a little parental pride, there are three generations of Carays here today. My son, Skip, a great broadcaster in his own right in Atlanta (applause) and his son, my grandson, Chip Caray, who's just been named the television voice of the Orlando Magic of the NBA. (applause) Just think of it a moment. Three generations of Carays. All broadcasting major-league sports at the same time. It seems a mathematical impossibility. I must have been married when I was five years old. (applause)

"You know, I've been privileged to have as important broadcasting partners, such wonderful baseball players as Gabby Street, Gus Mancuso, Joe Garagiola, Jimmy Piersall, Hall of Famer Lou Boudreau, and Cy Young Award winner Steve Stone, and we in Chicago are so proud of our other Ford Frick recipients such as the late Bob Elson and Jack Brickhouse. Nor can I overlook my long partnership in St. Louis with another Ford Frick recipient, Jack Buck. (applause)

"Yes sir, baseball has given me many happy days and fine rewards, but this day, the day of receiving the Ford Frick Award, is the pinnacle, the zenith, the most important day of my baseball life. I feel honored and privileged today to be here with you. My wife, Dutchy, thanks you. Our children all thank you, and from the very, very bottom of my heart, I thank you. Thank you very much." (applause)

St. Louis has been blessed with some of the best baseball writers in the country. Two of the greatest, J. Roy Stockton and Bob Broeg, have received the J. G. Taylor Spink Award, named after the long-time editor and publisher of the Sporting News *and given each year at the Hall of Fame "for meritorious contributions to baseball writing." Stockton, who received the Spink award in 1972, was a sportswriter for the* St. Louis Post-Dispatch *for forty-one years, beginning in 1917. Bob Broeg, who began his long career as columnist and editor for the* Post-Dispatch *in 1945, received the award in 1979.*

The Stockton essay on the Cardinals' most colorful team is from his baseball classic, The Gas House Gang and a Couple of Other Guys, *first published in 1945. It was originally ghostwritten by Stockton in 1936 for Frankie Frisch. The Broeg essay on the personality of Stan Musial, destined to become the most popular figure in Cardinal history, appeared in a 1954 issue of the* Saturday Evening Post. *The essay gave readers "the inside story of the St. Louis Cardinals star nobody knows."*

The Gas House Gang

Ghostwriting was a common practice and a big business back in the lush twenties. Christy Walsh had a newspaper syndicate in those days, and ghostwriting was the bulwark of his business. The press-box boys called the ball players, who were supposed to be writing daily stories about World Series drama, color and inside stuff, "Trained Seals," but the boys with the typewriters knocked off some useful extra change by writing stuff to appear under the by-lines of Walsh's Seals.

Ghostwriting has faded out of the picture to a great extent, but occasionally a publisher gets the idea that the by-line of a performer in athletics will give an article more authority.

That's how the writer happened to do the following article in 1936, his last—so help me—piece of ghostwriting. Frisch kindly gave permission to use the piece in this collection. And the Old Flash did let down his hair and tell a lot during the process of collaboration.

By Frank F. Frisch ――――――――――――
As Told to J. Roy Stockton

The Cardinals were playing the Cubs at Chicago. We were one run behind in a late inning, with one out, Pepper Martin on third base, Ernie Orsatti on second, and Lonnie Warneke pitching, Ken O'Dea catching for the Cubs.

Burgess Whitehead hit to Bill Jurges, who fumbled momentarily, but recovered and threw to the plate to cut off the tying run.

Pepper Martin and the ball arrived at the same moment. Catcher O'Dea went sprawling in one direction and the ball in another. O'Dea scrambled to his feet, retrieved the ball and threw to Warneke, covering the plate. The ball and Orsatti arrived at the same moment. Again there was the thud of bodily contact. Warneke went sprawling, the ball slithered across the infield, and there was another ball game for the Cardinals. It was a fine demonstration of a one-two punch.

That night, Warren Brown, Chicago baseball writer and one of the wittiest wags in the business, climbed aboard the Cubs' train, New York–bound. Curtains were drawn. All the little and big Cubs apparently had turned in for the night.

"What's the matter?" Brown wanted to know in a loud voice. "Are you boys afraid that Pepper Martin is on the train? You all had better stay on your side of the tracks, or the Gas House Gang will get you."

It was during that summer of 1935 that the Gas House Gang name was pinned on the Cardinals. Perhaps Brown did it. Perhaps it was our uniforms. You can't play the game for all it is worth and keep your uniforms clean through a three weeks' road campaign, with the sun broiling you each day and saturating your clothes before the game even starts. And the Cardinals do play the game for all there is in it.

Pepper Martin and Joe Medwick probably were responsible more than any other individuals for the club's Gas House reputation. Martin is one of the most spectacular players the game has ever known. Barrel-chested, broad-shouldered, with a great competitive spirit, he is a picturesque figure as he charges down the base line like an express train, or takes off in a flying leap on one of his hands-first slides.

After one time at bat on a sultry summer day, he is grimy from spiked shoes to finger tips. He looks like a member of a Gas House Gang. Medwick, whose remarkable improvement after joining the Cardinals was one of the most satisfying things about managing the ball club, is another gasser. He goes after every fly ball and slides into every base as though a world championship were at stake, and he, too, picks up plenty of diamond dirt as he battles for his base hits and buckerinos, as he calls the financial emolument of his labors.

Late that summer we played a doubleheader in Boston and caught an evening train for New York. It rained during the second game, there was considerable sliding on the base paths, and our uniforms were a sight. There was no time to have them dry-cleaned, as we didn't reach New York until after midnight. The next afternoon we played before a large crowd at the Polo Grounds in the worst-looking uniforms I ever saw. They were grimy, stained, and wrinkled, and the New York writers completed the job of tagging us the Gas House Gang.

It never was a team of tough individuals, as might be expected of a group associated in newspaper headlines with the shadows of a vaporous-fuel establishment. We probably had less trouble with umpires, for instance, than any other club in the league. But it was a colorful collection of ballplayers, a team that put on a great show as it fought for pennants.

[Collaborator's Note: It might not be wise to ask the umpires for confirmation of one statement above. One day in Boston there were several close plays and Umpire Ziggy Sears finally had to put Frisch out of the game, for, of course, he kicked at each ruling. The next day Sears told Dizzy Dean that he had played ball for years in Texas, where spaces were wide open and men knew all the words, but that in all his life he had never heard a man who could compare, even remotely, with Frisch when it came to making swearing one of the elegant arts. *See* Magerkurth. *See* Moran. *See* Stewart. *See* Dolly Stark.]

Naturally, with a squad of twenty-three young men in fine physical condition and on edge mentally, there occasionally were outbursts of temper and mischief. But discipline was not a problem with the Gas House Gang.

One day in Brooklyn, one of the boys made three hits which were important on the attack, and then failed to catch a fly ball which had a bearing on the outcome. One of the players thought the ball should have been caught and told the other player as much in the clubhouse. One word led to rougher ones, and before it was even a good argument the boys were swinging at each other.

Cooler heads tried to stop the fight, but I called off the pacifists and told the fist-swinging pair to go to it. They swung viciously for several minutes, without doing any damage, though I thought they might dent some of the lockers. They were trained for baseball, not for the prize ring, and soon were out of breath. When I saw that each had enough, I stopped them.

"Come here, you birds," I told them. "Stand right there."

Soon they regained their breath.

"Now shake hands."

They shook hands.

"Now put your arms around each other." They did that.

"Now forget it. You're on the same side still."

If I had stopped them before they had expended a little steam and excess energy knocking out a lot of air, they might have nursed a grudge against each other. But they had made some dandy swings, each felt that his honor had been maintained, and I didn't hear them exchange an angry word after that afternoon.

Ball players do not always expend all their surplus energy on the ball field, and occasionally the efforts to entertain themselves after the day's work of entertaining the public make a manager wish his men could be more serious. But a sense of humor helps.

I was standing in front of the Kenmore Hotel in Boston one evening, drinking in the fine New England air, when something exploded at my feet, drenching me and several other persons who were standing with me. It was a paper bag full of water that had been tossed from an upper window. If it had scored a clean hit, we could have dried off by jumping into the Charles River. It must have been a laundry bag.

There is a dignity to be maintained, even when you are packing a Gas House Gang around the country, and I went in search of the joker. It was not difficult. In such cases, *cherchez le* Pepper Martin, as we say in the Bronx. I found him, and when I saw his eyes and the grin, I knew I had my man. But what could I do?

"Frank," he said, "that was a slip. Honest it was. Now, if you'll just forgive me this once, I'll go out tomorrow and hit a home run for you and win a ball game." And that's exactly what the Wild Horse did the next afternoon.

Nobody plays any harder than Martin, but he has a highly developed sense of honor and fair play. Just a few days before this was written, he was at the plate at a critical time and I thought an inside pitch had touched his uniform shirt. I stopped the game and asked him.

"No, Frank," he grinned. "I wish it had a hit me, to force in that run. But I can't lie just to win a ball game. I'm John Brown if I can. The ball never hit me."

I'm devoting considerable space to Martin, because he really is the head entertainer on the ball club. He personifies the Gas House Gang spirit to the cash customers. He has boundless energy.

During the 1935 season he got the midget-automobile fever, which really was just a complication of an old trouble. His ambition, he always has said, is to win the five-hundred-mile automobile race at the Indianapolis Speedway. As a compromise, he bought a midget racer and called it the Martin Special.

Naturally, this did not make a hit with his manager or with his employers. A ball player ought to think in terms of baseball in all his waking hours, if he wants to be a success. But Martin bought the midget. It took up plenty of his time, too, not to mention the expenses. Telegrams were being delivered to him day and night, telling about the choked gas line, the inadequate cooling system, blown gasket, and other things that prevented the car from burning up the midget-racing world.

One night in Chicago I journeyed out to see a program of the races, taking a seat far up in the stands. A group of men pushed a midget car around the track. They gave up, one and two at a time, until only a pair of pushers remained. They were Pepper Martin and Dizzy Dean. And, mind you, Martin had to play a doubleheader the next afternoon.

Dean was an excellent partner for Martin as Pepper went through the world entertaining his public and himself. They did much to make the Cardinals a fine exhibition-game attraction. Martin was head man in a fancy juggling pepper-game act that never failed to wow the spectators, be it in Dublin, Georgia, or Bridgeport, Connecticut. When the actual game got under way, Martin or Dean, or both, would find the public-address system and entertain the spectators with a wise-cracking running account of the game, calling from time to time for members of the Cardinal troupe to step out and take a bow. This really served a purpose, giving the baseball public in the small towns a chance to see all the members of the Gas House Gang, though you might question the wisdom of a perspiring athlete risking pneumonia on a wind-blown roof, where frequently the microphone is installed.

Martin and Dean both had a highly developed sense of humor and gift of showmanship. On a burning summer's day, with the thermometer at 110 degrees, they found scraps of paper and sticks of wood, and built a fire in front of the dugout. They obtained blankets and mocked the blazing sun as they squatted, Indian fashion, in front of the fire. Of course, their public guffawed.

A rodeo was in progress in St. Louis, and Dizzy and Pepper were invited to appear before their public. Ignoring the dangers of equitation, they mounted horses and engaged in a calf-roping contest. The horse wasn't fast enough for Dizzy, so he leaped to his own feet, pursued the calf and wrestled with it in great glee as the crowd roared. And the next day the boys had to play a ball game.

Naturally, some of the pranks tried managerial patience. It was nothing unusual to find the clubhouse dressing room cluttered up with volunteer entertainers that Martin had picked up on the streets. Pepper loves music, as long as it is hillbilly music. At Sportsman's Park I was making my way from the field to the clubhouse after batting practice, for the meeting that a major-league club holds almost every day, and always before an important series or game. I heard strains of music and thought that Doctor Weaver, the club trainer, had the radio turned on unusually loud in the rubbing room. But when I entered the clubhouse, it was bristling with hillbilly musicians. Pepper had chanced upon a father and his five children wandering the streets with guitars, mandolins, and fiddles, and had piloted them to the ball park, through the press gate, and into the clubhouse to entertain the athletes. Hillbillies were perched on uniform trunks and benches, and Martin actually was hurt when I insisted that we could go over the hitters more advantageously if the hillbillies would scram back to the hills. He pleaded for just one more tune, so the musicians obliged before getting the gate.

Martin and Dean frequently carried the playful stuff too far. Late in 1935 we played the Dodgers in a doubleheader at St. Louis, and Dizzy was scheduled to pitch the first game. Mind you, we were in the thick of the pennant race, with a fine chance to win, as things looked then. Before Dizzy and Pepper went to the field, the question of their wrestling ability was brought up, and they grappled there on the concrete floor and stayed at it for half an hour. When they got through, Dizzy had hurt his arm and Martin had scraped a piece off his nose and had a cut above his eye, where he had struck a wire locker during the bout. Dizzy pitched and won his game, sore arm and all, but I believe we lost the second.

Another afternoon, Martin entered the clubhouse after we had finished with our batting practice. He had on a shirt that had been white, but which now was black with mud and grit. His face was grimy. He had to take a shower before he could put on his uniform. Chided about missing batting practice, he broke down and confessed he had been out at the midget-automobile speedway, in St. Louis County, racing several professional drivers. The stakes were a gallon of ice cream.

"Anyhow, Frank," grinned the irrepressible Martin, "Johnny Leonard Martin won the ice cream."

Shortly after that incident, Branch Rickey persuaded Pepper that it would be wise to lock up the midget car during the remainder of that baseball season and all other seasons.

Pepper's love of play runs up and down the scale. If he can't race midget automobiles, he'll find something else to do. If he offers you a cigarette, don't take it. If he tenders a match, beware. Either or both will explode. If you hear a wave of sneezing in the hotel lobby, Martin probably has been scattering powder to make the guests think they are catching their death of cold.

The World Series of 1934 prepared baseball observers to accept the Cardinals as the Gas House Gang. It was a cut-and-slash series, with no holds or slides barred, and we happened to win. It was bitterly fought, and there was much jockeying between the benches. A jockey is a player who verbally rides the opposition from the dugout, and we had some great ones on our side. One of the quietest, most gentlemanly members of our team was Pat Crawford, and it probably will be a surprise to hear that he turned out to be one of our great jockeys.

Of course the Tigers left themselves wide open for quips, and when you have Dizzy Dean, Crawford, Vance, and Durocher on a ball club, you have some pretty fair country quipsters. Publicity occasionally boomerangs against an individual. Schoolboy Rowe, for instance, was unfortunate enough, while broadcasting over the radio, to interpolate a "How'm I doin', Edna?" I dare say the Schoolboy wished many a time during that 1934 series that he had skipped that rhetorical question.

Then, the Detroit newspapers went to it in a big way as they covered the series. Mickey Cochrane was injured slightly and the next day a loud caption over a photograph in one of the papers proclaimed Mike as "Our Stricken Leader." Our jockeys got considerable mileage out of that one.

Sam Breadon and his lieutenants in the Cardinal organization, a far-flung farm system, deserve much credit for the color the team has had for years. They are always on the lookout for players who have that intangible thing called color, as well as mechanical ability.

The Cardinals have been colorful, spectacular, as long as I can remember them. They have won many spectacular games. Paul Derringer was pitching for us against the Dodgers in Brooklyn. Dazzy Vance, on the hill for the Dodgers, had an old trick that he used in trying to pick a runner off first base. Taylor Douthit was on first in a late inning, with George Watkins on third. Neither team had scored. Vance threw leisurely to first, giving Douthit plenty of time to get back easily. The Vance trick was to follow that leisurely throw with a fireball that frequently caught the base runner off guard.

Watkins took time out to tie a shoestring, so he could tell the third base coach to signal Douthit to try to draw another pair of throws, a slow one and a fast one.

Vance fell for the trick and as he leisurely tossed the ball, Watkins dashed for the plate and slid over safely, to win as fine a ball game as the Brooklyn customers ever saw. That was Gas House Gang baseball.

Many major-league clubs take exhibition games lightly, but not the Cardinals. We played four spring games in Havana, and the Gas House Gang played as though in a title series. They gave all they had on every play, and the spectators were happily surprised to see that the games were actual contests. The people were paying their money, and it was up to us to give them a fair return. Had we played in a half-hearted way, using second and third string players through most of the contests, the Cubans would have been disgusted with major-league baseball and would have wanted no more of it. I hope other teams that visit the island in the future will maintain the standard we set.

To be a great ball player, a man must love the game. If he is merely putting in a day's work, waiting for the first and fifteenth, he'll never go very far. And if the money angle is considered, as, of course, it has to be, because the game is the ball player's business, there is ample incentive for the will to win and the desire to excel.

Salaries go up as a club prospers. It is routine that players will get increases if the club wins a pennant and attracts large crowds.

Then there is the world-series extra money. A man who can get into four or five world series during his big-league career will have a substantial profit for his extra effort. The world-championship player gets a check from Commissioner Landis that calls for from $5,000 to $6,000, and the loser's share, in recent years, has run from $3,500 to $4,500.

That reward is worth trying for, and with that possibility always ahead, it is not asking too much to expect the ball player to give everything he has during the few hours he is on duty. It is not necessary to be vicious to play Gas House Gang baseball. No player wants to cut another one with his spikes. But the aggressive player is the one who breaks up the double play by upsetting the pivot man, and who slides hard for that extra base—the man who can give it and take it.

[Collaborator's Note: Frisch really does not care at all about the player who takes too much. In fact, despite his modesty, he was largely responsible for the team spirit, the daring baserunning and the belligerent aggressiveness that brought the Gas House sobriquet to the Cardinals. One spring the Cards were playing the Senators in an exhibition game at Bradenton. The Washington coach, on the third-base line, caught a signal and called loudly to the batter that the next pitch would be a fastball.

Such information makes it pleasant for the batter, and this particular one hit the fastball against the fence. The coach and the Washington players on the bench laughed uproariously.

An enraged Frisch charged in toward the young pitcher who happened to be working that game, and shouted to him, so the Washington bench could hear: "The next time he calls a pitch, hit the batter squarely between the eyes with all you've got."

Washington's bench was startled and somebody inquired if Frisch meant that. He barked back that he did; but, of course, he did not mean it literally. No manager ever orders a pitcher to hit a batter. But what Frisch meant and what all his men understood was that Frisch resented the Senators' heaping ridicule on the young Cardinal pitcher, and that if they did that again, he wanted the pitcher to make the batter do a bit of ducking.

"It's all right to catch signs if you're smart enough," Frisch explained to me after the incident, when he had cooled off. "And it's all right to take advantage of it. But when they try to make a laughing stock of you, it's time to do something about it."

As a matter of fact, the young pitcher narrowly escaped being sent to Houston, Rochester or Columbus, because he had to be told that he had been grossly insulted and that he ought to resent it.]

Maintaining discipline, of course, is one of the manager's most important jobs. It is not pleasant to have to take money away from your ball players. I have fined and I have been fined, and I'd say readily that I'd rather pay one than impose one. But that probably is the most effective way of discouraging offenders. You can talk yourself blue in the face to some men and they'll keep on breaking rules, but if they find their pay check short, they'll think a long time before breaking any more. I did not have to fine many members of the Gas House Gang. But in the few cases, a fine never was rescinded after being imposed. The fair way to look at it is that a player who does not stay in condition is jeopardizing the pennant and extra-money chances of his comrades. If one fine is rescinded, the effect of all such future disciplinary measures is lost.

Another important point is that you can't have two sets of rules for members of a club—one for the rank and file and another for one or two stars. That, of course, brings up the interesting and sometimes perplexing problem of the Deans.

To say that the Deans never caused anybody any trouble or worry would not be telling the truth. Paul, had he been the only Dean on the ball club, never would have caused a moment's vexation. But as the younger brother of the great Jerome Herman, he unavoidably was mixed up in most of the scrapes in which Dizzy found himself. However, the Deans never were granted any special favors. They were expected to observe the same rules that were in force for other members of the team, for the other members were just as important. Great as any pitcher or player may be, he could not ride to fame and riches without the necessary vehicle of a good ball club.

There were times when members of the Gas House Gang were very angry at Dizzy, to put it mildly. For instance, it would have been easy to start a fist-swinging riot that 1935 day in Pittsburgh when Dizzy lost his temper and made a spectacle of himself. But when the elder Dean recovered what might be nicknamed his equilibrium, he pitched so brilliantly and won so consistently that the boys quickly took him back as one of them.

Eccentric as Dizzy was, he stood out as a great pitcher, and his ability meant much to the team members financially. Dizzy's teammates will always remember his brilliant pitching and that of Paul as the Gas House Gang dashed down the stretch in 1934. The Deans could not have won without the team's attacking power and its defensive skill. The loss of a Durocher or a Collins would have been fatal to our pennant chances. But the boys all realized also they could not have won without the Deans.

The Deans caused me many vexatious moments, days, and weeks. I'll never forget one Eastern trip we made—a journey of bickering, threats, and conferences. Dizzy, who has a greater-than-average regard for his brother, Paul, got the idea that the younger boy had not been compensated properly in the contract that had been signed in the spring. I heard rumblings that he wasn't going to pitch unless Paul's contract was reopened and the salary increased, and finally the thing came to a head. He declared himself.

I talked to Dizzy and told him that it was not the time or place to start a controversy over a contract that had been signed a long time before. I suggested that if he and Paul thought they had a complaint, to wait until they returned to St. Louis and take up the business with the proper officials.

Time and again I thought I had the situation under control, but each time I was mistaken. Finally Coach Gonzales brought Paul to my room and, in front of coaches and a player, Paul said that he had no complaint, that he had signed his contract and was going through with it, and that he wasn't going to go on any strike. I summoned Dizzy to hear that, and it struck me that it ought to be convincing. But after listening to it all and saying that everything was all right, Dizzy decided that Paul really didn't mean it, and he guessed he'd better keep on with his strike for Little Paul. Each night, it seemed, there was an endless argument which led nowhere and, remember, on each next day I had to go out and play a ball game and manage a ball club.

There were excuses, of course, for a young man like Dizzy. Fair-weather friends, who always take a delight in basking in reflected glory, did much to put incorrect ideas in his head. A businessman in Florida told Dizzy he'd give him a fine job. Dozens of others told him the same thing. He overlooked the important point that without his baseball background, his value in other fields immediately would have diminished. If he had been J. H. Dean, clerk in a citrus exchange, no manufacturing company would have paid him $15,000 a year for endorsing a product. And if he had been J. H. Dean, a clerk, the fair-weather friends would have faded away, to appear at the side of some other new hero of the sport world. As Dizzy grows older, he doubtless will appreciate this fact.

I could see him learning as we went along. I tried to impress on him the fact that many a close game could be salvaged by a capable pitcher, if he'd continue to bear down, even in the face of discouraging breaks. And after the second game of the 1936 season, during which several things happened that might have been upsetting, he took hold of my arm going through the runway on our way to the clubhouse.

"Frank," he asked, "did I act all right?" He knew he had, and it was quite a satisfaction to him, but the boy in him wanted that pat on the back. He's all right. I wish I'd always have five just like him. I wouldn't mind going nuts winning pennants.

When I took over the management of the Cardinals, stepping from the ranks, I had to take what looked at the time like drastic steps, and there was considerable newspaper comment about my being a "John McGraw, Jr." There could never be another John J. McGraw. To me, he was the greatest manager that ever lived and there will never be another one like him. He was the real boss of his ball club and one of the most colorful characters I ever knew. I'll never forget some of the clubhouse scenes while Mr. McGraw was running the Giants.

He really was a tough manager. If you made a mistake, or what he considered a mistake, he'd slap a fine on you. But there were compensations. If you were fortunate enough to hit in the pinch and drive in the winning run, you were likely to find a check for $100 in your locker the next day.

John McGraw thought everybody should be able to "take it," and he spared nobody. Larry Doyle had been captain of the Giants, and a short time after I joined the club from Fordham, I was given that honor. The first time I made a mistake, or maybe it was my hundredth, McGraw ranted. He said he couldn't understand why fate was so unkind to him; that he thought he had the worst possible when he had a pinhead for a captain, but that colleges apparently turned out concrete heads and he'd never have another collegian on his ball club.

We lost a 2–0 game in St. Louis, and McGraw thought that Earl Smith, the catcher, had blundered. As we entered the clubhouse, McGraw began his harangue. Smith was the kind who would answer back and knew all the words. It was a great show. McGraw would talk till he was out of breath, and then Smith would swing into action. The players never thought of leaving the clubhouse under such circumstances. It would have been all your life was worth. And it was difficult at times to keep a straight face, for some of the verbal exchanges were gems. We'd just sit back in our lockers and wait. I managed to hide my face when I felt I would have to laugh, but Grover Hartley made the mistake of letting McGraw see him laugh. McGraw said that meant a trip to Indianapolis for him.

"It's all right with me," Hartley replied. "I'd just as soon play in Indianapolis as here." And the next morning Hartley was on his way to Indianapolis.

It was about five o'clock when McGraw and Smith started that argument in the clubhouse, and when McGraw finally dressed and departed, which meant that we could leave the park, too, the moon lighted our way.

There was another game with the Cardinals, in which we had a two-run lead going into the ninth. St. Louis had filled the bases, with Hornsby coming to bat, and, as captain of the Giants, I went to the dugout for instructions.

McGraw told us to be sure not to give Hornsby anything high and outside, and, as a matter of fact, not to give him anything good. We were to walk him and force in a run, rather than to give him one he could hit out of the park.

The first pitch to Hornsby was high and outside, and then it was high and outside the park, and the game was lost.

I knew what was coming as we made our way to the clubhouse, and I warned the pitcher to keep his mouth shut and let McGraw do the talking. But when the manager jumped on him, the pitcher couldn't restrain himself. He explained that the ball slipped out of his hand.

"Slipped, eh?" said McGraw. "Well, just slip me a $100."

McGraw was a hard taskmaster, unrelenting. We were playing an exhibition game in the South—Augusta, Georgia, or Jackson, Tennessee—and McGraw, a fine host, was entertaining some friends. During the night of festivities, in the Pullman-car drawing room, the question of base running and sliding was discussed, and as the sun was coming up about that time, they all decided to repair to the ball park for a demonstration of the proper sliding technique.

They must have demonstrated well, for at breakfast time we saw them climbing, grimy from head to foot, into a dining car on the railroad siding near us.

That morning at practice, we figured the boss was getting some needed sleep and we were making a merry joke of the day's work. But suddenly from an upper corner of the grandstand came a voice—the voice.

"Get to work, you rich so and so's," it said. It was John J. McGraw, never oblivious or neglectful of the duties of directing his ball club. We got to work.

McGraw was a fine character as well as a great baseball man, and it was a privilege to be associated with him. Hard taskmaster that he was, and brutal at times, he never carried a grudge. Things that were said in the heat of battle were forgotten quickly. There is no room for likes and dislikes in baseball, and he had none except a burning desire to win. You don't like your players or dislike them. You can't go far with a friendship team. There's no room for sentiment in baseball if you want to win.

The Mystery of Stan Musial
Bob Broeg

Among the myths which have matured with Stan Musial is the belief that the only interesting thing about him is his ballplaying. In this view, once you've described the $80,000-a-year star of the St. Louis Cardinals as the greatest player of his era, you've said it all.

Characteristically, the men who have competed with and against him get far more annoyed at this notion than Musial does himself. One of his distinguishing qualities is the amused tolerance with which he reacts to the misconceptions that have grown up about him.

It is true that Musial, unlike the usual big star, has done nothing to impress his personality on the fans by his conduct on or off the playing field. He has not disregarded training rules with the reckless abandon of a Babe Ruth, once fined $5,000 for failing to keep in shape. He has not feuded with sport swriters and spectators in the manner of a Ted Williams. He has not held himself aloof with the intriguing moodiness of a Joe DiMaggio, nor kept sounding off on controversial matters like a race-and-social-conscious Jackie Robinson.

However, while Stan Musial is no temperamental star, neither is he any colorless automaton. He is a bright-eyed, lighthearted thirty-three-year-old businessman who laughs heartily at all jokes, including his own, performs parlor magic tricks with a professional patter, and thrives on everyday living.

He has a zest for conventional diversions such as sprinkling his sun-parched patch of lawn in a ranch-style section of Southwest St. Louis. He used to pass a lot of time that way when the Cardinals were home, exchanging small talk with his neighbors or gleefully dousing his three young children under the cooling spray. He gave this up, though, after incurring a painful, strength-sapping sunburn.

"After a ballplayer is thirty," he says, smiling, "he's got to baby himself in the daytime to be strong and full of zip at night."

Stan the Man, an awesome term awarded him by shuddering Brooklyn fans several years ago, recognizes the financial gain to club owners and players, himself included, from the use of artificial illumination to play a game he firmly believes was meant for "the good ol' sunshine." However, he insists that night ball and the related schedule scrambling have shortened other careers and will cut his. Yet, over the years—and this had to be proved to him with cold statistics—he has hit better under the lights than in the daytime. The suspicion, therefore, is that the irregular hours and living habits have interfered more with his casual desires than with his career.

If it weren't for the frequent hurry-up demands of baseball schedules as now constituted, this poor boy who struck it rich would make every meal a production, home or away. He owns a half interest in a prospering St. Louis restaurant noted for its cuisine, but prefers the culinary art of his wife, Lillian, whose Polish cooking is surpassed only by her pastries. She hasn't forgotten, either, that since his mother sold him on the blood-building virtues of liver when he was a boy, he dutifully expects to eat it at least once a week.

On the road, when the night-day-night complications of the schedule don't interfere, Musial and roommate Red Schoendienst are the last to leave the clubhouse. Unless the traffic of autograph seekers is too heavy or unruly, Stan obligingly signs his name for one and all, quipping with the kids as he puffs a cigar at a rakish angle. He doesn't drink in his own restaurant, because of the ugly gossip that would be bound to result, but elsewhere he and Red stop for a beer or two, and if they've played an afternoon game, a few d'oeuvres to kill their hunger. Then they retire to their hotel room for an hour's rest before tackling the thickest steak or the most succulent lobster in town.

"The only time he'll hurry," says Schoendienst, who has come to enjoy the leisurely dining, long-sleeping routine, "is to catch a good live show on Broadway. We seldom see a movie—we eat too late and too long."

Schoendienst and Musial's wife are the best authorities for the statement, amply supported by people in Donora, Pennsylvania, that fame and fortune haven't changed Stan.

"Except to have—what would you call it?—more finesse and polish, he's still the same," says the star's pretty spouse of fifteen years, the former Lillian Labash, daughter of the corner grocer back home in Donora. "He's as patient with me and the children as he is with people who insist on taking up his time."

Musial's roomie of eight years' standing, Schoendienst, the Cardinals' master second baseman and their second-highest-paid player at $45,000, has a more amusing appraisal. "Sure he's changed," Red says blithely. "He's hitting the ball harder."

Stan never hit the ball harder than on May second of this year. In the reddest-letter day of his brilliant thirteen-year big-league career, he became the first player in major-league history to hit five home runs in one day. After getting the first three in the opening game of a double-header with the New York Giants, he was relaxing happily with a ham-and-cheese sandwich and a glass of milk when his excited wife, who attends about half of the team's home games but did not get to the park that day, called on the clubhouse phone to congratulate him.

Lil and Stan laughed as happily as school kids, remembering the only previous time he had hammered three home runs in one game. That had been during the penny-pinching past, in 1941, when he was playing with Spring-field, Missouri, in the Class C Western Association. Lil hadn't seen those three home runs, either, even though that time she had been at the game. Their first child, son Dickie, was then an infant, and his needs for maternal diaper service had coincided exasperatingly with the innings in which Stan cleared the fences.

When this time Musial hit two more homers in the second game, reporters who crowded into the clubhouse to ask him how it felt to set such a record found Musial actually open-mouthed in pleased surprise.

His lopsided grin was even more pronounced than usual as he asked, "You mean that none of those real sluggers—men like Ruth, Gehrig, Kiner, and the others—none of them ever hit five in one day?"

Musial meant it. He wasn't being coy. Neither was his son, Dickie, now a fourteen-year-old playground player of note, when Stan strode into his living room that evening, beaming proudly and scooping up daughters Geraldine, ten, and Janet, five. "They must have been throwing you fat pitches today, Dad," Dickie stated gravely. Musial chuckled the next night at the ball park when he retold that deflating anecdote with the same humor that makes him appreciate any good story—even at his own expense.

It's in the company of his teammates or with close friends that Stan Musial, the champion nobody knows, sheds his shyness to become a cutup. He has a prankish nature and a keen sense of musical depreciation that would have made him right at home with Pepper Martin's Missouri Mudcats of the Gas House Gang era a Cardinal generation ago.

Back before he went into World War II service, Stan acquired a taste for sleight of hand from Claude Keefe, a St. Louis insurance man and semipro magician. In the Navy, Musial practiced up. He was ready with a surprise for Cardinal players who welcomed back their slugger during spring training in 1946. With his lips pursed to suppress his inward giggles, he would gravely shake hands with each old buddy—then roar with laughter as the startled teammate withdrew, clutching a false right thumb.

At parties, if encouraged sufficiently, he'll demonstrate with a partial strip-tease the elastic qualities of a diaphragm developed through extensive calis-thenics and gymnastics as a boy. He sucks in his stomach to the backbone, then exhales to an aldermanic paunch. In the locker room he beats out juke-box tunes with a slide whistle, and drums coat hangers on an aluminum-backed chair. On trains, kibitzing a Pullman card game, he'll serve as water boy, stumbling at critical moments with paper cups—empty—that send less imaginative teammates scrambling.

Musial in turn takes good-humored kidding from fellow players, who may imitate him groaning under the weight of money bags. This doesn't bother him. However, he does recognize his position as the highest-salaried player in National League history. He is known as a lavish tipper around the league by bellhops, waiters, and redcaps. Musial shares with rookies and veterans alike the samples of hair oil, shave cream, cigarettes, and other products that manufacturers flood him with.

He declines to sit in on the penny-ante card games enjoyed by his teammates. "He wouldn't want me to say this," roommate Schoendienst confides, "but he makes so much money he doesn't want to take anything—no matter how little—from the others."

Only once back in 1940, when he was a Class D pitcher at Daytona Beach, Florida, was Musial ever thrown out of a game by an umpire. National League men in blue applaud him as a star who has made their job easier. "If he thinks you've missed one he'll say so, but that's all," explains Bill Stewart, senior National League umpire. "He's a perfect gentleman and a helluva ballplayer."

Baseball players' wives, frequently critical in their Kaffeeklatsches, have a high regard for him, too, on the testimony of Mrs. Charley Grimm, wife of the Milwaukee manager. Mrs. Grimm, who has seen players come and go for thirty years, describes the blushing Musial as a "sweetheart, so clean-cut and neat, friendly and polite—and such a fine family man."

Off the field, he would be as inconspicuous as any ribbon clerk were it not for the fact that people recognize him as Stan Musial. More than one headwaiter has been reproached for bringing to his table a friendly note or get acquainted offer of a drink from an attractive and fashionable female of leisure and boredom. Musial's answer is always the same. "Please don't let it happen again," he tells the headwaiter. "As for the lady, tell her I'm a happily married man with three children—one about ready to start high school."

Stan's family never meant more to him than early in the 1946 season, when the Pasquels, of Mexico, were raiding the United States baseball ranks for top talent. Musial, then earning a salary of less than $15,000 after eight years, was nearly popeyed when Bernando Pasquel dumped $75,000 cash on the kitchen table of his home in St. Louis and promised $125,000 more for five years if Stan would jump his contract with the Cardinals. Musial's head swam. He needed time to think and talk to Eddie Dyer, then St. Louis manager. Finally he refused the tempting offer.

"Like Eddie said," Musial told reporters softly, "people might point to Dickie or Gerry later and say, 'There go the kids of the guy whose word was no good.' I couldn't stand that."

As it developed, he was handsomely rewarded for staying. He is neither naive nor anybody's fool. He hasn't forgotten what it was like to face fatherhood at the age of nineteen on a meager $100 a month for seasonal baseball employment. Musial knows how to speak up for himself at contract time. For all his modesty, he is well aware that except for a weak-to-average throwing arm, he would be—as most baseball men say—the perfect ballplayer. So the four club owners for whom he has worked these last thirteen years have had to pay and pay.

Counting some $10,000 to $15,000 extra income a year for endorsements, plus his restaurant proceeds, Musial today pays taxes on close to $125,000 a year. From baseball alone, his pay comes to more money per game—$519—than it did for the entire season during his first three professional years.

The restaurant from time to time has caused him as much distress as the temptation—only occasionally succumbed to these last five seasons—to swing for home runs. He has licked both problems pretty well by frankly facing up to things.

To his sorrow, Stan tried to become home-run king after putting together in 1948 one of the greatest seasons ever enjoyed by any player. Hitting .376, he barely missed becoming the first major-league batter to sweep the board offensively since James (Tip) O'Neill of the gaslight 1887 St. Louis Browns. Musial finished first in hitting, runs scored, base hits, doubles, triples, and runs batted in. Only in home runs did he fall short. His total of thirty-nine was one behind the co-leaders Johnny Mize and Ralph Kiner.

"Kiner is right," Musial said the night he left for spring training in 1949, quoting a remark often attributed to Ralph. "Singles hitters drive Fords, home run hitters drive Cadillacs. I'm going out for the home-run title this year."

That might have been the right prescription for Kiner, but it wasn't for Musial, who for once was both wrong and greedy. He already was about to draw $50,000 a year on a two-season contract. And for one of only two times—the other had been in 1947, when he was weakened physically by an inflamed appendix—pitchers gloatingly learned they had The Man at a disadvantage.

Musial soon was manfully owning up to his mistake. "I've got myself to blame," he said. "Swinging for those home runs, I'm all fouled up. My timing's off. Pitchers are getting me out on stuff away from me because I've been trying to pull the ball too much. I know now I've got to hit the ball where it's pitched."

Happily, Stan recovered his Swiss-watch timing. He has had other slumps, of course. One of the most exasperating aspects of a slump for Musial is that some Cardinal fans and at least one former owner of the ball club have always been quick to blame it on his restaurant activities. Rumors invariably spread that Musial has been wasting too much energy on gladhanding customers and worrying over the financial state of his business.

Just for the record, the restaurant has done so well that Musial and his partner now have two of them. His associate on a fifty-fifty basis is a stout, close-to-forty character named Julius Garagnani. Most people call him "Biggie." Biggie is a malaprop who "prescribes" to this magazine, for instance. But although he murders the language, Garagnani knows his sirloins and his Musial.

"This kid," says Biggie thickly, "is the nicest guy I ever met. I don't want him around too much. It ain't good for him, or," Biggie adds slyly, "for the business neither. Bing Crosby doesn't sing every day in public."

Musial makes it plain that he sought out Biggie, that the restaurant man didn't come to him. "I hope," he says firmly, "I don't hear any more about my restaurant connection. If I did as well as the restaurant, I'd hit .400 every year. I wanted it as something to fall back on. One serious injury in this game and you could be through."

The worst injury scare Musial has had came in May of 1950, when he slipped in loose dirt rounding first base at Pittsburgh's Forbes Field. At the time he was hitting .450, the early-season figure he has always felt would be necessary for him to finish over .400. Gamely, because on one leg he was still the best hitter on the ball club, he continued to play, wearing a steel-ribbed elastic band to support his left knee.

The injury, though handicapping his hitting, was not serious. The night it happened, though, Musial's tan Slavic face and apple cheeks were pale as he related, "I tried to get up once, but I couldn't, and fell back. I said to myself, *This is it. I'm through. Thank God for the restaurant.*"

Even during the winter, Musial sees to it that the business doesn't interfere with the limited social life he and wife Lil prefer—a show with the neighboring Schoendiensts or a home party with a small circle of friends. Invariably, he'll excuse himself at the restaurant before nine o'clock, jump into his car—he drives a Cadillac, Lil has a Pontiac—and breeze the half mile to his home to kiss the kids good night and help tuck them into bed.

When the Cardinals are at home in the baseball season, Musial drops in at the restaurant at noon to confer with Biggie and go over fan mail carefully sorted by their secretary, efficient Shirley Anne. She estimates that Stan answers 10,000 postcards and letters a year, most of which request autographs, pictures, baseballs, public appearances, contributions, or answers to questions about hitting.

Since the winter of 1946–47, when he ran himself down physically chasing from one banquet to another, Musial understandably has tried to limit his speaking engagements. He's still a soft touch, however, for a religious group or school. He routed himself out of his living room on fifteen minutes' notice late one blustery, cold afternoon last winter because a Memphis high-school band, passing through town, had expressed a desire to meet him. Then, when the band's arrival was delayed by the weather, he waited two hours until they showed up.

Home or away, Musial has learned that a newspaper doesn't begin and end with the sports pages and comics. He reads slick magazines, preferring articles to fiction, and tackles an occasional well-recommended novel, especially one with a religious flavor. He'll go for a big prize fight or other top-drawer sporting event, and he has discovered the golfing thrill of shooting in the low eighties despite a long-hitting left-handed slice.

"Pretty good hunter now, too," says Schoendienst, a farm boy who was taken aback the first time he took the obviously inexperienced Musial on a quest for quail. However, Red relates that lefty Stan drew a right-hander's bead and knocked off the first bobwhite that whistled his way.

His sharp batting eye has won Stan the Man numerous record achievements as well as six batting championships and a chance to become the eighth hitter to pound out 3,000 hits. His only counterpart today is Ted Williams, who, going into this season, led Musial in lifetime average by .348 to .345, and in home runs by 337 to 257. Most baseball men give Williams a splinter's edge in hitting—and hitting alone.

"When it comes to team value, to trying for an extra base, to risking injury in a somersaulting catch, to playing when he's hurt and taking orders, Stan is in a class by himself," says Cardinal manager Eddie Stanky. He is echoing Billy Southworth, Eddie Dyer, and Marty Marion, Musial's previous bosses on the Cardinals.

The myths about the champion nobody knows include a belief that he doesn't care whether he plays any of the three outfield positions or first base. He does care, preferring right field, but it's not his nature to sulk. Besides, "I really don't care that much," he explains with an amateur's enthusiasm, "just as long as I get a tremendous feeling every time I put on a uniform. I think I'd quit if I couldn't hit .300, but I wouldn't want to guarantee that, either, because it's such a thrill to play."

Despite a deceptively streamlined physique, the six-foot, 175-pound Musial has been one of the most durable players over a long haul since Iron Horse Lou Gehrig, who ended a fourteen-year string of 2,130 consecutive games in 1939. Since his first full season of 1942, when he was exposed briefly to the two-platoon treatment, injuries have caused Musial to miss only sixteen games.

Ironically, it was an injury that converted him in one incredible year from a dead-armed Class D pitcher to a major-league hitting sensation as an outfielder.

Stan says, though, that he never doubted, from the day he began playing ball as a kid, that he'd reach the big leagues, and not necessarily as a pitcher.

"I could hit then, too," he declares, belying his shrinking-violet reputation and confirming his possession of an athlete's No. 1 asset—complete self-confidence.

Born on November 21, 1920, Stanley Frank Musial was the first son and second youngest of six children. His parents were Lukasz Musial, a small, wiry Polish immigrant, and Mary Lancos, a sturdy New Yorker of Czech descent. She was the daughter of a coal miner, who moved the family to Pennsylvania when she was a baby. There, at the age of sixteen, sorting nails in a Donora mill, she met Lukasz, twenty years old and recently from Warsaw. He wrestled 100-pound bundles of wire in the shipping department of the American Steel and Wire Company.

The community into which Stan Musial was born lies about thirty miles south of Pittsburgh in the industrial valley of the Monongahela. Donora crawls up a barren hillside as though to escape the belching smokestacks that line the riverfront like a king-size picket fence. To survive and flourish there requires ruggedness in its 15,000 people, most of whom are descended from the steppes of Russia, the forests of Germany, and the plains of Poland.

By all health and material measurements, Stan Musial, his wife, and his children are fortunate to have left Donora, twenty of whose inhabitants were victims of a death-dealing chemical smog in 1948. However, Stan retains a strong loyalty to his unprepossessing hometown. When the Cardinals play in Pittsburgh, Musial frequently runs over to Donora not only to see his mother—his father died wearily in middle age five winters ago—but also to visit other relatives and old friends.

As long ago as 1948, Stan backed off apologetically from a proposed biography in which he would have shared profits. The book necessarily would have detailed a family of eight's existence in a four-room, brown-shingled house on the north hill of the town.

"Look," he said haltingly, not trying to offend. "I don't quite know how to say this, but while my folks were poor, they were good to me. I don't want to do anything to hurt my family. I'm afraid this would be embarrassing." The project was dropped.

The story of how Stan Musial signed to play baseball is a legend now—how he cried until Papa Musial, set on his son taking a college athletic scholarship, relented and gave approval to a Cardinal farm-team baseball contract for sixty-five dollars a month. Few know, however, that Stan also had letters of inquiry from the Cleveland Indians and the New York Yankees, and that his heart really belonged to the nearby Pittsburgh Pirates and their hard-hitting Waner brothers. He signed with the Cardinals in 1937 only because their Andy French came to see him, while the others merely wrote.

By his own admission, Musial never would have reached the major leagues as a pitcher, though he delights in warming up on the side lines and kidding his Cardinal teammates that they're lucky not to have to face his "blazer." He did show enough in his third season of Class D pitching—at Daytona Beach in 1940—to merit spring consideration the following year by Columbus, Ohio, of the American Association, them Class AA.

By then, though, his strong left arm was almost lifeless as the result of a tumble late in the 1940 season, during which he saw considerable double duty as an outfielder for little Dickie Kerr, a veteran baseball man who managed the Cardinals' Daytona Beach farm club. The shoulder injury came just about the time Lil, with whom he had eloped on his nineteenth birthday, was to give birth to their first child.

Another Musial legend has it that the discouraged young expectant father was all set to quit baseball until Kerr, an untainted pitching hero of the scandalous 1919 Black Sox World Series, talked him out of it. To help the Musials hold down expenses, the Kerrs supposedly even rented a larger home.

This romantic little tale has appeared in print countless times, and until questioned about it for this article Musial has never bothered to straighten it out. "Lil had none of her family nearby, so the Kerrs invited us in as the baby was about to be born," he said. "Mrs. Kerr is as fine a person as Dickie. But they didn't take larger quarters, and I never considered quitting. I loved baseball too much. One hundred dollars a month"—five months a year—"was a lot of money then. Besides, I picked up a few extra dollars by clerking winters in Lil's father's grocery store."

The Musials remained grateful for the Kerrs' help—they named the baby after Dickie—and still correspond and visit with the Kerrs. Possibly the only time Stan has ever threatened to punch another ballplayer in the nose was at Daytona when a teammate spoke disparagingly of Kerr.

Something else that Musial has never before troubled to set straight is the pronunciation of his name. Back home, the family and foreign-born friends called it "*Mew*-shil." The closest that Stan himself can come to it now is "*Muze*-yil."

"I've heard it so many different ways, I'm confused myself," Stan says with a grin, "but it's properly pronounced as two syllables." The name gets its worst kicking around in St. Louis, whose fans readily went along with the unique baseball broadcasting of Dizzy Dean, extolling the hitting of that "*Mew-see-l.*"

While Dickie Kerr's help to Musial is well known, Stan says that Burt Shotton hasn't been given sufficient credit. Shotton, later a pennant-winning manager at Brooklyn, already was a baseball graybeard as leader of the Columbus club to which Musial was assigned for spring training in 1941. Sore-armed Stan couldn't pitch, but, oh, how he could hit!

"Shotton took me aside one day and told me he thought I could make it as a hitter and that he'd recommend to Mr. Rickey that I give up pitching for the outfield," Musial recalls.

Because Branch Rickey always has been one to push a prospect of intriguing potential, Musial's bat exploded in one season from Class C at Springfield, Missouri, through Double A at Rochester, to the Cardinals. In his first full season, in 1942, he batted .315 to help St. Louis to the world championship. The next year he climbed to .357 to win the first of his six batting titles—and the first of his three Most Valuable Player awards.

Although he runs and fields brilliantly and throws with an arm that has regained some of its earlier strength, there is only one really colorful touch in Musial's play—his picturesque and unorthodox batting stance. When he steps into the batter's box, he plants his left foot on the back line, loosens his hips with a hula wiggle that brings a titter from female fans, and describes a relaxing preliminary arc with his bat. He rests his right foot gracefully about twelve inches in front of the left, dips his right knee, crouches and comes set. He holds his thirty-three-ounce, thirty-four-and-a-half-inch bat farther from his body—twenty-four inches—than any other current major-leaguer.

From this position, poker-faced, his intent brown eyes peer over his ample nose and right shoulder. Ted Lyons, former American League manager and now a Brooklyn coach, once said, "He looks like a kid peeking around the corner to see if the cops are coming."

The peculiar stance, followed by a flat, level swing, is completely natural. Former teammates Terry Moore and Enos Slaughter, two of his greatest admirers, maintain that after spending 1945 in the Navy, Musial returned crouching more than before, but Stan acknowledges only two changes. In the service he edged a bit closer to the plate to oblige his buddies with more home runs. In 1948, stronger after off-season surgery for removal of an infected appendix and tonsils, he slipped his hands down from a one-inch choke grip to the knob of the bat.

Explaining his ability to combine a high average with more homers than usual into August this year, he says frankly, "I'm favored now by a livelier ball than before."

Approaching thirty-four, Stan the Eighty-Grand-Man hopes he can play long enough—"three or four more years"—to make the exclusive 3,000-hit club. He would also like to win two more batting championships and tie Honus Wagner, who also came out of the Western Pennsylvania hills, for the all-time National League record.

But records and statistics aren't all-important to Musial. He's too busy to worry—too busy hitting, helping the Cardinals win ball games, and raising his family in a style to which he was not accustomed.

Besides, he already has an epitaph which transcends anything in the record books. It's on a plaque that holds the position of honor in the trophy case of his first restaurant. It was presented to him by his teammates on a Stan Musial Night at the ball park several years ago. It reads:

To Stanley Frank Musial, an emblem of esteem from his teammates. An outstanding artist in his profession; the possessor of many baseball records; a gentleman in every sense of the word; adored and worshipped by countless thousands; the perfect answer to a manager's prayer; to this we (the Cardinals) attest with our signatures.

The Beginnings of St. Louis Baseball

In 1910, Alfred H. Spink, the founder of the Sporting News, *published* The National Game, *the first serious attempt at a comprehensive history of baseball. It preceded by one year Albert G. Spalding's* America's National Game, *a book often regarded as the first history of baseball. When the book was first published, it was embraced by prominent baseball officials, including American League president Ban Johnson, who praised* The National Game *as "the only real and complete history of baseball ever written."*

In his foreword, Alfred Spink declared that the goal of The National Game *was "to cover all the great happenings of the game," but his St. Louis bias is apparent in the high number of local personalities in his biographical sketches, including Jeremiah Fruin, portrayed by Spink as the father of St. Louis baseball. In a second edition, Spink published a letter from Merritt W. Griswold, who refuted the claim for Fruin.*

Jeremiah Fruin
Alfred H. Spink

Tall and straight as an arrow, standing over six feet in height, is Jeremiah Fruin, the father of baseball in St. Louis.

Mr. Fruin is at the head of the Fruin-Colon construction company, works out in the open air every day in the week, is as active as most men at 50, and yet in July next he will have completed his 80th year.

Mr. Fruin is a fine specimen of the advantages of outdoor sport and especially of baseball.

"Yes," said Mr. Fruin to me as I sat on the broad porch of his grand home in Arloe, "I have heard it said that I was the first to introduce baseball into St. Louis.

"But I make no such claim. I know there was some such game here before I arrived in the year 1862. But perhaps it was not the real simon pure article.

"I came to St. Louis direct from the cradle of baseball. I came from Brooklyn where at that time there were two great baseball teams at play—the Atlantics and the Excelsiors.

"The Excelsiors were the swell team and the Atlantics were a rough and ready set made up almost exclusively of Irish-American players. They could fight as well as play baseball. I played with the Excelsiors first and then with the Atlantics.

"The great players of the later famous Atlantic team were just budding into manhood. Start, Pearce, Crane, Charley Smith, Chapman, O'Brien, Pidgeon, and others of them were just beginning to be recognized as great players.

"Having played with them I had learned to catch the ball by giving to it as it was thrown, with the hands low down or high up as the occasion demanded.

"I had, of course, learned the rules of play that were in vogue then. I was able on my arrival in St. Louis, therefore, to give the boys I found playing out on Gamble Lawn a few lessons on the improved Eastern method.

"I played my first game as near as I can recollect with the Empires of St. Louis on May 10, 1862, the Unions being our opponents. I covered second base for the Empires. Two years later I was made captain of the Empires and I remained captain of the team for four successive years.

"When I went to the nine I found it composed of a rough and ready set who were ready at any time to call a halt in the regular proceedings to engage in a game of fisticuffs. But I quickly put a stop to that sort of thing and taught the men that the game could be carried on in a gentlemanly and sportsman's-like manner.

"The game at this time resembled much of the game as it is played to-day except that the player was out where the fielder caught the ball on the fly or first bound. There were few catchers then who had the nerve to stand up close to the bat. Most of the catchers stood fifty feet or more behind the home plate and even then often threw out men on the bases.

"Many of the great players who were playing with me then are now a power in the business world.

"The first battery of the Unions was made up of Bob Lucas, pitcher, and John H. Turner, catcher. When Turner let a ball get by him Bob cursed the little 'Red Head.'

"Gerald Fitzgibbon was the pitcher for the Empires. He is still alive and in the contracting business here and so is John W. O'Connell, now a wealthy painter in St. Louis, who used to handle the speedy underhand pitching.

"E. C. Simmons, now at the head of the Simmons Hardware Company, was I think the first captain of the Unions. But he was so overbearing and arbitrary that his players fell out with him and he went in another direction and started a team of his own.

"Charley Cabanne, Supreme Court Judge Shepard Barclay, Rufus Lackland, J. B. C. Lucas, and other prominent men of St. Louis were then playing baseball with the rest of us on Gamble Lawn. No, I do not claim to have been the first to introduce baseball to St. Louis, but I was perhaps the first to show the boys how to catch the ball easily rather than by fighting it, how to trap the ball, to make a double play and that sort of thing. Do I love baseball yet? Why, certainly. One who has ever played the game in real earnest will never lose his love for it."

The First Baseball Games in St. Louis
Merritt W. Griswold

Dear Sir—One of the reporters of "The Standard Union" of Brooklyn N.Y. showed me a few days ago a book written by you entitled the history of baseball.

To start at the commencement of the game in its first introduction into Missouri I would refer you to the files of "The Missouri Democrat" for the Winter of 1859 and 1860, wherein you will find published "the rules of the game," also a diagram showing the field and the position of each player made from a rough sketch I gave to Mr. Magee and Fishback, the publishers, or to Mr. Houser, at that time their bookkeeper, cashier and confidential office man (and, by the way, a mighty fine young man).

At this same time I was organizing the first baseball club, "The Cyclone," which name was suggested by one of its members, Mr. Whitney, of the Boatmen's Savings Bank.

Other members of "The Cyclone" were John Riggin, Wm. Charles and Orvill Mathews (the latter the late Commodore Mathews of the U.S. Navy), John Prathers, Fred Benton (later a captain under Gen. Custer), Mr. Fullerton (later a General U.S.A.), Mr. Alfred Berenda and his brother, Mr. Ferd Garesche, Mr. Charles Kearney (son of Gen. Kearney), Mr. Edward Bredell, Jr., and a number of other young men of St. Louis.

Soon after the organization of "The Cyclone" several others were started, viz: "The Morning Stars," "The Empire," "The Commercial," and later on several others.

The first match game played between the Mississippi River and the Rocky Mountains (if not to the Pacific Coast) was between "The Cyclone" and "The Morning Stars" and was played in 1860, just back of the Old Fair Grounds in North St. Louis, "The Morning Stars" winning the game, the score I now have. It is 50 years old and the ball used in that first match game was for years used as the championship trophy, it going from one club to the other, and the last the writer ever heard of it, it was in possession of "The Empire Club." I personally sent to New York for the ball to be used in this first match, and after the game it was gilded in gold and lettered with the score of the game.

"The Morning Star Club" was a "town ball" club and played from 5 a.m. to 6 a.m. on Tuesday and Friday mornings in "Carr's Park," but after considerable urging and coaxing on my part they passed a resolution at one of their meetings that they would try the national rules for one morning if I would coach them, or more properly, teach them, which I consented to do if they agreed to stick to it for the full hour without "kicking," for as I told them they would not like it until after playing it for a sufficient length of time to become familiar with some of its fine points, all of which they agreed to and kept their word like good fellows as they were, but in ten minutes I could see most of them were disgusted, yet they would not go back on their word and stuck to it for their hour's play. At the breaking up of the game to go home they asked me if I would coach them one more morning as they began to "kindly like it." I was on hand their next play day, or rather play morning at 5. Result, they never played "town ball" after that second inning and in their first match, as stated above, "waxed" my own club. I could give you many incidents up to the breaking out of the civil war and the disbanding of "The Cyclone" by its members taking part on one side or the other.

Hoping you will excuse my intruding with these little facts in regard to early ball playing in St. Louis. I am,

Yours Respectfully,

Merritt W. Griswold.

P.S.—Although I am now in my 77th year, I take just as much interest in that splendid game as when a kid at school in old Chautauqua Co., New York, or when a member of the "Putnams" of Brooklyn in 1857 and the "Hiawathas" of the same place in 1858–59 in which latter year I went to St. Louis.

When Charles Spink died in 1914, the Sporting News *passed into the hands of his son, J. G. Taylor Spink, the "alphabetical Mr. Spink," as Red Smith once described him. Under Taylor Spink's leadership, the* Sporting News *rose to prominence as "the Bible of Baseball." Spink's contributions to baseball were formally recognized in 1962, when he received the first Hall of Fame Award for "meritorious contributions to baseball writing." The annual award was also named after Taylor Spink.*

Alfred H. Spink, the uncle of Taylor Spink, published the first issue of the Sporting News *on St. Patrick's Day, 1886. Al Spink was an enigmatic figure who saw his new publication as an opportunity to cultivate his role in the sporting life of St. Louis. When the* Sporting News *became an early success, he brought his younger brother Charles to St. Louis to serve as business manager. In the 1890s, Charles eventually took control of the publication.*

Steven Gietshier, Director of Historical Records for the Sporting News, *wrote this biographical essay on founding editor Al Spink for a reprint of* The National Game.

Alfred H. Spink
Steven Gietschier ——————————————————

About the time Union soldiers were introducing the game they called Base Ball to the Confederate South, the Spink family immigrated to the United States from Canada. William Spink, at one time a Quebec legislator, and his wife, Frances Woodbury Spink, together with their eight children, settled on the west side of Chicago. The elder Spink boys, Frederick, William, and Alfred—Charles was but a baby—brought with them a Canadian enthusiasm for cricket, but they soon became devoted to the game already dubbed the National Pastime. As they grew older, the Spinks played on one of Chicago's prominent teams, the Mutuals, named after the famous New York nine bankrolled by Boss Tweed. Frederick Spink became a businessman and later served as adjutant general under Illinois Governor John Peter Altgeld, but his three brothers parlayed their youthful interest in baseball into colorful and varied careers.

The second Spink son, known as Billy, had become a telegraph operator while still a teenager in Quebec. He carried this expertise from Chicago to St. Louis, working for Western Union, but lost his job when the telegraphers union, of which he was secretary, went on strike. Vowing never again to work for the company that dismissed him, Billy entered the newspaper business, where he could use his telegraphic skills, first in Cincinnati and then back to St. Louis for the *Globe-Democrat*. According to his brother Al, who boasted of his sibling's accomplishments in *The National Game*, Billy persuaded his editor to introduce sports coverage to the *Globe-Democrat*, coverage that he often wrote himself. "Billy Spink was, in fact," wrote Al, "the best all around sporting writer of his day, if not the best all around sporting editor who ever lived."

Alfred Henry Spink, the third son, joined his older brother in St. Louis and became a journalist too, probably with his brother's encouragement. He worked for the *St. Louis Post* about the time Joseph Pulitzer was merging it with the *Dispatch* and later became sports editor of the *Missouri Republican* and then of the *St. Louis Chronicle*. The brothers used their positions to promote amateur and professional baseball and worked to restore the game's image after the city's National League club was tainted by a gambling scandal. For financial support when things ran low Al turned to an immigrant German saloonkeeper, Chris Von der Ahe, the man generally credited with making the connection between baseball and beer. Von der Ahe became "Der Poss Bresident" of the St. Louis Browns, a team that entered a new major league, the American Association, when it began play in 1882.

Al served the Browns as secretary and press agent and was at least partially responsible for hiring the players who won four straight Association pennants starting in 1885. Despite this success, a year after the Browns' first pennant win Al left the team to start a weekly newspaper devoted entirely to sports. Perhaps he was motivated by his friend Pulitzer's assertion that "given a good business manager and an editor who can really write, any newspaper should fast become a good paying institution." Or perhaps he was encouraged that there was only one other national sports publication extant, the *Sporting Life,* and that it was in faraway Philadelphia. At any rate, the *Sporting News,* eight pages long, hit the streets for the first time on St. Patrick's Day, 1886.

The *Sporting News* was an immediate success, so much so that Al soon summoned his youngest brother, Charles Carl Spink, to abandon a homesteading venture in South Dakota for an offer of fifty dollars a week as business manager. As the story is told, Charles arrived in St. Louis with ten dollars in his pocket. Al promptly borrowed the money and bought his brother dinner with it. Charles was not the great baseball fan that Al was, but he certainly was a business manager to fit Pulitzer's mold. He skillfully solicited advertising, mailed each edition to all sections of the country, and sent unsold copies to newsdealers as samples. Moreover, he got several minor leagues to name the *Sporting News* as their "official organ," thereby cementing its place, even at a young age in the baseball establishment.

In 1890, the *Sporting News* took an editorial position supporting the Players League, a one-season effort to wrest control of the professional game from the owners, and fell on economic hard times when the league collapsed. Simultaneously, Al was losing interest in his creation and turning his attention from baseball to his other love, the theater. He wrote and produced a play, *The Derby Winner,* that required a cast of forty-two persons (including Tod Sloan, later a famous jockey) and six horses. A moderate hit in St. Louis, the play flopped monumentally on the road. Al was wiped out financially, and Charles bought up *Sporting News* stock that Al had pledged as collateral for loans he could not repay. Al then tried homesteading in the Dakotas with his nephew Ernest Lanigan, later a prominent baseball statistician, and when he returned to the family business, he did so as an employee.

Al wrote about horse racing and boxing and baseball. He lampooned his old boss, Von der Ahe, now owner of the National League Cardinals, for turning his ballpark, Sportsman's Park, into a Coney Island–like sideshow, complete with rides, a Wild West show, an all-girls band, and betting pools. Von der Ahe was driven from the game, and Al, no doubt resentful and jealous of his brother, left the *Sporting News* around the turn of the century. He operated two race tracks in St. Louis for a while and then liquidated these interests to found the *St. Louis World,* a generally unprofitable newspaper that lasted about a decade. He turned to writing books, publishing the first edition of *The National Game* in 1910 and the three-volume *Spink Sports Stories: 1000 Big and Little Ones* in 1921.

Al sued his brother over the loss of his *Sporting News* stock in 1913, but the suit was never tried. The brothers reconciled, fortunately, for Charles died suddenly at age fifty-one on April 22, 1914, after attending the home opener of the St. Louis Terriers in the upstart Federal League. Control of the *Sporting News* passed to Charles's son, J. G. Taylor Spink, who prevailed upon his uncle to write a moving tribute to his late brother. Uncle and nephew remained in contact, Al once writing Taylor a letter strewn with pithy advice and signing it "Dad." Al Spink died in Chicago on May 27, 1928. His eulogy was delivered by Judge Kenesaw Mountain Landis.

In 1935, the Sporting News *publisher Taylor Spink hired Frederick J. Lieb for his writing staff. For nearly a quarter of a century, Lieb was Spink's cover reporter for the All-Star game and the World Series. He wrote so many obituaries in the* Sporting News *for Hall of Fame players that Bob Broeg called Lieb the "baseball undertaker." In 1973, Lieb became a recipient of the J. G. Taylor Spink Award and was inducted into the writers' wing of the Hall of Fame.*

One of baseball's most prolific writers, Fred Lieb was the author of seven of the fifteen team histories in the Putnam series, including The St. Louis Cardinals: The Story of a Great Baseball Club, *first published in 1944. In the book's opening chapters, Lieb discusses the early history of the Cardinals franchise, from its dubious beginnings, through its 1886 world championship as the American Association Brown Stockings, to its reentry into the National League in 1892.*

A Charter Member
Frederick J. Lieb ────────────────────────────

That colorful, picturesque word, Cardinals, so typical of the modern flamboyant Redbirds, the National League championship club which won 211 league games in 1942 and 1943, goes back only to 1899, when Willie McHale, then a cub St. Louis baseball writer, suggested it in his column in the old *St. Louis Republic.* St. Louis National League clubs then were the Browns, as are the city's American Leaguers of today, and Willie thought some of the brownish taste of years of second division baseball might disappear with a new, more vivid nickname. Frank DeHaas Robison, the St. Louis clubowner at the turn of the century, figured: "What can I lose?" and the team has been the Cardinals, or Redbirds, ever since.

However, St. Louis representation in the National League goes all the way back to 1876, the nation's centennial and the year the old National was born. In fact, it was a St. Louis jurist with a baseball bent, Judge Orrick C. Bishop, who drew up the young league's first constitution and wrote the first player contract. With a few changes here and there, that early constitution and style of player contract remain in force today. Though a charter member, St. Louis's sojourn in the league has not been continuous. There were two breaks: from 1878 to 1884 and 1887 to 1891.

While the Breadon-owned Cardinals of this century didn't move to their present location at Grand Avenue and Dodier Street until 1920, when they became tenants of Phil Ball, then the owner of the St. Louis American League club (both clubs now rent the grounds from the Phil Ball estate), that first

St. Louis National League club of 1876 played on the same field on which Terry Moore, Stan Musial, Whitey Kurowski, Marty Marion, and Mort Cooper romped and did their stuff the last few years.

While St. Louis fans frequently have held their fingers to their noses as they beheld some of the teams which followed, they had no need to apologize for their first National League club. It won 45 games and lost 19 in a 64-game schedule. There was only one better team in all the land, Al Spalding's Chicago White Stockings. The Chicagoans rolled up a percentage of .788 against .703 for the St. Louis Nationals, called the Browns. It was to be exactly 50 years later, when Rogers Hornsby's inspired club crashed through to a sensational pennant, before another St. Louis National League club would finish that high.

No 25-player St. Louis roster, with an additional 15 rookies, was mailed to big league reporters of 1876—a pre–World War II procedure, by the early secretary of St. Louis's first National League entry. Most of the players had come to St. Louis the year before, when a group of Mound City sportsmen, headed by John R. Lucas, put the Browns in the National Association, an early quasi–major league of which the present National League is the offshoot. As players went in the '70s, there was some pretty smart talent on the 1876 St. Louis aggregation. George Washington Bradley and Joe Blong did the pitching, and John Clapp and Tom Miller, known as "Little" Miller, caught their deliveries bare-handed from the old catching position some distance behind the home plate.

The St. Louis infield was made up of Herman Dehlman, first base; Mike McGeary, second base; Joe Battin, third base; and Dickie Pearce and Denny Mack, shortstop. Edgar Cuthbert played left field, Lipman Pike center field, and Joe Blong right field, when he wasn't pitching. In those days the fifth wheel of a ball club was stuck in right field. John Lucas was president of the club and Mason Graffan was manager, though Captain Dehlman directed the Browns on the field.

Bradley was one of the early pitching wizards of the game, and tossed the first no-hitter into the National League records, throwing back Hartford (yes, they were once in the league) without a hit on July 15, 1876. Bradley liked to have "Little" Miller work with him as his battery partner. Bradley, Al Spalding of Chicago, later the big sporting goods manufacturer, and Bobby Mathews of the New York Mutuals were considered the "Big Pitching Three" of the first National League season.

Lip Pike was one of the early fence-busters of baseball, while Cuthbert, along with Al Spink, an early St. Louis sports writer, were the chaps who later introduced Chris Von der Ahe, Der Poss Bresident, to St. Louis baseball. Joe

Blong, the alternate pitcher, probably was ahead of his time. Whenever a 1944 baseball writer speaks of a hypothetical pitcher, he always is Joe Blotz—perhaps a lineal descendant of Joe Blong.

The National League cut down to six clubs in 1877, and the St. Louis club didn't do itself or its fans much good, slipping to fourth with a .467 percentage. John R. Lucas, the president, also took over the management. Dehlman was reduced to substitute roles, as Arthur Croft took over first base, while Jack Remsen, who had played with the famous Atlantics of Brooklyn, and Mike Dorgan of the Syracuse Stars were outfield acquisitions.

No-Hit Bradley moved to Chicago to help Al Spalding on the White Stocking staff, and Fred "Tricky" Nichols, a former New Haven star, took his place as the No. 1 St. Louis boxman. Before the 1877 National League season got under way, the Browns played a 15-inning, 0–0 tie on May 1 with the Syracuse Stars, a strong independent team. For days the game was the talk of the town. Tricky Nichols was such a trickster that day that the Stars made only two hits; St. Louis garnered only eight off McCormack, the Syracuse pitcher.

Lucas and his fellow St. Louis boosters weren't satisfied with their 1877 showing and for the 1878 season signed the cream of the second-place Louisville club of the preceding campaign, captain and shortstop Charley Snyder, pitcher W. H. Craver, third baseman James A. Devlin, pitcher A. H. Nichols, and left fielder G. W. Hall; also shortstop Johnny Peters of the Chicago club. Pennant hopes were running high for 1878, when the roof fell in on the St. Louis baseball structure. Four of the Louisville contingent—Craver, Devlin, Nichols, and Hall—were accused of throwing games in 1877 and were permanently barred from professional baseball in the first of the two great scandals to rock the game, the second being the Black Sox World's Series scandal of 1919.

What stung Lucas and his fellow St. Louis organizers to the quick were intimations that they had knowledge of the nasty business when they acquired the players and were about to let them practice their wiles on unsuspecting St. Louis fans. In a huff, John Lucas and his associates resigned from the league, ending the first chapter of St. Louis in the National League.

2

St. Louis was without league baseball for several years, but in 1882, the original American Association, then a major league, put a club in St. Louis. Chris Von der Ahe, one of the legendary characters of the game, was the backer, assisted by Al Spink, who with his brother, Charles, founded *Sporting News,* the baseball bible, in 1886. Al was uncle to Mr. Baseball of today, the high-powered J. G. Taylor Spink, present publisher of *Sporting News.* Von der Ahe took over the name of the original St. Louis National League club, the Browns, and at Al Spink's suggestion engaged Charley Comiskey, a former Chicago sand-lotter, as first baseman and playing manager. Comiskey later organized and owned the Chicago White Sox of the American League and was the founder of the Chicago baseball fortune. Commy, as he was affectionately called, was the pioneer of the great first basemen, the first player in that position to play away from his bag. Up to Comiskey's time, the first basemen were heavy-buttocked fellows, who packed a healthy wallop at the plate, but who played their position with their left foot glued to the bag—even when no runner was on base.

Comiskey's Browns became the most famous club in the country, winning their association pennants four successive years, 1885, 1886, 1887, and 1888. In World's Series with the National League champions, they won one series and tied another (it broke up in a fight) with Anson's great Chicago White Stockings, and lost to the Detroits of 1887 and Jim Mutrie's "We Are the People" Giants of 1888.

The Browns of the American Association also played at Grand Avenue and Dodier, the site of St. Louis's present-day Sportsman's Park. Originally baseball was only a side issue with Chris, a means of getting customers to his beer gardens and amusements, especially on Sunday, for St. Louis, with its population made up largely of German, Irish, and early French, always was a friendly open town, and had Sunday baseball when that still was considered wicked and sinful by more sedate cities. The Browns' ball games were played between Von der Ahe's beer tables. St. Louisans of the eighties said rather truthfully: "The Browns were built around a keg of beer and a barrel of pretzels." Well, between selling a scuttle of suds for a nickel and a baseball admission ticket for two bits, Chris did a thriving business, and eventually "paseball" became his first enterprise.

Von der Ahe was one of those characters who could have existed only in St. Louis of the eighties and nineties. Chris gets quite a little attention here, as he later became the president and owner of the St. Louis National League club and almost wrecked it. He was pudgy and had a nose on which Jimmy Durante and W. C. Fields would have looked with envy; as Chris seldom passed when drinks were on the house his proboscis usually was lit up like a red bulb on a Christmas tree. While he eventually lost his ball club, and operated a small, frowsy saloon in his later years, in the eighties he was one of St. Louis' best known citizens. He wore a stove pipe hat, gaudy waistcoats, and in his flush days almost as many diamonds as Jim Brady, who dazzled New York around the same time.

Where other clubs went to the ball park in prison van–like buses, Chris made a parade of his team's trip from hotel to the ball grounds. Nothing less than open barouches, with St. Louis Brown blankets on the horses, were good enough for Comiskey and his "poys." Chris was a lavish entertainer, and every night was party night. Like most of St. Louis's sporting fraternity, he loved the ladies, and never was squeamish about their social standards. He had a well-trained horse who knew the way home in the early hours of the morning without the benefit of "Whoas," "Ghees," and "Giddy-upps." One morning faithful Dobbin drew the buggy to the curb of Chris's house. He was asleep on one side of the front seat, as was his lady friend on the other, while Dobbin, having done his job, vainly tried to drown out Chris's snores with his impatient neighs. An old *Sporting News* cartoon shows Von der Ahe with a buxom blonde on one knee and a shapely brunette on the other.

3

While the Browns flourished, St. Louis had another brief spell of National League baseball. In 1884, a league terming itself the Union Association invaded the field in various National League and American Association cities. Its platform was that the reserve clause, put into the contracts by the St. Louisan, Judge Orrick Bishop, was undemocratic, unAmerican, and made serfs of the ballplayers. And, hadn't Lincoln freed the slaves only two decades before?

The backer of the club in St. Louis was Henry V. Lucas, a wealthy realtor and club man and nephew of John R. Lucas, the first St. Louis National League president. The Lucases came of a prominent, well-to-do St. Louis family; one of the downtown streets is named after an earlier Lucas. Henry Lucas called his team the Maroons, and they played at Jefferson and Cass Avenues, in the heart of the Kerry Patch, once a famous hotbed for St. Louis home-grown ballplayers. Under the management of Arthur Irwin, a crack early shortstop, the Maroons won the Union Association's only pennant hands down, as franchises were shifted during the season to such smaller cities as Wilmington, Del., Altoona, Pa., and St. Paul.

The Union Association's brief career aroused considerable bitterness. Not respecting the reserve clause, the league had raided freely in the two established leagues and lured some good players. But when it blew up after one season, animosities soon were forgotten, and the National League voted a franchise to Henry Lucas and his pennant-winning Maroons. Henry managed his own club, and moved it to Vandeventer and Natural Bridge Avenues, which also became the home of the latter-day Cardinals.

The two seasons the Maroons were in the National League, 1885 and 1886, were an evil augury of the many lean Cardinal years before the sun was to shine through the clouds years later during the Breadon-Rickey reign of plenty. In 1885, Lucas's team won only 36 games, and the Union Association champs of '84 finished behind the 8-ball in the National League cellar. It was the first of many St. Louis tailenders. Lucas won seven more games in 1886, and boosted the club to sixth, but it was rough and hard going.

Von der Ahe's Browns won the first two of their string of pennants in those two years and the city went into the seventh baseball heaven when Comiskey's club defeated Anson's Chicagos in the 1886 World's Series, four games to two. The city was Brown-conscious; Von der Ahe, Comiskey, and the Browns were kings and could do no wrong; the Maroons were poor baseball relatives who ate scraps at the second table. Henry Lucas took a bad financial licking. He sold the St. Louis franchise to John T. Brush of the When Department Store of Indianapolis, and John moved the club to the Hoosier capital. Brush later moved up the baseball ladder, buying bigger and better clubs, as his trail led to Cincinnati and New York. He was the wealthy and influential owner of the New York Giants when he died in 1912.

However, Lucas had several pretty fair ballplayers on his team, including Fred Dunlop, a second baseman, and Jack Glasscock, one of the early short-stop greats and later a National League batting champion in New York. Stage and radio funster Phil Baker may be amused to know the Maroons had a catcher by that name, and in 1886, Sam Crane, who for many years wrote baseball for the *New York Journal,* was the Maroon second baseman.

II Der Poss Bresident

1

St. Louis was back in the National League in 1892, and has been represented in the oldest major ever since, but the next seven years in the old 12-club National League were the darkest, dankest, and direst in St. Louis baseball history. In those seven years the St. Louis club—they still were the Browns—dug through the league cellar into the subcellar and then excavated even below that level. In the seven lean years, St. Louis had two twelfth-place clubs, three elevenths, one tenth, and once rose as high as ninth. It was difficult to stay under the misfit teams which represented Washington and Louisville, but bad as they were, the Brown National Leaguers succeeded in being just a little worse.

But, we've got to hark back to the previous decade. The present Cardinal club actually is the direct lineal offspring of the American Association Browns of the eighties, rather than of the St. Louis National League clubs of 1876–77 and 1885–86. While the National League and the old American Association usually respected each other's territory and players, there was little love between the two leagues. The animosity and bitter feeling was even more acute than that which frequently existed between the two majors, the National and American Leagues, of today.

In 1885, when the Browns played the Chicago White Stockings in the World's Series, two of the games were played in Cincinnati and Pittsburgh to spread around the interest. In the second game, played in Chicago, Comiskey took exception to an umpire's decision in the sixth inning and marched his club off the field. The game was forfeited to Chicago, and the series later was called off in an air of bitterness with each club having three victories. The incident only heaped coals on the fires of animosity and ill will between the two circuits. Anson accused Comiskey of quitting in the series; the then not-so-Old Roman replied in kind; while Al Spalding, president of the Chicago club, vowed he never again would have anything to do with the Association, or any of its clubs, particularly Von der Ahe and Comiskey.

However, a year later—the same clubs won again in their respective leagues. Von der Ahe, who didn't let grudges interfere with business, sent Comiskey to Chicago to see Spalding and Anson and to challenge them to a World's Series for the baseball championship. The Chicagoans were cool, and Anson snapped: "We will play you under only one condition, and that is winner take all, and by all, I mean every penny that is taken at the gate." Spalding and Anson thought that would dispose of the St. Louis managerial upstart, but to their surprise Comiskey accepted.

Commy then was afraid to break the news to Von der Ahe; he knew Chris liked to see the money coming through the gate, and didn't know whether he would gamble on such high stakes. But Chris expressed his pleasure at the success of Comiskey's mission. "Sure, we will take them up and teach those fellars a lesson. No club is goot enough to beat the Browns."

No club was goot enough that year. The Browns won the series, four games to two, on one of the great plays of the eighties, always referred to later by Comiskey as "Curt Welch's $15,000 slide." With the Browns leading three games to two, the score was 3–3 in the ninth inning of the sixth game, with the famous White Stocking battery, John Clarkson and King Kelly, working for Anson. Welch was taking quite a lead off third, and Kelly signaled for a high pitch—out of the reach of Bushong, the St. Louis batsman. However, Curt came in with the pitch and when the great Kelly slightly juggled the ball, Welch slid home in safety with the run which made the Browns World's Champions.

The entire gate of the series was far below that of the first game of a present-day World's Series. However, after expenses, including champagne for everyone after it was over, Von der Ahe had some $15,000 left. He shared it liberally with his players. The two clubs also had put up $500 to wager on themselves; Von der Ahe had offered to bet Spalding another $10,000, which the Chicagoan ignored. Chris, who had his generous side, even helped out quite a few of the Chicago players who went broke backing the White Stockings with side bets.

The Browns continued to win pennants, and despite his liberal spending—and squandering—Von der Ahe made lots of money in baseball and beer. Starting in with a little German grocery store at Spring and Sullivan Streets, just north of the present Sportsman's Park, Von der Ahe built rows of houses, with space for saloons on the corners. His own saloon and expanded grocery business also showed substantial profits. After each game, Chris's grocery wagon backed up to the ball park and hauled the dollars to the bank. He went deeply into politics and was reputed to be a millionaire.

He was well pleased with himself, frequently patted himself on the back, and once told interviewers: "I am the smartest fellar in baseball." Once he even boasted: "I have the largest diamond in baseball," when Comiskey reminded him that all baseball diamonds were of the same size. "Vell, Charley, maybe I vas mistaken dis time, but I got de biggest infield, anyway." Someone sold him the idea that a great man like Chris Von der Ahe should be preserved for posterity. He had a life-size statue of himself sculptured; later it was placed over his grave.

2

When the Chicago White Stockings sold the great Mike "King" Kelly, then baseball's most colorful star, to the Boston Nationals in the winter of 1886–87 for $10,000, Von der Ahe was much impressed. In the following winter, Chicago sold the King's battery mate, John Clarkson, to Boston for another $10,000, and that gave Chris ideas. Why not do the same; sell some of the good players, pay less in salaries, and have Comiskey develop some new ones. Charley could do it. Without consulting Commy, he sold pitchers Dave Foutz and Bobby Carruthers and catcher Doc Bushong to Brooklyn for $10,000 and outfielder Curt Welch and shortstop Gleason to the Philadelphia Athletics for $5,000. Comiskey saw red when he heard of it; he threatened to resign, but his Brown salary was $8,000, a princely sum in the eighties, and he reconsidered.

St. Louis fans also were wild with rage; the indignation spread to nearby cities and towns, where the menfolk had been loyal supporters of the Browns. It was much like the turmoil thirty-nine years later, when Sam Breadon, the present Cardinal owner, outraged St. Louis fans by trading Rogers Hornsby, his World's Championship manager of 1926, to New York for Frankie Frisch. There was talk of boycotting Chris's club, and many predicted a last-place finish for the 1888 Browns. But Comiskey had amazing luck with sand-lotters and minor league replacements. Silver King, Chamberlain, and Devlin turned into winning pitchers; Big Milligan took Bushong's place behind the plate; a youngster, Shorty Fuller, filled the shortstop gap, and Tommy McCarthy was so sensational in center field that he made the fans forget Welch of the $15,000 slide. And, to the surprise not only of St. Louis but the entire nation, the Browns won another pennant, making it four straight. It would be thirty-eight years before pennant lightning again would strike in St. Louis!

But Von der Ahe was supremely happy. His club had lost the World's Series to the New York Giants; a predecessor to the four St. Louis (Cardinal)—New York (Yankee) Series of present day baseball. It was a well-attended, profitable series, and if the Browns lost, they made a good showing, winning four games to New York's six. Even in defeat, Chris rubbed his hands with glee. "They talked of poycotting my team," he laughed. "I made more money than with my old wonder poys. I guess I am a pretty smart fellar."

Chris engaged a special train to take the team and loyal St. Louis fans to New York, Der Poss Bresident paying all expenses, even hotel bills. He had Al Spink put big streamers from the windows of the Special, reading: "St. Louis Browns; Four Time Pennant Winners."

But, he wasn't so smart a fellar. Though he won the 1888 pennant and his teams were in the race the next three seasons, his downfall really started with the sale of his stars to Brooklyn and the Athletics the winter before, for from that time things never again were quite the same.

3

The Browns finished a close second in 1889, the new Brooklyn club, built around Carruthers, Foutz, and Bushong, winning the championship. Then came a year, 1890, which wrecked many early baseball fortunes. The crack players of the National League and American Association, claiming they were tired of grasping owners getting all the money in baseball, formed an association called the Players' Brotherhood, which procured backers for their own circuit, the Players League. The great bulk of stars and top ranking players went to the new league, feeling they were the drawing cards and the fans would support them against their old greedy bosses. They were to divide the profits equally with the backers.

Even such later-day wise men as Connie Mack and John K. Tener, later governor of Pennsylvania and president of the National League, fell for it. Tener, who had been a great pitcher for Anson in Chicago, jumped to the Pittsburgh Players League team and was treasurer of the Brotherhood. The new league put clubs in New York, Brooklyn, Philadelphia, Boston, Buffalo, Chicago, Pittsburgh, and Cleveland. Von der Ahe was spared Brotherhood competition in St. Louis, but his crack manager, Comiskey, went over to the Players League as manager of the Chicago club. After one season, the backers of the new league went broke, and the club owners of the established leagues were only one jump behind. Many fans became disgusted, lost their regard and esteem for big-named players, and there was such general ennui after the 1890 World's Series ran into some bad weather that the series was called off because of lack of interest, with each contending club, the Brooklyn Nationals and Louisville A. A. Colonels, having won three games, a seventh resulting in a tie.

The Players League lasted only one season, and in 1891 the players, hats in hand, were glad to return to their former employers. Comiskey returned to the management of the Browns, but his relationship with Von der Ahe was not the same. The game had been rocked to its very foundations, and it was some time before baseball regained its former hold on the American public. The season of 1891 was a lean one, especially for Chris's league—the battered American Association.

With the Players League war out of the way, the two leagues again got to bickering and fighting among themselves. Two Association stars, Louis Bierbauer and Harry Stovey, had jumped from the Athletics to the Brooklyn Players League club. Jumping players were ordered back to their former clubs, but through an oversight the American Association had neglected to place Bierbauer and Stovey on their reserve list; the Pittsburgh Nationals signed the former and the Boston club the latter. The American Association charged the conduct of the Pittsburgh club was "piratical," and ever since the Pennsylvania team has been known as the Pirates. A board of arbitration awarded the disputed players to Pittsburgh and Boston, whereupon the Association withdrew from the National Agreement, and another baseball war was on.

The upshot of the matter was that after a season of scrapping, player-snatching, and name-calling, the two leagues agreed to merge into one 12-club organization. At a special meeting in Indianapolis in December 1891, the National League purchased the Association clubs in Chicago, Boston, Columbus, Milwaukee, and Washington for $135,000. The Washington franchise was awarded to George Wagner of Philadelphia, and the St. Louis, Baltimore, and Louisville clubs were admitted to the National League.

It was in this manner that Chris Von der Ahe and the Browns came into the National League, an unhappy experience for both Chris and the league.

In St. Louis, on May 6, 1875, Chicago and St. Louis professional baseball teams met for the first time. When the St. Louis Brown Stockings defeated the Chicago White Stockings, their rivals in the National Association of Professional Base Ball Players, by the lopsided score of 10–0, the St. Louis Republican *boasted that the Brown Stocking victory proved that the city had "the greatest population, the most flourishing trade, the biggest bridge, and the prettiest women."*

A decade later, the Brown Stockings, now champions of the American Association, met the White Stockings, pennant-winners in the National League, in what was proclaimed as a world championship series. The 1885 series ended in a disputed tie, but in 1886, the teams repeated as league champions, and met again in a $15,000, winner-take-all, seven-game series, won by St. Louis, four games to two. In the sixth and deciding game, Curt Welch, who once dedicated his season to beer, scored the winning run on what became known as the "$15,000 slide," though newspaper accounts, like the one in the St. Louis Daily Globe-Democrat, *reported that Welch trotted home after a wild pitch or passed ball.*

The St. Louis Browns Are Champions

The St. Louis Browns are champions of the world at the national game of base ball for another year at least. That was decided at Sportsman's Park yesterday afternoon by their great victory over the Chicagos in the sixth game of the world's championship series. No one—not even the most devoted friends and admirers of the Chicagos—can dispute their right to the title, or can say that it was won in anything but a fair, square, and honest manner. The struggle was not such a hard one for the Browns, after all. Taking everything into consideration, they won the battle with comparative ease. Their victory, however, was not due to any luck, but was only secured by playing a superior brand of ball. Their hard, steady, and all-pull-together style of playing landed them on top on more than one occasion when defeat seemed inevitable. The Chicagos are an excellent team of ballplayers, but, as already has been mentioned, they are out of their class when they face the Browns in a contest, as has been plainly shown in the six games played between them. The Browns have made more runs, more hits, more total bases, less errors, have presented stronger batteries, and outplayed the Chicagos all around. It does not require many more facts to convince people which is the better club. Since the initial game was played in Chicago last Monday, there have been a number of people shouting hippodrome and claiming that the Chicagos would win the series without any trouble; that they were merely toying with the Browns; that they were merely working things to increase the gate receipts, but yesterday's play dispelled all suspicion.

Analysis of the Play

The contest between the two clubs yesterday afternoon was the most exciting and brilliantly played game ever seen in St. Louis, or any other city, in the history of the national sport. It was the hardest battle of all the six games, and it was not decided until a wild pitch allowed Welch to cross the plate with the winning run in the tenth inning. The Chicagos started out to play in a manner that meant business, and it looked like defeat for the Browns. The home club never once gave up, though, and with the score standing 3–0 against them at the end of the seventh inning they played just as hard and steady as they did at the opening of the game. For six straight innings they went to the bat and six straight times they were retired without a hit, much less a run, or anything that looked like one. Bushong got his base in the first inning, but never advanced from the base. In the seventh inning O'Neill made the first hit of the game for the Browns. He drove the ball far up in the air and out in the field beyond all reach of the fielders for three bases. But Jim in his effort to make third base in safety ran over the bag. The ball was fielded quickly and returned to Burns and as O'Neill went over the base, he was touched by the ball and put out. This terrible luck did not dishearten the Browns, but they kept on striving to get a run. In the seventh they tied the score and Latham assisted no little in doing it. With one run in, two men on the bases, two men out, and two strikes and three balls called on Latham, the latter lifted the sphere to the left field over Dalrymple's head for three bases, sending in the two men.

Crazed with Delight

The demonstration on the part of the spectators when the score was tied was such that has never been equaled at any game of baseball before. The immense crowd seemed to go crazy. They yelled and cheered until they grew hoarse. Men and boys shook hands and embraced each other, turned somersaults on the grand-stands and in the field, and many actually wept tears of joy. The air was full of hats, handkerchiefs, and umbrellas, and it was nearly five minutes before the crowd could be quieted sufficiently to go on with the game. It was a sight that will never be forgotten by those who were present. But the scene in the tenth inning when the winning run was scored and the Browns had secured the championship is almost beyond description. As soon as Welch had crossed home plate, and the 10,000 people who filled the grandstand and stood in rows ten or twelve deep in a circle around the field knew that the game had been won, more than half of them made a grand rush for the players, yelling and making all manner of noises and demonstrations. As soon as they would run up against a man in a Browns' uniform, they would throw him upon their backs and carry him off the field. The entire nine were taken to the dressing room in this manner. At various places in and around the park a crowd would congregate, and when someone would propose three cheers for the championship, they would be given with a will. Everybody was happy and everybody wanted to shake hands with everybody else. A crowd numbering, perhaps, 3,000 lingered around the park until after the members of the club had dressed. Wherever one of them was seen, a big crowd immediately circled around and cheered him heartily. It was long after dark before Sportsman's Park and vicinity had settled down to its usual quiet state. It is not likely that such scenes of enthusiasm will be seen again at St. Louis base ball parks for a long time to come.

Tie on the Ninth Inning

The tenth inning was commenced. Clarkson struck out and both Gore and Kelly knocked flies to left field. Welch was the first batsman for the Browns. He took a position pretty close to the plate and Clarkson hit him with the ball. Welch took first. Anson protested and a wrangle ensued. The umpire finally called Welch back, claiming that he tried to get hit with the ball. To the great delight of the audience, however, Welch knocked the first ball that was pitched to him for a single to the center field. Foutz was the next man to handle the stick. He batted a grounder back of the pitcher, between short and third. Williamson made a run for it and fumbled it. Foutz, of course, got safe on the error, and Welch went to second. Robinson advanced both men on his sacrifice from short to first. With a man on second and another on third and only one out, the chances were good for a run. Bushong came to the bat, but he did not get an opportunity to hit the ball. Clarkson, who is usually so cool, was visibly nervous. He rolled and twisted the ball around in his hands several times before he got into position to pitch it. He finally delivered it, but it was far over Kelly's head. The latter made no effort to get it, and like the other members of the team, stood in a half dazed manner and watched Welch come in with the deciding run. The Chicagos packed up their bags and got off the grounds as quickly as possible.

Impatient for Returns

The scenes down-town and around the pool halls, yesterday, have not been equaled for a long time. There was a very general idea and fear of a hippodrome, but it did not prevent crowds from assembling to get the bulletined result of the game as it progressed, and at the same time to increase instead of diminish the interest. The biggest jam and of the wildest enthusiasts of the season was seen around the *Globe-Democrat* office, filling the streets and both sidewalks, even for distances from where the bulletin boards could not be seen. The pool-rooms were the same way, hundreds standing patiently all afternoon, though able to hear only the cheers and shouts of those near the boards, and form an idea from those demonstrations. The Chicagos certainly had the call in the betting, with odds of $10 to $8. The Browns' friends wanted to sail in and take the offering, but in the general idea of a hippodrome it was Chicago's day, and the betting was limited, and became worse and worse as the Chicagos made one run, then a second, and then a third. John Donovan at that time offered $100 to $10 on the Chicagos, having a large amount already on the Browns, but though it was estimated there were one thousand men in his rooms the bet went begging until finally Bob Golsan took it. Then he made another of $50 to $10 and $25 to $5, but the crowd was all of one way of thinking, and there were not many takers of such bets. When the Browns piled up three runs in the eighth and tied the score the faith of their friends in the honesty of the game returned, and a number of bets were made at $10 to $7 in favor of the home club. Then the bulletins favored Chicago's probability of making runs, and the betting moved up to even money, and a number of bets were made at Donovan's, Wiseman's, and other places. At that time the scene around the *Globe-Democrat* was one that will not be soon forgotten. Men and boys, silk hats and common ones, mingled together, yelled together, and, in fact, went crazy together, and during the playing of the ninth and the tenth innings it was impossible to get through the crowd. The shouts when the winning run was scored in the tenth were deafening.

Departure of the Chicagos

The vanquished Chicago nine quietly and unostentatiously took their departure from the Union Depot last evening. There was an immense crowd of

Saturday night travelers, but none of them knew that the windy city nine from Michigan Lake was about to make its retreat. There was no flag or proud banner to announce their presence, nor the sound of a fife or drum to tell where the breezy crew could be found. They refused an escort, preferring to straggle by ones or twos in the disguise of dudish attire into a Pullman, rather than attract humiliating attention from the busy throng. So quietly did they take passage that no one but the conductor knew who they were. There was no bluster in their midst, and they made a mournful-looking crowd, that reminded one more than anything else of a delegation of undertakers who had performed the last sad offices for a friend. The name of Chicago was not spoken, and the defeated ballplayers who came from there looked sad at the thought of having to return. All the gush and sentiment usually displayed by them was suppressed and they were silent. A Texan, who was escorting a Mexican band to the state fair at Dallas, discovered them and insisted on giving them a few lively beats of the drum, but St. Louis hospitality prevailed, and the crestfallen crowd was allowed to leave with out any demonstration to emphasize their idea of fallen pride.

Results of the Series

After the game last evening President Von der Ahe sent a note to President Spalding, suggesting that an exhibition game between the Browns and Chicagos be played in Cincinnati next Tuesday. This was Mr. Spalding's reply:

> Friend Von der Ahe: We must decline with our compliments. We know when we have had enough.
> Yours Truly, A. G. Spalding
> P.S. Anson joins me in the above message.

Under the reign of beer baron Chris Von der Ahe, professional baseball in St. Louis experienced the best and the worst of times. A late-nineteenth-century combination of Bill Veeck and George Steinbrenner, Von der Ahe gave St. Louis four years of championship baseball from 1885 to 1888, while entertaining them with beer gardens, amusement rides, and an all-girl band. But, while proclaiming himself "the smartest fellar in baseball," he also ruined his franchise and his personal life with his wild antics and his interference with the operations of the team. Jon David Cash in Before They Were Cardinals *describes the fall of Chris Von der Ahe, which unfortunately coincided with the entry of his Brown Stockings into the National League in 1892. His career as a baseball owner finally ended after a disastrous fire on April 16, 1898, at the new Sportsman's Park.*

Farewell to Chris Von der Ahe, 1892–1899
Jon David Cash ——————————————————————————

Fans and players of the younger generation will only laugh, perhaps, at the German dialect stories that are told on the late Chris Von der Ahe as part of his obituary, and their main impression of the once famous owner of the old St. Louis Browns will be that he was a clown, given to much drink and squandering of money.

But the veterans of the long ago, remembering what Chris really was and did, felt a choking in the throat and a scalding in the eyes when they read that he was no more. Mr. Von der Ahe had what convention terms faults, but they were only those of a plain and simple foreigner, suddenly elevated into a whirl of wealth and popularity. . . . As for Von der Ahe's virtues, they were those of a good-hearted, generous, loyal character. . . . It is significant that those who knew him best held him in greatest regard.

—the *Sporting News* obituary for Chris Von der Ahe, June 12, 1913

Throughout the 1880s, Chris Von der Ahe received appropriate public acclaim for saving major-league baseball in St. Louis from extinction. In June 1883 he had enhanced his favorable civic image even further, organizing a charity baseball game between his Browns and a team put together by the St. Louis Merchants Exchange that benefited local flood victims. Later, as the Browns claimed American Association championships from 1885 to 1888, Von der Ahe had been hailed for his role in building the "Four Time Winners." Along the route of the city's parade to celebrate the Browns' first Association pennant, the *St. Louis Globe-Democrat* observed that "cheer after cheer rent the air" as soon as Von der Ahe arrived. Von der Ahe lost some public support over his 1887 trades of five of the most popular Browns. However, despite his increasingly controversial reputation within national baseball circles, Von der Ahe remained generally popular in St. Louis as long as the Browns kept winning.

After the Browns entered the National League, the public's perception of Von der Ahe became less positive. In the National League the Browns, stripped of practically their whole lineup, never gave Von der Ahe another winning record. Without the assistance of first baseman–manager Charles Comiskey, Von der Ahe lacked the skill and the patience to rebuild the team. Over the next seven years he employed eighteen managers, even trying the job himself. Von der Ahe faced trouble off the field as well. Real-estate values collapsed in the late 1880s, leaving him overextended and heavily indebted to the Northwestern Savings Bank of St. Louis. To pay his debts, Von der Ahe resorted to selling the services of many talented players. In the last two years of his ownership, the Browns finished last in the National League.

As the nation slipped deeper into the economic depression of 1893–1897, Von der Ahe continued to squander his wealth in efforts to satisfy his passions for women and alcohol. In 1895 his affairs with two St. Louis women, Della Wells and Kitty Myers, provoked his wife, Emma, to sue him for divorce after twenty-five years of marriage. Emma received a generous alimony settlement, and Von der Ahe wed Wells. Edward Von der Ahe, son of Chris and Emma, never spoke to his father again. Meanwhile Chris Von der Ahe delighted in buying rounds of drink, especially champagne, for "a numerous army of flatterers and hanger–ons." While establishing himself in St. Louis, Von der Ahe had been known as a thrifty businessman. But after baseball brought him fame and fortune, he frequently "handled $1000 bills as if they were peanuts to feed to monkeys."

The new Sportsman's Park, built in 1893 at the corner of Vandeventer Avenue and Natural Bridge Road, was one of Von der Ahe's many risky real-estate ventures. On April 16, 1898, a disastrous fire virtually destroyed the ballpark. Von der Ahe sank his dwindling cash reserve into rebuilding it, but the fire hounded him. Some spectators, trampled in the rush to flee the burning ballpark, filed personal injury lawsuits against him. Confronted by too many creditors, Von der Ahe declared bankruptcy. He could not pay off the bonds used to finance the original construction of the new Sportsman's Park, and in March 1899 the Browns were sold at a public auction.

Von der Ahe faded into the obscurity of the St. Louis saloon business. He did not prosper, and in the spring of 1908 a benefit baseball game was staged for him at the old Sportsman's Park on Grand Avenue. Amidst the other troubles of 1898, Von der Ahe had been divorced by his second wife, Della. He later married a third time, and this wife, the former Anna Kaiser, survived him. Von der Ahe died on June 5, 1913, of cirrhosis of the liver. Hundreds attended his funeral. Comiskey, then owner of the White Sox, eulogized his former boss as "the grandest figure baseball has ever known." Von der Ahe is buried in Bellefontaine Cemetery in St. Louis beneath a life-sized marble statue of himself. His major-league franchise lives on, now known as the Cardinals.

The American League Browns

By the time Fred Lieb got around to writing the team history of the St. Louis Browns for the Putnam series, the franchise had moved to Baltimore. First published in 1955, The Baltimore Orioles: The History of a Colorful Team in Baltimore and St. Louis *begins and ends with the history of baseball in Baltimore, but it also includes chapters on the history of the Browns, beginning with their entry into the American League in 1902 during its baseball war with the National League, their adoption of the old Brownies team name abandoned by the now National League St. Louis Cardinals, and their early popularity with St. Louis fans, before they fell into the second division and earned the city the dubious title of "first in booze, first in shoes, and last in the American League."*

Browns in American League since 1902
Frederick J. Lieb ───

And what about the club the Orioles inherited, the St. Louis Browns? Actually, they had a sad heritage, only one pennant and eleven first-division clubs in 52 years. Twelve Brown clubs finished seventh and ten more wound up in the cellar. Five of the first-division clubs came in the six seasons between 1920 and 1925, the years Jack Dunn had his pennant trust in the International League.

The modern American League Browns couldn't even claim to be descendants of Von der Ahe's and Comiskey's fabulous St. Louis Browns of the old major American Association, four straight winners in 1885–86–87–88. This Brown club was taken into the National League in 1892, at the same time that the Baltimore A.A. Orioles were admitted to the twelve-club National League. Actually, the present-day Cardinals are lineal descendants of the original Browns.

It may seem paradoxical today that the American League Browns started as the Milwaukee Brewers of 1901. Ban Johnson, first American League president, was a sagacious man, but he couldn't look forward a half-century and visualize a Milwaukee club averaging close to 2,000,000 a season for the years of 1953 and 1954. In 1902, St. Louis was the fourth city in the nation, and rated highly as a ball town. During the latter stages of the National-American baseball war, Johnson thought it a smart move to enter St. Louis and fight the Robinson interests there. So, he shifted his early Milwaukee club to the banks of "Ol' Man River." The new club took over Sportsman's Park, the old home of Von der Ahe's Browns. The old nickname, "Browns," also was kicking around since the St. Louis Nationals abandoned it in the late nineties, so Johnson and

Jimmy McAleer, the new St. Louis American manager, appropriated it, and hung it on their new team.

The 1902 Browns first were backed by a group of St. Louis sportsmen headed by Ralph Orthwein, but after one season Ralph sold the new franchise to Robert Lee Hedges, a Cincinnati carriage manufacturer. Johnson had known Hedges during Ban's baseball writing days in Cincinnati. Hedges was a smart early operator, knew how to get 100 cents out of a dollar, and whether his clubs were up or down, Robert Lee almost invariably showed a profit.

The club Ban Johnson shifted to St. Louis in 1902 had been a tailender in Milwaukee the season before. It was almost the same situation as the shift of the 1953 St. Louis Browns to Baltimore in 1954. And, how Baltimore wishes the same happy climb could have been brought about! In one season, this transferred club leaped from eighth to second. However, Clarence Miles, Art Ehlers, and Jimmy Dykes were in no position to raid the St. Louis Cardinals of such stars as Stan Musial, Red Schoendienst, and Harvey Hendrix as were Johnson, Orthwein, and McAleer 52 years before when they took the cream of the St. Louis National League's war-torn team.

Obtaining a first-division team in 1902 was quite simple, even though it baffled McGraw in Baltimore. You went into the rival camp with pockets stuffed with greenbacks. In wholesale raids on the Cardinals, the Browns obtained Jesse Burkett, who batted .400 three times; Rhoderick "Bobbie" Wallace, a shortstop then considered second only to the great Hans Wagner; pitchers Jack Powell, Jack Harper, and Willie Sudhoff; and two other outfielders in addition to Burkett, Emmett Heidrick and Billy Maloney. Another ace pitcher, Frank "Red" Donahue, a 22–11 performer in 1902, was snared from the Phillies. With this aggregation of filched talent, Jimmy McAleer ran second to the Athletics the season Connie Mack brought his first of nine pennants to Philadelphia.

The runner-up finish of 1902 was not an augury of good things to come. Only one other second-place club followed in the next 51 years. McAleer's club tumbled into the second division in 1903 and hit bottom for the first time in 1905. Brownie fans got some measure of comfort in 1906 when their outfielder, George Stone, beat out the great Nap Lajoie for the American League's batting title.

If the Browns suffered five successive second-division teams after their first second placer, Hedges prospered. The Cardinals, ruined by the war, were considerably worse, and the Browns became St. Louis's favorite ball club. Hedges did so well that by 1908 he increased the capacity of Sportsman's Park to 18,000, considered a big park for that period.

Hedges's enlarged park was nicely timed. In 1908, the American League had a freak race, with all of its strength massed in the West. Hedges and McAleer pulled a great deal for St. Louis when they purchased the playful left-handed star, Rube Waddell, from the Philadelphia Athletics. Connie Mack had tired of Rube's shenanigans after the left-hander blew the 1907 pennant for the A's. Waddell was the same zany in St. Louis that he had been in Philadelphia: he chased fire engines, tended bar, rang strangers' door bells, imitated a circus barker, and wrestled with admiring bar flies. But he had one more good season, winning nineteen games, losing fourteen, and striking out 232 batsmen. Rube's high spot in 1908 was the first game in which he faced his old team, the Athletics, in Philadelphia on July 29. Rube was out to show Mack what a blunder he had made and struck out sixteen of his erstwhile teammates, which stood as an American League record until Bob Feller knocked it out of the book.

With the aid of Waddell, Bill Dinneen, and Barney Pelty, one of the early Jewish players, the Browns fought abreast with the Tigers, Clevelands, and White Sox until Labor Day. St. Louis slumped in September, leaving it up to the remaining three clubs to battle it out to the finish line. McAleer's team couldn't win, but they knocked out Nap Lajoie's Cleveland Naps. With only two days of the schedule left, the Naps could assure themselves of the pennant by taking three games from the Browns, a double-header and single game. But, Bill Dinneen stopped them in one game of the twin bill, and Detroit defeated the White Sox for the flag on the last day of the season. Cleveland lost the pennant by four points, as the fourth-place Browns finished eight games off the pace.

McAleer's second baseman was Jimmy Williams, the infielder John McGraw had snatched from Barney Dreyfuss's Pirates when "Mac" was manager of the American League Orioles. St. Louis had a Texan pitcher–outfielder–pinch hitter in 1908 named Dode Criss. Dode batted .341 for 64 games against .324 for Ty Cobb, who played the full season. Many St. Louisans were angered when Ban Johnson named Cobb, rather than Criss, the batting champion. St. Louisans then took their Brown baseball most seriously, and anyone suggesting the Browns be moved out of town would have been considered daffy. They finished a close second to the White Sox in American League attendance, 636,096 for the Sox to 618,947 for the Browns.

However, this fourth-place finish had to satisfy Brown fans for a full decade. The club skidded to seventh the following year, and it was 1920 before the Missouri club again saw the light of the first division. McAleer left after 1909 to pilot Washington, and was followed by a succession of managers, Jack O'Connor, Bobbie Wallace, George Stovall, Branch Rickey, Fielder Jones, and Jimmy Burke. The careers of O'Connor and Stovall came to turbulent ends, the former for trying to help Lajoie win a batting championship and the latter for squirting tobacco juice in the face of one of Ban Johnson's umpires.

O'Connor was involved in a lively rhubarb at the end of the 1910 season. An automobile company was offering cars to the batting champions of the two majors, and young Ty Cobb and Lajoie were coming down the American League home stretch neck and neck. Cobb was most unpopular with fellow players at the time, with 90 percent rooting for Lajoie to beat out Ty. The Browns wound up the 1910 season at home, playing Cleveland in a doubleheader. O'Connor went to such extremes to have Lajoie win that he had a kid third baseman, Johnny "Red" Corriden, play back on the outfield grass for King Larry. As a result, Lajoie closed with eight hits, six of them safe bunts. And Larry, by that time thirty-five, never was a particularly fast base-runner. A seventh Lajoie hit was a ball fumbled by shortstop Wallace; the scorer first recorded it as a Wallace error but a few minutes later changed it to a hit.

One set of unofficial averages had Lajoie the batting champion and car winner; another set had Cobb the winner by a fraction. The official averages eventually gave it to Cobb, .385 to .384. But, the manner in which Corriden played Lajoie and other shenanigans at Sportsman's Park on that final day raised a smell like a pig sty. It also developed that the St. Louis official scorer had been offered an expensive suit of clothes if he gave Lajoie the benefit of the doubt on all questionable hits. Ban Johnson held an immediate investigation to which he summoned O'Connor, Harry Howell, a pitcher-coach, Corriden, and the umpires. Howell, a former National and American Oriole, got into the act with frequent trips to the press box asking how Lajoie's doubtful hits were being scored. Johnson absolved Corriden as a kid who only was obeying instructions, but ordered the Browns to fire O'Connor and Howell, even though Jack's contract ran into 1911. O'Connor later brought suit in the civil courts and was awarded his 1911 Brown salary, with which he started a St. Louis saloon. Jack never got back into baseball, but Howell later was employed as a minor league umpire.

Stovall's expectorating job in 1913 brought Wesley Branch Rickey, who then didn't use tobacco and never took a drink, to the fore. Third baseman Jimmy Austin followed Stovall briefly as a fill-in manager, and then Lee Hedges named Rickey. It started Branch up the ladder on his way to baseball fame and fortune. Rickey wasn't a newcomer to St. Louis baseball. As a young college catcher from Ohio Wesleyan, he had joined the Browns late in the season of 1905. Just the opposite from the swearing, badgering O'Connor-Stovall type, Branch's worst cuss word was "Judas Priest"; he didn't even play ball on Sunday in a town which derived much of its revenue from big Sunday crowds. Perhaps that's why Hedges traded Branch to New York despite a .284 batting average and fair promise as a catcher in 1906. Rickey lasted only one season with the early Yankees, and next became baseball coach at Michigan, where he also studied law. His health broke down from overstudy and overwork, and he went to Montana and briefly put out his law shingle. But baseball soon lured him back. Hedges remembered Rickey as a young man with ideas; he invited Branch to return to St. Louis as presidential assistant. From that job, he moved on to the Brown management. Because Branch wouldn't manage the club on Sunday—wouldn't even go near the ballpark on the Sabbath—outfielder Burt Shotton, who won pennants in recent years in Brooklyn, became Rickey's Sunday manager.

Rickey managed the Browns for the latter half of 1913 and in 1914 and 1915; the enthusiastic collegian tried a lot of new ideas and experiments as his clubs finished eighth, fifth, and sixth. Rickey's coaching years in Michigan paid off when he signed one of his Michigan boys, George Sisler, a fellow Ohioan of Swiss descent, to a Brown contract in 1915. Pittsburgh also claimed the crack collegian. As a high school boy in Akron, Ohio, George foolishly had signed a contract with his Akron town team. Though Sisler never reported to Akron, that club sold his contract to the Columbus American Association club, and Columbus, in turn, sold the contract to the Pittsburgh Pirates. After Sisler was graduated from Michigan, Barney Dreyfuss, Pirate president, insisted the player report to his team. It started one of baseball's greatest rows. It finally was put up to the old three-man National Commission; president Ban Johnson voted to send Sisler to the Browns, National League president John K. Tener favored Dreyfuss's claim, and Garry Herrmann, commission chairman, sided with Johnson. Dreyfuss was so infuriated that he started a lengthy campaign to unseat Herrmann from the chairmanship, which reached success in 1920.

The signing of Sisler, nicknamed "the Sizzler," was the greatest thing that ever happened to the Browns. Though George did some early pitching, played the outfield, and even took a whirl at third base—a strong position for a left-hander—he eventually settled at first base, and became one of the super-stars of baseball. Sisler and Lou Gehrig of the Yankees usually are the men selected for first base on mythical All-Star All-Time teams. Gorgeous George was one of baseball's greatest hitters, a fielder whose brilliancy was compared to that of Hal Chase, and a top-ranking base runner. Sisler's star would have twinkled even more brilliantly in the baseball heavens but for a sinus and eye affliction, which kept him on the sidelines for an entire season and handicapped him severely in his later career. Even so, Sisler left the big leagues with a lifetime batting average of .340.

The Browns acquired a new owner, cantankerous, irascible, blustery Philip deCatesby Ball, shortly after the arrival of Sisler. Phil Ball, millionaire manufacturer of ice-making machinery and cold storage plants, and brewer Otto Stifel backed the St. Louis Terriers during the Federal League years of 1914 and 1915. In 1915, the Terriers, managed by Fielder Jones of old Chicago White Sox Hitless Wonder fame, lost the Federal League pennant to Chicago by one point. It gave Ball the yen to stay in baseball. Among the terms of the Major Leagues–Federal League peace agreement was that Ball should be permitted to buy the Browns. He purchased the club from Bob Hedges on December 18, 1915, for $425,000. Phil moved into Sportsman's Park, merged the best of his Federal League runner-up with the 1915 Browns, put the club in charge of his Fed manager, Jones, and kicked Branch Rickey upstairs as business manager. Though Branch had a five-year contract, he left the club a year later to accept the Cardinal presidency under a syndicate of new owners. It infuriated Ball; he tried to stop Branch by court proceedings and never forgave the man from Ohio Wesleyan. Ban Johnson later retaliated by inducing Miller Huggins, successful Cardinal manager, to leave St. Louis for the better-salaried managerial berth on the New York Yankees.

Ball was a character. He bought the Browns largely as a personal hobby. With the exception of a few years, he lost money constantly, but it never bothered him. When Rickey left the club, Ban Johnson told him, "Don't worry; I'll get you a better man as business manager, Bob Quinn of Columbus." Quinn came in, and did a really fine job. But, he got nowhere trying to save Ball money. When an early rain chilled the outlook for any patronage, Quinn called off a game with the Red Sox at 2:30. Ball arrived at the ballpark at 2:45, being driven there post-haste by his Negro chauffeur. When Ball saw no action on the field, he went into a high dudgeon and stormed into Bob Quinn's office.

"What's the reason for this? Why isn't there a game?" he demanded.

"Oh, there were only a few hundred fans in the stands," hemmed and hawed Quinn. "A double-header later on will be more profitable."

The truculent Ball shook his fist. "Bob Quinn, let me tell you something," he roared. "I worked myself to a frazzle at the office so I could see this game, and if you want to keep your job, don't ever do anything like this to me again."

He feuded with his managers and ball players. Once he openly accused his second base pair, second baseman Del Pratt and shortstop Johnny Lavan, of not giving the Browns their best. They brought legal action against Ball for intimating they were "laying down." Both players soon were traded.

During the war season of 1918, the Browns, leading the Senators, 4 to 0, blew the game in the ninth as Washington batted out five runs to win, 5 to 4. After the game, Ball was in one of his crabbiest moods, and Fielder Jones, his manager, threatened to quit.

"So, you want to quit," shouted Ball. "You haven't an ounce of courage. Get out of my office; I wouldn't take you back if you'd work for nothing. I want men who like to tackle a tough job. Quinn, get me a new manager." Bob engaged Jimmy Burke, former big league third baseman and product of St. Louis's famed Kerry Patch, in the early century a breeding spot for big leaguers.

However, despite Ball's truculence and quirks, he was intensely loyal. Though a former Federal Leaguer, he stuck to American League president Ban Johnson through thick and thin, in Johnson's fight with the National League, in Ban's battles with his own club owners, and later with Commissioner Landis. In fact, Ball was the only one of the sixteen major-league club presidents who refused to sign the contract with Judge Landis in late 1920. Bob Quinn, as vice-president, signed for the Browns.

When Sam Breadon, at that time president of the run-down Cardinals, first asked Ball to let him come into Sportsman's Park as a tenant, Ball ordered him out of the office. "Are you crazy, Sam?" he exploded. "I wouldn't let Branch Rickey [by then Cardinal vice-president–general manager] put one foot inside my ballpark. Now, get out yourself."

After being repulsed a second time, the persistent Breadon made a third attempt. He begged Ball to hold back his temper for a few minutes and listen. "I was a poor boy—a very poor boy—in New York," he began. "I came here to St. Louis, nearly starved at first, but eventually made some money in the automobile business. I got into the Cardinals with that fan group—soon got in over my head—and much of my money is in the club. We're heavily in debt, and our only chance to salvage what we put into it is to sell the Cardinals' real estate for $200,000, get out of debt, and move to Sportsman's Park. You're a rich man, Mr. Ball; money doesn't mean anything to you, but I'm about to go broke, and only you can save me."

Ball gulped. "Sam, I didn't know you were hooked so bad," he said. "I admire your frankness, and what's more I admire a fighter, a man that doesn't quit easily. Get your lawyer to draw up a contract, insert a rental figure you think is fair, and I'll sign it. Even if it includes having that Rickey around the place."

Ball often had much to criticize, but in 1917, he felt he got some of his investment back when on May 5 and 6, two Brownie pitchers, left-hander Ernie Koob and right-hander Bob Groom, pitched no-hitters against the powerful White Sox, 1917 World's Champions, on successive days. "No matter what they do to us this season, that's a Brownie mark that will stay in the books a long time," Phil exulted.

Wales-born Jimmy "Pepper" Austin, after being traded to the Browns in 1911, stayed in St. Louis as a player and a coach for twenty years. He actually appeared in a Browns game in 1929 at the age of fifty. In this excerpt from Lawrence S. Ritter's The Glory of Their Times, *Austin remembers playing third base in the same infield with shortstop Bobby Wallace, who, in 1953, was elected to the Hall of Fame, and later with the great Browns first baseman George Sisler. He also recalls the day Browns manager George Stovall spit himself out of a job and changed the course of St. Louis baseball history. After Stovall was fired for spewing tobacco juice on an umpire, he was replaced the following year by the relatively unknown Branch Rickey.*

Jimmy Austin
Lawrence S. Ritter ————————————————————

When I went to St. Louis in 1911, the Browns were *the* team in that town, you know. It wasn't until the late twenties and the thirties that the Cardinals became the big team in St. Louis.

When I got to St. Louis, Bobby Wallace was the manager. One of the greatest fielding shortstops who ever lived, you know. It was a delight to play third base next to that fellow. Bobby played most of his career with the Browns. He was their regular shortstop from 1902 to about 1914 or so. Anyway, they made Bobby a playing manager in 1911, but he wasn't very happy as a manager, and in the middle of the 1912 season they got George Stovall to replace him. Bobby stayed at shortstop, though, for a few more years. George was a playing manager, too. He managed and played first base.

However, George spit himself out of a job the next year. Yeah, that's right, he expectorated himself right out of a job. He got himself into an argument with an umpire by the name of Charlie Ferguson. It was an awful rumpus. They were hollering at each other and one thing and another, and Ferguson finally threw George out of the game.

Well, before he left, George had to go back to first base to get his glove. Our dugout was on the third-base side. So Stovall walked, as slow as he could, all the way around the umpire and to first base, picked up his glove, and then started back the same way, maybe even slower. Well, the longer he walked the madder he got. And the longer he took, the madder the umpire got.

As George came around behind Ferguson on the way back to our dugout, the umpire told George to hurry it up. I guess that was the straw that broke the camel's back, because George let fly with a big wad of tobacco juice—

p-tooey!—that just splattered all over Ferguson's face and coat and every-where else. Ugh, it was an awful mess. It was terrible. George always did chew an uncommonly large wad, you know.

Well, they suspended George for that. In fact, they went and threw him clear out of the League. I don't believe he ever played another game in the American League, although I think that George did manage the Kansas City club in the Federal League later on.

So there we were in the middle of the season—that was 1913—without a manager. So who did Mr. Hedges, the president of the club, ask to be tempo-rary manager until they got a new one? Of all people, *me*.

Mr. Hedges called me in after Stovall was suspended and said, "Jim, will you come out to my apartment tonight?"

"Sure," I said. "Where is it?" How the devil was I to know where he lived?

He told me, so I went out there, and when I got there, here's this Branch Rickey fellow. He'd been a second-string catcher years before with St. Louis, but since then he'd become a lawyer and was at the University of Michigan as a teacher or a baseball coach, or something.

"Jim, I want you to meet Mr. Rickey," said Mr. Hedges. "Mr. Rickey is going to be the manager next year, but we'd like you to finish out as manager for the rest of the season." Which, of course, I did.

So that's how I met Branch Rickey. A year or two later Branch brought George Sisler to the Browns. Branch had been his coach at the University of Michigan. And you know the tremendous ballplayer Sis became. One of the greatest who ever lived. Golly, he hit like blazes: .407 one year, .420 another. He was unbelievable with that bat. Really, you had to see it to believe it.

You know what happened last December? The phone rang and some guy with a real rough voice says, "Are you going to be home tomorrow?"

"Yeah, I'll be home tomorrow," I said.

"Well, I expect to be there about lunchtime."

"Who the hell is this?" I said.

"It's Branch Rickey," he says.

So old Branch showed up and we spent hours talking about old friends and replaying old ball games. It was great.

I was Branch's Sunday manager, you know. He promised his mother and father he'd never go near a ballpark on Sunday, so I managed the team for him every Sunday all the time he was with the Browns.

Just think of me, a third baseman, playing most of my years throwing over either to Hal Chase or George Sisler at first base. Why, that's *heaven* for a third baseman. There's no doubt that they were the two greatest fielding first base-men who ever lived, and that's in *anybody's* book.

Of the two, I guess I'd have to say that Chase was the better fielder. I hate to say that, but you have to give the devil his due. Sis was a better all-around ballplayer. He started with us as a pitcher, you know. I was at third base one day in 1915 when he outpitched Walter Johnson and beat him 2–1. And, of course, Sis was a better hitter, one of the best of all time. But just on fielding alone, I'm afraid I'd have to pick Chase.

And pitchers—boy did we ever have 'em. Lefty Grove was fast and Sandy Koufax is, too. But you should have seen Walter Johnson. On a cloudy day you couldn't see the ball half the time, it came in so fast. That's the honest-to-goodness truth. But I'd rather bat against Walter than some of those other fastball pitchers because Walter was so damn careful. He was too good a guy, scared stiff he'd hit somebody. A lot of the others didn't care—the hell with you, you know.

I remember one day Walter had us beat, 10–2, or something like that, and he yells into me, "Here's one right in there. Let's see you hit it."

Well, he threw a medium fast one in, letter high, and I hit it clear over the right-field fence. Laugh? I don't know which one of us was laughing harder as I was going around the bases. But of course that was the exception. Usually I couldn't come close to hitting Walter, and neither could anyone else. I was playing against him that day in 1913 when he pitched his 54th consecutive scoreless inning, to beat Jack Coombs's record of 53 in a row. He reached 56 straight scoreless innings before we finally got a run off him. I guess that record stands even today, over half a century later.

And old Rube Waddell. What a card that big guy was. You know, when I first came to the Big Leagues they didn't have clubhouses in most parks, especially not for the visiting teams. We'd get into uniform at the hotel and ride out to the ballpark in a bus drawn by four horses. They used to call it a tally-ho in those days. We'd sit on seats along the sides and ride, in uniforms, to the ballpark and back.

That ride was always a lot of fun. Kids running alongside as we went past, and rotten tomatoes once in a while. Always lots of excitement when the ball club rode by, you know, with plenty of yelling back and forth, as well you can imagine.

But what I started to tell you about was Rube Waddell. When I was with the Highlanders, Rube was with the St. Louis Browns. He'd left Connie Mack by then and was near the end of his career. This day I'm thinking about we were riding to the ballpark in the tally-ho to play the Browns, knowing Rube was going to pitch against us. As we got near the park somebody yelled, "Hey look, there's Rube."

And darned if it wasn't. He was scheduled to pitch that day, but there he was, standing out in front of the swinging doors of a saloon with a mug of beer that big. He's waving and yelling to us, and while we're yelling and laughing back and forth he holds up the beer, like as to say "Skoal," and downs the whole thing, chug-a-lug, right like that. And as the tally-ho continued on, we saw Rube go back into the saloon.

Doggone it though, when game time came, darned if Rube weren't out there ready to pitch. I'll never forget it as long as I live. He went along all right for three innings, but in the fourth we got two men on base and then Rube grooved one to me, which I promptly hit over the fence. As I'm trotting around the bases Rube is watching me all the way, and as he kept turning around on the mound he got dizzy and by golly he fell over right on his rear end. Fell over right flat on his can!

Oh, that started everyone to laughing so hard we could hardly play. Some guys laughed so much they practically had a fit. All except the St. Louis manager Jack O'Connor. He came running out and yelled, "Come on out of there. You didn't want to pitch anyhow." Somehow that made everybody laugh all the more. Good old Rube. In his life he gave a lot of people a lot of enjoyment.

Before Branch Rickey built a dynasty for the St. Louis Cardinals and revolutionized baseball with his farm system, he spent a few years managing the St. Louis Browns. A former major league catcher with the Browns and the Yankees and later head baseball coach for the University of Michigan, he left his law practice in Montana to become an assistant to Browns' president Robert Hedges. After Hedges fired manager George Stovall near the end of the 1913 season, he asked Rickey to manage the Browns. Rickey lasted until the end of the 1915 season when new owner Phil Ball removed him from the position and made him the team's business manager. An unhappy Rickey left the Browns the following year to join the Cardinals front office as team president.

In Hunt Stromberg's interview with Branch Rickey in the Sporting News, *the new Browns manager expounds on a variety of topics, ranging from managerial strategies and the handling of players to his religious convictions and his refusal to play or manage on Sunday.*

Rickey Tells How He'll Boss Browns
Hunt Stromberg

Just for one minute jostle your imagination, pinch yourself to be sure that you're awake and shift the scene from a busy office of a major league base ball company to a college campus in far-off Michigan. Imagine a messenger boy entering the side exit and while you're in the act of instructing a group of collegiate hopefuls in the correct manner in which to step up to the plate, you are handed a message that commands you to quickly travel to a far-off metropolis, assume supreme reign over an eighth-place ball club and elevate the standard and the league standing of that pitiable organization! Perhaps you would cry "tut-tut" meaning something else in the conservative vexed vocabulary of one of our most esteemed executives and, perhaps, you would look ahead to great honor, publicity, etc., and bid your students farewell to show the hapless fans the manner in which a real manager takes up the task of guiding a cellar club.

Branch Rickey chose the latter course. Advancing from an amateur player to a semi-pro star, hence to the big leagues to head coach at the University of Michigan, the manager of the St. Louis Browns tossed to the winds the forlorn and thorny path ahead to bear the massive burden of leading a team which has proved a dismal, gloomy failure for many, many years.

Mr. Rickey—as suggested by a musical comedy strain—is "A Manager All His Own." Just what bitter formula has been compounded by Messrs. McGraw and Mack in building championship teams is nothing to Rickey. He has ideas, suggestions, plans, schemes, and a system which is ocean-wide different from any system employed by a major league manager. He doesn't hanker for the stamped approval of the base ball world in his dealings with a losing club; in fact he does not care one way or the other who agrees with his methods, or vice versa. Mr. Rickey's platform, an educational one, stands firm in the belief that he has been called upon to lend a helping hand in showering a ray of light upon St. Louis balldom. Before we go into lengthy detail as to Mr. Rickey's exclusive personality, mannerisms, and impressive tact in dealing with more or less pessimistic critics, Mr. Rickey, when interviewed, decided to answer every question we sprung as to his exact plans for running the St. Louis Browns. Rickey at first refused to respond to our plea, but, after he was assured that the base ball world at large was commonly interested in the chart for smoothing out a losing combination, he gladly consented to enlighten as to the inner composition of his repair outfit brought to St. Louis to hammer down the seemingly closed door and begin work on nailing together a first division club. Not possessed with an explicit faith in our ability to memorize intelligently every question we wished answered, Mr. Rickey was presented with a typewritten sheet of interrogatives.

Off hand, he swung in his chair uneasily, peered beyond the edge of the foolscap, blinked, frowned—he didn't say a word. Ten minutes later, Mr. Rickey asked if we were in the habit of exploding bombs while a natty detail of police patrolled the street along the busy thoroughfares of St. Louis. After the plaintiff and defendant had presented their respective case, Mr. Rickey, two days later, declared he had plowed through the list and was prepared to publicly announce his every little suggestion and idea in managing the Browns. Below is a copy of the questions presented to the American League pilot, his answers and his attitude in attaching himself to a losing team:

1) How is your general system calculated to elevate an eighth place club to a higher rank?

Ans: I am not thoroughly acquainted with the condition of our club, or the personnel of the Browns, therefore any system I might formulate would be subject to change. The question is so general that it is difficult to answer.

2) Do you believe in keeping aloof of your men or shall you mingle freely with them off the field to personally gain their support?

Ans: I do not believe in keeping aloof from my men. I shall mingle freely with them off the field, however, not to gain their support, but just because I like to "mingle."

3) Are you in favor of retaining recruits who show signs of greatness and giving them a chance to get acquainted with your methods before sending them to the minors?

Ans: Depends upon the size of the "signs." I expect to keep some young-sters on the club.

4) What has religion to do with base ball?

Ans: It has no more to do with base ball than it has to do with any other le-gitimate pursuit.

5) Do you contend that it is better for a player to attend church once a week and pay proper respect to his religion in order to get on in base ball?

Ans: Doubtless every man should pay proper respect to his religion, if he has one. Going to church once a week has no connection whatever with the playing ability of any man.

6) How shall you handle your men—firm—or shall you speak to their sense of right to give the club their most worthy services?

Ans: Impossible to give categorical answer; depends entirely upon the man, the offense, the time, the place, how he feels and how I feel.

7) How about perfect harmony among the players?

Ans: Don't believe in feuds among ballplayers.

8) Have you any system in mind for keeping the men friendly?

Ans: Every man should have his mind so set on winning ball games that he cannot remember petty grievances.

9) Shall you have "smokers" or congregate in friendly mass meetings?

Ans: I do not know anything about such things on a ball club. There will be frequent "meetings" and I expect them to be friendly.

10) You do not play ball or don your uniform on Sunday. Would you cen-sure any one of your men should he feel about the sabbath in the same man-ner as yourself?

Ans: The St. Louis American League Base Ball Company signs the players to their contract. Beyond a doubt both parties will observe their contract.

11) Would you permit him to remain away from the park on Sundays?

Ans: Answered in ten.

12) Just for argument, suppose that every man on the team would decline to play Sunday ball. What would be your policy if this were the case?

Ans: Answered in ten.

13) Do you favor in detail the demands of the Base Ball Players' Fraternity?

Ans: Many of the demands are reasonable, and I believe they will be given proper consideration by both major leagues. I prefer not to discuss the de-mands in detail.

14) What shall be your policy in trading or purchasing players?

Ans: Distinctly for the benefit of the St. Louis Browns.

15) Is Mr. Hedges to be considered in the matter of trades, etc., or shall you have supreme power to run your ball club as you see fit, one way or the other?

Ans: Mr. Hedges employed me to assist in making a ball club for St. Louis.

He has so far supported me in all my plans and I have no doubt that he will continue to do so.

16) When a man pulls a "bone" shall you reprimand him briefly or is it your policy to take him aside and explain in detail his blunder, as the case may be?

Ans: Answered in six.

17) How about the pitching? Shall you permit one man to hurl nine innings, even though the Browns are winning, or do you contend that a pitcher must be replaced towards the final innings to assure his arm for duty as relief man the next day or to assure his not "exploding" in the crucial moment?

Ans: Impossible to answer.

18) Have the Browns the material to rank higher than eighth place?

Ans: The Browns have 12 old players and 25 new ones. I do not know the new men. The 12 old ones are too good to be in last place.

19) Do you think that the past management has failed to pull the full strength from the Browns?

Ans: I have never made criticism of any past manager and know comparatively little of the material each had.

20) If, after leading the club for several years, say four, the team fails to advance—shall you continue as manager, even though Mr. Hedges desires your services?

Ans: If your supposed case actually happens, my opinion is that Mr. Hedges will be dead long before this time. I AM DECIDEDLY more optimistic about the future standing of the Browns than the author of this question, I am sure.

21) Do you think a club should profit by shifting the lineup and batting order occasionally?

Ans: If you mean arbitrarily to "juggle" the lineup, the answer is no.

22) Do you think a team may be strengthened considerably by persistent trading and changing about?

Ans: A good team has more or less fixed identity.

23) Do you contend that collegiate players, in time, round into more efficient players than the sand-lot variety?

Ans: A college education is no more a necessity in base ball than it is in any other business. It is the exceptional ball player on any major league club today who is not recognized as having a very good so-called education.

24) What part in base ball do brains actually play?

Ans: The kind of brains I have in mind play a big part.

25) Is it more physical ability and so-called "natural" genius which produces a phenom or is it necessary to educate a youngster from the very start?

Ans: Splendid physical ability, rare judgment, a perfect coordination of mind and muscle makes what I suppose you mean by a "phenom." There are few such combinations. The Browns welcome recruits with any one of the three qualities.

26) What aid is a school of baseball?

Ans: I believe in every man having a thorough mastery over his business and if so-called "school of base ball" should be instrumental in this respect, I should certainly employ it.

27) How about the spring training trip? What course shall you follow in prepping the men?

Ans: I am unable to answer this question as would be advisable here.

28) Will you submit the players to rigid rules while in the South or do you believe that permitting them to follow the honor system will develop the proper attitude, etc.?

Ans: I believe about as much in rules as I do in the honor system and vice versa. Discipline on a ball club is largely personal. There will be some general rules as a matter of course, breakfast hour, practice hour, etc.

The long list of queries and answers in the above list are self-explanatory.

Mr. Rickey's reply in Number 10 is of whole-cloth material. It is a known fact that Rickey and the American League Base Ball Company came to a compromise on the black-and-white agreement that Rickey should not be compelled to enter within the portals of a ball yard on the Sabbath. The question was compiled to ascertain his valued opinion as to his much-vaunted religious fortitude. The answer is comprehensive.

Theory? Bosh! Says Rickey

Mr. Rickey takes this opportunity to deny the tempestuous reports that his base ball platform is on a basis of theory, law of averages and keen intellectual proficiency. Rickey declares that he doesn't give a snap of the fingers for theoretical base ball. He desires his subordinates to play intelligent ball, use their brains when brains are necessary in outwitting the competitor and the other part of the game can wend its own course.

"I want no theoretical base ball," said the manager of the Browns, "in plain words to hell with that report. I have never made such a statement. I know absolutely nothing regarding the 'law of averages,' but if it is thought playing an intelligent game and watching closely the fine points, call it that if you wish. I do not care what any body wishes to style it. I am not a grand stand manager and I am not a silent fixture from a school of base ball. I played the game myself, professionally and every other way, in the big leagues and in the minors, and I know the kind of base ball that produces winning teams. I wish you to know also that I am not "religious" and a church fanatic, as many have been led to believe. I have my own religious ideas and wish to conform with these ideas. The others may do as they see fit."

As Rickey was seated, his body bent forward, his fist time and time again hitting his desk with a thud when he wished to impress certain facts, one cannot desist from expressing admiration for his individual convictions, his concrete power, his aggressive personal manner in which he expresses a desire to give St. Louis a pennant winner and his many realistic ideals. Mr. Rickey is an idealist pure and simple. He has a goal; a long journey faces him as he sweeps aside the thorns en route his destination, and his odd singular map which will direct him to this golden gate may be taken as base ball's history. Jeered by man, accused by a tiny multitude, Rickey only smiles at the religious missiles thrown his way. He has fixed resolutions. Base ball or volcanic outbursts could not deprive the collegian of his moral pursuit. He is different. You'll admit that the new pilot of the Browns is not the kind to be presented to balldom every fortnight. Perhaps his manner, his personality, knowledge and practical judgment may swell the coffers of the St. Louis club.

Branch Rickey's tenure with the St. Louis Browns was brief and undistinguished, with the exception of his signing of George Sisler after the National Baseball Commission released Sisler from a contract that he had signed before his collegiate career at the University of Michigan. With the Browns, Sisler batted over .400 twice, hit better than .300 thirteen times, and had a lifetime average of .340. His 257 hits in 1920 remained a major-league record for eighty-four years.

After Sisler's remarkable season in 1920, F. C. Lane's popular Baseball Magazine *published a special George Sisler issue. Lane's own article celebrates the brilliance of baseball's "Sizzler" and favorably compares his record with that of Babe Ruth. In the Hughie Jennings interview, Ty Cobb's former manager examines Sisler's talent and temperament and whether the Browns star is a worthy successor to the great Cobb.*

The Dazzling Record of George Sisler
F. C. Lane ─────────────────────────────

George Sisler was the most brilliant player of 1920. His dazzling exploits dominate the records as those of Ty Cobb used to do. In batting, he was easily first with the phenomenal average of .407. In run scoring he was tied with Tris Speaker at 137 tallies. In stolen bases he was second only to Sam Rice, the flying mercury of the Washington Senators. In number of runs driven in, he tied at second place with his teammate Jacobson at 122 tallies, acknowledging no superior but Babe Ruth. Nor was his wonderful batting record in any sense a fluke, for Sisler took part in the full schedule of 154 games and appeared at bat more often than any other player, 631 times. In the number of his hits, he not only exceeded all competitors, but he broke the previous American League record with a grand total of 257 safe hits. What is more, he led all competitors in number of total bases, even Babe Ruth with his 54 home runs being forced to take a back seat. Just one short of an even .400, Sisler piled up a grand total of 399 bases, a record unmatched in modern baseball. In two-base hits he was second only to Speaker. In three-base hits he was second only to Joe Jackson. In home runs he was second only to Babe Ruth. Such a record is an all-around masterpiece whose like may not be seen again for many years.

From his youth up a veritable gale of good fortune has blown George Sisler on his way. While he was still a schoolboy in an obscure Ohio town, prominent baseball men had their eye on him. While he was a college undergraduate, Big League clubs were eager to sign him. His entry into Major League baseball nearly precipitated a war of the magnates and was remotely responsible for the overthrow of the National Commission. His career with the St. Louis Browns has been a continuous triumph, always on the upward scale culminating in the grand climax of the season closed. Favored by every possible talent, fleet of foot as an arrow, a wonderful fielder, a phenomenal hitter, and when so minded, a brilliant pitcher, Sisler is one of the greatest all-round players, if not the very greatest, that baseball has ever produced.

This is high praise and yet the facts deserve it. In purely offensive departments of play, Sisler has not yet equaled Ty Cobb, though during the past season he fell little short of the Georgian at his best. In defense, however, Sisler is a better natural fielder than Cobb. He is furthermore an infielder and, of course, Ty with all his ambition was never a pitcher. Babe Ruth is a greater slugger, but does not shine either in the outfield or on the bases, though himself a remarkable pitcher. Other players have excelled Sisler in certain departments and still do, but we know of no one who at present can be compared with his sheer versatility and all around talent.

The baseball star is commonly allowed a certain latitude covered by the dubious epithet "temperamental." Most stars need this latitude to cover their angularities of conduct. Babe Ruth is gruff and unaccommodating. Ty Cobb is high strung with a touchy temper. Tris Speaker is inclined to be moody and taciturn. Eddie Collins is cold and distant. But George Sisler, younger than any of these save Ruth, used to the limelight from his earliest years, has remained entirely unspoiled by the profuse honors which have been heaped upon him or by his truly remarkable exploits and he is today as simple, straightforward, and unaffected as the youngest recruit in Organized Baseball.

In many respects Sisler's baseball career reads like a romance. His present manager, Lee Fohl, was the man who first brought Sisler to the notice of prominent baseball people as a find. His present boss, Bob Quinn, engineered his signing of a baseball contract and did his best to dispose of Sisler's contract to Barney Dreyfuss and the National League. Now, by a strange freak of fate, all three of these actors in that little Ohio drama, which centered in the city of Akron years ago, are again gathered together with one Club, the St. Louis Browns, and what is more, though shifting interests might have caused enmity among these three, they are in reality the best of friends.

The story of Sisler's first contract and the battle between the National and American Leagues for his possession has been told before. There are, however, one or two points in that story which have been frequently misstated. For example, Branch Rickey, the manager of the Cardinals and former manager of the Browns, has been credited with discovering Sisler. Undoubtedly Rickey, as athletic coach at the University of Michigan, had great influence with Sisler when the latter was an undergraduate at that institution. Doubt-less he was largely instrumental in securing Sisler's name to a contract with the Browns. But he did not discover Sisler, and now, by an equally strange twist of fate, Rickey finds himself in the National League, while, of course, Sisler will always remain in the American. The man who turned Sisler from profes-sional baseball after he had wandered into the meshes of a contract was Pro-fessor Thomas of the University of Michigan. Lee Fohl, then Manager of the Akron Club, had seen Sisler play and was greatly impressed with his ability. He called up Robert Quinn, who was then head of the Columbus Baseball Club, and told him of this young phenomenon. "I doubt, however, if we can sign him for the price we could afford to pay," said Fohl. "If he is as good as you say he is," responded Quinn, "do not let a few hundred dollars stand in the way." And so George Sisler was signed, not by Fohl himself, but oddly enough, by an umpire in that obscure League who was friendly with Sisler and had great influence over him.

So, for the matter of that, did Professor Thomas of the University of Michi-gan. As soon as this gentleman heard that Sisler had affixed his signature to the fatal document, he immediately got in touch with the youngster and showed him how that act would prevent his playing baseball or indulging in any other form of amateur athletics at the University of Michigan. He also explained to the impressionable youngster how his extraordinary abilities would enable him to gain a college degree. And so it came about that Sisler went to the University of Michigan and turned his back for the next three years on professional baseball. At college, Sisler was one of the greatest pitch-ers and batters that ever represented any institution of learning. In fact, in the light of what has since transpired, it would be no exaggeration to claim that he was the very greatest. And yet all through his college course, the spectre of that contract haunted him. Influential friends, who saw the mistake he had made, rose to defend him, and Barney Dreyfuss, who stood ready to pay Columbus $5,000.00 for his release, found himself bilked of the best Pitts-burgh prospect since Honus Wagner was a cub. In baseball law, Dreyfuss's claims to Sisler were doubtless sound and the Pirate leader has never ceased to bewail the hard fate which robbed him of his superstar.

At St. Louis, Sisler started as a pitcher and a good one. But his abilities as a fielder and a batter were too conspicuous. Like Babe Ruth he was too good a player to be a pitcher. Even now Sisler mounts the slab occasionally and twirls a few innings merely to show what he might do if he set his mind on it. But needless to say, his days as a pitcher are over. The men who can hit .407 are needed in the game oftener than once every four days.

Sisler might, if he chose, lay off in the Winter-time, like many less favored stars. But he came of a frugal Swiss family where money was not abundant and where the value of thrift and industry was fully appreciated. Though he draws one of the largest salaries in baseball, which is indeed his due, Sisler has always worked at some useful occupation in the off-season. Just now he has embarked rather deeply in the printing business and is Vice-President of the River-City Press, Inc., of St. Louis.

So extraordinary a record as Sisler made last year deserves a closer analysis than common. Eight years ago when Ty Cobb passed his zenith, the .400 hitter became extinct until Sisler resurrected the breed in 1920. The records show that last year Sisler went hitless in only 23 of the 154 contests in which he played. Only twice during the season did he fail to hit in two consecutive games. The balance of the time he hit with a deadly persistence which knew no let-up and which rather increased up to the close of the season. As proof of this, the records indicate that in the closing months of September and October, Sisler hit very nearly .450. As his season's average was .407, it may easily be seen that he was growing better toward the finish. The ability to do this has been long recognized by ballplayers as the proof of a good hitter. The weakling may hit well at first, but he is bound to slump later on. Only the man who can really deliver the goods can improve as the season advances and the opposing pitching and fielding defense grow more impenetrable. In the final game of the season Sisler made three hits in five times up, scored two runs and stole three bases, including a clean steal of home. He also mounted the slab and pitched the final inning of the year, retiring two batters on strikes and allowing never a hit. The climax of a great season's work can scarce be improved upon. Although Sisler is himself a left-handed batter, the portsiders fail to bother him. Only five left-handers were able to hold Sisler hitless during the entire season.

Sisler's baserunning also improved as the season advanced. September was his best month. Evidently this superstar had not fairly got started until June when he first began to hit at a .400 clip. In August he was hitting at a rate of .442, while in September and October he hit for .448. Evidently, if Sisler ever starts a season hitting at his top form he will hang up a record which will make any other batter pale with envy merely to look at.

For years experts have picked Sisler as the man who would inherit Ty Cobb's batting crown and Ty Cobb's laurels. The experts were not at fault: Sisler has fulfilled all expectations, if indeed he has not exceeded the brilliant predictions which were made for him. And yet, by a curious piece of ill-luck he finds his name somewhat obscured in the very hour of his greatest glory by another player of noisier if not so substantial merits. That annihilator of pitcher's hopes, Babe Ruth, by his thunderous salvo of 54 home runs, has quite drowned out the plaudits due to Sisler's wonderful work. For the crash of splintering fences is too impressive to the ear of a fan to permit of a sober appreciation of all-around baseball merit. And yet, while Ruth is and doubtless will remain for some time to come, baseball's biggest drawing card and most popular idol, it is doubtful if he can compare in true worth to his club with the slender, agile, and modest first baseman of the St. Louis Browns. Since Sisler has already passed Ty Cobb on the downward decline and since Babe Ruth is the only man who can challenge his supremacy, let us pause for a moment to contrast these two superstars. While Ruth is a very fair outer gardener, he is of less value to his club as a fielder than is the St. Louis first baseman. Ruth is a pretty fast man, for a big fellow, but obviously Sisler can run rings around him on the bases. As a hitter, Ruth is unquestionably the greatest slugger who ever lived. But Sisler, though a lighter hitter, is something of a slugger himself. As we have seen, his batting average is some 30 points higher than Ruth's, which is perhaps a minor consideration. But he actually led Ruth in total bases, which is not a minor consideration by any means. Ruth drove in 137 runs, more than any other batter, as we would expect. But Sisler was not far behind him with 122. No one will rob Ruth of the honor due him and a comparison of these two players is hardly fair to either. And yet, the most superficial analysis of the season's records will show that even in batting, what is more, even in slugging, Sisler was not an unworthy rival to the redoubtable Babe. For example, Sisler made 49 two-baggers. Ruth made 36. Sisler made 18 three-baggers. Ruth made 9. To be sure, when it comes to four-base wallops Ruth is undisputed king and his 54 circuit smashes is perhaps the most amazing record ever hung up. But even here Sisler was no mean antagonist. He himself scored 19 home runs, second only to Ruth in either League, a feat which in most seasons would have attracted a world of notice in itself. Evidently there is honor enough for both of these stars, but don't think for a minute that George Sisler readily yields the palm even to Ruth.

There is really some little resemblance in the careers of these two worthies, though that resemblance might not be apparent at first blush. Both started as poor boys with few advantages. Both were naturally left-handed. Both began their professional careers as pitchers and proved to be good ones. Both were obliged to relinquish that position by virtue of their extraordinary talents elsewhere. Both have climbed to the pinnacle of baseball greatness and share that pinnacle between them with no close or likely competitor. And lastly, though Sisler is not often looked upon in that light, both are sluggers whose total of extra bases finds no close parallel elsewhere. There, perhaps, the resemblance ends, but it is really quite striking so far as it goes.

Sisler recently refused the managership of his club. He did so after mature

deliberations. The man who perhaps more strongly than any other champi-
oned his candidacy was Ban Johnson, President of the American League. "I
had a conversation with Sisler some time ago," says Mr. Johnson, "and I was
greatly impressed with his apparent good sense and sound judgment. It
seemed to me that he would be an ideal club leader, though I understand why
he should decline that honor at this particular time, and urged his candidacy
for the position. Sisler in my judgment is one of the very greatest players the
American League has ever produced. I am glad that he wears an American
League uniform, for he is a distinct credit to his profession in every particular. It seems impossible to improve upon such a record as his for last year, and
yet, I hope he does this. Surely, if he cannot do it, no one can."

This estimate of Ban Johnson's might well be the opinion of all other well-
informed baseball people. It is safe to say that among an army of friends,
Sisler numbers not a single enemy. And if there is a player now in uniform
who can surpass his record in 1920, that player is George Sisler himself.

Will George Sisler Equal Ty Cobb?
Hugh Jennings ————————————————————————

People seem fond of comparing George Sisler with Ty Cobb just now. It has
become a popular sport, almost a fad. As I have been associated on the same
club with Ty Cobb for many years, and as I watched Sisler break into the
League and develop into the great player he is, perhaps my opinion is as good
as the next man's.

So far as sheer natural ability is concerned, Sisler is certainly as well
equipped as Cobb. He is as fast as Cobb ever was, and speed after all has been
the basis of Cobb's success. Sisler is a brilliant fielder and great hitter. He
would no doubt have been a successful pitcher if his other qualities had not
demanded his regular presence in the line up. I am told that he makes an
earnest study of the game and he evidently possesses a keen, well-equipped
mind. In some ways it is quite possible that he may excel Ty, but there are two
important particulars wherein I believe Ty has something on him.

Sisler's personality is at once his strong point and his weakness. He is, I am
informed, a very likable young fellow and his temperament is of the type that
never antagonizes or makes enemies. Such a disposition is an admirable one
in the business world or in social intercourse. But it has its drawbacks on the
diamond. Baseball is far from a parlor sport and while it is lacking or should

be lacking in the blood and bruises which too often characterize football, it is, nevertheless, a pretty strenuous sport. The domineering, aggressive type of player who rides rough shod over everything between him and his goal is the type who will carry furthest on the diamond. Cobb is distinctly of that type. He is restless and ambitious and aggressive. He is fair, but wants all the law will allow him. Any advantage which comes his way he will utilize to the full. It is his temperament quite as much as his extraordinary talents which has carried him at a tremendous pace through fifteen years of strenuous work. Sisler is entirely different. He is quiet, almost backward in his way. He never seems to court the limelight as Cobb loves to do. He evidently hasn't the knack of pushing himself forward. He depends entirely upon his marvelous ability and strict application to business. A very worthy ideal, but unless he changes somewhat, or uncovers talents to outshine those of Cobb, if such a thing be possible, I doubt if he will ever be Cobb's equal as a personality on the diamond. After all, it is color quite as much as anything else which attracts the public to a player. Cobb has a lot of vivid color. Sisler has little. Cobb has that about him which makes him a great drawing card. People admire Sisler and appreciate his record but they are hardly thrilled by his exploits as Cobb used to sway the audience. In short, Cobb outclasses Sisler in his direct appeal to the public.

Whether Sisler is as great a hitter as Cobb, time will tell. Up to date he has done as good work as Cobb ever did. But he hasn't led the League in nine consecutive years as Cobb did. This is his first experience. When he has played eight more years, it will be easier to compare his batting with Cobb. Personally, I am inclined to believe that he is good as Cobb in natural ability as a hitter. And he seems to be making the best use of his abilities on the bases. Sisler is just as fast as Cobb in his prime, and he is certainly not lacking in intelligence. But I doubt if he will ever be Cobb's equal as a base runner. Cobb has developed a slide into the bag which no modern player can equal. The only men I ever saw in my experience who could approach it were Joe Kelly and Wild Bill Dahlen. Cobb's baserunning is not altogether a matter of speed or knack or even brains, though he uses all three. His slide easily puts him in a class by himself. It is more than a fall-away slide, although it is generally called that. He throws himself away from the baseman and around him, catching the bag with his toe or hand. This is a stunt for a contortionist. It has caused endless arguments in the stands when Cobb has seemed to be out at second or third and the umpire insisted on calling him safe. Most of the time, at least, he was safe. Other players would have been out, but not Cobb. He had eluded the baseman's groping hand and wriggled back to the base like an eel. It is certainly a masterpiece, that slippery, baffling slide of Ty's. Sisler has a good slide and is a finished base runner in every respect, but when you compare him with Cobb, you compare him with a master who has no equal as a base runner, at least in recent years.

From what I have said, it might appear that I thought Cobb outclassed Sisler. This is not the case. I have indicated, as best I can, two important particulars in which Cobb does outclass Sisler. But there are many other things to consider. Sisler, from what I know of him, seems fully capable of picking up the burden where Ty lays it down and carrying it to even greater heights.

Of course, it is impossible to speak of leading stars without mentioning Babe Ruth. Ruth deserves all the notice he has been getting. He is the king of sluggers. And the public likes sluggers. A slugging team like the Yankees will always be a drawing card. In the long run, however, it isn't slugging so much as other things which win pennants and it isn't slugging which sticks in the public memory. Thirty years ago the Baltimore Orioles were known as a brainy team. Men are still talking about the Orioles and will be talking about them thirty years hence. But when the Orioles flourished, the Phillies were known as a team of sluggers. Pitching may not have been equal in those days, but surely their like as sluggers was never seen. But slugging never got them very far, and who now-a-days knows or cares anything about that old team of fence smashers. Slugging will always appeal to the crowd because it is so obvious. If the batter knocks the ball over the fence you can see it go. That is Ruth's favorite stunt. Of course, the man has uncommon batting ability, but, after all, it is the beef that does it. Let a brainy player, however, like Eddie Foster engineer a hit and run play that would win the game equally well, and the fine details of that play would be lost on the crowd. Baseball, at least baseball popularity, is a fine example of the old adage, "Seeing is believing."

Batting should always flourish at New York for two reasons. In the first place the stands are near, and overhanging stands are a continual menace to the pitcher. Second, a ball batted into the crowd seldom comes back. This necessitates the use of many new balls. A new ball means a straight, fast one, or possibly a slow ball, with a curve entirely eliminated. And the batter knowing this, fattens his average immensely. A batted ball into the stands always did run the risk of being a dead issue. But last season hardly anybody thought of returning such a ball. Once in the stands it was out of the game and the pitcher had to take another reef in his belt accordingly. Earlier in the season the umpires helped a bad cause along by being extra fussy over shine balls or sailers. I remember a game at Detroit in which the umpire continually threw out the ball. We used several dozen new balls in one game. It was a considerable expense as well as a perpetual nuisance. We complained to Ban Johnson and he instructed the umpires to be more lenient. The next game we played throughout with three balls. The following game we used but six.

People have asked me what was the matter with the Tiger club last season.

I have commonly replied that nothing was the matter with the Club, only that it would have to be rebuilt. That is a long and difficult process. If you do not think so, ask Connie Mack. When he broke up his great club years ago, he told me he would have another pennant winner by 1918 or 20 at the latest. I told him if he had one by 1925 he would be doing well. Judging by Connie's progress up to date, I was very conservative. He is a great manager, but he could not perform miracles.

*The Beginning of a
St. Louis Dynasty*

At the beginning of the 1920s, inspired by the heroics of Babe Ruth, Red Grange, and Bobby Jones, America entered a golden age of sports. It was also the decade when St. Louis fans finally had a good reason to cheer for their baseball teams. The Browns, still the most popular baseball franchise in St. Louis, nearly won a pennant in 1922 before finishing the season one game behind the New York Yankees. The Cardinals, infused with talent from Rickey's new farm system, began to look like a pennant contender. Negro League baseball, with stars such as Oscar Charleston and Cool Papa Bell, also came to prominence in St. Louis.

In this excerpt from Baseball in St. Louis: 1900–1925, *Steve Steinberg describes the exciting baseball events in the first five years of the Roaring Twenties that were prelude to the city's first modern world championship.*

The Rise of Baseball in St. Louis, 1920–1925
Steve Steinberg

St. Louis's pro baseball teams became contenders for their leagues' titles. With the exception of the 1924 Cardinals, they both were close to or above .500 each of these seasons. In 1922, both clubs were in the pennant race deep into the summer, and for a few heady days that August, both occupied first place. The Browns fell just one game short of the Yankees and the pennant that season, and the Cardinals finished in third place, just eight games behind the New York Giants. St. Louis continued to be an American League city, as the Browns outdrew the Cardinals in five of these six seasons. They also finished in the first division five times.

At the time, 1920 did not seem to be one of the most significant years in St. Louis baseball history, yet it was. First, as the year began, one man emerged from the Cardinals' ownership group to consolidate control. Sam Breadon was an automobile dealer who bought $200 of stock in the team in 1917. He soon increased his holdings to $2,000 and then loaned the team $18,000. Why? To protect his investment, when the team was in danger of defaulting on a payment to Helene Britton. He became team president in December 1919 (Branch Rickey became vice-president) and reduced the team's large board to a more manageable seven members. Civic ownership of the team was ended for all practical purposes. Decision-making was streamlined, and the team was able to act more clearly and quickly. By 1922, Breadon owned a majority of the stock, and one year later he controlled more than 75 percent of it.

Second, in June 1920, the Cards played their last game at their ramshackle ballpark. Known as League Park early in the century, and then Robison Field after the death of both Frank and Stanley Robison, the name was changed to Cardinal Field in 1917. Breadon and Rickey had convinced Phil Ball to let them become tenants at his Sportsman's Park for $35,000 a year.

Breadon soon sold his old ballpark property to the city's Board of Education for $200,000. (A few years later, Beaumont High School was built on the site.) The team then sold another part of the property to the city's public transit company for $75,000. Mrs. Britton had sold her club (and assets, which included the ballpark and property) for $350,000 (the original $375,000 included legal fees of $25,000, which attorney Jones later waived). The new owners recouped more than 75 percent of that price just a few years later. $275,000 was an enormous amount of money in 1920. It allowed the team to pay down debt and still have a substantial amount of cash left over.

At the same time, Branch Rickey wanted his Cardinals to compete with wealthier teams for promising minor league players. He decided to bring to fruition what he and Robert Hedges had visualized back in 1913: the concept of a formal and structured farm system, whereby the Cardinals would acquire minor league teams that would feed players up to St. Louis. The plan was remarkably simple: sign many players at low salaries, place them in different levels of minor league teams, and let the talent develop and bubble up. Since the Cardinals would own the teams, they would not have to get into bidding wars with other, richer teams. With the money they had from the sale of their ballpark property, the Cardinals bought the Ft. Smith, Arkansas, and Rochester and Syracuse, New York teams. Just a couple of years later, the first players from this farm system took their place in the Cardinal lineup: Jim Bottomley and Ray Blades.

Nineteen-twenty was also a significant year for black baseball in general and in St. Louis in particular. The Negro National League, consisting of eight midwestern teams, was created and provided structure. While barnstorming continued even during the season, there were schedules and rules against contract jumping. Charley Mills's St. Louis Giants was one of the eight teams, but he sold out after the 1921 season—not before a spirited pennant race with the Giants falling just short of the pennant. And not before a member of the Giants, Oscar Charleston, put together one of the finest years in Negro League history. He was in the midst of a long and spectacular career, one that would result in his election to the Baseball Hall of Fame in 1976.

The team was renamed the Stars and moved from a small park on North Broadway to one that held 10,000 fans on Compton and Market. In their first three seasons (1922–1924), the Stars finished in the middle of the pack. At the top, the Kansas City Monarchs were replacing the Chicago American Giants. Something significant was going on at the player level in St. Louis. A young pitcher, who would soon be converted to a position player, arrived on the scene and began to give black fans someone to cheer for. His name was James "Cool Papa" Bell. In 1925, with a new split-season format in place, the Stars and Bell won the second half and faced Kansas City in the playoffs. The Monarchs eked out a 4-games-to-3 victory. The difference was a man by the name of Bullet Joe Rogan. He won all four of their victories and hit .455.

There were also fall exhibition games between organized baseball's teams and Negro League teams. In 1920 and 1921 the Cardinals (without Rogers Hornsby) beat the St. Louis Giants in series. A year later, the new Stars' team faced off against the Detroit Tigers (minus Ty Cobb and Harry Heilmann) and won that series. While the money was important for both sides, there was more to prove and more at stake for the black teams.

The Browns and Cardinals of the early 1920s were both imposing offensive teams. Consider the batting averages and league rank:

Batting Average:	Cardinals	Browns
1920	.289 (1st)	.308 (1st)
1921	.308 (1st)	.304 (3rd)
1922	.301 (3rd)	.313 (1st)

Superstars Hornsby and Sisler drove these numbers with spectacular hitting performances in Sportsman's Park virtually every day of the baseball season—when the Browns were on the road, the Cards were home, and vice versa:

Batting Average:	Hornsby	Sisler
1920	.370 (1st)	.407 (1st)
1921	.397 (1st)	.371 (4th)
1922	.401 (1st)	.420 (1st)

While George Sisler did not replicate those numbers after 1922, Rogers Hornsby did. He led the National League in hitting for another three years in a row, 1923–1925, with batting averages of .384, .424, and .403.

Had the two teams' pitching talent been equally strong, there might have been some pennants during these years. In only one of these seasons did a St. Louis club have one of the league's best earned run averages: the 1922 Browns, who finished one game short of the pennant, actually had major league baseball's lowest earned run average that year.

Both teams fell back to fifth place in 1923. The Browns lost George Sisler for the entire year, due to a sinus condition that caused a serious eye ailment. They also lost their capable and unassuming manager, Lee Fohl (who had replaced Jimmy Burke in 1921), and their talented business manager Bob Quinn. Fohl was fired, ostensibly over the Dave Danforth controversy [Danforth was suspended for throwing illegal pitches with doctored baseballs] and Quinn left to assemble the ownership group that bought the Boston Red Sox from Harry Frazee. His replacement, Billy Friel, simply did not have the background that Rickey and Quinn had.

In both instances, the hand of owner Phil Ball was evident. His interference frustrated Quinn, and without him, Fohl no longer had a buffer between himself and his owner. George Sisler became the skipper for the 1924 season. His eye condition improved, yet he never again approached the high level of performance he had in the past. Like Browns' star Bobby Wallace more than a decade earlier, managing was not a role Sisler particularly enjoyed or was best suited for.

With the Cardinals, as different as the personalities of Sam Breadon and Branch Rickey were, Breadon recognized Rickey's strengths and especially the potential of the farm system, which he funded freely. He gave Rickey both the authority and the limelight that his vice-president needed to thrive and be effective, something Phil Ball could not do. There was one exception. In late May 1925, with the Cardinals floundering in last place, Breadon relieved Rickey of his managerial responsibilities, which he turned over to his star player Rogers Hornsby. While it was a difficult blow to Rickey at the time, it allowed him to focus on what he did best, in a position we today know as the "general manager."

As 1925 drew to a close, the prospects of both teams seemed similar. The Browns had just gone 82–71 (good for third place), after two seasons with 74 wins. Phil Ball felt so optimistic about his team's prospects that he undertook a major expansion of Sportsman's Park that winter, increasing the capacity from 24,000 to 34,000. The Cardinals improved after Hornsby took over and finished 77–76, after averaging 72 wins the two previous seasons.

Two of the greatest hitters ever were player-managers of their teams, a popular combination at the time. Detroit's Ty Cobb, Cleveland's Tris Speaker, and Washington's Bucky Harris had similar roles on their clubs. After Washington won the American League pennant in 1924 and repeated in 1925, there were only two of the sixteen major league teams who had not won a pennant in this century. Both were in St. Louis, yet the prospects were positive for both. Even the city's Negro League team, the Stars, seemed to be on the verge of the Negro National League pennant.

*After decades of mediocrity, the St. Louis Cardinals won their first National
League pennant in 1926 and defeated the New York Yankees in one of the most
dramatic finishes in World Series history. In his essay, J. Roy Stockton tells the
"rags to riches" story of the Cardinals' rise to glory and the crucial role played by
Branch Rickey's innovative farm system, with the backing of owner Sam
Breadon, in developing a championship franchise. When the Cardinals won the
World Series in 1926, fifteen of the twenty-five players on the club's roster, including future Hall of Famers Jim Bottomley and Chick Hafey, had spent their
entire professional careers with the Cardinal organization.*

From Rags to Riches: A Baseball Success Story

J. Roy Stockton ————————————————————————————

Branch Rickey, president and manager of the St. Louis Cardinals, covered
his eyes with his hands. He could not bear to look. Out there on the infield at
the Polo Grounds, his second baseman and batting star, Rogers Hornsby, was
lying unconscious. Johnny Lavan, the St. Louis shortstop, had fielded a
grounder, and the ball, which he had thrown mechanically, without taking
time to look, had struck Hornsby on the head.

Only the night before, Rickey had been offered $350,000 for Hornsby. That
is a lot of money, no matter what your background. And what was Rickey's
background? Born in a small Ohio town, his parents had made great sacrifices so he could go to school and college. The Rickeys always had to count
their nickels. And here was Rickey, president of a poverty-stricken baseball
club, a club deep in debt, offered $350,000 for one player.

Rickey had met Charles A. Stoneham, president of the New York Giants, by
appointment in a café at 110th Street and Broadway. With Stoneham were
Manager John J. McGraw and Judge Francis X. McQuade, of the New York club,
and Oscar Cooper, a banker. Stoneham's first offer was $150,000, but Rickey
laughed and stood firm even when Stoneham berated him for a foolhardy
and irresponsible club president.

"Your board of directors will hang you for betraying their trust," Stoneham
told him. "You must have a price—what is it?"

"Half a million dollars," Rickey replied, and it was Stoneham's turn to laugh.
But he raised his bid to $200,000, then $300,000 and finally $350,000.

"You, the president of one of the richest clubs in the world, offer me three
hundred and fifty thousand dollars for the greatest player in the business,"
Rickey said. "Hornsby is an established star and you have a wealthy club in a

great population center. My club is poor. But poor as we are and small though our city is, I'll give you one hundred thousand dollars for one of your players who has been in only four or five games. I'll give you one hundred thousand dollars for Frank Frisch. Or I'll give you Hornsby if you'll give me Frisch and two hundred thousand dollars."

McGraw vetoed that proposition and the conference broke up.

How a Baseball Idea Was Born

"I'll never forget those moments on the bench," Rickey said afterward. "Three hundred and fifty thousand dollars suddenly mobilized out there on the turf at the Polo Grounds. They were large silver dollars. They had arms and legs and wings and faces that mocked at me. They did squads right and squads left, and right oblique and left oblique. They turned cartwheels, and as they rushed on their way, out toward the exits and over the fences, each one laughed at me.

"Hornsby recovered, but I didn't. Three hundred and fifty thousand dollars, and I had offered one hundred thousand dollars for Frisch. A total of four hundred and fifty thousand dollars, and all for two men. If I had the two men, I could sell them to Stoneham for four hundred and fifty thousand dollars. But I had no Frisch and, I feared, then, I no longer had a Hornsby.

"But I said to myself that I could find other Hornsbys and other Frisches. I would find them young, but I could find them and develop them. Pick them from the sand lots and keep them until they became stars. All I needed was the place to train them."

That's how the idea of chain-store baseball was born, on that afternoon at the Polo Grounds in the summer of 1919. Sired by necessity, the idea has carried the Cardinals from poverty and a sea of red ink to affluence and championships.

On that afternoon when Hornsby was knocked unconscious, the Cardinals owed $150,000 and he was their only player worth important money.

Today the Cardinals are champions of the baseball world for the third time in nine years, during which they have won five National League pennants. They expect to be stronger than ever in 1935, and Bill Terry, of the Giants, Charley Grimm, of the Cubs, and Pie Traynor, of the Pirates, building and planning for the coming race, build and think in terms of beating St. Louis.

The Cardinals are not standing pat just because they won the 1934 pennant and world series. The process of rebuilding, of adding strength here and there, has been going on through the winter. Many promising young athletes who could have been sold to other clubs for fancy prices will report to Manager Frisch at Bradenton, Florida.

Center-field trouble developed in the St. Louis machine last season and Rickey has attended to that. Baseball scouts will tell you that the best young center fielder in the minors last year was Terry Moore, of Columbus. He is the answer to a scout's prayer. He can throw a baseball into a barrel at 100 yards, is a ten-second sprint man and can hit a ball a country mile. Last spring, in an exhibition game with his uncles, the Cardinals, Moore hit one over the fence at Avon Park—the only time the feat ever was accomplished.

Moore will be one of many. There will be young pitchers, catchers, infielders and outfielders, knocking at the big-league door. If they are ready for the majors, the door will be opened and they will be added to the Cardinal roster or sold to rival clubs.

Replacements for any need are easily available now. No longer is it necessary to scour the minors or bid in the open market against the wealthier clubs. When a weak spot develops through the failure of a man to measure up to big-league requirements or because a veteran is fading, Rickey sends orders to Rochester, Columbus, and Houston for delivery of the cream of the year's crop. The manager then picks the men he wants to keep.

A Treasury of Horsehide Recruits

When Chick Hafey developed contract trouble and Sam Breadon ordered him sold or traded, Rickey summoned half a dozen outfielders. Joe Medwick, from Houston, was one of them and he made good immediately.

Right field was not covered satisfactorily in 1933, Manager Frisch asked for help, Rickey summoned Johnny Rothrock from Columbus, and he knew his man. Johnny played every inning of every game for the 1934 Cardinals.

When Sunny Jim Bottomley seemed to be on the down grade with a salary that was rather high, James (Ripper) Collins was called from Rochester and, after a short apprenticeship, he replaced Bottomley as the regular first baseman, making Bottomley available as trading material.

Charley Gelbert suffered an accident while hunting after the 1932 season, forcing him out of baseball when he was reaching the peak. The Cardinals were not prepared within the organization to replace so young a man, so Rickey selected Leo Durocher, of Cincinnati, as the shortstop he wanted and obtained his services by giving Pitchers Paul Derringer and Allyn Stout—two farm products—and Infielder Sparky Adams.

The Cardinals have money now. Before the Rickey idea began to function, it was necessary to economize in every possible way. The Cardinals lived at the cheapest respectable hotels they could find. Regulars, in the game every day, and a few pitchers, were given lower berths, but if you were a rookie player or a rookie newspaperman, you rode from city to city in an upper.

Today, if one of the better hotels doesn't give the boys the service to which they have become accustomed since leaving La Plata, Missouri, or Sylacauga, Alabama, the Cardinals move to another. Instead of crowding into the uppers and lowers of one Pullman car, the team uses only the lowers, frequently having three cars to itself.

In the old days, business was transacted by mail. Today Rickey flies from farm to farm, and has asked Breadon to buy him an airplane. At regular intervals, business managers are summoned from the chain stores for round-table conferences at the St. Louis headquarters. Transportation, telephone, and telegraph bills stagger the office help each month.

The Cardinals' Acres of Diamond Stars

Branch Rickey did it all with his chain-store idea. The Cardinals now have development farms in leagues of every classification. They own the Rochester club of the International League, Columbus in the American Association, and Houston in the Texas League, the three big proving grounds. Their holdings in smaller leagues include Springfield, Missouri; Greensboro, North Carolina; Huntington, West Virginia; Greensburg, Pennsylvania; and besides these clubs, owned outright, there are optional agreements with more than a dozen others in various small leagues, from which the outstanding stars will be graduated to larger circuits, until they are ready for the major-league tests in St. Louis uniforms.

There is today no more important figure in baseball than Branch Rickey, the penniless president of the struggling Cardinals of 1919. When he goes to a major or minor league meeting, club owners, managers, and scouts wait upon him. They ask his advice and are eager to buy his players. At the recent minor-league convention at Louisville, there was a line of seven men in the lobby of the Brown Hotel, waiting for a few words with Branch Rickey. He and his party, including scouts, club presidents, and managers, occupied twenty-seven rooms at the Kentucky Hotel.

Rickey could have had the National League presidency when John A. Heydler resigned. If or when Judge Kenesaw Mountain Landis retires, Rickey will be the outstanding candidate for the commissioner's job.

When the St. Louis National League club, in a badly run-down condition, was purchased in 1917 from Mrs. Helen Hathaway Robison Britton, it was a civic enterprise, to prevent the sale of the team to outsiders. There was a bally-hoo dinner at the Mercantile Club and teams of stock salesmen were formed. The Knothole Gang Idea, conceived by J. C. Jones, a St. Louis attorney, was explained. Anyone buying a share of stock at twenty-five dollars was to have the right to give a season's pass to some deserving boy, so that the youngsters of the community could have their big-league baseball without having to depend on knotholes in the fence. There was to be a Knothole Gang and the members would develop into loyal Cardinal fans who, in later years, would keep the turnstiles busy.

The price was $350,000 and the first payment was to be $75,000, but the early stock-selling drive netted only $50,000. However, Mrs. Britton really wanted to sell and agreed to accept the amount.

Rickey resigned his position as business manager of the Browns, the American League club in St. Louis, and became president of the Cardinals. To make the road rougher for the project, the country went to war, Rickey entered the service, and when he returned in January 1919, he found the Cardinals in a bad way.

The 1918 team had finished last in the pennant race and the turnstiles had rusted for lack of customers. The cash box was empty, Major Rickey was broke, too, and because there was no money to pay a manager, Rickey, along with the duties of president, assumed the task of directing the team on the field.

A spring training trip to Florida or Texas was out of the question. There was no money for railroad fare. And so it was decided to condition the athletes in St. Louis, using the baseball field and gymnasium of Washington University.

An angel came along in the person of A. M. Diez, a stockholder who had made a fortune out of shoe findings. He was a baseball fan and, as a sporting proposition, agreed to advance enough money to finance the modified training program.

As the opening of the league season drew near, the problem of equipping the team with uniforms arose. It was out of the question to buy a set of new ones. The money advanced by Diez had been used to feed the players, transport them to and from the university campus, and to provide baseballs and bats. The cash box was empty again.

Rickey rummaged around among the uniforms of the 1918 season and found a dozen that could be patched and repaired. He canvassed the sporting-goods houses until he found one that agreed to match the old ones as nearly and as cheaply as possible and to extend credit.

And so, with half the squad wearing old uniforms and with Rickey serving as manager and president to save money, the Cardinals went to the baseball wars of 1919. It was no wonder that Charles A. Stoneham confidently expected to buy Rogers Hornsby.

With not even enough money to provide the smaller necessities of baseball life, it was natural that the Cardinals found themselves severely handicapped as they sought to build up the team with player talent. Even when the club found an exceptional bargain, there were many difficulties.

First Link in the Cardinal Chain

At that early time, Rickey had convinced the baseball world that he was an unusually keen observer, an astute judge of ball players. His chief scout, Charley Barrett, was just as outstanding when it came to seeing future greatness in the awkward youths of the minor leagues, the sand lots, or the college campus. But in effect, Rickey and Barrett frequently found that they were serving other clubs, indirectly, but effectually.

Barrett would see possibilities in a young player and inquire as to the sale price. Perhaps the minor-league-club owner or manager had not seen the hall mark of a Hornsby or a Sisler or a Grove in the player, but when the astute Barrett made inquiries, that was different. Scouts of the wealthier clubs would be informed that Branch Rickey and Charley Barrett had made an offer for Pitcher Joe Doque. If Barrett offered $3,000 for Doque, he must be worth more than that to a club with money, and time and again Barrett would come back empty-handed from his bargain-hunting trips, having learned that Joe Doque had been sold for two or three times $3,000 to New York, Detroit, or Chicago.

When, despite handicaps, promising players were picked up, the Cardinals found it difficult to keep them during the necessary period of development. It is customary for major-league clubs to send young players to minor-league teams under optional agreements. This amounts to a loan of the player's services; the minor-league club, in return, giving the player instruction in the fine points of the game.

This arrangement does not always work out satisfactorily. Good pitchers are overworked by overzealous minor-league managers. Others are neglected. Minor-league clubs make much of their profits, or did when there was profit in the business, by selling young stars to the majors. Naturally, they prefer to devote their time and attention to players whom they own outright.

Rickey visualized a chain of minor-league teams of various classifications, a kindergarten, grade school, preparatory school, and a university of baseball, which eventually would graduate shining Phi Beta Kappa students of the game—Hornsbys, Frisches, Sislers, Cobbs, Speakers, and Mathewsons—who would lift the Cardinals out of the doldrums of red ink and who could be sold to the Stonehams, Rupperts, and Navins for battalions of silver dollars.

Rickey talked about his dream at every opportunity, and in 1920 a man came along who listened to him.

The man was Sam Breadon, aggressive, with a square jaw and a willingness to back up his judgment with his dollars.

Breadon, a former bank clerk who moved from New York to St. Louis in 1904 and decided that the automobile industry offered more to a young man than did a bookkeeper's stool, was one of the early investors in the Knothole Gang Idea. He bought eighty shares in 1917, investing $2,000. He was a baseball fan as well as a successful business man, and though the Cardinals were staggering on their way, he saw the possibilities of the future. In 1920 he put $5,000 more into the club, became a member of the board of directors, and looked around for other blocks of stock.

Breadon quickly became outstanding among the stockholders because of his interest, his enthusiasm, and his holdings, and on January 13, 1920, he replaced Rickey as president. Through that year and the next he increased his holdings, and in November 1922, he bought 1,048 shares of common stock from J. C. Jones, thereby gaining a controlling interest.

Rickey's idea was just a dream to most of the stockholders, but to Sam Breadon it was something real, with a dollars-and-cents fabric, and in February 1921, the two men forged the first link in the Cardinal chain. They purchased 50 percent of the stock of the Syracuse club, of the International League, from E. C. Landgraf, for $20,000.

At last the Cardinals had a place where young players could be sent for development, and so many promising juvenile stars were found and placed that in October of the same year the board of directors voted to further the project. They placed a fund of $25,000 at the disposal of the president and manager, to be used at their discretion for buying players and to increase minor-league holdings.

A Pitcher Knocks Himself Out

Rickey and Breadon soon discovered that the 50 percent arrangement was not satisfactory. James Leroy Bottomley, who wrote from Nokomis, Illinois, that he thought he could play major-league baseball if he had an opportunity, was given the chance, and by the time he graduated to Syracuse, it was evident that he was to be a star.

Landgraf had continued as president at Syracuse, and when major-league clubs began to make attractive offers for Bottomley, Landgraf wanted to accept.

It was with great difficulty that he was persuaded to return Bottomley, for a more modest sum, to the Cardinals, who had found him and farmed him to Syracuse.

Experience at Houston in the Texas League also proved the folly of trying to operate with only a part interest in a chain store. From California had come a sturdy young fellow named Charles Hafey. Hafey reported as a pitcher, but Rickey, sitting in the grandstand during a morning workout, quickly classified him properly. Branch heard the crack of a bat against a baseball that was particularly sweet to his ears and saw a line drive whack against the lumber in the left-field bleachers.

"Judas Priest, who hit that ball?" he wanted to know.

"That's a boy named Hafey, from California," Old Joe Sugden replied. "He's a pitcher."

"You mean he was a pitcher," Rickey replied. "Tell him he's no longer one. He's an outfielder. Throw away his toe plate and buy him sun glasses."

It was law, and Hafey became an outfielder. He went through the kindergarten stages and reached Houston. The Cardinals' first investment there was the purchase of nineteen shares of a total of 100 for $19,000. The holdings were increased until the Cardinals owned 59 percent. However, because of objections within the Texas League to ownership by persons in a higher circuit, the stock was in a straw man's name.

Hafey became a sensational hitter at Houston, and Rickey awoke one morning to learn that the president of the Texas League club was inclined and eager to sell the slugger to a rival major-league club for $35,000.

The Cardinals were at a disadvantage. They could not shout from the housetops that they owned 59 percent of the stock and that the club president was not doing right by them in selling Hafey. So they had to dig into their left pocket and pay $35,000 to Houston, their pain being alleviated in part by the fact that 59 percent of the purchase price eventually found its way into their right pocket.

It was apparent that straw men and part ownership were not satisfactory, so the emergency fund was used during 1922 to purchase the other 50 percent of the Syracuse stock, and the Cardinals then challenged the situation at Houston. Increasing their holdings there to 90 percent, they called for a showdown, opened their books, showed what the stock had cost, what they had spent for a new baseball plant, had a fair price set by an impartial committee, and asked the league to buy them out or forever keep its peace.

No one advanced to pay the fair price of approximately $500,000 and the Cardinal ownership of the Houston club has been out in the open ever since.

Expansion of the chain of farms might have been impossible if it had not been for a profitable year at the box office in 1922. The club was beginning to show the results of Rickey's careful planning and shrewd trading, and when it made a noise like a pennant contender, half a million persons attended the home games, almost as many the contests on the road, and the books at the end of the season showed a profit of $138,000.

Pennants over St. Louis

If Breadon needed convincing that Rickey's idea was not an empty dream, here was the proof. The final payment to Mrs. Britton was made in 1923, the club was out of debt, and the business of expansion continued. Sioux City, Iowa, was added to the chain in 1924, and in 1925 the Cardinals owned that farm, all of Fort Smith, Arkansas, all of Syracuse, and 90 percent of Houston.

Then, in 1926, after a total of $160,000 had been invested in minor-league holdings, the Cardinals won St. Louis's first pennant in thirty-eight years. On that Cardinal squad of twenty-five players, fifteen had spent all of their baseball careers in the St. Louis organization. There was not a man on the team who had cost more than $10,000. It was tangible proof that players could be picked green, trained, polished, and developed into valuable major leaguers.

Rickey had stepped down as field manager when the Cardinals gained their great triumph of 1926. If Rickey had any flaw, it was that he was too intelligent for his players. He talked over their heads. His baseball was sound. Rogers Hornsby recently said there wasn't a smarter man in baseball than Rickey, that he was always a jump or two ahead of the opposition. He also was far ahead of his men in his ideas. They never quite caught up with him. The team was in last place in 1925 when Breadon persuaded Rickey to turn over the managerial reins to Hornsby and take the full-time job of business manager.

Hornsby, practical and unimaginative, took the excellent club that Rickey had built and quickly whipped it into a pennant contender. He recalled shortstop Tommy Thevenow from Syracuse, arranged a trade with the Cubs for catcher Bob O'Farrell, claimed the great Grover Cleveland Alexander from the Cubs for the waiver price—a mere $4,000—traded Heine Mueller to the Giants for Billy Southworth, and in 1926 led his men to a pennant and the world championship.

The country's baseball fans still talk about that world series and the dramatic seventh game, played in New York on a drizzly afternoon. Persons who saw the contest will never forget the picture as Grover Cleveland Alexander trudged from the bullpen through an October mist and saved the championship for the Cardinals.

Bases Full, Lazzeri Up

Alexander—Old Pete to his teammates—had pitched a full game the day before and followed with a night full of celebration, an old Alexander custom. Hornsby feared the combination might have impaired the efficiency of the great right arm, but in the seventh inning, when Jesse Haines developed a blister on a pitching finger, Hornsby called a halt and signaled to the bullpen for Old Pete.

"People always ask me what I said to Alec when I went out to meet him," Hornsby explains. "I left my position and met him halfway between the bullpen and the infield. I wanted to find out if he could see. He recognized me all right, which was encouraging. He had been dozing in the bullpen, but his eyes were about open when he met me. So I told him we were ahead, but that the bases were filled, two out in the seventh inning, with Lazzeri at bat. I had told him he was our best bet and that, if we needed help, I'd call him.

"'Don't worry, Rog,' Alec told me. 'I guess there's nothing to do but give Lazzeri a lot of trouble.' And so, after I saw that he could see and walk, and didn't have anything in his hip pocket, I told him to go in and pitch."

Alexander took five practice pitches, struck out Lazzeri with the bases filled, to end that dramatic inning, and then turned back the Yankees for two more innings to make the underdog Cardinals champions.

"And there never will be another thrill like that one for any of the Cardinals of 1926," Hornsby confided.

Now there was money to carry out the chain-store idea in a big way, and Rickey made the most of it. Each year there were additions. Unsatisfactory links were discarded and more desirable ones substituted. In 1928 Syracuse was sold and Rochester bought in its place. The chain also included Houston, Danville, Laurel, Waynesboro, Fort Wayne, Scottdale, and Shawnee, and the investment in minor-league holdings amounted to $946,000.

At first baseball ridiculed Rickey and his idea. Then opposition crystallized. It was encountered first at Houston, where, as told, the other club owners legislated against the entry of major-league capital. Later Judge Landis took up the cudgel. But by that time the Cardinals had established property rights and an order to discontinue would have been tantamount to confiscation. Other clubs, too, were adopting the idea, and finally the commissioner, though he never has changed his mind, was forced to surrender, as far as active opposition was concerned.

Final victory for the chain-store idea was gained when the major leagues at joint session forced into their agreement with the commissioner a clause in which it was stipulated that he would treat all player transfers alike, whether or not they involved minor-league clubs owned or controlled by a club in another classification.

This ended the last threat to the chain store as part of the structure of organized baseball, and since then the building has been done with confidence. The New York Yankees have a chain and Tom Yawkey, new owner of the Boston Red Sox, is building one.

It has been said that local ownership of minor-league clubs is the ideal situation; that it is not proper for one club to control as many players as are at the beck and call of the Cardinals; that advancement of players in their profession is blocked or hindered by all the strings attached to them by the St. Louis organization.

Rickey replies that the Cardinals turned to the chain-store idea as a matter of self-preservation. If a near monopoly exists now, there was a worse one in the field when the Cardinals were unable to compete with the checkbooks of the wealthy Giants, Yankees, Tigers, and White Sox, he contends.

Rickey denies all the allegations against his idea. He can prove that players are not retarded by reason of Cardinal control. Last year there were in the major leagues more than seventy-two players who had been found by the Cardinals or trained in what flippant critics call Rickey's Chain Gang.

Baseball's Proving Ground

The annual surplus of talent has been used to good advantage. In 1928, St. Louis needed a catcher to replace O'Farrell. Young players from the farms were used in an exchange with the Philadelphia National League club whereby Jimmy Wilson was obtained by the Cardinals. Similar deals have been made when the need arose.

The Cardinals sold pitcher Bill Lee to the Cubs, pitcher Fritz Ostermueller to the Red Sox, Bob Worthington to the Braves. When the major-league teams gather shortly in spring training camps, there will be dozens of Cardinal-grown players trying for positions. In lean years these sales have balanced the budget for the larger farms.

Rickey and his chain-store idea saved many a minor-league club, even leagues, from the scrap heap during the depression. Loans were made to clubs and to entire leagues, to carry them through a season. In return, the Cards got the pick of the players at the end of the year. These arrangements were not always profitable. But the far-sighted Rickey realized that without the minor leagues, baseball soon would dry up at the roots and die. With no grade or high schools, there would be no use for a university, and much of the Cardinal attention has been devoted to the Class D and C leagues, the grade schools of baseball training.

Each year the Cardinals sponsor free-for-all trial camps or training schools in various parts of the country. In 1919 the youth with baseball ambitions thought only of playing with the Giants, Yankees, Tigers, or White Sox. But Rickey has made the youth of the land Cardinal-minded. Winter and summer, the mail brings letters from young men who want to play baseball. And the Cardinals answer all letters.

In 1934 more than 450 rookies reported at the Cardinals' spring camps, 85 percent of whom had never before signed a baseball contract. For them the Cards were opening, for the first time, the door to a baseball career.

Four schooling and trial camps were held during the summer, attended by almost 1,000 boys with no previous professional experience.

Seldom have the Cardinals encountered serious competition in persuading young men that their chain stores opened up the widest and easiest avenue to the majors. Rickey has a way with men. A college graduate, a former professional player, former baseball coach at the University of Michigan, an attorney and a fine public speaker, he has a compelling personality. The average father, after an hour's conversation with Branch Rickey, jumps at the chance to entrust his son's future to the man.

Rickey can sway an audience. He can't find time to accept a fraction of the speaking engagements he is invited to fill. The first order of business for the program committee at any civic, fraternal, church, or athletic function is to ask Rickey to make an inspirational address.

Lulu Loses Out

Jack Smith, an outfielder with the club several years ago, had high regard for Rickey's ability as a talker. He decided one winter that he was not satisfied with the contract offered. He journeyed to St. Louis and informed the newspapers that he was a holdout. A week passed without a conference between the player and Rickey, Smith still reporting from his hotel stronghold that he was a steadfast holdout.

Finally a friendly scribe suggested that Jack ought to visit Rickey at the Cardinal office and save himself time and money by trying to reach a compromise agreement.

"Not me," Smith replied. "I ain't going to see Mr. Rickey. Five minutes with him and I'll sign anything he hands me and I won't be a holdout any more."

Rickey, feeling responsibility as guardian of the young men in the organization, frequently makes clubhouse talks to warn and arm them against temptation. Occasionally a youth takes him seriously.

Clarence (Heine) Mueller, a product of the St. Louis municipal diamonds, signed a Cardinal contract, went to training camp with other young men who had been chased to the train by the cows, and heard one of Rickey's clubhouse exhortations.

Heine had relatives, including a comely girl cousin, in the town where the team was training, and that evening, after the day's practice, he was escorting Cousin Lulu to an ice-cream parlor. As he approached the parlor he saw Rickey walking down the street in his direction. Unceremoniously, Heine pushed Cousin Lulu into the nearest doorway, with orders to stay put, and then sauntered away to avoid his manager. When Rickey disappeared, Heine returned and found the girl cousin indignant.

"I don't care how mad you get," Heine retorted. "That was Mr. Branch Rickey, manager from the St. Louis Cardinals, coming down the street, and, after all, I'm down here already to train for the Redbirds, not to run around with women."

Thoroughness marks the Cardinal training and trial camps. Managers, scouts, club executives, and coaches attend, and each boy is card-indexed. Each is watched and checked individually, and if, at the nightly conferences, one inspector reports tagging a young man as having a single asset, he is retained for further trial.

Few stars have slipped through the hands of the St. Louis owners, once they have been caught in the great dragnet. Lonnie Warneke, of the Cubs, was an exception. He once belonged to the Cardinals. A slender youth from Arkansas, with a burning fast ball, he was sent to Houston, then shunted to Laurel, Mississippi, tagged as a fine prospect.

A Find Who Got Away

Laurel's manager did not see the future greatness in Warneke. He informed St. Louis that he was about to dispose of the young pitcher to a club outside the organization. The card index at headquarters showed that Warneke from the beginning had been labeled as having promise. A scout was sent to Laurel to pass final judgment. He grudgingly gave his consent to the release and Warneke passed out of the organization, to develop later into a brilliant master of pitching.

But the mistake served a purpose. In annual instructions to camp inspectors, the case is mentioned. Warneke must have had that fast ball at that early date. Let there be no such blunders in the future.

At the outset, the Cardinals, wanting to make the farm clubs as nearly self-supporting as possible, knew that it was essential to have the good will of the customers in the minors. They decided, therefore, never to take an important player from a farm during the playing season. At the end of the pennant race, the fans expect and want to see their heroes graduate. But never, during a season, have the Cards wrecked or impaired a farm team by taking away a player, no matter how crying the need in St. Louis might be.

Minor-league clubs in the chain have had more than their own share of success. Rochester, shortly after it came under St. Louis ownership, won three consecutive pennants. Houston won in the Texas League and also gained the Dixie Series championship under the Cardinal banner. Columbus won American Association titles and the Little World Series, in competition with the International League, in 1933 and 1934.

Instead of resentment today among the minor leagues, there are more requests than the Cardinals can take care of, for assistance and ownership.

The 1934 personnel of the Redbirds proved how well Rickey built. St. Louis dashed gallantly down the stretch to win the pennant and make Bill Terry and the Giants sick of all wisecracks, and especially those concerning the presence of Brooklyn in the league. Then the Cardinals defeated Detroit in a dramatic seven-game world series and the chain-store stamp was on the outstanding Cardinal heroes.

Dizzy and Paul Dean, who pitched the National League team to victory, each winning two games and the hearts of the country outside of Michigan, were picked up as boys and trained in the Cardinal chain stores. "Me and Paul" are being hailed as the outstanding box-office attraction in baseball, successors to Babe Ruth. Babe cost the Yankees $125,000. "Me and Paul" cost the Cardinals nothing but a few headaches.

Bill DeLancey, the juvenile catcher, who did all of the backstopping in the series, was obtained in the same way, for nothing. Joe Medwick, hard-hitting left fielder and idol of the Detroit fruit and produce merchants, was found on a Jersey sand lot and developed at Scottdale, Pennsylvania, and Houston.

Collins, the first baseman, became Cardinal property when St. Louis sold Syracuse and obtained Rochester and its roster.

John Leonard (Pepper) Martin, who galloped to national fame in the 1931 world series as the Wild Horse of the Osage, making a one-man show of the victory over Connie Mack's Athletics, also was a product of the chain stores, costing only the trouble of developing him and teaching him that a Pullman car was safer than riding the rods.

Two of the infielders were obtained in trades. Frisch became a Cardinal in the 1926 Hornsby trade. Durocher figured in the 1933 swap with Cincinnati.

Chick Fullis was the only St. Louis outfielder in the series developed outside the organization.

Color and courage are two assets the Cardinals are glad to find in rookies, and the team of today has both in large quantities. The Deans stand out. They figured prominently in that drive down the stretch, during which St. Louis won twenty of its last twenty-five games. And when Detroit was leading, three games to two, in the rough-and-tumble world series, Capt. Leo Durocher remarked that the situation was made to order for the Cardinals.

"We haven't cracked on a hill yet," he said. "When the fighting gets tough, that's where we shine."

The Breadon-Rickey Alliance

The Breadon-Rickey combination has been an efficient one. Rickey, whose contract calls for a share of the profits, has a free hand in shifting, trading, buying, and selling players. He has a blackboard, covering one wall of his office, on which transfers are posted during the winter trading months. He consults Breadon only when a deal involves first-line strength.

Breadon decides questions of business policy and hires and fires managers. As Rickey's shrewdness is a by-word with baseball people, so is Breadon's luck. Every time Breadon meets a dilemma—and he has tackled many of them—he comes out of the scuffle with a solid gold, diamond-studded horn in either hand.

Rogers Hornsby was sitting in the city's lap after leading the Cardinals to the 1926 triumphs, and when Breadon, two months later, traded the Rajah to New York for Frisch, because harmony didn't live there any more, the indignation was tremendous. Pro Bono Publico, Vox Populi, and Beowulf Q. Phan vowed never to make another turnstile click. The customers were determined to show Breadon he couldn't do that to their Rogers Hornsby.

But Frisch, in 1927, was the greatest second baseman and probably the best player in the business; the Cardinals finished just a nose behind the pennant winners without Hornsby and the turnstiles clicked merrily.

During a controversy with the Browns over the rental of Sportsman's Park—owned by the American League club—because a clerk forgot to mail a check Breadon had signed a month before as he departed for a Florida vacation, Sam bought an abandoned quarry and was prepared to turn it eventually into the site for a baseball plant. The trouble was settled satisfactorily, a building boom came along, and the quarry was used profitably as a dumping ground by excavators and became a valuable property, as it paid for itself several times over in fees from the dump trucks.

Subsequently, the Browns enlarged their park, adding materially to its seating capacity, but it was Breadon and the Cardinals who cashed in on the improvements, because the next year the Redbirds won the pennant.

There was indignation when Breadon demoted Bob O'Farrell after one year as manager for finishing second, and then traded him to the Giants, but George Harper, obtained in the swap, had the best year of his career and his batting carried the team to the 1928 pennant.

Nothing Succeeds Like Success

Fans stormed again when Breadon fired Bill McKechnie after the Cardinals won that pennant, but Breadon picked Gabby Street from nowhere, and again the customers forgot their resentment when the Old Sergeant won two flags and a world title in 1930 and 1931.

Street, in turn, was fired to the tune of the usual indignant protests, but Frisch, taking charge late in 1933, drove the Cardinals and the Dazzling Deans to the 1934 world championship. If success is a convincer, the customers believe now in Breadon's judgment and luck.

The value of the Cardinals has grown tremendously since that afternoon in 1919 when a vision of 350,000 silver dollars swayed Branch Rickey. Recently Tom Yawkey, of Boston, bought Joe Cronin from Clark Griffith, of Washington, and good authority has it that the price was $250,000 and a $35,000 player. Using that as a basis of values, Rickey and Breadon could get back more than the 1917 purchase price of the Cardinals if they wanted to part with Dizzy and Paul Dean. If they chose to sell on a wholesale scale, they undoubtedly could clear half a million dollars and still have their franchise, minor-league clubs, and a respectable roster of players.

Lew H. Wentz, Oklahoma multi-millionaire, recently negotiated for the purchase of Sam Breadon's holdings, approximately 77 percent of the stock. The price was to be $1,000,000, and except for the fact that baseball-minded men with $1,000,000 bank rolls are exceedingly scarce, that would have been a bargain. Breadon said he was glad Wentz didn't buy—that the club was worth $2,000,000.

At the three larger minor-league farms—Rochester, Columbus, and Houston—real estate and new baseball plants represent a total investment of $1,200,000. Baseball men will tell you that if times were more nearly normal, the Cardinal property, at a conservative estimate, would be worth $2,500,000.

Here is a team which has won five pennants and three world championships under four different managers in nine years, with other triumphs ahead, an artistic as well as a financial success. And Branch Rickey did it.

Grover Cleveland Alexander's dramatic strikeout of Tony Lazzeri with two outs and the bases loaded in the seventh inning of the deciding game of the 1926 World Series has become one of the most memorable moments in World Series history. Because of Alexander's notorious drinking problem, the strikeout has also become a part of baseball's fabled history. Claims about Alexander's condition when manager Rogers Hornsby summoned him into the game have varied over the years, but, fortunately, Alexander's own account has been preserved by oral history as well as an account by Alexander's battery mate, Bob O'Farrell. Alexander's story, first published in the Chicago Daily News, *was reprinted in* My Greatest Day in Baseball. *O'Farrell's version first appeared in Lawrence Ritter's* The Glory of Their Times, *along with an account of Babe Ruth's base-running gaffe that ended the 1926 World Series.*

Grover Cleveland Alexander
Francis J. Powers

My greatest day in baseball has to be the seventh game of the 1926 World Series between the Cards and the Yankees. If I picked any other game the fans would think I was crazy. I guess just about everyone knows the story of that game; it has been told often enough. How I came in as a relief pitcher in the seventh inning, with two out and the bases filled with Yankees, and fanned Tony Lazzeri to protect the Cards' 3–2 lead. Actually that was my biggest game, for it gave me not one, but three, thrills. But if it wasn't I'm stuck with it like George Washington with the hatchet.

There must be a hundred versions of what happened in the Yankee Stadium that dark, chilly afternoon. It used to be that everywhere I went, I'd hear a new one and some were pretty far-fetched. So much so that two-three years ago I ran across Lazzeri in San Francisco and said: "Tony, I'm tired of fanning you." And Tony answered, "Maybe you think I'm not." So I'd like to tell you my story of what took place in that game and the day before.

There are stories that I celebrated the night before and had a hangover when manager Rogers Hornsby called me from the bullpen to pitch to Lazzeri. That isn't the truth. On Saturday, I had beaten the Yankees 10–2 to make the series all even. To refresh your memory on the series, the Yankees won the opener and we took the next two. Then the Yankees won two straight and needed only one more for the world's championship and I beat 'em in the sixth.

In the clubhouse after that game, Hornsby came over to me and said: "Alex, if you want to celebrate tonight, I wouldn't blame you. But go easy for I may need you tomorrow."

I said: "Okay, Rog. I'll tell you what I'll do. I'll ride back to the hotel with you and I'll meet you tomorrow morning and ride out to the park with you." Hell—I wanted to win that series and get the big end of the money as much as anyone.

Jesse Haines started the seventh game for us, pitchin' against Waite Hoyt. We figured Jesse would give the Yanks all they could handle. He was a knuckle-baller and had shut 'em out in the third game. Early in the game Hornsby said to me: "Alex, go down into the bullpen and keep your eye on Sherdel [Willie] and Bell [Herman]. Keep 'em warmed up and if I need help I'll depend on you to tell me which one looks best."

The bullpen in the Yankee Stadium is under the bleachers and when you're down there you can't tell what's going on out in the field only for the yells of the fans overhead. When the bench wants to get in touch with the bullpen there's a telephone. It's the only real fancy, modern bullpen in baseball. Well, I was sitting around down there, not doing much throwing, when the phone rang and an excited voice said, "Send in Alexander."

I don't find out what happened until the game is over. Haines is breezing along with a 3–2 lead when he develops a blister on the knuckle of the first finger of his right hand. The blister breaks and the finger is so sore he can't hold the ball. Before Rog knows it the Yanks have the bases filled.

I take a few hurried throws and then start for the box. There's been a lot of stories about how long it took me to walk from the bullpen to the mound and how I looked, and all that. Well, as I said, I didn't know what had happened when I was called.

So when I come out from under the bleachers I see the bases filled and Lazzeri standing at the box. Tony is up there all alone, with everyone in that Sunday crowd watching him. So I just said to myself, "Take your time. Lazzeri isn't feeling any too good up there and let him stew." But I don't remember picking any four leaf clovers, as some of the stories said.

I get to the box and Bob O'Farrell, our catcher, comes out to meet me. "Let's start where we left off yesterday," Bob said. Yesterday [Saturday] Lazzeri was up four times against me without getting anything that looked like a hit. He got one off me in the second game of the series, but with one out of seven I wasn't much worried about him, although I knew that if he got all of a pitch he'd hit it a long piece.

I said okay to O'Farrell. We'll curve him. My first pitch was a curve and Tony missed. Holding the ball in his hand, O'Farrell came out to the box again. "Look, Alex," he began. "This guy will be looking for that curve next time. We curved him all the time yesterday. Let's give him a fast one." I agreed and poured one in, right under his chin. There was a crack and I knew the ball was hit hard. A pitcher can tell pretty well from the sound. I spun around to watch the ball and all the Yankees on base were on their way. But the drive had a tail-end fade and landed foul by eight-ten feet in the left-field bleachers.

So I said to myself, "No more of that for you, my lad." Bob signed for another curve and I gave him one. Lazzeri swung where that curve started but not where it finished. The ball got a hunk of the corner and then finished outside. Well we were out of that jam but there still were two innings to go.

I set the Yanks down in order in the eighth and got the first two in the ninth. And then Ruth came up. The Babe had scored the Yanks' first run of the game with a tremendous homer and he was dynamite to any pitcher. I didn't take any chances on him but worked the count to three and two, pitching for the corners all the time. Then Babe walked and I wasn't very sorry either when I saw him perched on first. Of course Meusel was the next hitter and he'd hit over 40 homers that season and would mean trouble.

If Meusel got hold of one it could mean two runs and the series, so I forgot all about Ruth and got ready to work on Meusel. I'll never know why the guy did it but on my first pitch to Meusel, the Babe broke for second. He (or Miller Huggins) probably figured it would catch us by surprise. I caught the blur of Ruth starting for second as I pitched and then came the whistle of the ball as O'Farrell rifled it to second. I wheeled around and there was one of the grandest sights in my life. Hornsby, his foot anchored on the bag and his gloved hand outstretched was waiting for Ruth to come in. There was the series and my second big thrill of the day. The third came when Judge Landis mailed out the winners' checks for $5,584.51.

I guess, I had every thrill that could come to a pitcher except one. I pitched 16 one-hitters during my time in the National League and that's coming pretty close, pretty often.

You know you think of a lot of funny things that happened in baseball, sittin' around gabbing like this. I remember when I was with the Cubs, and I was with them longer than any other club, we were playing the Reds in a morning game on Decoration Day. The game was in the 11th when I went up to bat and I said: "If they give me a curve ball, I'll hit it in the bleachers. My wife's got fried chicken at home for me." They gave me a curve and I hit 'er in the bleachers.

Bob O'Farrell
Lawrence S. Ritter

In 1924 a foul tip came back, crashed through my mask, and fractured my skull.

It was my own fault. It was an old mask and I knew I shouldn't have worn it. You know a catcher's mask gets so much banging around it gets dented here and there. If you try to bend it back the way it's supposed to be, it weakens it. Well, I put on an old mask that day and asked the clubhouse boy to get me my regular one. Before he could get back with it, the ball spun off the bat, smashed through the mask and knocked me unconscious.

I had caught almost all the Cubs' games the two previous seasons, and hit a solid .320 both years. Gabby Hartnett had come up to the Cubs in '22, and he was sort of crowding me. But the catcher's job was mine until I got my skull fractured. I didn't play much for the rest of that season, however, and the next year the Cubs traded me to the St. Louis Cardinals. A good break for me, I guess, now that I look back on it. At the time, though, I was brokenhearted. Still, it turned out for the best because the Cardinals won the pennant in 1926, and I was even voted the league's Most Valuable Player that year. We won the World Series, too.

That was *the* World Series, the famous one against the Yankees, where old Grover Cleveland Alexander, at the tail end of his long career, came in late in the seventh game to strike out Tony Lazzeri and save the Series for the Cardinals. I guess that's maybe the most famous strikeout in the whole history of baseball, wouldn't you say?

I had caught Alex for years on the Cubs before we were both traded to the Cardinals. I think he was as good as or better than any pitcher who ever lived. He had perfect control, and a great screwball. He used to call it a fadeaway, same as Mathewson.

I don't believe Alex was much of a drinker before he went into the army. After he got back from the war, though, he had a real problem. When he struck out Lazzeri he'd been out on a drunk the night before and was feeling the effects. See, Alex had pitched for us the day before and won. He had beaten the Yankees in the second game of the World Series, and *again* in the sixth game, pitching the complete game both times. He was thirty-nine years old then, and naturally wasn't expecting to see any more action.

However, after the sixth game was over, Rogers Hornsby, our manager, told Alex that if Jesse Haines got in any trouble the next day he would be the relief man. So he should take care of himself. Well, Alex didn't really intend to take a drink that night. But some of his "friends" got hold of him and thought they were doing him a favor by buying him a drink. Well, you weren't doing Alex any favor by buying him a drink, because he just couldn't stop.

So in the seventh inning of the seventh game, Alex is tight asleep in the bullpen, sleeping off the night before, when trouble comes. We had each won three games in the Series and now all the chips are down. The score is 3–2 in our favor going into the bottom of the seventh inning of the seventh game, Jesse Haines pitching for us against Herb Pennock for the Yankees. Suddenly Haines starts to tire. The Yankees get the bases loaded with two outs, and the next batter up is Tony Lazzeri.

Rogers Hornsby and I gather around Haines at the pitching mound. Jesse's fingers are a mass of blisters from throwing so many knuckle balls, and so Hornsby decides to call in old Alex, even though we know he'd just pitched the day before and had been up most of the night. So in he comes, shuffling in slowly from the bullpen to the pitching mound.

"Can you do it?" asks Hornsby.

"I can try," says Alex.

We agree that Alex should pitch Lazzeri low and away, nothing up high. Well, the first pitch is a perfect low curve for strike one. But the second one comes in high, and Tony smacks a vicious line drive that lands in the left-field stands but just foul. Oh, it's foul by maybe ten feet. Actually, from home plate I can see it's going to be foul all the way, because it's curving from the time it got halfway out there. Of course, I'm giving it plenty of body english too, just to make sure.

The pitch had been high, so I run out to Alex. "I thought we were going to pitch him low and outside?"

"He'll never get another one like that!" Alex says.

And he didn't. The next pitch was a low outside curve and Tony Lazzeri struck out. Fanned him with three pitches.

Most people seem to remember that as happening in the ninth inning and ending the ball game. It didn't. It was only the seventh inning and we had two innings to go. In the eighth Alex set down the Yankees in order, and the first two men in the ninth. But then, with two out in the bottom of the ninth, he walked Babe Ruth. Bob Meusel was next up, but on the first pitch to him the Babe took off for second. Alex pitched, and I fired the ball to Hornsby and caught Babe stealing, and *that* was the last play of the game and the series.

You know, I wondered why Ruth tried to steal second then. A year or two later I went on a barnstorming trip with the Babe and I asked him. Ruth said he thought Alex had forgotten he was there. Also that the way Alex was pitching they'd never get two hits in a row off him, so he better get in position to score if they got one. Well, maybe that was good thinking and maybe not. In any case, I had him out a mile at second.

Then the most fantastic thing of all happened. That winter the Cardinals up and trade Rogers Hornsby to the Giants for Frankie Frisch and Jimmy Ring! They trade away the manager of the World's Champions, who also happens to be a guy who had hit *over* .400 in three of his last five seasons! Boy, that really shook us up. Traded away a national hero. And to top it all off who do they make the new St. Louis manager? Me!

What a position to be in, huh? Hornsby couldn't get along with the owner, Sam Breadon, and in a way I ended up the goat. I didn't want to be the manager. I was in the prime of my career, only thirty years old, and managing always takes something away from your playing.

Nevertheless, we almost won the pennant again in 1927. Lost out to the Pirates by only 1½ games. But we *didn't* win it, so the following season I wasn't the manager any more, and I found myself traded to the Giants in 1928.

Hornsby was a great manager as far as I'm concerned. That year in St. Louis he was tops. He never bothered any of us. Just let you play your own game. He was fine. Of course they say later on he couldn't get along with his players. Got a little bossy, they say. Seems like he changed. But as far as I'm concerned, he was great.

Now McGraw, he was rough as a manager. Very hard to play for. I played for him from '28 to '32, when he retired, and I didn't like it. You couldn't seem to do anything right for him, ever. If something went wrong it was always your fault, not his. Maybe it was because he was getting old and was a sick man, but he was never any fun to play for. He was always so grouchy.

I remember one time Bill Terry was at bat with the count three balls and no strikes on him, and McGraw let him hit. Bill hit a home run. Right out of the park. As he came back to the dugout, McGraw said, "I'll take half of that one!" Meaning he should get some credit for letting Bill hit away with the count three and nothing.

"You can have it all!" Terry says.

No, McGraw was never a very cheerful man to be around. At least that's my opinion.

The greatest player I ever saw? Oh, I don't know, there were so many great ones. Guys like Paul Waner, Hornsby, Alex, Terry, Hubbell, Ruth, Vance, Mel Ott, Rixey, Roush. There were too many great ones to say any one is *the* greatest.

Although I'll say this: the greatest player I ever saw in any one season was Frankie Frisch in 1927. That was his first year with the Cardinals, when I was managing him. He'd been traded to St. Louis for the man of the hour, Rogers Hornsby, and he was on the spot. Frank did *everything* that year. Really an amazing ballplayer.

Today I'm still a Cardinal fan, even though I never caught as many games as I did for the Cubs. Or later for the Giants, for that matter. I was in the Big Leagues an awfully long time, you know, I think longer than any other catcher. Twenty-one years, from 1915 through 1935.

Over the years, Grover Cleveland Alexander's pitching heroics in the 1926 World Series overshadowed an equally brilliant performance by Jesse "Pops" Haines. After shutting out the Yankees in Game 3 to give the Cardinals a 2–1 edge, Haines started Game 7 and took a 3–2 lead into the seventh inning. He needed relief help from Alexander only after the blisters on the finger tips of his pitching hand, caused by throwing his knuckle-ball, became so painful that he had to leave the game.

On the occasion of Jesse Haines's election into the Hall of Fame in 1970, Red Smith, who started his distinguished sportswriting career in St. Louis, wrote this glowing tribute to Haines, both for his many accomplishments and his modest character. When Haines passed away in 1978, Si Burick, like Smith a recipient of the Hall of Fame Taylor Spink Award, eulogized his good friend as "a great, a wonderful, human being."

Country Boy
Red Smith —————————————————————————————————

It is a poor supermarket where the customer can't get Jerry Koosman's autograph with her Rice Krispies, ogle Nancy Seaver's hairdo among the detergents, or shake hands with Ed Kranepool at the cash register. They make the scene these young ones. They sell stocks and bonds, give organ recitals, take university courses, espouse causes, and sing in Las Vegas saloons.

They are with it. They know where it's at. They are typical of the major league ballplayer of today.

Jess Haines was fairly typical of another day. He was a country boy out of southwestern Ohio and he loathed cities. The fleshpot didn't interest him, one suit was all he needed to cover his nakedness, and he would sooner put the winning run on base than make a speech.

When the Cardinals were in New York, he could usually be found outside working hours killing time near the 71st street entrance to the Alamac hotel, where all the clubs stayed then. He'd stand on the sidewalk with his back to the building, hands in pants pocket, and as he watched the traffic pouring past on Broadway, distaste would show on every line of his face. He couldn't wait, he would say, for the season to end so he could get back home, where you could stand in the doorway at sunrise and hear a quail whistling or stand there at twilight and watch the dog bring the cows in for milking.

Blood, Toil, and Sweat

Jesse Joseph Haines earned his living in cities because that's where they played major league ball. He played it better than most. The Old Crocks Committee made no mistake when it selected Haines to the Hall of Fame along with Ford Frick and Earle Combs, the stylish centerfielder of Babe Ruth's Yankees.

Jess Haines was a knuckleball pitcher, but not like the knucklers who practice the art today. He wasn't at all like the wonderful Hoyt Wilhelm, for example, who'll be a Hall of Fame candidate himself one of these days. Wilhelm, who will be 47 years old in July, has been a relief pitcher throughout his career, except for one season. He arrives late, works briefly, and the butterfly pitch which drives men mad never seems to be thrown any harder than you'd expect a 47-year-old to throw.

Haines was a starting pitcher who was good at finishing what he started. In his first big league season he had 19 completed games, and in other seasons his figures were 25, 23, and 20.

Like Winston Churchill, what Jess Haines had to offer was blood, toil, and sweat, though perhaps not tears. Because of the way he gripped a baseball and the way he threw it, it was a common occurrence for him to finish a game with his finger tips bleeding.

The Fiercest Knuckler

He threw the knuckler harder than anyone you ever saw. He must have had exceptionally strong fingers, which he used like talons. He gripped the ball with the very tips, went up high on his toes in the middle of his delivery, and came over the top with a furious motion.

Many times when he failed to finish a game it wasn't the batters who drove him out; blisters on his finger tips would break and he'd take himself out, using language.

Still vivid in memory is a game he pitched against the Phillies in the house of horrors called Baker Bowl. This was a park slightly larger than a hockey rink, but not so big that the right field wall cast its shadow on the pitching mound. The Philadelphia team had one inviolable rule: even the batboy had to hit .300.

Seen from the press box behind the plate, Pop Haines was tremendous that day. Seen from the stands behind first base, he was bloodcurdling. From there you could see him go up on his toes, come through with that fierce, flogging motion, and the ball was a blur of white across the field of vision. Haines shut out that mob—Chuck Klein, Lefty O'Doul, Spud Davis, Don Hurst, Pinky Whitney, and those other predators—on two or three hits.

Pappy Guy

The game for which Jess Haines is most frequently mentioned went into the records as a victory for him, but he wasn't the hero. It was the seventh and deciding match of the 1926 World Series when Grover Cleveland Alexander relieved Haines with the Cardinals leading, 3–2, and the bases full of Yankees with two outs in the seventh inning. Alexander struck out Tony Lazzeri, allowed no hits in the eighth and ninth, and saved the game.

As the story usually is told, you get the impression that it was the New York hitters who drove Haines to cover. It wasn't. It was the unbearable pain of his bleeding fingertips.

The skin wore out because this was his third World Series appearance within eight days. Haines relieved Bill Sherdel in the first game, started, finished, and won the third with the most spectacular win of the Series. He not only shut out the Yankees, 4–0, with a five-hitter, but in the fourth inning he broke a scoreless tie with a two-run homer off Dutch Reuther. Sixteen years went by before another National League pitcher shut out the Yankees in a World Series.

Neither memory nor the record book identifies the young player who first called him Pop Haines, but the name suited him. He pitched through his 44th year, so at the end he was old enough to be the father of teammates like—well, like Dizzy and Paul Dean.

He did have a more or less fatherly appearance and manner. He was friendly in an undemonstrative way.

● The Downtown Exploded

On Sunday, October 10, at 3:20 p.m., when the Cardinals defeated the Yankees 3–2 in the seventh game of the 1926 World Series, the city of St. Louis erupted into a wild celebration that lasted for more than nine hours. Though the seventh game was played in New York, the moment Rogers Hornsby tagged out Babe Ruth on his ill-fated attempted steal, St. Louis fans, many listening to the game on the radio, poured into the streets of St. Louis. The account from the St. Louis Post-Dispatch *called the celebration "a city-wide detonation," as the downtown exploded with noise and painted itself red until the early hours of the morning. It was one of the wildest street celebrations in the history of St. Louis.*

Fans in Nine-Hour Rampage
Staff Reporter ──

From game's end at 3:20 o'clock yesterday afternoon to an early hour this morning, St. Louis abandoned itself to tumultuous celebration of the Cardinals' baseball championship of the world.

The downtown thundered with unceasing din for more than nine hours. Thousands of automobiles wormed and twisted in an unending circle of the business district. Machines chalked with exultant jibes at the Yankees, extravagant praises of the Cards—windows painted with paeans of victory—cars draped with Cardinal red, their horns sounding ceaselessly, filled with costumed, shouting men, women, and children.

Thousands Mill in Streets

The sidewalks overflowing into the street with milling thousands—a mob with cowbells, horns, rattlers, musical instruments, tin pans, gongs, bells, and lusty voices that never seemed to hoarsen. A crowd garbing itself grotesquely, snake-danced in the street, elbowing its way, throwing paper, slapping backs, shoving ticklers into one another's faces—a grinning, laughing, happy crowd.

The celebration spread itself throughout the city, beyond the city into the suburbs, beyond the suburbs into the State, beyond the State into the Southwest and Southeast. Telephones and telegraph brought word that hundreds of loyal Cardinal towns were celebrating.

It all began on a quiet Sunday afternoon. However, it was only a surface quiet, for the entire city was waiting and eager to shatter the calm if the right sort of news came from Yankee Stadium in New York. Groups were gathered about radios in downtown. Throughout the city, in private homes, there were

radio parties. Each block had several. The whole city had its ear to one voice—
the voice of the announcer on KSD from the scene of the decisive contest.

Roar Goes Up from the City

Twice before the city had given itself up to celebration of the Cardinals—
on the winning of the National League pennant and when they came home—
but here was a world's pennant in the weaving.

The eighth inning. The city held its breath through three outs. Now the
ninth. One out, two out, but outburst is not safe yet. The mighty Ruth at bat.
One strike, two strikes. Now a ball—two—three. Was ever torture more
acute? The flash—the Cardinals win.

It was like a city-wide detonation. It was as if dynamite had been planted in
a hundred scattered spots and all touched off at the same instant. The downtown exploded in noise. Two minutes after the din was deafening. Automobile horns and sirens, back-firing of motors, tin horns, bells that had been
muffled in silence, all turned loose.

Shouts of men and women at their radios in their homes telegraphed the
victory to their neighbors. Men, women, and children poured into the streets,
shouting and laughing.

They rushed for their automobiles and headed them into the downtown.
From all directions they came, north, south, and west—even east, because
within half an hour the Municipal Bridge was jammed with a one-way traffic—everyone coming, no one going. In 30 minutes all the east and west
streets east of Twelfth Boulevard were a solid mass of cars from curb to curb.
The noise now was almost entirely from automobiles. The sidewalks were virtually deserted.

Now the buses and the streetcars begin to be loaded. The sidewalks fill. On
every corner street-hawkers of noise-makers, of pennants, of buttons are
mobbed. The crowd outfits itself for a deafening night.

The complexion of the celebration changes. Automobiles quiet down and
the sidewalk takes up the noise—a great babel running block after block and
above it the shrill notes of the mechanical noise-makers.

Grotesque Costumes Appear

Grotesque costumes appear in number. Flappers in boy's clothes and boys
in flapper's clothes. A girl with a Charlie Chaplin mustache. A group carrying
red lanterns. Red crepe paper, cut into ribbons and festooned on automobiles,

wrapped about heads in turbans, worn as sashes, neckties, and belts, tied about legs. Other paper conveniently cut into strips. Girls with red birds plastered upon their stockings. Another with a red bird painted upon her cheek.

Grandma and the Children

A whole family, from grandmother to little tots, all with noisemakers. Police trying to divert the traffic jam into the side streets. It obeys and comes back on another street. Automobile loaded to the gunwales. At least 25 in that one. Riding on top, on the running board, on the hood, on the fenders, clinging to the back. A girl all in red sitting on top of a coupe. Red headlights on automobiles. Harlequins. One, a red devil. A baby sound asleep in its father's arms, oblivious of the racket. Two men with their faces smeared from ear to ear with Cardinal red. Another group with blackened faces. Youths with their coats turned front to back and trousers rolled to their knees. Two others clad only in red bathing suits.

A parade with the leader carrying a baton, the end of which is a great red bird. Automobiles trailing wash tubs, cans, boilers that strike sparks from the pavement. A man riding in a wash tub. Another riding on a bed spring.

Back-Firing Autos Heighten Din

Red stickers, picnic trucks loaded to the guards. An ear-splitting backfire of motors caused by racing them and turning the ignition off and on again. A traffic policeman directing traffic with a horn and finding time for occasional toots. Six traffic policemen needed at the Hotel Statelier corner. Girls in baseball uniforms—red caps and red stockings. A man with a placard: "Alex the Greatest." Another with a second man on his shoulders and a taxicab sign on his coat-tail—"For hire."

Faces rouged red with excitement. A sign: "We waited 40 years for this." Another—"They're walking the floor with the Babe tonight." A downtown department store unveils a double window dedicated to the Cardinals, champions of the world. An automobile carrying aloft a broom and a mop—a complete cleanup. Men wearing women's hats.

Smiles, smiles, smiles.

Elderly men, young men, elderly women and flappers—ticklers. A group carrying three sets of sleigh bells. Where did they get them? Thirty or 40 straw hats tied in a bunch and being dragged along. Everyone bent on being seen or seeing. Men dressed like clowns and acting worse.

A middle-aged man with a walking stick buys every victory extra that a newsboy has and distributes them along the curb. Boys with tin cans salvaged from dump strung together, offering them for 15 cents a string and selling out instantly.

That Ford has the name of every Cardinal player chalked upon it. "And the greatest of them all is old Alex." A group enter Hotel Statler and commandeer a page. He shouts, "Call for Babe Ruth." And the invaders shout in chorus: "He's in Mr. Hoyt's mortuary." Red balloons. One painted to resemble Babe Ruth's scowling face. Men with red sashes and little else, stripped to underwear.

Rowdyism Develops

It is growing late. The elder folks are going home. Rowdyism lifts its head. Slapsticks. The snatching of hats, hitting with horns. A fight there. Quieted by the belligerents' friends. Scuffling and milling. Police take a hand. Groups are broken up.

Past midnight. The noise trails off. The celebrators start home. It is early morning before the last banging dishpan is stilled in some garage.

Immediately following the game, each neighborhood business center duplicated the downtown celebration, though on a smaller scale. Toward game's end, numerous radio owners turned their loud speakers through open windows into the street. Passersby gathered in groups before them. The result of the great sport event was known instantly by a great majority of the population. For several hours, the larger outlying business centers, beginning with Grand and Olive, were whirlpools of celebrants and noise. The din extended from the city limits, Baden on the north to Carondelet on the south, down to the river. Eads Bridge poured in thousands from the East Side communities.

Vaudeville and motion-picture theaters were convulsed with excitement. Most of them gave the returns, some in detail, others by inning. The Orpheum matinee was delayed 40 minutes while the radio report of KSD was given. When victory came, the house burst into applause to bring envy to the heart of any comedian. Those in the balcony tore their programs to bits and showered the first floor.

At the Ambassador, someone called for 15 "rahs" for the Cardinals. The band played "There'll Be a Hot Time in the Old Town Tonight." In Grand Boulevard theaters there was ten minutes of cheering. Some persons left their seats in anticipation of the bedlam that was to break outside.

Shotgun Signals on Meramec

The radio did not meet all sections of the Meramec River, so a pre-conceived plan of firing shotguns was resorted to. Three shots were to mean Cardinal victory. The firing rang for miles up and down the river and the clubhouses rang with cheers.

During the height of the celebrations in the downtown, all Olive street cars were turned back at Twelfth Street and as many of the crosstown lines as possible were diverted around the area of congestion.

The streets for the third time in this baseball crisis were littered with paper, though not so thickly as on two previous occasions. Some throwing from office buildings—which mainly were closed—was indulged in. Denied the opportunity to paint the town white, the crowd was contented with "painting it red."

After winning six straight National League batting titles with St. Louis, Rogers Hornsby, as player-manager, led the Cardinals to their first modern world championship in 1926. When Hornsby was traded during the off-season to the New York Giants for Frankie Frisch, St. Louis fans were understandably outraged at the deal. In the years after the trade, the Cardinals went on to further greatness, but Hornsby, despite his batting prowess, was haunted by his growing reputation as a malcontent and by rumors of a gambling problem.

In this December 29, 1938, article in the Sporting News, *Hornsby gives his version—"as told to" Dick Farrington—of the controversial trade, responds to those critical of his gambling, and explains the reasons for his turbulent career as a baseball manager.*

'Me an Underminer? Not on Your Life,' Says Hornsby

I don't want this to sound like a squawk because everyone knows I can take it. But since I've been asked for this piece by the *Sporting News,* I might as well tell you right off the bat that you can't believe everything you hear. For years now, they've had me marked down a hard guy, a bull-dogger and a self-centered mug. They said I couldn't get along with my players; that I quarreled with everybody from the batboy to the club president; that I had a habit of undermining managers and, because I bet on the races, I was first cousin to the devil. Horsefeathers.

I'll dismiss the betting indictment first and let the readers draw their own conclusions on the other allegations.

Yes, I do wager on the horses and if it's a sin, a lot of guys gambling on the markets in Wall Street—or the horses for that matter—will burn in oil for a long time.

Betting on the billygoats—and that's what some of them run like—is a hobby with me. It gives me my only recreation off the ball field. I don't smoke, chew, or drink and I guess a fellow has to have some way to let himself out a little. But never—get that—never has my wagering in any way interfered with my affairs on the diamond. A ball game is always a fight to me and nothing else enters into it.

The races have cost me a lot of money, it is true, but it's my dough and as a free-born American citizen, I can do what I want with it.

If I had my last 20 years to live over, I'd do just as I have done. It's the only real fun I get—betting on horses.

Now, about my supposed undermining of managers and that sorta thing. I never tried to get another fella's job in my life and I want to tell you fans—and newspapermen, too—a few things you didn't know now that I've got warmed up.

When I was manager of the Cardinals, May 31, 1925, I never wanted Branch Rickey's job. In fact, I always felt like I saved his job for him during spring training that year at Stockton, Cal. For some reason, Mr. Breadon got sore at Branch. Breadon sent for me, and in the presence of Charley Barrett, told me Rickey was going to be fired.

At that time, nothing was said about me taking charge of the team, but I did tell Mr. Breadon that he would make a mistake in getting rid of Branch. Rickey stayed. So, you see, I couldn't have been gunning for the place.

Tried to Duck Job in May, But Breadon Had His Way

There is quite a story connected with my taking the job in May, 1925. We were in Pittsburgh and the team was going pretty bad. So, who pops into town, the morning of Memorial Day, but Mr. Breadon. I was eating breakfast at the Schenley Hotel when Clarence Lloyd, our traveling secretary, came to me and said Mr. Breadon wanted to talk to me. I told Lloyd I'd go up to see Mr. Breadon in his room as soon as I got through with my bacon and eggs.

Before I left the dining room, Rickey, who was having breakfast at another table with Burt Shotton, our coach, nailed me. He knew what Mr. Breadon was in town for and told me what was going to happen.

"Sam wants to relieve me as manager," Branch said, "and you're going to get the job."

I told Rickey I didn't want to be manager of the team.

"You mean that?" asked Rickey.

"I sure do," I told him, "I wouldn't manage any ball club."

"Are you going to tell Breadon that?" asked Rickey. And I told him that I was.

Well, I saw Mr. Breadon and he laid his cards on the table. But I protested that I didn't want to take the job.

"Why don't you keep Rickey on, or give the place to Shotton?" I asked him.

Mr. Breadon, however, was dead set. He is stubborn when he makes up his mind.

"I don't want Rickey or Shotton to run the team," Mr. Breadon shot back, his face flushed. "I want you to take charge—nobody else."

I stood off Mr. Breadon for a while and then was told that Rickey, who was also the vice-president of the club, was willing to let go of 1,165 shares of stock he held in the Cards. I guess he was peeved at Mr. Breadon's plan to fire him. Anyhow the prospect of getting into the club in a financial way began to interest me because I knew the Cards would make money if the team ever started winning.

Mr. Breadon arranged it so I could take over the Rickey stock and with certain inducements along this line, I accepted the management, taking charge the next day, May 31. Well, the team began to click and we pushed up from last place to a fourth-place finish. The club made some money.

I was getting $30,000 a season as a player and this contract was not changed when I took over the team. Neither was it changed for 1926, but I felt I was still on trial as a manager and besides, I was cutting in on profits as a stockholder. However, when we won the pennant, and beat the Yankees for the world's title in 1926, I decided that I ought to be stepping into the big dough as a manager.

Insisted on a Three-Year Pact; Offered $50,000 for One Season

Mr. Breadon and myself had several conferences on what my salary should be and the figure finally agreed on was $50,000 for 1927. He wanted me to take a one-year contract, where before, as a player, I had always signed for three years at a stretch. So, I insisted on three years, or no dice, at $50,000 per. How was I to know that my head wouldn't be cut off in 1927 if I didn't win another pennant!

It is true that Mr. Breadon and I got pretty hot over the contract that I wanted, and some things were said that wouldn't look good in Mr. Spink's family newspaper, but Rickey never entered the picture on that debate, as press comment had it at the time.

I never said anything about "Rickey goes or I go" at that time. I might have said something like that during the season, but not then. We had our disagreements when I was playing under him, but those things will happen on any ballclub. I still think he is one of the smartest men in the business.

Anyhow, Mr. Breadon and myself couldn't get together on the three-year contract, and in December, 1926, we came to a parting of the ways. I steamed up, told him where he could go, slammed the door as I left his office and the next thing I knew I was traded to the Giants for Frankie Frisch and Jimmy Ring.

There was some trouble over the sale price for my stock. You remember, they said I couldn't play for the Giants and continue to hold a financial interest in the Cards. That was perfectly right.

I figured that I had helped to increase the value of the stock by winning the world's title in 1926 and held out on bids made for it. However, at a special meeting of the National League, followed by an analysis of the value by a brokerage firm, the price was fixed at $116,000. It cost me about $50,000 when I bought it. But it was a business matter when it came to me selling and you couldn't blame me for getting what I could in the way of a profit, could you?

Another thing that ought to be cleared up for good is the reason why I left the Giants after the 1927 season. Some people said I had trouble with John McGraw. That isn't true. He was my friend.

Late in the 1927 season, Mr. McGraw got sick and he told me that he wanted me to pinch-hit as manager for him. We were on the road and the team made a pretty good showing.

In Chicago we won the first three games of a series, but in the fourth game, Travis Jackson, our shortstop, booted one that cost us a clean sweep. I made a practice of riding back to the hotel with Jim Tierney, then the club secretary, and no sooner had we got into the cab than Tierney began laying out Jackson to me for making that error.

As a manager, I never could tolerate mental blunders, but when it came to physical mistakes, such as an honest error, that was something else. I always stuck up for my players when officials butted in on the playing end.

I guess I was a little hasty, but I jumped on Tierney for criticizing Jackson.

"You run your end of the club and I'll run mine," I told him, among other things. "See that our players are taken care of properly at the hotels and don't be grabbing the best accommodations for yourself."

Tierney was red with rage at the crack and he must have run right to headquarters with a complaint about me. At that time he was just-like-that with Charley Stoneham, owner of the club. So, during the winter, while McGraw was in Havana, I was traded to the Boston Nationals.

Did I run Jack Slattery off the Braves as manager in 1928? Not on your life. Judge Fuchs, president of the club, called me to his office one day soon after the season opened, told me he wasn't satisfied with the way things were going and that he wanted me to take charge of the Braves. I took the job, realizing that Boston was paying me $40,000 and that it was a heavy drain on a losing club. It meant a saving to Judge Fuchs to have me in there as playing manager.

That was all there was to it. I never asked for the job, never had any trouble with Slattery, and all that press stuff at the time was so much baloney.

"I'm No Politician and Didn't Crowd Out Joe McCarthy"

Now then, about the Chicago Cubs and Joe McCarthy. I was branded as an underminer when McCarthy was released as manager in September, 1930. But Joe knows as well as I do that I had nothing to do with his losing out.

I never was a baseball politician. As a player I went it alone, giving my bosses the best I had and seldom saw the front office. As a manager, I ran my end the way I thought it should be run and if the bosses didn't like it, they could always find somebody else to do the job for them.

When I was playing with the Cubs, I tended to my own business and took my orders from McCarthy just like the other fellows. If I undermined him, I certainly don't know how I did it, because, as I say before, I always kept away from the front office and the club officials.

McCarthy was let out—as I got it—for the simple reason that the late Mr. William Wrigley didn't think the team was showing enough pep. When he gave me the job as manager of the Cubs, I didn't sit on anybody's lap to get it. It came out of a clear sky. McCarthy and myself are good friends today. And I'm not even jealous of his record of being the only manager ever to win three World's Series in succession!

I got in bad with the late Bill Veeck and lost out with the Cubs in a rather unusual way. We were two runs behind, with two outs in the ninth inning of a game in Pittsburgh on August 2, 1932, at which Mr. Veeck was a spectator. The club had just bought Frank Demaree, a young outfielder with a fine batting record in the Pacific Coast League, for $30,000 and Mr. Veeck had been after me to give the kid a chance.

So, I decided that here would be a good place to test the nerve of Demaree, and sent him in as a pinch-hitter for Pat Malone. He didn't do anything and after the game, Mr. Veeck told me he thought I should have gone up there myself, instead of sending in Demaree. I explained why I used Demaree, but Mr. Veeck insisted that I showed poor judgment.

"Even if I had gone in to hit and made a homer, we still would have been a run behind," I told him. But he was irritable and we had some words. Maybe I did say: "If you think you can run this team better than I can, run it yourself."

Nothing more was said and I figured the incident had been forgotten, but it wasn't long before I was notified of my release and Charley Grimm took the team and won the pennant. I still think the Cubs would have won for me, but that ain't here nor there.

I've learned to take the tough breaks with the good ones. That's baseball.

"Always Run to the Horses When They Want an Excuse"

As manager of the Browns, I was supposed to have been fired for betting on the horses. They always run to that one. But you'll never hear me squawk when the breaks are going against me. There are a lot of cry-babies in the game and I'm glad I'm not one of them.

I've been asked what I thought of these rookie managers who are coming up from the minors to handle big time teams. Well, there's no reason why a successful minor manager cannot get by in the majors, for he should know his baseball.

But I see club officials turning toward that type of manager for a reason. Business managers sometimes run out of excuses for the showing of an inferior club. So, they decide to throw out a new line and bring in new leaders.

It's easy to see through it. The business manager sells his boss on a minor leaguer who has had from good to ordinary success, the idea being that the business office can dictate to a newcomer brought in from a lower league. Then, too, if the minor pilot happens to get the club going, the B. M. is a hero. If the manager doesn't do anything with the club it's an easy thing to fire him and then try somebody else.

I have no particular quarrel with the front office, but if some of the fellows who think they know it all, would keep their nose out of the managerial end, which they know nothing about, baseball would be lots better off.

I'll always stick up for what I think is right and won't say "yes" when I mean "no."

But don't believe all you hear about me.

As I look back, I like to think that the Cardinal team of 1926 was the pluckiest outfit I ever managed. Get me now, I don't say the best team I ever played on, but the gamest and hardest to lick that I ever handled.

It was a team that went along—everybody fighting for just one thing—to win. There were no second-guessers on that club and nobody was better than the other guy.

Older fans recall that the team came from nowhere and then battled it out in a seven-game series to beat the Yankees. Those Cards were a real throwback to the earlier days of the game and made every contest a personal battle.

Today, I'm afraid there are too many of what you newspaper fellows call individualists. By that I mean, if a guy can hit home runs, that's all he aims for. Some of these individualists might have weaknesses, but they don't give a whoop about 'em, just so they can do their specialty.

These fellows go to camp and instead of working on their weak points, they practice on their strong points. And managers let 'em get away with it.

What I liked about my 1926 Cardinals was that nobody was too proud to freshen up on fundamentals. So, when we took the field, everybody knew what to do and how to do it.

Youngsters in the minors are not properly drilled in the fundamentals. Some of these lads perhaps will go to the majors and yet not know all they should know because they were never taught to do certain things right.

I remember a first baseman who became a star in the National League. He's through now, but up to the very end of his career, he couldn't make the force throw to second base without hitting the advancing runner, or coming pretty close to it. Of course, he got by because that play does not come up very often, but he could have been a better first baseman had he learned this trick when he was a kid.

That is one reason why I like the idea of a school for youngsters such as I am going to run at Hot Springs. If they've got any brains at all, they'll at least know the fundamentals when they leave me and some minor league manager will not have to spend his good time teaching ABC's to these lads.

Of course, you can't make a pitcher throw any faster than he is physically able to. But you can show young hurlers how to hold men on bases, conceal their pitch, field their position and that sort of thing.

Batters can improve themselves, too. All they need is some natural ability and the guts enough to stay up at the plate and hit good pitches.

Rog as 135-Pound Recruit Tried Higgins's Choke Style

When I came up to the Cards in 1915 from Denison, Tex., I was a chump for all pitchers because I was only a kid and my weight was against me. I weighed only 135 pounds.

Miller Huggins, who managed the Cardinals at that time, saw that I wasn't getting anywhere and he figured I could never do anything with major-league pitching with my step-in style and skinny arms. You know Hug was a little fellow and he got pretty fair results by choking the bat. So, he decided that I might do better by gripping the bat shorter.

When the season closed, Hug also suggested that I try to put on some weight. Well, I put in a whole winter in Texas building myself up and when I reported at camp in the spring of 1916, I weighed 160 pounds. Because of my weight, Hug and scout Bob Connery agreed that it would probably be better for me to shift back to my old style of striding into the ball.

There was another advantage to this stance. This was in the fact that the pitcher had a wider zone in which to try to find the strike area than when I was standing up there near the plate, giving him an outline of the strike zone on the inside of the plate.

I have never advocated my stance for any other players, because every one more or less has a style of his own and I don't believe in changing a fellow if he can hit under his own system.

Nor do I believe in switch-hitting. When I see a youngster who says he can swing from either side of the plate, I ask him what side is his natural way to hit. I then tell him to hit that way and not change from his natural position unless he finds he can't do as well and he thinks he might the other way.

Hell, you never heard of Cobb, Wagner, Ruth and the other great batters switching to meet right or left-handed pitching, did you?

The real secret of hitting is knowing the strike zone and hitting good balls that are in the strike zone. What difference does it make if you have a strike or two called on you? It's the big one that counts.

There are fellows who are guess hitters. Too many of them try to guess what the pitcher is trying to throw to them. Then there are certain type hitters on whom the pitcher's delivery has an effect. These fellows watch the hurler as he lets the ball go, instead of keeping an eye on the ball. I call these "delivery hitters."

What would I do to give the pitchers a better break? I'd deaden the ball and raise the seams. For nearly 20 years they've been playing into the hands of the batters to the sacrifice of pitching.

It would be a better game to watch if they gave something back to the pitchers. They've become a lot of throwers.

Until the Cardinals were swept by the Red Sox in the 2004 World Series, the 1928 World Series against the Yankees was the one that St. Louis fans would most like to forget. Not only did the Yankees sweep the Cardinals in four games, they also put on an awesome power display, highlighted by Lou Gehrig's four home runs and three more by Babe Ruth. To make matters even worse, Yankee pitcher George Pipgras claimed that when he shook hands with Grover Cleveland Alexander before they opposed each other in Game Two, it was clear that Alexander, the hero of the 1926 World Series, had been drinking before the game.

Fred Lieb, who covered his first World Series games in 1911, gave this account of the 1928 World Series in his team history of the Cardinals.

The 1928 World's Series
Frederick J. Lieb ————————————————————————

The 1928 World's Series is one of St. Louis's touchy baseball subjects. The 1928 Yankees, pretty much the same club that lost to the Cardinals two years before, were not regarded as supermen on the eve of the series. The Yankees almost blew a thirteen-game July lead in their own league, just barely limping in ahead of a fast-coming Athletic team. And the New York club was riddled with injuries. Herb Pennock, the pitcher, who had won two of the three New York victories in 1926, was out of the series with a lame arm. Earle Combs, crack centerfielder and lead-off man, who hit .357 in the 1926 event, was out with a broken finger. Huggins was planning to start Lazzeri, but Tony's arm was so dead he could scarcely get the ball to first base. And even Ruth supposedly was hobbling on one ankle. St. Louis licked its chops in happy anticipation; this was going to be good.

With Babe Ruth and Lou Gehrig putting on the greatest two-man show of all World's Series play, it proved a lark for the rampaging New Yorkers. They won four straight games, repeating the dose they handed Pittsburgh the year before. But, it was how the Cardinals lost which hurt Breadon and the St. Louis fans; the Birds were blown out of their roost by scores of 4 to 1, 9 to 3, 7 to 3 and 7 to 3. Ruth rose to his World's Series heights, and hit .625, getting three home runs, scoring nine runs and driving in four. Unlike Hornsby, whose pitchers walked Ruth 12 times in 1926, McKechnie let his pitchers pitch to Ruth, and he walked only once. It was good sportsmanship, but it was fatal. Young Gehrig was almost as tough as the "Big Guy," hitting .545, his six hits including four homers and a double. The young first baseman walked four times, scored five runs and drove in nine. There was no doubt that the Yankees earned their marbles; they outhit the Cardinals, .308 to .207.

Sherdel, who lost a three-hitter to Pennock to start the 1926 Series, again ran into a three-hit game, this time pitched by Hoyt in the first game in New York, October 4. The Yankees won handily, Bottomley's homer accounting for the lone Redbird run. Bob Meusel homered for Huggins.

Alexander, now forty-one years old, tried to repeat his second game victory of 1926, but Gehrig promptly showed old Grover that this was another year, when he lashed the veteran for a four-bagger in the first inning with Durst and Ruth on base. The Cardinals gave National League fans something to cheer about in the second inning, when they tied the score with three runs on young Pipgras. George walked Harper as a starter, and Wilson's double, Maranville's single, and Lazzeri's wild throw on Aleck brought in the runs. Unfortunately it would be the last time Cardinal rooters had a real chance to shout in the series. Pipgras settled after that, allowing no further scoring; the Yankees regained the lead with a run in their half of the second, and then knocked Grover out with four runs in the fourth.

When the series shifted to St. Louis, October 7 and 9, it was more of the same, the Cardinals twice going under by the same lopsided score. Jesse Haines, the 1926 whitewasher, tried to stop New York's thunderers in the third game, but was also clubbed out, Gehrig hitting a pair of round-trippers. Huggins got away with this one with old Tom Zachary, a Washington southpaw discard, in the box.

In desperation, McKechnie benched center fielder Douthit, who had made only one hit, in the fourth game, putting in the rookie Ernie Orsatti, while Earl Smith, the former Giant, went behind the plate in place of Wilson. Those moves worked well, as Ernie hit a double and single and Earl three singles, but it couldn't change the verdict. Hoyt again vanquished the unlucky Sherdel, as Willie went down to four defeats in two series.

This was the game of the famous quick pitch, which nettled the Cards and finally sent the deck crashing all over the field. St. Louis stayed in this game longer than in the others, leading 2 to 1, as the Yanks came up in the seventh. Sherdel had two strikes on Ruth, and then shot a "quick return" right over the heart of the plate. The Cardinals and the crowd thought it was a strike-out, but Pfirman refused to allow it. In his instructions to the umpires, Judge Landis had ruled against this quick pitch. Ruth, amused at the annoyance of Sherdel, McKechnie, and Frisch, knocked the next pitch into the stands for his second homer of the day, and Gehrig followed with an even longer one. For good measure Babe hit his third four-bagger in the eighth, matching his great three-homer performance at the park two years before.

With Lazzeri suffering from his lame arm, Huggins relieved him in each of the four games with a pesky flea of a rookie infielder, who rode the Cardinals unmercifully. He was later to become a great shortstop on the Redbirds in another World's Series—Leo Durocher, the famous Lip, now manager of the Brooklyn Dodgers.

The most disappointed man in all St. Louis was Sam Breadon. He couldn't understand it; he admitted the Yankees were good, but not that good. He could take defeat, but four straight shellackings left an ugly taste in his mouth. All during the series he felt his club lacked inspiration.

So, he demoted his manager, Bill McKechnie, to the Class AA farm in Rochester, and brought Billy Southworth, playing manager of the Rochester Red Wings in 1928, to St. Louis for Billy the Kid's first fling at the Cardinal managerial job.

The Gas House Gang

After the 1930 pennant-winning season and the Cardinals' loss to Connie Mack's Philadelphia Athletics in the World Series, Branch Rickey hired Gene Karst to do some publicity work for the ball club. While St. Louis, with the rest of the country, kept sinking into the Great Depression, the Cardinals offered some relief by playing uplifting baseball. During the four years that Karst worked in the Cardinals' front office, the team won two pennants and two World Series.

In this article written for a Society for American Baseball Research publication on St. Louis baseball, Karst remembers what it was like living in St. Louis in the early 1930s and working for the championship Cardinals.

The Cardinals' First Publicity Man
Gene Karst

Sixty years ago there were no millionaire ballplayers in St. Louis. No night baseball, no artificial turf, no exploding scoreboards, no plane travel, no West Coast baseball teams, no helmets, no batting gloves, no blacks in the grandstand, no luxury air-conditioned boxes, no stadium club. No parking problems—most people used a streetcar or a bus—and oftentimes no crowds!

Sam Breadon owned the Cardinals and Phil Ball was the owner of the Browns. Anheuser-Busch, the brewery which owns the Cardinals nowadays, had nothing to do with baseball back then. In fact, the brewery had nothing to do with Michelob, Budweiser, Bud Light, or even Busch beer—it was manufacturing Diesel engines, truck bodies, soft drinks, "near beer," corn sugar, syrups, whatnot. August A. Busch and his son Gussie, just 32, were too busy with the problems of doing business in the days of Depression and Prohibition.

You could get into the Missouri Theater for 25 cents in the afternoon until 6:30, after which it cost 50 cents to see a double bill like this: *Dude Ranch*, with Jack Oakie, Mitzie Green, Stewart Irvin, June Collier, and Gene Pallette; and *Too Young to Marry*, starring Loretta Young, Grant Withers, and O. P. Heggie (Who was he? Do any of you remember?).

Hellrung and Grimm was ready to sell a "distinctive" 4-piece bedroom suite for $89, reduced from $139. Newspapers featured used car ads for sedans and coupes in fine condition, one or two years old, for $415 and all the way down to $275—or less. Two bars of Lifebuoy soap could be had at a Walgreen's for 11 cents.

That's when a new world opened up for me, not long out of St. Louis University and my days as a cub reporter for the *Globe-Democrat* helping to pay my college tuition. Branch Rickey, the vice-president and general manager of the Cardinals, liked my scheme to do publicity work for the club, the first time any major league team had employed a publicity man. Nowadays, all sports organizations have publicity departments, usually with several hands grinding out statistics and information, to say nothing of promotion and marketing specialists.

Rickey sent me to spring training in Florida that year, 1931, and soon I was getting acquainted with the likes of Frankie Frisch, Jimmy Wilson, Chick Hafey, Jim Bottomley, Charles Gelbert, Jesse Haines, Burleigh Grimes, and the rest of that great ballclub. By mid-May the Redbirds were on top with a record of 14 wins and four defeats, while the hapless old Browns, who had players like Goose Goslin, Oscar Melillo, Red Kress, Rick Ferrell, George Blaeholder, Sam Gray, and Dick Coffman, held title to last place in the American League.

The Cardinals, of course, went on to win the pennant by 13 games. The Browns, under Bill Killefer, rose to fifth place before the season ended.

The Cards and the Browns had interlocking schedules which meant the old ballpark, Sportsman's Park at Grand and Dodier, was in use almost every day from early April to October, save for an occasional rainy day or a rare time when there was an open date. The infield grass got browner and scraggier as the summer progressed. The outfield wasn't much better.

Ballparks were more restful, relaxed in those days. The scoreboards were simple affairs which gave the ball and strike count, the number of outs, and the line scores from other major league games. No messages about visiting groups from Carbondale, Decatur, or Festus. No animated cartoons, no instant replays. No "hit" or "error" signs—Sam Breadon believed posting an error on the scoreboard might make a home player unduly nervous.

Umpires on the field wore coats and ties as part of their dignity. And everybody, from players in their wool uniforms to spectators in the stands to scribes in the press box, sweltered, sweated, ate peanuts, Eskimo Pies, and soft drinks. Prohibition did not end until midnight, April 7, 1933, when Gussie Busch declared, "It was the greatest moment of my life, the greatest, I guess, that I will ever know." At that moment trucks loaded with Budweiser—real beer—began rolling out of the Anheuser-Busch brewery.

In the 1980s, when Busch hired Whitey Herzog to manage the Cardinals, they won three pennants and one world championship. Busch used to ride that big wagon led by a team of Clydesdales triumphantly around Busch Memorial Stadium, and we believed he did enjoy those moments more than he had the end of Prohibition.

But back to 1931 when Sam Breadon, Cardinal owner, also owned the

Pierce-Arrow automobile agency. They were like the Cadillacs and Lincolns of today, and were selling for $2,895 delivered. Gabby Street was field manager of the Cardinals, reportedly earning $7,500 in annual salary. Gabby, as a player, had gained some notoriety as the catcher for Walter Johnson with the old Washington Senators. Gabby also got some passing attention for catching a ball dropped from the top of the Washington Monument.

Gabby had been a sergeant in the army (he lived on Sergeant Street in Joplin, Mo.). At one time Branch Rickey, in an off-the-record remark, confided to me the difference between Street's strategy running a ballclub with that of John McGraw, the master minding the New York Giants. "Gabby was a sergeant—but McGraw would have been at least a major general."

Gabby had so many good pitchers in 1931 that he didn't need Dizzy Dean, still in the minors at the Cardinal farm club in Houston. Undoubtedly he could have been a winning pitcher in the majors that year. On May 17 Dizzy experienced a victory and defeat pitching against Dallas. He won his ball game, 7–1. But during the contest he threw a "purpose pitch" dangerously close to the skull of Al Todd, husky Dallas catcher. Todd promptly dashed to the mound, decked Dizzy with quick blows to the arm, the eye, and the mouth, knocking him to the ground. Thus ended any idea Dizzy might have had for a boxing career. From then on, he used his pitching arm and his hyperactive tongue, which earned him good money over the airways long after his arm went dead.

In 1931 Paul Dean, Dizzy's brother, was just getting started at the Cardinal farm club in Springfield, Mo., where Eddie Dyer was getting his first managerial experience in the Class C Western Association. Tex Carleton and Joe Medwick were teammates of Dizzy at Houston, then managed by the original Joe Schultz, the St. Louisan who had been a Cardinal outfielder in the 1920s.

It was a colorful, glorious, fun year for an awful lot of people in St. Louis, despite the ominous, growing national economic depression. The Cardinals traded Taylor Douthit, "the ball hawk," to the Reds in mid-June, paving the way for Pepper Martin to bat .300 for the season, en route to a fabulous World Series against the Philadelphia Athletics.

Thomas Patrick and Bob Thomas (the Convey father and son) regaled radio fans with their enthusiastic boosting of the Cardinals on KWK, headquarters at the Chase hotel. France Laux did a calmer, more workman-like job covering baseball for KMOX, whose studios were located on Twelfth Street, about a block south of Market Street.

My job included singing the praises of the Cardinals to newspaper editors, sportswriters, and announcers in places like Princeton, and Terre Haute, Indiana; Cairo, Peoria, and Springfield, Illinois; Union City, Tennessee; Paducah, Kentucky; Moberly, Jefferson City, and Cape Girardeau, Missouri—and most towns and hamlets in between. It also included writing and editing *The Cardinal News,* the first fan publication.

I dug up statistics, made them available to sportswriters like J. Roy Stockton, John E. "Ed" Wray, Sid Keener, Red Smith, Jim Gould, Dick Farrington, Glen Waller, Martin J. "Mike" Haley, Herman Wecke, Kid Regan, and Sam Muchnick, predecessors of guys like Bob Broeg, Bob Burnes, Dick Kaegel, Rick Hummel, and other later scribes. J. G. Taylor Spink of the *Sporting News* used our material occasionally, as did some of the sportswriters for New York and other metropolitan dailies.

What a season! It came to a climax October 10 when the Redbirds vanquished the Philadelphia Athletics by a score of 4–2. The Cardinals had overcome a powerful team which included Lefty Grove, Al Simmons, Jimmy Foxx, Mickey Cochrane, Rube Walberg, Jimmy Dykes, George Earnshaw, and managed by Connie Mack.

Pepper Martin, alias the Wild Horse of the Osage, was the superstar of that series, earning a salary of $4,500. All he did was bat .500, steal a lot of bases, and completely discombobulate Mickey Cochrane and the Philadelphia pitchers. Old Burleigh Grimes, the last of the legal spitballers, pitched most of that final game into the ninth inning. Bill Hallahan relieved him, got the final out when Martin squeezed a fly ball in center.

By that time Martin had captured the imagination of the American people through his stellar World Series play and was besieged with offers for stage appearances, requests for endorsements, business propositions, to say nothing of those who merely wanted his autograph.

Pepper accepted an offer to go on stage for $1,500 a week. After a few weeks the call of the great outdoors overcame any latent ideas he might have had about acting. "Hell, I ain't no actor," said Pepper, "I'm a ballplayer." So he turned down a chance for additional weeks and returned to St. Louis.

They gave me the job of handling Pepper's mail. Every day brought letters and telegrams by the basketful. We sorted out offers of contracts and business propositions, and turned them over to Bill DeWitt, Cardinal treasurer who was acting as Martin's business manager. We tried to answer all other letters with form letters.

Most of the mail was filled with superlatives, congratulating Martin on his exploits, his modesty in the face of national adulation, with a sprinkling of mash notes, requests for handouts, invitations to turkey dinners, hunting trips, and requests to speak at service clubs luncheons, church suppers, and boys' clubs.

We packaged the fan mail in several large bales and presented it to Pepper when he was ready to drive back to Oklahoma. He loaded it onto his trailer and took off for the winter. Soon he was out quail hunting, duck hunting, and trampling through the wilder sections of Oklahoma.

Next spring when Pepper appeared at the Cardinal training camp in Bradenton, Florida, I asked him what he thought of all those flattering, congratulatory letters he had taken home with him. "You know, Gene," he said, "I never got around to opening those bales of mail all winter long. Maybe I will some day." I doubt that he ever did.

In 1932 the world champion Cardinals fell on evil days. Pepper came up with an insect bite which led to infection. He broke a bone in his hand. He tried too hard, slumped, and couldn't get out of the doldrums. The rest of the team also faltered badly and finished a poor sixth. When the 1933 season rolled around it looked like Martin might not even make the club. The Cardinals had problems at many positions, among them third base. Sparky Adams had faded as Redbird hot corner man and in desperation Gabby Street gave Martin a chance at the job. After all, he had started out as an infielder in the minors and still had a powerful throwing arm.

Pepper was an incredibly horrible third baseman. He couldn't field cleanly. When he did pick up the ball after it hit his chest, his great arm often sent the ball miles above the first baseman's head or into the dirt. He wasn't hitting either.

Then came a Sunday game when he was particularly futile, fumbling grounders, making wild throws, and striking out two or three times. After his last strikeout he threw his bat toward the dugout. His head down and muttering imprecations, when he reached the bat rack he kicked at the collection of bats. One of them uncannily bounced into the box seats and landed in the lap of Mrs. Sam Breadon, wife of the Cardinal owner.

When the crowd saw this they roared their disapproval with resounding boos. It was a tragic moment for the fallen star—the hero of 1931. Probably no hometown player had suffered such ignominy in St. Louis.

The Cardinals fortunately went on the road that night. Gabby Street kept Pepper in the lineup. If he made errors or struck out on the road it wasn't the same as suffering before the home fans. Martin couldn't get worse than he had been on that fateful Sunday. He bounced back. By the time the team returned home he had settled down and become a pretty fair third baseman.

The nation's fans voted for players to be on the National League All-Star team—the first time ever—and apparently they remembered Martin's 1931 World Series, as he was selected. So was Pie Traynor, at that time the greatest third baseman anywhere. John McGraw, managing the National League team, used Martin as his third baseman throughout the contest. Traynor rode the bench. Quite a compliment for the comeback of a man who had been on the verge of being relegated to the minors a few weeks earlier.

Locally, that 1933 season wasn't much of an improvement over 1932. Rogers Hornsby, after managing the Cardinals to their first pennant and World Series ever in 1926, came back to the team contrite and penitent. He and Breadon had come to a parting of the ways late in 1926 after Rogers demanded a three-year contract at $50,000. Breadon countered with a one-year contract at $50,000 or a three-year pact at $40,000 a year. St. Louis fans at the time thought of Hornsby as a demigod and a miracle worker, and the Rajah fully expected Breadon to capitulate. Instead, Breadon grabbed the phone and traded Hornsby to New York for Frankie Frisch and a mediocre pitcher, Jimmy Ring.

St. Louis fans were furious at the Cardinal owner, and wanted to lynch him or run him out of town. They talked about court action to nullify the trade. But it stood. During that period between 1926 and 1933 Hornsby had become playing manager at Boston and again for the Chicago Cubs. In the field he had slowed down considerably, but he still could hit. Though he made big money for those days, he frittered it away at race tracks and elsewhere. So when the Cubs fired him well into the 1932 season he was unemployed and broke.

The Cardinals signed him to a 1933 contract. He hit .325 as a sub and pinch hitter, but the team continued to flounder. Frisch was also slowing down. Changes were also in order, so in mid-season Hornsby was released so he could become manager of the Browns, and Frisch replaced Gabby Street as boss of the Cardinals. The Redbirds finished above the .500 mark but still ended up in fifth place.

When the 1934 spring training season rolled around, the Cardinals had the nucleus of the team which later would become "The Gas House Gang": Dizzy Dean, Rip Collins, Joe Medwick, Lippy Leo Durocher, Pepper Martin, Virgil Davis, and three rookies of considerable promise, Paul Dean, a pitcher, catcher Bill Delancey, and Burgess Whitehead, an infielder.

Rickey took me to spring training camp in Bradenton, Florida. I helped him drive, took care of the voluminous correspondence—mostly telegrams in those days—and roomed with him in the old Dixie Grande Hotel.

After watching the team workouts a few days, Rickey told me he had spotted two glaring weaknesses in the Cardinal lineup—catching and second base. "We can't win the pennant with Davis catching and Frisch playing second base," he said. "What I really ought to do is try to trade for a catcher and put Whitehead at second base. I'm sure I could trade Frisch to Boston for catcher Al Spohrer. What I should do would be to catch a plane and sell the idea to Sam Breadon."

Rickey toyed with the idea quite a while, swearing me to secrecy. "Mike Gonzales could manage the team and we could win," he ruminated. But he soon realized that Breadon probably would not go along with the idea of trading Frisch, so Rickey gave up the idea completely.

Still the 1934 Cardinals weren't going to win the pennant without a struggle. They were headed nowhere in particular as the pennant race went along into August. Dizzy and Paul were the starting pitchers in a Sunday doubleheader. Both of them lost. Unhappy about their fate, Dizzy stayed in St. Louis that night when he should have been on a train headed to Detroit, where the club was scheduled to play an exhibition game that next day.

Frisch, with Breadon's approval, plastered a small fine on Dizzy, who was making $6,500 that year. In the argument which ensued, Dizzy tore up his uniform, complained to the press that Paul also was underpaid, and both of the Deans walked out of the clubhouse. Suspensions followed and both were off the payroll. Paul's 1934 salary was $3,000.

During their absence the Cardinals had just 19 men on their roster. The player limit at that time was 23 but the Cardinals were carrying just 21 players. Short-handed, the remaining players "came together" as a team and seemed to be showing what they could do without Dizzy and Paul. Pepper Martin volunteered to pitch—and did. When the Cards began to win consistently, first Paul, and later Dizzy, decided to get back on the payroll. Both promised to be good boys, and they were for the rest of the season. Paul won 19 games and Dizzy came up with 30 victories despite missing at least two or three starts during the strike.

Rickey believed the strike of the Dean brothers was a blessing in disguise. He felt the rest of the team had resented the Deans hogging the limelight and that during the strike they proved they could win a lot of games without Dizzy and Paul. When the Deans repented, a spirit of togetherness bolstered the unity of the team.

Manager Frisch, slowed down by aching legs, was stimulated by the chase, and proved himself still a great "money player." Leo Durocher, who had been called "the All-American Out," found romance with a classy St. Louis fashion designer, Grace Dozier. At first Rickey tried to discourage Leo from marrying Miss Dozier until after the season. But the couple was married anyway and matrimony seemed to result in great play in the field for Leo. He fielded in top form and got numerous hits.

Frisch, like Rickey, wasn't too happy with Virgil Davis as a catcher, and gave rookie Bill Delancey more and more time behind the bat. By the season's close, Bill was definitely the Cardinals' first-string catcher—and he hit a healthy .316 in 93 games.

The Cards went 33–12 after the Deans' walkout, and when the Giants collapsed at the wire, St. Louis had a surprise pennant.

No need to repeat the stories about the 1934 World Series against the Detroit Tigers, a formidable club with stars like Hank Greenberg, Goose Goslin, Charley Gehringer, Bill Rogell, Schoolboy Rowe, Eldon Auker, Tommy Bridges, and Fred Marberry. Mickey Cochrane managed the team and was still a fine catcher and good hitter.

But we who were rooting for the Cardinals suffered a terrible shock during the fourth game of the series, played in St. Louis on Saturday, October 6. The Redbirds were leading at the time, two games to one. But in that fourth game after three-and-a-half innings the Tigers were ahead, 4 to 2. In the last of the fourth inning the Cardinals were trying to get back in the game. Pinch hitter Virgil Davis got a single and Frisch sent Dizzy Dean in to run for him. Dizzy was much faster than Davis, of course. But, trying to break up a double play a moment later, Dizzy tried to go into second base standing up. Shortstop Billy Rogell's throw hit Dizzy in the noggin and he dropped to the ground like he was shot. He was carried from the field with his lanky arms and legs flopping over the makeshift stretcher. Cardinal fans feared the worst. Would he be out for the rest of the World Series? Did he suffer a fracture of the skull? Would he ever pitch again? After play resumed the Tigers continued to bash Redbird pitchers and won the game, 10–4.

Fortunately Dizzy must have had an awfully hard head. X-rays showed no fracture and Dizzy was ready for the seventh and crucial game the following Tuesday. All he did was hold the Tigers to six scattered hits, get a single and a double, and win the game, 11 to 0. The rejuvenated Frankie Frisch held his own, driving in the first three runs of the game with a double with the bases loaded. The Cardinals made 17 hits in all. Pepper Martin, Jack Rothrock, Leo Durocher, and Dizzy had two hits each. Fun-loving first baseman Rip Collins came up with four hits. That also was the game when Judge Landis removed Joe Medwick from the premises when Detroit fans took out their frustrations by pelting him with all kinds of garbage and debris, threatening to stop the game.

Thus ended my four eventful years as publicity man for the Cardinals—two pennants, two world championships in four seasons. As they say, I didn't make much money but I certainly had a lot of fun. Before the pennant had been decided Larry McPhail, general manager of the Cincinnati Reds, came to town and offered me a 50 percent salary increase and a contract for the 1935 season. I accepted Larry's offer, spent a couple of years with the Reds, and later did publicity work for the Hollywood Stars in the Pacific Coast League, and spent three wonderful years in Montreal with the Royals in the Brooklyn Dodger organization.

Bill Hallahan had the distinction of playing in four World Series with the Cardinals, beginning with his rookie year in 1926 and ending with the Gas House Gang in 1934. In 1930, though the Cardinals lost in six games to the Philadelphia Athletics, Hallahan pitched a shutout in Game 3. In 1931, he shut out Connie Mack's A's in Game 2, outpitched Waite Hoyt in Game 5, and relieved Burleigh Grimes in the ninth inning of Game 7 to preserve the Cardinals' victory and World Series triumph.

In Donald Honig's oral history, October Heroes, *Hallahan recalls his most memorable moments with the Cardinals and his colorful teammates, ranging from Grover Cleveland Alexander to Dizzy Dean.*

Bill Hallahan

I was satisfied with my career. I put in twelve years and some of them were very rewarding. I played on four pennant winners with the Cardinals and three world championship teams. One nice thing about baseball is that, generally, you're remembered for the successes you had rather than the failures, unless those failures are of themselves memorable. I never had any memorable failures, and I'm grateful for that.

I was fortunate, though, to become a teammate of one of my boyhood heroes—Grover Cleveland Alexander. I was a rookie on the Cardinals in 1926 when we bought Alec from the Cubs in midseason. I'll never forget the first time he pitched for us. I was sitting on the bench with another young pitcher and naturally we glued our eyes on Alec when he went out to warm up. He flipped a few into the catcher, then stopped, put his glove under his arm, took out a piece of chewing gum, very casually took the paper off, put the gum in his mouth, looked around through the stands, then put his glove back on and started throwing again. He threw just a few more pitches, very easily, with no effort. Then he was through. He came back to the bench, put on his sweater—we wore those big, red-knit sweaters on the Cardinals—and sat down.

I looked at this other fellow and said, "This is going to be murder. He isn't throwing *anything*." Well, Alec went out that day and stood the other team on its ear. Control, that's how he did it. Absolute, total control. He had this little screwball that he could turn over on the corners all day long. Amazing fellow. Born to be a pitcher.

No, I never talked pitching with him. Alec never said much about anything. When he did talk it was seldom above a whisper. As a rule we didn't see him around after a game. He was a loner. He would go off by himself and do what he did, which I suppose was drink. That was his problem. But he was a good-natured fellow. You never heard him say anything against anybody.

He liked to go out before a game and work in the infield, generally around third base. One day we were taking batting practice and there's Alec standing at third, crouched over, hands on knees, staring into the plate. A ground ball went by him and he never budged, just remained there stock still, staring at the batter. Then another grounder buzzed by and same thing—he never moved a muscle. Then somebody ripped a line drive past his ear and still he didn't move. That's when Hornsby noticed him—Rog was managing the club at the time.

Hornsby let out a howl and said, "Where in the hell did he get it? Where did he get it?" he kept yelling. He ordered a search made and they found it all right. In old Sportsman's Park in St. Louis there used to be a ladies' room not far from the corridor going down to the dugout, and that's where he had stashed it, up in the rafters of the ladies' room. One of those little square bottles of gin.

We won the pennant by just two games in 1930. Beat out Chicago. I pitched the game that was probably my best ever in Brooklyn right at the end of the season. At least that's what a lot of people think. I'll never forget that one, and for plenty of reasons.

We finished a series at the Polo Grounds against the Giants and went over to play the Dodgers. I think we were a half game out of first place. The night before I was going to pitch, I went out with Ray Blades and another fellow to see a show on Broadway. When we came out of the theater we figured we would take a cab back to the hotel. We hailed a cab and Ray got in first and I followed him. Then the other fellow jumped in, and when he did he pulled the door in with him, very quickly. Well, some how that door closed right across the fingers of my right hand.

When we got back to the hotel the hand was killing me. And here I've got to pitch an important ball game the next day. The only lucky thing was it was my right hand and not my left. But all the same, when a door slams on your hand it hurts just as much whether it's the right one or the left. So when I went to my room they sent our trainer, Doc Weaver, to work on me. He sat up most of the night with me, applying hot and cold packs and massaging my arm. Branch Rickey, who was our general manager at the time, came into the room and asked me if I thought I would be able to pitch the next day.

"I pitch with my left hand, Mr. Rickey," I said.

Well, I've got to tell you what else was going on at the same time. It became one of the stories they're still talking about to this day. Sometime late that night somebody noticed that my roommate, Flint Rheum, hadn't shown up.

Do you know about Flint? Well, he was a pitcher and a pretty good one too. But he had the same problem Alec did—a fondness for booze. He was a very nice fellow, but now and then he did some strange things.

Flint never did show up that night, nor did he show up the next night either. When he finally did reappear the reporters asked him where he'd been. Flint kind of hemmed and hawed, until one of the reporters jokingly asked him if he had been kidnapped.

You could see Flint think about it for a minute, and then he said, "That's right. I was kidnapped by some gamblers who wanted to make sure I didn't pitch." Hell, he wasn't even scheduled to pitch.

"Is that so?" somebody asked.

"That's right," Flint said. He was really getting warmed up now. "They kidnapped me and took me to a room someplace. Then they held a gun to my head and made me keep drinking whiskey until I passed out."

That was the best part of the story, and one of the writers remarked in the paper the next day: "Imagine kidnapping Flint Rheum and forcing him to drink whiskey?"

What happened, we found out later, was some friends of Flint had come up from South Carolina to see games in New York and Brooklyn. After the games in the Polo Grounds they went out for a few drinks and just kept going.

Meanwhile, I was having my own troubles. I was still in considerable pain the next morning. But there was never any doubt in my mind that I was going to pitch. It was an important game and I wanted to be in it. Two fingers on my right hand were packed in some sort of black salve and I had to cut my glove so they could protrude on the outside.

Dazzy Vance was pitching for the Dodgers and he was really firing that day. But so was I. I had a no-hitter until the eighth inning. At one point I retired twenty in a row. At the end of nine there was no score. In the top of the tenth we got a run on a couple of hits by Andy High and Taylor Douthit. In the bottom of the tenth the Dodgers gave us a scare. They loaded the bases with one out. Then Al Lopez hit a grounder to Sparky Adams at short. Sparky threw to Frisch at second and Frank made the fastest pivot I ever saw in my life and just did nip Lopez at first. There was a full house in Ebbets Field that day and the crowd was just stunned, absolutely stunned. You didn't hear a sound.

I would say it was probably my best game, and not just because I pitched well but because it meant so much. We were right at the end of the season and really needed that one.

You had to be at the top of your game to beat Vance. When Dazzy had his stuff he was almost unhittable. He was one of the greatest pitchers I ever saw. He could throw hard. And he had an exceptional curve, too. I saw many a right-handed hitter fall away from that curve and then be highly embarrassed when it was called a strike.

I got to know Dazzy very well later on. He joined the Cardinals at the end of his career and was with us when we won the World Series in 1934. I remember a group of us went out to a Greek restaurant in St. Louis to celebrate the victory. Dazzy decided he would mix the drinks. The owner of the place let him go behind the bar and Dazzy got a big glass and poured a little bit from just about every bottle into it. Then he brought it over to the table and said it was the "Dazzmarine Special." He offered the glass around the table, but nobody would touch it. So he downed the whole thing himself. He was practically kayoed on the spot. Later, when we were helping him across the hotel lobby, he suddenly stopped and took hold of our arms and really squeezed tight.

"Stop boys," he said. "Wait a minute."

"What's wrong, Daz?' we asked.

"Don't you see it?" he said.

"See what?"

"All the chairs in the lobby," he said. "They're jumping at me."

Dazzy wouldn't move until Joe Medwick, who was with us, walked ahead and told Vance he wouldn't let the chairs get at him.

Dazzy was always a great character. When he was with Brooklyn he loved to play tricks on his manager, Uncle Wilbert Robinson, who was a lovable and gullible old man. One time somebody hit a scorcher past Chick Fewster, the second baseman. It was a low line drive that went out there like a pistol shot, as sudden a base hit as you'd want to see. Vance was in the dugout and he turned to the fellow sitting next to him and, just loud enough for Uncle Robbie to hear, said, "What's the matter with Fewster? He didn't even move on that ball."

So when the inning was over and Fewster came into the dugout, Uncle Robbie said to him, "Say, Chick, what happened on that ball? Why didn't you pick it up?"

Fewster was ready to explode, but then he looked around and saw Dazzy sitting there with a big grin and he knew what happened.

It's hard to believe today what an unusual personality Uncle Robbie was. I remember coming out of Ebbets Field after a game one day and there he was, talking to a group of cab drivers, explaining to them what had happened in the game and giving the reasons for his strategy. Can you imagine a manager doing that today?

Dizzy Dean was another colorful one. I guess I don't have to tell you that. In the '34 Series he and his brother Paul won two games apiece to beat the

Tigers—just as Dizzy had said they would. There was one game in that Series when Dizzy went in as a pinch runner. Frisch, who was managing the club then, has received a lot of criticism for putting a thirty-game winner in to pinch-run. Well, here's how it happened. We needed somebody to run, and while Frisch was looking up and down the bench trying to decide who to put in, Diz ran out there, on his own. Somebody said to Frisch, "Dizzy's already out there." Frisch took a look and sure enough, there was Dean, standing on first base. Frisch frowned; he didn't like the idea. But the guy was already on the field, so he said, "Okay, let him be." Wouldn't you know it, but the batter hits the ball to Charley Gehringer at second, who picks it up and flips to Billy Rogell, who crosses the bag and cocks his arm to throw to first for the double play, and here's Diz coming in standing up. Well, Rogell threw it all right. *Pow!* The relay hit Dean right in the head and he went down like he'd been shot. We all stood up in the dugout and you could just feel what everybody was thinking: there goes the series.

They carried Diz off the field and carted him away to the hospital. That night Dean came into the hotel with a big grin on his face and told everybody, "It's okay. They X-rayed my head and didn't find anything."

But that's how it happened. There was no way Frisch would have sent him in to run. No sir. You don't do that with thirty-game winners.

You know, there was a funny thing after the second game in Detroit. We lost it, and after the game our team bus got a big police escort back to the hotel, with motorcycles and blaring sirens. But when we *won* in Detroit, it was, "Get back the best way you can. You're on your own."

In the 1930 World Series we were up against one of the greatest teams of all time—the Philadelphia Athletics. Jimmie Foxx, Al Simmons, Mickey Cochrane, Mule Haas, Bing Miller, Max Bishop, and so on. Not to mention three of the best pitchers you'll ever want to see on one staff—Lefty Grove, George Earnshaw, and Rube Walberg.

But we had a pretty good outfit ourselves. This might be hard to believe, but every man in our starting lineup hit better than .300. There was Jim Bottomley, Frisch, Charlie Gelbert, Sparky Adams, Chick Hafey, Taylor Douthit, George Watkins, and Jimmy Wilson. Those were the regulars. In addition, we had men on the bench hitting better than .300—Ray Blades, Gus Mancuso, Showboat Fischer, Ernie Orsatti. Overall the team hit around .314.

We ran against Grove and Earnshaw in the first two games and lost. I started the third game and drew Rube Walberg. I had a rugged first inning. They filled the bases with two outs and Bing Miller came up. He was a very tough hitter. As a matter of fact, they didn't have a soft spot in their lineup either. I went to a full count on Miller and I can remember standing there on the mound rubbing up the ball and thinking to myself, "Well, what do you do when you've run the count full and the bases are loaded?" The answer was easy: you put everything you've got on the ball and hope he doesn't hit it. That's just what happened. Miller was one of the most deadly curve ball hitters that ever lived. So I threw him my best fastball and he swung and missed. I went on from there to pitch a shutout, which was a pretty good trick against that team.

I was basically a fastball pitcher, but every now and then I would change speeds a little. You just can't throw every pitch as hard as you can for nine innings. But, gee, every time I did that I would hear one of my infielders, Frisch or somebody start yelling, "Bear down! Bear down!" I remember Frisch hollering at me during that World Series, "Stop experimenting out there! Who do you think you are—Thomas Edison?"

Well, they came back to beat us in six games. Grove and Earnshaw each won two. That was the second world championship for them and people were saying that nobody was going to be able to stop that team for years to come. They sure were a great team, but we had a secret weapon waiting for them when we played them in the Series again the next year. The name of the weapon was Pepper Martin.

That was Pepper's first full year with us. He showed up well, too, hitting around .300 and proving to be a real hustler. A good ball player all right, but then came the Series in 1931 and he just tore it apart. He got twelve hits, hit .500, caught everything in sight in center field, and the thing people remember most, stole five bases. Another thing about his record in that Series, and I don't imagine a lot of people realize this, is that Pepper did all of his hitting in the first five games. In other words, he went twelve for eighteen until they finally stopped him in the last two games. Now and then individual players have taken charge of a World Series, but I don't think anyone ever did it as dramatically or as colorfully as Pepper did in 1931. What he did in that one week caught the fancy of fans all over the country and established his reputation forever.

Mickey Cochrane, the A's catcher, got a lot of criticism for letting Pepper steal so many bases. But that was nonsense, of course. We ball players knew that. Pepper was stealing on the pitchers—most bases are stolen on the pitcher. He stole all of his bases against Grove and Earnshaw because those fellows just didn't hold a runner on very well. You give a catcher like Cochrane a chance to throw you out and he's going to do it. Nobody can out run a ball.

I started the second game against Earnshaw. George had beaten me just a year before, but this time I got the edge. I shut them out, 2–0. Pepper had a hand in both runs, or I should say he had his feet in both runs. He doubled with one out in the second and then the son of a gun stole third and scored on Jimmie Wilson's fly ball. Later in the game, he singled, stole second, and came around on a ground ball and a squeeze play.

I went into the ninth up by those two runs and experienced an inning I'll never forget as long as I live. Jimmie Foxx led off and I walked him. Then Bing Miller flied out. I walked Jimmie Dykes. I got a called third strike passed by Dib Williams. Then Connie Mack sent up a fellow named Jim Moore to pinch-hit for Earnshaw. Well, I got two strikes on him and then broke off a beauty of a curve and he struck out on it. Or so I thought. It was a low pitch and Jimmie Wilson caught it right down on the ground, figured it was strike three and for some reason fired it down to third base to Jake Flowers, thinking the game was over. I don't know why in the world he did that; maybe it was some sort of reflex.

Eddie Collins was coaching first base for the A's. He started hollering at Moore to run to first base—Moore had already turned to start back to the dugout. So Moore ran to first base and the other two runners moved up. We didn't know what was going on. Jake Flowers was just standing there with the ball in his hand. You see, the umpire ruled that Wilson had scooped up the third strike—the ball hit the ground first—and in that particular situation you have to put the batter out at first base, or tag him, if you can. Eddie Collins, who was as sharp a baseball man as ever lived, was the only one who realized what had happened, and that's why he yelled at Moore to run.

You know, Flowers came up to me later and said he nearly threw the ball into the stands, that it had been his impulse to do so. That would have been great—all three runs would have scored, or at least two of them anyway. Can you imagine two or three runs scoring on a strikeout? Well, it nearly happened. Then Jake said he thought that maybe I would want the ball back as a memento. Memento heck; I needed the ball back to get the next man out with.

I already had some of the infielders patting me on the back and saying, "Nice game." The outfielders were running in. But then somebody told us to get back there; that the man was safe and the bases were loaded.

There was an argument, of course, which we lost, of course. So I had to go back onto the mound and do it again. You don't like to give a team like the A's four outs in an inning, but that's what I had to do. The batter was Max Bishop, a fellow I didn't like to pitch to. He was a smart little hitter who generally got the bat on the ball. I always preferred working to the big free-swingers because they gave you a lot of pitching room, the way they wound up with those bats. But a fellow like Bishop—they called him "Camera Eye"—guarded the plate like a hawk and it was hard to get a ball past him.

I put everything I had on it and Bishop popped one up in foul ground that Jim Bottomley chased down and then dove over the Athletics' bullpen bench and caught by reaching into the stands. It was a really remarkable play by Jim. That ended the game for real. I always said it was a lucky thing we were playing at home, because the fans got out of the way and let Jim make the play. If we had been in Philadelphia I'm sure they wouldn't have been so helpful.

We won the next day with Burleigh Grimes and then lost the next one. In that fourth game Jimmie Foxx hit a home run over the left-field pavilion that was hit just as hard and as far as any ball I've ever seen. One of our bullpen pitchers, Jim Lindsey, said later, "We were watching that ball for two innings."

I started the fifth game against Waite Hoyt. I beat them 5–1, and again I had a little help from Pepper. Just a little. All he did was drive in one run with a fly ball, two more with a home run, and another with a single. It was after that fifth game that he had all of his hits. There was a story that came out later, about Mr. Mack asking Earnshaw what Pepper was hitting. "Everything we throw," George said. He was just about right.

Late in the game, I think it was the seventh inning, Foxx hit a line drive that whacked me in the shin. Boy, I can tell you how hard he could hit a ball! Speaking from personal experience, you might say. The ball caromed off into right field and I felt for a moment like it had taken half my leg with it. I stood there on the mound with that foot lifted, not wanting to put it down for fear it might be broken. It swelled up so fast that by the time I got back to the bench it looked like I had a baseball tucked into my stocking. But I finished up all right.

We went back to St. Louis on the train that night and Doc Weaver was putting ice packs on my leg to try and keep the swelling down. Pepper and some of the fellows were sitting around watching. Pepper was by this time a national hero. Judge Landis was making the trip with us and he came walking through the car. He stopped to ask me how I was and then somebody introduced Pepper to the Judge.

"Well, Mr. Pepper Martin," the Judge said with a big grin, shaking hands with Pepper. "What I wouldn't give to be in your shoes."

Pepper looked at him and said, "I'd be happy to make the switch, Judge. I'd trade my sixty-five hundred a year for your sixty-five thousand any day."

We all laughed, the Judge the loudest.

The next day Lefty Grove came out firing bullets and they beat us 8–1. That made the Series three games apiece.

Burleigh Grimes started the seventh game for us against big George Earnshaw. We jumped off to a 4–0 lead by the third inning and Burleigh nursed it along until the top of the ninth. Then he got into some rough waters and gave up two runs and had men on first and second with two out. Burleigh had been having some trouble with his side, a pulled muscle or something, and he decided he had better come out right then and there. You can be sure he must have been in great pain, because he was a tough customer, that Grimes, and he hated to come out of a game.

So they brought me in to pitch. The batter was Max Bishop. Again, here was this fellow I didn't like to pitch to. I went to a full count with him and burned one in there. He lifted an easy fly ball to Pepper in center, and that's how the Series ended—the Pepper Martin Series—with a fly ball right into the glove of the man himself.

John "Pepper" Martin burst upon the baseball world like a thunderbolt. After struggling early in his career to find a place in the Cardinals' regular lineup, he became the starting center fielder in 1931 and batted .300 for the pennant-winning season. But it was in the 1931 World Series victory over the Philadelphia Athletics that Martin became an overnight sensation and a national celebrity. He batted .500 with 12 hits against the A's great pitching staff and had five stolen bases against future Hall of Fame catcher Mickey Cochrane. But it was his daring play and his head-first slides that dazzled fans around the country.

Ray Robinson, the biographer of Lou Gehrig and Christy Mathewson, wrote this tribute to one of the most colorful characters in baseball history.

Redbird Who Stole a World Series
Ray Robinson ————————————————————————

In the crisp, Indian summer days of early October, 1931, "Pepper" Martin became a household word. He was the tough, fun-loving, stomach-sliding galoot on the St. Louis Cardinals who literally stole a World Series right from under the noses of the proud Philadelphia Athletics, just when sixty-nine-year-old Connie Mack was trying to guide the A's to their third straight world title.

Before the Series got under way, few people, outside of dyed-in-the-wool baseball fans, knew anything about Pepper Martin. By the time the seventh game had been reached, Pepper had emerged as a true national hero and the Douglas Fairbanks, Sr., of the base paths. He came out of nowhere to dominate the Series, the newspaper headlines, and the conversation in almost every hotel lobby in America. Nobody in baseball since Ty Cobb had ever run bases that way, especially with a world championship at stake. Pepper had made the best defensive catcher in the game, Mickey Cochrane, look silly as he stole everything from the A's catcher except his chest protector.

In that unforgettable Series, Pepper batted an even .500, with 12 hits in 24 times at bat, an incredible mark, considering he failed to connect with a hit in the last two games. He had five stolen bases, just one short of the mark of six made by Jimmy Slagle of the Chicago Cubs in 1907. He scored both runs to beat the princely George Earnshaw, 2–0, in the second game. He hit one home run, four doubles, batted in five runs, and scored five runs.

At the start of the Series Pepper went up to the Old Sarge, Gabby Street, who managed the Cards, and insisted that he be given the green light to cavort on the bases.

"Lemme run on this guy Cochrane," Pepper pleaded, ignoring the reputation that Mickey had built up over the years as one of the greatest catchers in American League history.

Gabby glared at his barrel-chested, unshaven center fielder and made one of the most important decisions off the field of battle. Yes, he would let the twenty-seven-year-old rookie run at will. (Pepper still had to be regarded as a rookie, since he'd played only a few games in 1928 and 1930 before winning a regular job in 1931.) And run Pepper did, like a depression farmer for a month's pay.

"That Martin," Ripper Collins, the Cards' first baseman said, "is the kind of fellow who'd kill you with a slide just to get to first base. If you survived, he'd stay up all night nursing you back to good health. Then, the next day he'd be at you again!"

John Leonard Martin was born in Temple, Oklahoma, on February 29, 1904, appropriately enough, a leap year. His dad was George Washington Martin, a Nebraska carpenter, who took an Oklahoma land grant from the government and developed it into a modest farm.

As a youngster Johnny worked on farms, enjoying the physical work that made him sweat and which put hard muscles on his arms and shoulders and legs. He grew up to be a kid with a weather-beaten, corrugated face that always reminded people of a pirate out of Robert Louis Stevenson's novels.

It is said that at an early age he could chase jack rabbits in and out of the mesquite bushes of Oklahoma until the long-eared animals pleaded "enough." Even if the tale is false, it epitomized the type of youngster Johnny Martin was. As he grew older he took odd jobs as a newspaper delivery boy and dug telephone pole holes for an electric power company. He was as good a wrangler of ornery horses as you can find and he could pump gas, in his quiet moments.

But there was nothing Johnny liked more than playing ball. He left home to play ball in Missouri in the Tomato League, where stars like Hod Lisenbee, Buddy Myer, Memphis Bill Terry, and Bill Clark had got their start. Then he came back to Oklahoma City and played on Saturdays for the Second Presbyterian Church. Though Mr. Branch Rickey, who guided the far-flung chain system of the St. Louis Cardinals, had never heard of Johnny at the time, Martin was exactly the kind of player he was looking for in his business.

Mr. Rickey had repeatedly informed his chief scout, Charlie Barrett, what to seek in the way of baseball talent.

"I want boys who can run like deer, have slingshots for arms and hit the ball on the nose," said Mr. Rickey.

Barrett, scouring the sandlots and bush leagues, finally came across Johnny

Martin in Greenville, Texas, where Johnny had gone to play following a stint in Ardmore, Oklahoma, as a neophyte pitcher.

In those days able ballplayers like Martin could be purchased for a good deal less money than big-league clubs are apt to fork over today for talent. When the Cards, prodded by Barrett, bought Martin's contract from the Class D Greenville club of the East Texas League, little more than $500 was involved in the transaction.

Martin played in the outfield, then at second base, in his 1924 and 1925 seasons with Greenville. When the Cards transferred him to their Fort Smith farm club in the Western Association, in 1925, he became a shortstop. The next season with Syracuse in the International League, Martin spent most of his time at second and third.

With Houston, in the Texas League, in 1927, Pepper roamed the outfield, crudely and uncertainly, to be sure. But he looked far better there than he had in the infield, where he seemed to fight the ball as if it were a born enemy. After he batted .306 for Houston and stole 36 bases, Martin came up to the parent club in the big leagues. He played 39 games for the Cards in 1928 and batted .308, but he didn't seem to rate very high with management.

However, in the World Series that fall, when the Cards were losing four successive games to Miller Huggins's Babe Ruth-powered New York Yankees, Martin's name actually appeared, for the first time, in a Series box-score. Manager Bill McKechnie of the Cards waited until the ninth inning of the last game to unveil Pepper and then it was only as a pinch runner for catcher Earl Smith.

But, in a sense, Pepper permitted a preview of his 1931 performance. He immediately scampered around to third base, without drawing a throw (the Yanks led by 7–2 at the time) and then tallied on an infield out. A few minutes later the Series was over when Babe Ruth, playing left field that afternoon, grabbed a foul fly.

Pepper had got into the act, at last. The brief fling in the majors had whetted his appetite to be a permanent party on Mr. Rickey's team in St. Louis. But he still wound up back in Houston for the 1929 season. He batted .298 there and stole 43 bases, the high for his career. Such a record would seem to have earned him a place on the varsity, but Mr. Rickey, who later was to consider Pepper one of the truly great competitors of the game, decided the fellow needed additional seasoning. So Pepper was back with Rochester, in the International League, in 1930.

At Rochester, Pepper whacked the ball at a .363 pace and stole 27 bases. In the last days of the season he was back with the Cards for another look. But it was only for six games, and Pepper had the distinct impression, as the 1931 season approached, that he was destined to be a minor-league nomad forever, or nothing more than a spare tire in the Cardinal setup.

In the first few weeks of the 1931 season Pepper sat on the Cardinal bench, occasionally getting a call for a pinch-hitting shot or a pinch-running assignment. This was not what he had in mind for himself when he first decided to be a ballplayer. He wanted to play every day, to be part of the regular team fighting for the pennant. There were some outstanding players on that Card team, too, men like the bespectacled, league-leading Chick Hafey, in left field; Sunny Jim Bottomley, the first baseman, who batted in 12 runs in a game against the Dodgers in 1924; the Fordham Flash, Frankie Frisch, an all-time choice of many experts for his second-base play; the brilliant young shortstop Charley Gelbert, and battlers like Andy High and Jake Flowers, alternating at third base.

Pepper thought he belonged in there, with these men, hustling every day, fighting, scrambling, driving, sliding—those scary, fingers-first belly slides that later became the trademark of his play in every National League town on the map.

So one fine day Pepper went in to see Mr. Rickey about the matter. The general manager of the Cards was too astute to be bulldozed by any of his employees. But he was also as understanding and knowledgeable a baseball man as ever has lived. Some said, with certain bitterness perhaps, that he was as sharp as an official scorer's pencil.

As Mr. Rickey surveyed Pepper and listened to the man's complaint, he sensed that this bull-necked, hook-nosed player was making a good case for himself. It would be wrong to discourage him for too long; a man couldn't ride the bench perennially without losing confidence and the will to play, and this fellow certainly has these qualities in abundance.

"I want to play regularly, Mr. Rickey," Pepper said. "Either you give me that chance or I want to be traded to a club that will use me."

"Young man," answered Rickey, "I will see what I can do."

In mid-June the thoughtful Mr. Rickey made a trade. Taylor Douthit, the Cardinals' center fielder, was dealt to Cincinnati for Wally Roettger. From that time on, Pepper Martin became the Cards' starting center fielder. For the rest of the 1931 season he batted an even .300, stole 16 bases, and helped the Cards finish 13½ games ahead of the New York Giants.

However, when the World Series of 1931 opened on October 1 at St. Louis, little attention was focused on Johnny Martin. This, after all, was the year Robert Moses Grove, the bony southpaw from Lonaconing, Maryland, had won 31 games, including 16 in a row, for Connie Mack's Athletics and Al Simmons had copped the American League batting title with a .390 average.

These were the players, along with Cochrane; Jimmy Foxx, the home run slugger; Bing Miller; Jimmy Dykes and Mule Haas, who would lead the A's to another world title. How could they miss? Certainly an all but anonymous, unscrubbed Oklahoman named Pepper Martin couldn't stop Mr. Mack's juggernaut.

But he did. And it was the greatest one-man show the Series had seen since "Babe" Adams of the Pirates whipped the Detroit Tigers three times, as a freshman right-hander in 1909. Even Babe Ruth's .625 batting spree of 1928 didn't seem to come up to Pepper's performance.

"Pepper Martin went all out in everything," Mr, Rickey once said. "That's why he was such a great ballplayer."

In the 1931 Series he was a demon, at bat and on the base paths. Playing with the fervor of a sawdust-trail evangelist, he made every kid in America conscious of his speed-crazy efforts.

The day the Series began, Pepper was approached by a reporter who wanted to know what his feelings were as he faced his first World Series as a Card regular.

"I kinda feel like a kid with a red wagon," answered Pepper, who had less pretentiousness about himself and his talents than most players who have ever grabbed the spotlight. "But I'm a lucky guy. There've been lots of better players than me who have never gotten into a World Series."

A few days later, sportswriters were dreaming up new adjectives to describe his derring-do. One of them, H. I. Phillips, of the *New York Sun,* commented that he had traveled to Philadelphia "to see a World Series played between the A's and one John Leonard Martin of Oklahoma." The *New York Times* columnist, John Kiernan, suggested the A's might apply for a federal injunction to stop Pepper's peccadilloes. Others began to call this spectacular, catcher-defying ballplayer the "Wild Horse of the Osage." The tag stuck throughout Martin's 13 madhouse seasons with the Cards.

In the first game of the series Pepper and the Cards faced Bob Grove. As everybody expected, Grove won. The score was 6–2. The Cards had scored their two runs in the first inning, and one of them came across on Pepper's first hit of the classic, a double off the right field wall. It was the first of Pepper's twelve base knocks and put the A's on notice that he wasn't around simply to dirty up his uniform. He also stole the first of his five bases off the harassed Mickey Cochrane, and got two other hits.

"Stealin' bases on my stomach was as easy as pickin' berries," Pepper told a reporter many years later, in a moment of reflection about his past glories.

It was in the second game at St. Louis, before 35,000 wild-eyed fans, that Martin really came into his own as the world's happiest one-man gang. As the

Redbirds knotted the series at one game each, Pepper won the contest for Wild Bill Hallahan, 2–0.

"He ran the bases in a manner so heedless of his physical safety," Robert Smith has written, "that he had the fans screaming with excitement. . . . He slid into bases on his chest, smearing the dirt on himself and his uniform, spurting it high along the base lines, risking a broken nose, a split skull, cracked ribs."

A former Chicago sportswriter, Lloyd Lewis, paid an additional tribute. "Pepper sliding into third," he wrote, "will always lie sharper in my memory than Babe Ruth hitting a homer."

In the second inning of that second game, batting against George Earnshaw, who had just finished his third straight season with over 20 wins, Pepper socked a ball into left field, where Simmons was somewhat lackadaisical in returning it to little Max Bishop at second base. The oversight sent Pepper blazing into second, like a freight train on the loose. Then, hardly content with a two-base hit that he had gained by leg work and heads-up play, Pepper set sail for third as Earnshaw took his big windup. Cochrane's peg to Jimmy Dykes was low and accurate. But Pepper had beaten the ball, in a riotous, stomach-skidding slide that brought the crowd to its feet in a roar of delight.

Then, when catcher Jimmy Wilson belted one to center and into the outstretched hands of Mule Haas, Pepper came trotting home after the catch. It was to be the only run of the duel until the seventh inning. Again Pepper made things hot for Moose Earnshaw with a lead-off single. He didn't wait long to set sail for second, for he carried within his sturdy legs the hopes for a second and possibly crucial tally in a tight ball game. Cochrane, aware that his antagonist would go but unable to stop him, made a poor throw that ended up in center field, where Haas had to retrieve it.

Wilson managed to hit an easy one to Dib Williams at short. But while the catcher was being thrown out at first base, Pepper moved into third. Manager Street, eager for the second run, which would give Wild Bill Hallahan a cushion to work on going into the eighth inning, put on the sign for the "suicide" squeeze. That meant that as soon as Earnshaw's pitch was released in the direction of home plate, where Charley Gelbert waited to look it over, Pepper would break violently and with complete commitment, for home.

Gelbert's bat met the ball. It rolled toward the mound, where Earnshaw pounced on it and flipped it in almost the same motion to Iron Mike Cochrane, guarding the plate. But the toss was not fast enough to get Martin as he slid under Cochran's legs. That was the ball game. And Pepper, with Hallahan's mound help, had done it all by himself.

John Kiernan was fascinated by Pepper's brilliance. "His fighting spirit and speed," wrote Kieran, "carried him around the circuit twice. They say that Pepper doesn't bother with passenger trains when going to training camp because he doesn't like to pay railroad fare. After watching him on the base paths it seems he has another objection to passenger trains. They don't travel fast enough for him. . . . When Pepper next tries to steal second perhaps Cochrane will peg to third to be sure he doesn't get past that point."

As the Cards moved into Philadelphia for the third game of what was shaping up as a fiercely contested Series, the public began to take note of the bull-chested Redbird center fielder who ran as if his life depended on it. First they had asked who Martin was, where he had been all season, could he be more than a flash in the pan? Now they crowded around him wherever he went, tried to touch him to make sure he was for real, lapped up the sportswriters' stories about him.

In a Philadelphia hotel lobby a man confronted Pepper. "Tell me, Pepper," he asked, "where did you ever learn to run like that?"

"I guess I learned it back home in Oklahoma," said Pepper, puzzled at the adulation he was receiving. "When you're running around out there, there just ain't a thing to stop you."

In the third game the Cards faced Lefty Grove again. But this time they belted him around for 11 hits and beat him, 5–2. Pepper had a double and a single, scored twice, and roamed his position—between Hafey in left and Walter Roettger in right—as if he'd been born right there in the center of Shibe Park. However, he took it easy that day and didn't run on Mickey Cochrane—or Grove. He did, though, exhibit his flying legs once again in the second inning, when he reached third on Wilson's single. Gelbert hit a line drive to Bing Miller in short right, and Pepper rumbled home on it. Another player might have thought twice about going on it, but not Pepper.

Earnshaw came back in game four to shut out the Cards, 3–0, on two hits. Who got the two hits? Pepper, of course. One of the hits was a double. After his first hit, Pepper stole another base, his fourth of the Series.

Pepper was making a mockery out of Cochrane's reputation as a bulwark behind the plate. Many years later, Martin told a reporter, W. C. Heinz, that he really felt sorry for Mike during the frenetic week that made him famous.

"Once," said Pepper, "Cochrane said to me, 'Don't you ever make an out?'"

Pepper was hotter than a hamburger grill in the fifth game. He went three for four, including a bunt single, against Waite Hoyt, Rube Walberg, and ancient Eddie Rommel, scored one run and batted in four, enough to whomp the A's and give the Cards the go-ahead victory, 5–1. In the sixth inning, with Frisch on base, Pepper took a vicious swing at one of Hoyt's fast balls and missed.

"That's not like old Pepper," he muttered to himself as he edged out of the batter's box to rub dirt into the palms of his callused hands. Stepping back in, Martin belted the next pitch deep into the left field stands.

In the eighth inning, Pepper connected for his 12th hit of the Series, tying the all-time record. Once more he tested the vaunted throwing arm of Cochrane. But this time—for the only time in the Series—Mickey gunned him down with an accurate throw to Eric McNair. The Philadelphia fans, who had been cheering every move of Pepper's even if he was killing their club's chances, reacted to his first failure on the bases by showering torn-up paper around him in center field. Pepper waved back at them, then proceeded to pick up the isolated scraps that littered the grass. He was always superstitious about such things. His own teammates knew him as an avid collector of hairpins!

With a chance to pass the record for hits in World Series play, Pepper failed to hit in six times at bat in the final two games, as he batted in the fourth position. Gabby Street had moved him up to the clean-up slot after Pepper had started the Series as the Cards' sixth batter in the lineup. When Pepper finally went hitless in the sixth game, the *New York Times* made it front-page news. "PEPPER" MARTIN STOPPED read the blurb on the story. In the last game, as the Cards beat Earnshaw, 4–2, for the championship, Martin drew a pass his first time up. But after promptly stealing second, for his fifth stolen base, he finished the Series in quiet fashion, without another hit or steal.

However, Pepper was heard from for the last time in the ninth inning, as the A's staged a last-ditch rally. Behind 4–0, the Philadelphians banged two runs across and had two on base. Bishop, batting against Hallahan, who was brought in to relieve Burleigh Grimes, connected for a low, long drive into center field. It looked like it might fall in, but Pepper, running desperately, snagged Bishop's bid for a hit with one hand, fittingly putting an end to a Series that he dominated from first to last.

Hailed for his role in the St. Louis victory, Pepper became a national idol. Even baseball's high commissioner, Judge Kenesaw Mountain Landis, rushed to shake Pepper's hand and congratulate him for the spectacular job he had done.

"Young fellow," said the white-maned jurist, "I'd like to trade places with you."

"OK," said Pepper, who never was one to lose his perspective. "I'll take your $65,000 a year and you can have my $4,500."

Pepper probably was one of the lowest paid Series heroes in history. But he added $4,500 of his winner's share to his season's salary, then embarked on a vaudeville tour that paid him another $1,500 a week.

However, Pepper didn't consider himself an actor, and within a month he quit to go hunting.

"I'm a ballplayer," he said. "I don't belong on the stage. That's cheating the public."

In the next few years Martin, though he never again reached the heights he'd scaled against the A's, became one of the most colorful members of the St. Louis Gas House Gang. The Gas Housers, a throwback to the old Baltimore Orioles, were the weirdest assortment of major-leaguers ever assembled under one roof. They were ornery, tough, grimy, profane—and fighting was their favorite dish. They had the incorrigible Dean brothers—Dizzy and Daffy—on the mound and outfielder Joe Medwick, a tough kid from Carteret, New Jersey. They had the musical Ripper Collins at first base and Ernie Orsatti, a Hollywood stunt man, in the outfield. Lippy Leo Durocher, a strident dude, handled shortstop. They had a gravel-voiced Frankie Frisch at second. Frankie was also their manager. "They might have killed a half-dozen managers in a single season," Frisch once said in exasperation.

But the real guiding force was Pepper Martin. His personality—laughter-loving and rambunctious on the field and off—was contagious. When he was in high spirits and leading the way, the club always seemed to follow.

In 1932, for instance, when Pepper was injured a good deal and in bad slumps the rest of the time, the Cards fell to sixth place. Pepper played in less than 100 games, hit a measly .235, and stole only nine bases. After stealing five in the World Series of 1931, that was pretty poor going for the Wild Horse. In 1933, the Cards finished in the second division again. But Pepper had been shifted to third base and liked the job. He stopped ground balls with his chest, then scrambled in the dirt to pick them up and shoot them across to first. He also ran the bases with abandon and his batting average went up to .316 in 145 games.

In every way he personified the spirit of the Gashouse Gang. By 1934, the Gashousers had jelled into a winning combination. With the swashbuckling Dean boys winning 49 games between them, the Cards won the National League flag the final two days of the season, edging the Giants out of the picture.

In the World Series that followed against Detroit's Tigers, Pepper wasn't up to repeating his flamboyant one-man show of 1931. But with the large crowds in St. Louis and Detroit urging him on, he made life miserable again, at bat and on the bases, for the foe. He stole only two bases in this Series. Both steals came in the seventh game, as the Cardinals shelled the Tigers, 11–0, with Dizzy Dean working on the mound. But again the man who was subjected to his baseball chicanery was his old friend Mickey Cochrane. In 1934, Mike was the manager and catcher of the Tigers.

Pepper's Series mark this time was .355. He banged out 11 hits and scored 8 runs. Batting in the lead-off spot, he had three runs batted in.

Frisch, who inherited more headaches from Martin and Company than it is proper for a single manager to be subjected to, nevertheless had a soft spot in his heart for Pepper.

"I doubt if any player has ever enjoyed sliding, running, scrambling, fighting, and stealing everything on the ball field the way Pepper did," said Frisch.

But, recalls Frisch, Martin got his biggest kicks from midget auto racing, and harmless practical jokes.

"When I became convinced he was going to get himself killed in one of those autos," said Frankie, "I warned him he wouldn't be able to buy more insurance. But Pepper would tell me, 'Gosh, I'm just having fun.'

"Once right before an important series with the Pittsburgh Pirates, Pepper failed to put in an appearance for batting practice. When he finally showed up, I asked him where he'd been. 'Some wise guy bet me I couldn't beat him in a two-mile race through the streets,' Pepper told me.

"'Now isn't that nifty,' I exploded. 'We're trying to win ball games and stay in the race and you're betting on auto races. What did you bet?'

"'A coupla quarts of vanilla ice cream,' said Pepper. Of course it was the unvarnished truth. Pepper never took a drink of the hard stuff in his life."

More often than not Pepper would arrive at the Cards' ball park with grease covering every inch of him. He looked as if he might have spent a half dozen days getting rescued from a coal mine cave-in.

On another occasion Pepper conspired with Dizzy Dean to subtly inform the Cardinal management that, at 115 degrees or thereabouts, it was entirely too hot to play ball in St. Louis. On the day in question Pepper and Dizzy put together a neat little pile of paper and wood in the middle of the Card dugout and set fire to it. Then they wrapped themselves in blankets, like Indians in a tepee, and stoically watched the fire blaze. Somehow or other nobody got the hint. The Cards played that day anyway, and Pepper, as usual, gave it all he had.

"He was in a class by himself," said Frisch nostalgically. "They don't make 'em like him any more."

When Pepper became a minor-league manager in 1944, he managed the same way he had always played.

"I've always taken this game very seriously," said Pepper. "I'm a stickler for principle, honesty, and the all-out college try—even though I never went to college. That's the way I played it with the Cards, and that's the way I'll always play it."

The outrage that St. Louis fans felt when Rogers Hornsby was traded after the 1926 season to the New York Giants for Frankie Frisch was quickly dispelled by Frisch's outstanding play when he joined the Cardinals. He set fielding records at second base for chances and assists in 1927, batted .337, and led the National League with 48 stolen bases. After several seasons with the Cardinals, Frisch became player-manager during the 1933 season and led the Gas House Gang to the World Championship in 1934.

In his September 1, 1932, column in the St. Louis Star, *longtime St. Louis sportswriter Sid Keener questions Frankie Frisch on his first sub-par season with the Cardinals and asks him to respond to rumors that he wanted to be traded back to the Giants to become their manager. In his September 1933 article in* Baseball Magazine, *editor F. C. Lane offers his views on Frankie Frisch just after Frisch had been named to replace Gabby Street as Cardinal manager.*

Admits He Would Like to Be a Manager Some Day
Sid Keener ————————————————————————————

Frankie Frisch was starting on the first course of his breakfast at his suite in a hotel here when I called him. It was ten minutes past the noon hour—12:10 p.m., and rubbing his eyes, Frankie was just seeing the light of day through the windows. He apologized for appearing in his lounging robe and, spotting the clock on the table, he remarked:

"I suppose you think this is my daily schedule—breakfast at noon."

I was forced to admit that he could not hold a card in the Bread Wagon Drivers' Union.

"It's this way," he explained. "I lost seven pounds playing last Sunday's double-header in the terrific heat, my neck's as stiff as a canoe paddle, and I have a flock of blisters on my feet. A fellow in this condition cannot get up with the early birds and play ball in the afternoon."

That was okay with me, as I told him. I was a trifle sympathetic over the fact that he had to go through a grueling double-header, losing weight, contracting a stiff neck, and handicapping the feet that for many years had carried him to the leading honors for stealing bases in the National League. However, I had something in mind, far more important than his physical condition.

After exchanging a few short greetings I informed the Fordham Flash that I would like to hear his side of the story. For the first time in his brilliant career he has been put on the spot, so to speak, this year. I reminded him that fellow players, members of other clubs in the league, baseball writers, and cash customers have been putting him over the hurdles this summer.

He leaned back in his chair, relaxed, puffed on a fresh cigarette, and said: "Shoot the works! I've heard so much about myself, it is hardly possible that you have something new to offer."

In brief, I followed with these questions: "Is it true that as early as last May you decided to go joy-riding for yourself because the club cut your salary? . . . What nature of business transpired when President Sam Breadon held an unexpected conference with you in Cincinnati early in the season? . . . I understand someone close to the club informed Mr. Breadon that if he wanted to win the pennant this year he'd make a wise investment by returning to you the amount that was deducted from this year's contract . . . You have been accused of saying that club executives apparently displayed no desire to win the pennant for the Cardinals this year through the deals they arranged—Hafey to Cincinnati, Grimes to Chicago, Wilson to Brooklyn, and Rhem to Philadelphia . . . And you said something like this: 'Well, they won't see me hustling this season—I won't go in there to steady the pitcher and help out on other jobs.' Other members of the Cardinals have criticized you because of your listless play at times . . . Have you engaged in any tiffs or rows with Gabby Street? . . . Do you want the Cardinals to trade you back to the Giants? . . . Where you might get a managerial job in New York?"

Frisch was an attentive listener. He did not attempt to interrupt me at any time while I was spilling out the questions. When I finished he grinned a bit and said: "Well, that is a load, I've heard a few new things, about myself."

Frisch Comes to His Own Defense

Frisch, getting out of his chair, started strolling around his room leisurely. He turned off the radio, pranced back and forth a bit, and mentally seemed to be reviewing the entire season—or thinking up the answers for the questions. He returned to his chair and, leaning forward, showed the expression of a person who was prepared to defend himself.

"I'll start with something like this," he opened up. "I guess it's just a bad year for Frankie. They come to a ball player, you know, every now and then."

I stopped him at that point by cutting in with: "That's a weak alibi, Frankie, and you know it. It covers too much territory—just a bad season."

"All right, then I'll be more explicit for you," he replied. "I did not open this season with any intention of joy riding through the year. My meeting with

Mr. Breadon in Cincinnati was purely personal. I did not ask him to reimburse me to the extent of my salary reduction. I did not criticize the club for making those deals of last winter.

"To me it looks as though there may be a couple of eavesdroppers around. I may have said things about not going out and coaching a pitcher, talking to him, trying to get him to steady himself, but how many ball players don't pop off out of turn when a tough game has been lost or things are going against them?

"So someone is snitching a bit on me, eh? Listen—ball players say aplenty back in the clubhouse; things they don't mean. The club owner is this and that—the manager, too. Outfielders, infielders, pitchers, and catchers come in for criticism while the boys are under the showers, but the next day everything is forgotten."

Frisch paused several moments, straightened some newspapers that were on a table, and offered a cigar. "We can smoke this thing out, can't we?" he said with a smile. Frankie took another cigarette.

"Do you know what started me on the road to a grouchy spell?" he continued. "Well, everyone knows blame well I'm not laying down on the job. I'm not that kind of a ball player, but it was back here late in May—around that date I think, when I hit a grounder to Shortstop Jurges of the Cubs late in the game and didn't put full speed behind my dash for first place. It looked like an easy out for me. Jurges fumbled, recovered, and I was retired on a close play.

"The next day I was criticized in the papers for my actions, but I had been playing with an injured rib and a sore leg. We didn't have any available substitutes to relieve me and I had to play when I should have been home in bed.

"Gabby Street was the one who should have informed the newspaper boys that I was so badly crippled I could hardly run. Gabby muffed that one and I had to take all of those knocks. The fans read those stories and they started hopping on me.

"That incident put me down. I was furious when I read the stories about Frisch loafing. For more than a week things went from bad to worse with me. I didn't care whether I got a base hit or not. I can see now where I was wrong, but when a fellow gets down in this business it takes some time to bring him back, especially with things as they were on our ballclub. Our regulars were going out with injuries one after another and for a time I didn't think we'd have enough players with which to finish the season."

Admits He Would Like to Become a Manager

The Fordham Flash was getting warmed up with himself. He seemed to welcome the opportunity I gave him to say his own piece. "Ball players are seldom invited to defend themselves," he explained. "When he is traded or sold the club owner or manager makes an announcement something like this: 'He had a bum year and we had to get rid of him.' And away the ball player goes to the next city.

"I am not making a denial of all the charges or questions I have heard. I haven't had a good year. No one knows any better then myself. But I haven't laid down intentionally.

"We won two straight pennants, beat the Athletics in the World Series and when we started this spring I thought it would be another gallop for us. There's something with a winner that spurs a ball player. I'm that kind. I'd break a leg to win a ball game with something at stake.

"When things started breaking against us that fighting spirit seemed to die out, but it'll come back. This Frankie boy should be good for four more years and I'll prove it next season, whether I'm with the Cardinals or some other club."

Did Frisch hold a secret fancy of a trade? He did not—so he said. He denied that he had engaged in any long feuds with Gabby Street or that he was coasting along the road this summer for the express purpose of leading up to a transfer to New York where perhaps he'd become manager of the Giants, where he'd be playing back in his home town.

"I'd like to become a major league manager," said Frisch with an admission of frankness, "but not at the price of sacrificing my reputation by loafing for a magnate and forcing a trade. If I ever get that appointment I want to earn it.

"I should be talking about trades—that's funny. Owners, not players, make them. I'd like to remain in St. Louis. I hope I do, but I have no voice in the matter. Mr. Breadon is the one who will make that decision."

Before departing I reminded Frisch that ball players who have been held in higher esteem by the fans than the Fordham Flash have taken a lofty tumble from their high perch by falling into those temperamental moods—temperamental mood, just another expression for sulking on the job.

"I thought I was the injured party all year," said Frisch as he gave a hearty hand-shake. "I suppose I'm the guy who's been out of step."

The Fordham Flash Becomes a Manager
F. C. Lane ——————————————————————————————————————

They called him the Fordham Flash. And that colorful phrase expresses his career upon the diamond. Speed—brilliancy—dash—have characterized his work in the field and on the base paths and at bat. And now he steps out in a new role, that of manager of a major league club, a club with a background of victory, a pennant winner and a world's champion. It is a great opportunity for Frank Frisch.

The passing of Gabby Street was regrettable. He was one of the most likable personalities in professional sport. Moreover, he had done excellent work. Two pennants and one world's championship fell to the lot of the Cardinals while he stood at the helm. But baseball is a game of merciless competition. Sentiment fades from the picture when results are at stake. The Cardinals have faltered this season, have slipped into the second division. The owners felt that a new manager, particularly a playing manager with the dynamic personality of Frank Frisch, would do better than the grey-haired veteran of many campaigns. So exit Street, enter Frisch.

Ballplayers call him a money player, this spectacular second baseman. The epithet is deserved. Frisch, like Babe Ruth, has the indefinable talent which enables him to appear at his best when the call is the greatest.

In the recent all-star game at Chicago, Ruth was the hero with a home run and a single. Frisch was a step behind, but he also made a home run and a single. Both players rose to the occasion, beyond all their teammates.

Up to this season, Frisch had spent fourteen years in major league baseball. Exactly half that time he was on a pennant-winning team. Three times he has been with a world's champion club. Such experiences, which are prized by all ballplayers, have been deserved in Frisch's case. It was not alone that he was lucky to be on a pennant winner. He helped in every case to win that pennant.

Sam Breadon, president of the Cardinals, announced, when he appointed Frisch to the management, that he hoped to win a pennant by making the managerial change. That is improbable, but certainly not impossible. When Frisch assumed command, the Cardinals were in fifth place. They could climb to first, in fact, have done it before. But there was little more than two months remaining. The time was short. If Frisch accomplishes this goal, he will have won his spurs as one of baseball's foremost leaders. No one doubts that he will strain every nerve to accomplish this, for his is the winning spirit.

Early this spring Frisch was discussing with the writer some of his views on this winning spirit as shown by players and clubs. At the time he had no faintest inkling of climbing to the managership so soon. Like all great players, he hoped some time to lead a major league team, but that hope was in the distant future.

The conversation veered to players who were playing for an individual record. Frisch was outspoken in his criticism of such players. "I have never seen a base-hit hound yet," he said, "who was of much use to his ball club. So far as I am concerned, I never worried about base-hits in my life. But I have worried plenty about playing winning baseball. I've been on seven pennant winners, so I know the feeling. It's a pleasure to be on a winning team. The fellows are all hustling. Things are coming your way. You are sitting on top of the world. Besides, five thousand dollars more or less in World Series' money is something that a fellow doesn't want to kick around.

"A winning ball club is hard to define. It is made up of good players, with good pitchers. That goes without saying. But there's something else, a fighting spirit, a confidence, a determination to pull through. Everybody can sense this spirit but no one that I ever heard can quite define it.

"The same thing goes for individuals. There are winning pitchers and there are pitchers that look even better and have more natural stuff but they aren't winning pitchers. What's the difference? It's in the attitude, in the mind of the pitcher. There are winning ballplayers. They may not hit as well or be such capable fielders as certain other players, but they fight for every game and fight for their club. They have the winning spirit.

"You can search in the records for this spirit and you will never find it. It isn't there. Batting averages don't express it, nor fielding averages, nor pitching averages. But managers, in general, know these players and so do the owners.

"A team is made up of personalities. It is a kind of a combination of twenty-odd personalities. That combination confers a certain personality on the team. You know such teams and how they differ. There are smart teams and teams that get easily discouraged and teams that refuse to get discouraged, but fight. They are the teams that win.

"Let any tail-end team develop a real fighting spirit and hustle every minute, day in and day out, and they'll not stay long in last place. Let a good, strong team develop that spirit and they are a potential pennant winner."

Frisch's comments that afternoon, in the clubhouse, were quite expressive of his own personality and his own attitude toward baseball. For Frisch is a fighting ballplayer who always hustles. No doubt the Cardinal owners recognized this fact when they gave him his appointment.

That fact was also recognized long ago by John McGraw. McGraw took Frisch from the Fordham campus and gave him his opportunity to become one of baseball's greatest stars. McGraw looked upon Frisch as a probable successor. He told him more than once, that he planned some day to step aside and let him pilot the New York Giants. When McGraw did step aside he recommended Frisch for his place, but Frisch was the property of the Cardinals and there were many handicaps. Terry was chosen as McGraw's successor and he has fully justified that choice.

Frisch came to the Giants in 1919 when he was scarcely twenty-one years of age. He remained with them for eight seasons. Brilliant seasons they were both for him and the club. Then, in the winter of 1926, came the sensational deal which sent him to the Cardinals in exchange for Rogers Hornsby.

Hornsby was then at the peak of his career, the greatest star in the National League, with his fresh-won laurels as manager of the first world's champion team St. Louis has ever known. The St. Louis populace boiled and seethed when the trade was announced, and openly arraigned the Cardinal owners. But before the season was ended, they had forgotten Hornsby. Frisch covered second with so much aggressiveness and sheer brilliance that criticism simply died away and ever since that time he has been the star of the team.

His batting average in fourteen seasons, up to date, has been .321. His batting record in seven World's Series has been .313. A dangerous, aggressive hitter is Frank Frisch.

In fielding he has covered second base, third base, and shortstop and played them all with his usual restless urge to excel. He has been one of the flashiest infielders baseball has ever known. On the base-paths Frisch has always excelled. Several times he has led his league in stolen bases. Alert, resourceful, and always threatening, he is a thorn in the side of all opposing pitchers.

By an odd turn of fate, Rogers Hornsby returned to the Cardinal club this year, a veteran in the twilight of his great career. He has not been able to take a regular place upon the team, though he has hit with something of his old-time skill. Once rivals in the records and fellow actors in the most dramatic trade baseball has ever pulled, the older man found himself for a day working for the younger. It was a queer turn of the wheel of fate. Then Hornsby, like Frisch, blossomed out as a manager—the leader of the St. Louis team—the Browns.

The baseball world will watch with interest the success of these ancient rivals.

For both are managers of St. Louis baseball clubs.

The ringleader of the Gas House Gang, Jay Hanna "Dizzy" Dean is often re-membered more for his brash personality, his outrageous conduct, and his frac-turing of the English language than for his baseball accomplishments. But before an arm injury in 1937 shortened his career, he was one of the most dominant pitchers in baseball history. In his first five full seasons, Dean averaged 24 wins and led the National League in strikeouts four times. In the 1934 championship season he had a 30–7 record, the last time a National League pitcher would win 30 games. He dominated the 1934 World Series with his personality and his pitching and threw a shutout against the Detroit Tigers in the seventh and de-ciding game.

Bob Broeg's essay on Dizzy Dean, first published by the Sporting News *as part of a series honoring baseball's centennial, is a wonderful example of a great base-ball writer capturing the career of one of the game's most colorful personalities and greatest pitchers.*

Dizzy Dean
Bob Broeg

Jay Hanna (Dizzy) Dean warmed up for the first time in the major leagues on the last day of the 1930 season, a lean, lanky, long-armed righthander with a smooth, flowing delivery. Standing nearby at a box, next to the St. Louis Cardinals' dugout at old Sportsman's Park, manager Charles E. (Gabby) Street talked to the St. Louis mayor, Victor J. Miller, who had come out to congratu-late Street on a spectacular fourth-to-first, down-the-stretch drive to the Na-tional League pennant.

The mayor nodded toward the high-cheekboned pitcher, then only 19 years old, if you could believe anything about Dizzy, including his birth certificate.

"How about that Dean, Gabby?" His Honor asked. "Is he going to be as good as they say?"

Street smiled. "I think he's going to be a great one, Mr. Mayor," said Gabby in one of the most prophetic double-barreled pronouncements ever, "but I'm afraid we'll never know from one minute to the next what he's going to do or say."

Street should have gone into the Hall of Fame with Dean for putting that one in the side pocket. Ol' Diz, as the gangling guy called himself from the outset, did become a great pitcher, his career cut short by an arm injury when he should have been just reaching his peak.

And from the time he threw a three-hitter at Pittsburgh that first game,

3–1, helping himself with a hit, until he ballooned into a living legend as a baseball broadcaster, Dean fulfilled the second half of Street's prophecy, too.

Never has anyone, including the Great One, ever been sure what he'd say or do.

Ol' Diz helped thin the sparse gray thatch of Frank Frisch, manager of the Gashouse Gang, a colorful Depression-era ball club of which Dean was the most colorful member. And he never ceased to amaze, amuse—or anger—Frisch.

Like the time at Boston when an East St. Louis night-club comic, Johnny Perkins, as corpulent then as Dizzy became later, accompanied the Cardinals on a trip and heard Dean insist that he'd strike out Vince DiMaggio every time at bat the next day. The eldest ballplaying DiMaggio brother, a brilliant outfielder with power, struck out frequently and couldn't carry brother Joe's bat—or Dominic's, either.

Still, to fan any hitter four times isn't easy, as Perkins knew, and he offered a friendly bet that Dean couldn't do it. It was a small thing, no doubt, though later Ol' Diz would play golf for high stakes and was called in for some embarrassing questions in a Detroit gambling probe. The pitcher remembered the Boston bet with Perkins as only a nickel, to be redoubled, etc., if he kept striking out Vince, so that maybe no more than 80 cents cash was involved.

But for money, marbles, or fried channel cat with hush puppies, Dean was a deep-dyed-in-Dixie competitor. He wiffed DiMaggio three times and then quickly fired across two strikes as he faced the Boston outfielder a fourth time in the ninth inning with two out and the tying run on second base.

Suddenly, Vince got a piece of the ball, lifting a high foul behind the plate and toward the visitors' dugout. Young Bruce Ogrodowski, rookie Redbird catcher, ripped off his mask and headed for the ball, fist thumping his glove, a confident sign that he'd make a game-ending catch.

To Frisch's consternation in the dugout, Dean thundered down off the hill toward Ogrodowski, hands cupped to his mouth, screaming:

"Drop it . . . drop it . . . ."

Startled, Ogrodowski looked at Dean.

"Damn it, if you want to catch me again, drop it," Dizzy demanded.

Ogrodowski permitted the ball to fall, and Frisch, leaping to his feet, cracked his head on the concrete roof of the dugout. Before the dazed manager could recover, Dean calmly had gone back to the mound and fired—no, "fogged" is the word he always used—a third strike past DiMaggio. Thus Diz protected, in order, his pride, that 80 cents or whatever it was and, oh, yes, the ball game.

Dizzy was capable of the unexpected from the time he was choppin' cotton as the son of a poor sharecropper in Arkansas and Oklahoma. When a neighbor friend lost a son and grieved deeply over his loss, young Jay Hanna was quite comforting. He allowed as how it would be neighborly to change his name to that of the man's dead youth.

So Jay Hanna became Jerome Herman and if that doesn't throw you, you must be as perceptive as the Army sergeant who nicknamed him Dizzy at Fort Sam Houston when the skinny, big-footed country kid was pulling a peacetime hitch for Uncle Sam. These were—understand!—roots of an obscure background at least before author Bob Gregory in Tulsa promised to rearrange if not destroy Dean's image in an interesting book.

Dean's predilection for the unexpected never was more evident than in the 1934 World Series, the one in which he and brother Paul—Me 'n' Paul, as Dizzy called 'em—scored two victories each over the Detroit Tigers, a club that had four future Hall of Famers as did the Cardinals.

Catcher Mickey Cochrane, first baseman Hank Greenberg, second baseman Charley Gehringer, and left fielder Goose Goslin of the Tigers were on their way to Cooperstown. So, too, were Cardinals' second baseman Frank Frisch, left fielder Joe Medwick, pitcher Jesse Haines and, naturally, Dean himself.

Ol' Diz had a ball for himself from the time the Cardinals arrived at Navin Field for a pre-Series look and found the Tigers working out. Dean, in street clothes, took a bat out of a surprised Tiger's hands, stepped into the batting cage, hit a pitch into the left-field seats and said, "That's the way to do it, fellas."

Dean, the National League's last 30-game winner that year, won the Series opener, 8–3, and apologized for pitching poorly. He served as a pinch-runner in the fourth game and, leaping to break up a double play, was hit smack on the head by Billy Rogell, Detroit's shortstop, and was carried off the field.

You couldn't hurt Ol' Diz by hitting him on the head. Not seriously, anyway. Shucks, I saw him react slowly on a hot, steaming day, pitching against the Giants, when former teammate Burgess Whitehead caromed a line drive off Dean's head and into the left-field bullpen—on the fly—for a double.

So when newspaper headlines told the story—"X-Rays of Dean's Head Show Nothing"—Dizzy came out of the hospital and pitched the next day in the fifth game of the '34 Series, losing a tough one to Tommy Bridges, 3–1.

The Tigers, therefore, took a 3–2 lead in the Series, but Dizzy's brother, Paul, a 21-year-old-rookie, battled to his second victory, 4–3, sending the Series to a seventh and final game.

There were no open dates for Series travel after the second and fifth games, as now, so that Dizzy Dean would have to come back for the seventh game with just one day's rest. Besides, he'd pitched 11 times in the tense month of

September, winning seven games and helping save three. In the final nine National League games, when the Cardinals caught and then passed the slumping New York Giants, he'd pitched four complete-game victories, three of them shutouts, including one on the final day.

So the rangy righthander really had worked too often, Manager Frisch told the press after the sixth game, suggesting that lefthander Bill Hallahan would be the Cardinals' pitcher in the windup. A steaming Dean charged into the showers, where Frisch slipped in for the showdown the manager slyly sought.

"Dawgonnit, Frank," Dean protested, "I don't see how you can even think of pitching Hallahan tomorrow when I've brought you this far."

The Dutchman, as Dizzy ordinarily called Frisch, let the 23-year-old pitcher plea for the assignment and then promise to get a good night's sleep, which is what the manager wanted most. Then Frisch said the job was Dean's.

"And remember, Jerome," Frisch said, "if you win that ball game tomorrow, it can be worth $50,000 to you now and more over the years."

For a pitcher earning only $7,500—remember, this was deep in the Depression—50 grand had to sound, well, just grand.

Which is the way Dizzy felt for game No. 7. He posed for pictures with his good friend, Will Rogers, the cowboy humorist who spoke his same twang of the Southwest. He didn't horse around as he did in earlier games at Detroit, where he'd draped a tiger skin over himself and played a tuba for the first time, predicting he would "twist the tail of the pussy cats." But he still had time for the gamemanship that made him deadly in later life on the golf links.

Walking behind Elden Auker, submarine-throwing righthander who was warming up to start the blue-chip ball game for Detroit, Dean paused, shook his head and then said airily, as Auker glowered:

"You don't expect to get anyone out with that stuff, do you, podnuh?"

The game, however, was scoreless until the third inning when Ol' Diz, leading off, hit what amounted to a routine single to left field. Years later, justifiably, the Great One was proud because of the Pandora's Box he opened with his hitting and his hustle.

Always a good athlete, a loping runner who could let out, Dean watched Goslin in left field handle the ball casually. Rounding first base, Diz took off unexpectedly for second base and beat the startled Goslin's weak, late throw with a hook slide that, viewed today in films, is a classic.

The double meant far more than one base. When Pepper Martin, next up, grounded to Greenberg at the first baseman's right, Hank would have had an easy play at second if Dean had been on first. But now, required to make the stop backhanded, then wheel and throw across his body to Auker covering first, Greenberg couldn't retire Martin on a bang-bang play that went for an infield hit.

So instead of a man on first, one out, St. Louis had runners on first and third, none down. And when Martin quickly stole second, both runners were in scoring position, creating a problem for Detroit and leading to questionable strategy by Manager Mickey Cochran.

The great catcher ordered Jack Rothrock passed carefully to fill the bases, setting up a double-play situation. But Frisch, even in his athletic dotage a money player, slugged a bases-clearing double, leading to a decisive seven-run inning, which had been set up by Dizzy Dean's derring-do. The Great One tied a Series record with two hits that inning.

As the score mounted, so did Dean's enjoyment. When he began to cut up and laugh as he turned back the Tigers, taking particular delight in teasing Greenberg, Frisch stormed in from second base and threatened to remove him from the game.

"Aw, c'mon, Frank, you wouldn't dare take out Ol' Diz when he's pitching a shutout," Dean said.

"The hell I wouldn't," said Frisch. "Just try me. Just lose Greenberg."

Dizzy struck him out, the ninth time Hank had fanned in the Series. Despite the interruption for a barrage aimed at Medwick after a baseline incident with Marvin Owen, the Detroit third baseman, Dean breezed to a laughable 11–0 climax to an exciting World Series. And with personal appearances, endorsements, and other benefits of that season, the Dizzy who wasn't so Dizzy earned about $40,000.

As a pitcher with the Cardinals, for whom he won 82 games and lost just 32 over one three-year stretch, 1934 through '36, Dean got up to $25,500, the highest salary paid a National League pitcher until better times and a big bonus paid to young Johnny Antonelli prompted Johnny Sain of the Boston Braves to stage a brief sitdown strike at the All-Star break in 1948.

So Ol' Diz was off base and merely trying to stick the needle in his former boss, Sam Breadon, when he would tell how little he was paid the year he won 30. He was annoyed, for one thing, because Breadon forever removed competition from the Redbirds' radio broadcasts when he gave exclusive rights in 1947 to establishment of a network. Dean, then airing both the Cardinals' and Browns' games, was with the wrong beer sponsor and with the wrong station.

The gregarious, good-natured big guy with the blue eyes, wide grin, and western white hat could be spiteful at times, just as he could be difficult when he was a skinny kid wearing No. 17 and mowing down batters in a manner that brought him a 150–83 record, a good one that would have been great if he hadn't been hurt.

Even giving or taking a year in his age, Ol' Diz had won 133 big league ball games before he was 27. And if he'd followed his inclination—and his suitcase—as he wanted to at the All-Star interval in 1937, he might have escaped the unfortunate early end to what well might have been one of the greatest pitching careers.

In addition to supreme confidence, Dean had developed excellent control and a good curve and change-up to go with his high hard one, but when he was unable to "rare back and fog 'er through," as he used to put it, he became just another pitcher.

Even so, sore arm or not, forced to lob the ball side-armed rather than crank up and let fly with a fluid three-quarter delivery, Ol' Diz still managed to contribute a 7–1 record to the Cubs in 1938, after he had been sold to the Wrigleys for three players and $185,000. He walked just eight batters in 75 innings and posted a 1.80 earned-run average.

Dean had been in drydock for a considerable time when the surging Cubs collared sagging Pittsburgh in late September at Wrigley Field. Even the highly competitive Dean did a double-take when manager Gabby Hartnett asked him to pitch the pivotal middle contest of the decisive three-game series. But using cunning, control, and changing speeds, Ol' Diz blanked the Pirates into the ninth, 2–0, before giving way to wheelhorse Bill Lee, who wild-pitched home a run, then preserved the victory that put the Cubs in first place to stay.

Hartnett, playing a hunch, started Dean in the second game of the 1938 World Series at Chicago. Dizzy's nuthin' ball was painfully apparent, but his soft curves and off-stride pitches were so well directed that he held the slugging Yankees at bay until the eighth inning. By then, actually, he should have been ahead 3–0 if, weirdly, third baseman Stan Hack and shortstop Bill Jurges hadn't bumped heads on a slow second-inning grounder that trickled into left field with—of all people—the pitcher in pursuit of the ball.

Still, Diz led by a run into the eighth when he thought he'd slipped a third strike past Frank Crosetti, the Yankee shortstop and leadoff man. Crosetti then rapped a full-count pitch over the left field wall for a two-run homer.

As Crosetti trotted around the bases, Dean circled the pitcher's mound, cussing and fussing at the batter all the way. Finally, as Frank stepped on home plate with the run that put the Yankees ahead to stay, Dean said: "And, furthermore, if I'd had my old fast ball, you wouldn't have seen the ball."

To which Crosetti replied graciously, "Darned if I don't think you're right, Diz."

In the clubhouse later, a downcast Dean was startled—and pleased—to look up and see Connie Mack. The baseball institution patted Dizzy on the back and said, "My boy, you've given me one of the greatest thrills I ever had. It was magnificent, but it must have hurt you terribly. . . ."

As late as the last day of the 1947 season, when he was six years out of baseball and already beginning to bulge at the seams, Dean was given permission generously by the Cubs' Phil Wrigley, a man he respected highly, to pitch the final game of the season for the Browns. After all, he still was on Chicago's voluntarily retired list.

Broadcasting for the bumbling Browns, Ol' Diz hadn't been able to resist a remark here or there about the quality of what he was watching, which was pretty horrible. So, shrewdly, club president Bill DeWitt challenged him to try to do better himself, aware that the magic name of the popular pitcher and play-by-play announcer would draw a crowd.

Ol' Diz worked out a few times with the Browns and then toed the rubber for them in the season windup against the White Sox, still unable to throw hard, but still able to catch the corners with the changing speeds and curves. The overweight Great One worked four innings, yielding three hits and one walk, but not a run.

He'd have kept going, too, if he hadn't been too good at bat for his own good. In the fourth inning, he hit safely to left field, delighting the crowd and, sliding into second base, the out-of-shape pitcher pulled a leg muscle. He got up, limping, and his wife, Pat, seated in a box next to the Browns' dugout, leaned over and yelled to manager Muddy Ruel:

"Get him out of there before he kills himself."

Pat Dean, the former Patricia Nash of Bond, Miss., a Houston sales girl when Dizzy met and married her in 1931, frequently had the last word in matters dealing with Ol' Diz. At times it even had been profane, but, usually, it had been for the former pitcher's own good.

No wife probably ever acted in her husband's best interests more conscientiously than Pat Dean, who can be even more outspoken and direct than Jay, which is what she called Dean. Back in 1935, for instance, when Diz was holding out in Bradenton, Fla., Branch Rickey dropped by impolitely late one night and awakened the young couple.

"I'm not here to talk contract, Jerome," said Rickey pontifically, "but just to find out why Mrs. Dean doesn't like me."

Diz started to apologize, as Rickey shrewdly anticipated. "Now, Mr. Rickey, she really is fond of you," Dean began, but he never finished.

Pat interrupted. "He's a stinker," she said.

The former Patricia Nash, childless, babied Ol' Diz over the years when, after he had weathered cataract operations, she suffered heart attacks that prompted Jay to give her the attention she'd always shown him. As a good-hearted guy, by nature a gambler who had won as much as $8,000 on a round of golf, Dizzy could have lived life in constant jeopardy of easy-come, easy-go. But Pat insisted that they save $1,200 out of the $3,000 he earned the year they were married and, though they were quietly generous, she saw to it with even occasional hardboiled protectiveness that no one took advantage of her man, financially or otherwise.

The affluent Deans, whose wealth was made largely after Dizzy's playing days, divided their time between a farm in Bond, Miss., and a home in Arizona. They once had a handsome ranch-style bungalow in Phoenix, then later spent the winter months at a fashionable hotel so that Pat could take it easy and Ol' Diz could skin someone on the golf course. He was invariably just good enough to win the day's play.

In Mississippi, they thought so highly of Pat Dean's husband that they wanted Dizzy to run for governor at one time. Wisely, though flattered, Dizzy bowed out. Even though he could afford a pay cut from Falstaff Brewing Corp. to take the governor's salary in Mississippi, it just wouldn't do to keep him from the "darndest catfishin' you ever seen."

The fried "eat" sweet corn and hush puppies he favored contributed to the 6–3 Dean's bulk, which at times was uncomfortably close to 300 pounds, more than 100 greater than in his playing career.

On the golf course one time, President Dwight D. Eisenhower asked, "Dizzy, for a man who plays golf so well, how can you permit yourself to get so overweight?"

Dean had a ready answer. "Mr. President," he said, "I was on a diet for 25 years. Now that I'm makin' some money, I'm makin' sure I eat good to make up for the lean years."

They were lean, all right, leaner than Jay Hanna Dean grew into after he was born in Lucas, Ark., in 1911. Sure, he told three reporters one day that he was born in two other states and on two other dates, too, but as he confided to his favorite chronicler, J. Roy Stockton of the *St. Louis Post-Dispatch:*

"I give 'em each a scoop, Roy, so that their bosses can't bawl the three of 'em out for gettin' the same story."

If at times reading "The Gas House Gang and a Couple of Other Guys," you wonder which is the more amusing, Dean or Stockton, meaning the one and only Jay Hanna or the Dizzy as seen, heard—and helped—by the talented, puckish baseball writer, don't look at me. I find 'em both funny. They represented one of the happiest of coincidences by which a fresh, colorful character came along to be covered by an extremely able writer who not only wouldn't stand in the way of a good story, but even might be willing now and then to make it just a bit better.

Except, however, for the time that brother Elmer (Goober) Dean was left behind a string of cars at a railroad crossing and not seen for years when the family was scratching a pitiful living out of the land, there wasn't much funny in Dizzy's boyhood. His mother died when he was three years old and Paul was an infant. Pa—Albert Dean—drove 'em from job to job in Arkansas,

Oklahoma, and Texas in a sputtering jalopy. More than one community like Holdenville, Okla., can claim proudly, "Didya know that Dizzy Dean chopped cotton here?"

Jay left the school books behind after the fourth grade. At the tender age of 10, he was getting up at five in the morning and picking as much as 400 pounds of cotton a day. No wonder the Army was tempting with a three-year hitch when he was only 16. After all, Uncle Sam offered new shoes, clothes, three squares a day—and a chance to play baseball.

Shortly before his Army enlistment was to end, with his father's encouragement and $120 they'd scratched up, the brilliant pitcher that wise Army sergeant had called "Dizzy" bought himself out of service, a practice in those peace-time days. He took a job with the public service company in San Antonio so that he could pitch for the company baseball team. And that's where Don Curtis, a scout for the Cardinals' Texas League farm club at Houston, signed him in the fall of 1929.

At St. Joseph, Mo., in 1930, Dizzy topped the Western League in pitching, I.O.U.'s and wild stunts. Man, imagine getting paid to pitch! He rented rooms at three addresses, asked hitters what they wanted thrown to them and where—and then poured the ball past them.

When he was 17–8, the eccentric kid was transferred to Houston, where he pitched a night game, won by a 12–1 score, and then walked into club President Fred Ankenman's office the next day and apologized.

"I'm awfully sorry," he said. "I promise if you'll give me another chance, it'll never happen again. Can you imagine them bums getting a run off me?"

A few nights later, arriving in the hotel past curfew, the 19-year-old pitcher met the club president in the lobby.

"Well, I guess me and you will get the devil for this, Mr. Ankenman," the boy said, reassuringly, "but I won't say nuthin' about it if you don't."

After his major league debut in the final game of the 1930 season, Dizzy swaggered through spring training in '31, reporting later for practice than the sportswriters. When Gabby Street rebuked him, the hurt kid would strike out Al Simmons, Jimmie Foxx, and Mickey Cochrane of the world champion Athletics in one inning and then threaten to go back to Houston.

A pennant-winning ball club didn't need to put up with insubordination. When the cocky kid was optioned back to Houston, relief pitcher Jim Lindsey cracked, "A world's record—it's the first time a ball club ever lost 30 games in one day."

Without Dean, the 1931 Cardinals won 101 games, took the pennant by 13 games, and upset the Athletics in a bid for their third straight world championship. With Dizzy, that veteran, well-balanced team might have been the best ever.

So Dizzy cost himself a probable World Series share in '31, but by return- ing to Houston, where he won 26 games and struck out 303 batters, he met Pat Nash, who declined in a whirlwind romance to be married at home plate. Dizzy borrowed two bucks from a friend for the marriage license. And Pat took over the finances for a happy-go-lucky lad who'd been so irresponsible that in spring training the Cardinals had put him on a dollar-a-day allow- ance. Pat fortunately didn't reform or remake her Jay, but she helped to mod- erate him. And they had a happy, profitable marriage.

As a rookie in 1932, when a poorly conditioned championship club col- lapsed to a tie for sixth and seventh place, the bony, uncombed Dean was wild, but effective with a high-kicking fastball. He won 18, lost 15, and led the National League in strikeouts.

A year later, another second-division season, he was 20–18, again first in strikeouts. He began to skip exhibition games, collect fines, and became a "name" overnight. On July 30, 1933, he struck out 17 Chicago Cubs, which existed as a major league record until Bob Feller, Sandy Koufax, Don Wilson, Steve Carlton, and Tom Seaver came along.

Dean enjoyed horseplay with Pepper Martin, Rip Collins, and other fun- loving members of the Gashouse Gang, but he had a loose lip, too, and he found himself overmatched whenever he'd criticize the fielding of the smaller, but muscular, left fielder, Joe Medwick.

"Dawgonnit, that Medwick don't fight fair," Dizzy complained. "You argue with him and he whops you even before you've had a chance to speak your piece."

When brother Paul came up from Columbus in 1934, observers tried to tab 'em as Dizzy and Daffy, but the alliteration wasn't apt. If Dizzy wasn't really dizzy, certainly Paul was not at all daffy, though queasy would have fit after he'd watched the Redbirds' batboy, Kayo Brown, a boxing protege of Pepper Martin, get his block knocked off in a prize ring. P. Dean suffered an upset stomach.

He was quiet and poker-faced then, though he has become articulate, and considerably more affable in recent years, running his own baseball school in suburban Dallas and also serving as athletic director at the University of Plano, an institution designed to help young men who need remedial reading.

Paul got his lumps early in the 1934 season, but manager Frisch stuck with him, and brother Dizzy, bragging more about his brother's speed than his own pitching stuff, forecast reassuringly that "Me'n Paul will win 45 games."

For once, Ol' Diz was a piker. P. Dean chipped in with 19 victories, J. Dean with 30, despite two sitdown strikes. One was for more money for Paul, then getting only $3,000 a season, and the other for back pay after a fine and sus- pension for failing to show up for an exhibition-game train trip to Detroit.

It was mid-August and the Cardinals were a half-dozen games behind the league-leading Giants. Dizzy didn't think Frisch could afford to set down his best pitchers.

"The hell I can't," snapped Frisch. "I'll pitch Hallahan, Carleton, Walker, and the two old men (Haines and Vance) and we'll win."

They did, too, seven out of eight at a critical period when Dizzy was balking at paying for uniforms he'd torn up. After a hearing with the baseball commissioner, Judge Landis, the costs to Dizzy were $100 for missing the exhibition game, $350 for seven days' salary, and $36 for two torn uniforms. Paul was fined $100.

The Deans were miffed at Frisch, momentarily, but they took out their spite on the foe and they came down the stretch like gangbusters. At Brooklyn in September, Dizzy pitched a three-hitter in the first game of a doubleheader and Paul a no-hitter in the second contest.

"Gee, if I'd known Paul was gonna do it, I'd done it, too," said Dizzy, who had held the Dodgers hitless until the eighth inning.

A victory by Paul the next-to-last day of the season put the Cardinals into first place and Dizzy shut out Cincinnati in the clincher, 9–0.

Setting the tone for the raucous, rowdy, rough-sliding, knockdown pitching of the 1934 World Series, Dizzy apologized after throwing a home run ball to Hank Greenberg in his 8–3 opening game victory.

"Why, that Greenberg hit a curve that hung up there so that a kid could have hit it. I could bring four National League teams over here and win the American League."

In the next couple of seasons, Dizzy was as good as in 1934, on the strength of 28–12 and 24–13 seasons and working in and out of turn. The Cardinals were just a bit short both seasons, however, losing in 1935 to the incredible 21-game winning streak of the Cubs and in 1936 to the Giants.

The Giants' great lefthander, Carl Hubbell, bested Dizzy often in their famous duels of the mid '30s, but Hubbell would say, "For a few years, Diz was as great as any pitcher."

In 1937, after umpire George Barr had called a critical balk on him in a game at St. Louis, Dizzy spoke at a church supper in nearby Belleville, Ill., and was quoted as labeling Barr and National League President Ford Frick as "the two biggest crooks in baseball."

Frick suspended him, pending an apology, but Dizzy came up with one of the best-remembered quotes of his career. "I ain't signin' nuthin'," he said, and he didn't, winning a newspaper decision when the National League president lifted the suspension.

So he was 12–7 with a fourth-place ball club, a likable braggart, the popoff who would make good most of his boasts, and the last gasp of gas in the

Gashouse Gang when he tried to take French leave and pass up the 1937 All-Star Game in Washington.

When he showed up in St. Louis, even wife Pat advised him that he owed it to baseball, and when he flew to Washington, then a six-hour flight away, owner Sam Breadon accompanied him.

A shutout pitcher for three innings in the All-Star Game the year before, Dizzy started for the National League in '37 and was one out away from a three-inning runless stint. Then he shook off his catcher, Gabby Hartnett, and insisted on a fastball on a full-count pitch to Lou Gehrig, who hammered a two-run homer.

The next batter, Earl Averill of Cleveland, hit a hot smash back through the box. Dean, despite the full, free follow-through of a hard-throwing pitcher with a smooth delivery, ordinarily was quick enough to recover his fielding position because he not only was a pretty good hitter and baserunner, but also a fifth infielder, defensively. Averill, however, had a unique habit of knocking pitchers off the mound with line shots through the middle, and his hummer cracked the big toe of Dean's firmly planted left foot.

Dizzy was hurt, painfully, and the toe was put in a splint. The Cardinals' surgeon, Dr. Robert F. Hyland, cautioned him not to pitch too soon. But for a guy who ducked an exhibition at the drop of a railroad schedule—he preferred trains to planes—Dean was highly competitive and a team man who prided himself on showing up rather than showing off when it counted.

Frisch needed him, and Dizzy volunteered to pitch in Boston, where the perceptive and gentlemanly manager of the Braves, Bill McKechnie, coaching third base, counseled him:

"Don't, Jerome, don't. You'll hurt your arm by favoring that foot with an unnatural stride and delivery."

Late in the game when Diz was pitching to shortstop Bill Urbanski in a tight game, he felt something pop and his arm dangled at his side.

"You've done it, Jerome. You've done it," said McKechnie in prophetic anguish that Dizzy Dean never forgot.

Gone was the fastball that once was so good that in the same ballpark where it left him forever—Braves Field—Ol' Diz once had faced the Boston players and, grinning, taunted 'em this way:

"Tell you what I'm going to do, fellas. We won't use no signs today, and I'll throw nuthin' except fastballs—honest!"

They knew what was coming and he still shut 'em out.

When the bottom dropped out of his playing career, the loquacious, lively-larynxed Dean found himself in front of microphone, as you'd know if only because you'd seen movie actor Dan Dailey play Dizzy in a so-so film of his life.

Pride of St. Louis, as they called it most uninspiringly, was good for $50,000 for Ol' Diz, but it was good for fewer laughs than the Great One himself could generate.

As a radio announcer, he mangled the language so badly in St. Louis that school teachers protested the syntax-fracturing. Kids were talking how a guy "slud" into second base and the runners returned to their "respectable" bases.

Dean won 'em over, of course, just as he did most of the nation's baseball fans, especially the rural folks who talked his twang and homespun humor. New generations discovered him nationally, through television, just as St. Louis had in radio during the weather-enforced censorship of World War II when he explained a rain delay at the old ballpark by saying:

"I can't tell you what it's doin', folks, but if you'll stick your head out the window, you'll find out."

By his own modest self-evaluation, Dean wasn't the greatest pitcher, but he was "amongst 'em," as he put it. And whether squatting on the field in 100-degree weather, building a fire when seated with a blanket over his head, or bursting into song on one of his broadcasts to yodel the ballad of the "Wabash Cannonball," Ol' Diz dedicated a lifetime to fulfilling Gabby Street's prophecy the day he broke into the big leagues:

Before he died in 1974 at only 63, no one ever knew from one minute to the next what Jay Hanna (Dizzy) Dean would say or do.

Not every member of the Gas House Gang was famous for his colorful personality. Joe Medwick, nicknamed "Muscles" for his physique and "Ducky" for his waddling gait, was best known on the playing field for his toughness. Dizzy Dean once said that you could never win an argument with Medwick because he'd "whop you" before you finished your say. Medwick had a career average of .324 and hit over .300 in fourteen of his seventeen big league seasons. A great clutch hitter, he led the National League in RBIs for three straight years and in 1937 captured the National League's triple crown and its Most Valuable Player Award. He is probably best remembered for being removed from the seventh game of the 1934 World Series by Commissioner Landis after Medwick caused a near riot with his aggressive play.

"Muscles and Me" is a chapter from Donald E. Hood's acclaimed book, The Gas House Gang.

Muscles and Me
Donald E. Hood

The name Medwick comes from the Hungarian word *medve*, which means "bear."

A light wind blew, the temperature was near 80, and the cloudless sky was blue as a tourist's umbrella. It was the third week in March, the best time to watch baseball at an ideal site, a minor-league training camp, this one belonging to the St. Louis Cardinals.

I heard the crack of bat against ball and the cry of "Hat-a-baby." Through the wire fence I could see about a hundred young Cardinals cavorting on the practice fields. Interwoven among those huskies—like gray strands in a brown rope—were portly men standing with hands on hips and mouths working: managers and coaches, overweight and overwrought. Walking through the open gate, I stopped a towering youngster with powerful shoulders.

"Joe Medwick around?" I asked.

He pointed to his left. "Straight ahead, sir."

There stood old Muscles, the name MEDWICK stamped like an advertisement on his sturdy shoulders. He was talking to a group of outfielders, his voice carrying crisply in the spring air: "Don't make basket catches, fellows. You're not Willie Mays. He was a great one, but that's not the way the Cardinals teach you to catch a fly ball." The players moved thirty yards away to form a line in front of Medwick. They began bouncing the ball to him, simulating the throw made from the outfield to home plate. "Throw overhand, boys," Medwick instructed. "You can control it better that way." Now and then the ball skipped off-line a few feet, forcing Medwick to move to his left or right. Then he'd holler: "Take it easy, fellows. Remember I'm an old-timer." He limped after the ball, favoring his right leg which had been operated on twice.

He doesn't look too big, I thought, edging closer. A compact man (playing weight 180 pounds; five feet ten inches tall). The nearer I got the larger he looked, which made me wonder if he were built like Mickey Mantle who, it was said, grew bigger with each layer of clothes he removed. A careful look canceled out the analogy: Medwick was sturdy and muscular, but not massive like Mantle. He looked fit, though, and I remembered the first time I ever saw him, when he was playing for the Brooklyn Dodgers.

It was in 1942 at Ebbets Field during one of those crucial series that Brooklyn seemed forever to be having against the Cardinals. I had worked on a summer construction job, breaking rocks with a sledgehammer for fifty cents an hour to earn money to make a weekend trip to see the hero in action. I was sixteen years old, and made the trip with a "guardian," an old friend of my father's named George McDonald. A feisty little Irishman, who had been a prizefighter, he occasionally squared off against me to demonstrate his left jab. He was quick-witted and always took an adversary stance on whatever I said. "Medwick's the best right-hand hitter in the National League," I said, as we took our seats in the grandstand.

"He's washed up, Bobby," he said. "Why he's thirty-five years old."

"He's only thirty!"

"Have it your way, kid—but he's an *old* thirty."

Hearing that remark, a Brooklyn fan with a cigar stuck in his mouth turned in his seat.

"You can say that again, buddy. The bum couldn't carry Musial's glove. He ain't even going to play today—thank God for small favors. The bum. Not with Mort Cooper pitchin'!"

Not play today. I was devastated. Yet when the lineups were announced, there it was: "Playing left field for the Dodgers, Augie Galan, number . . ."

The Brooklyn fan turned when he heard the sound of anguish. "Ah, don't let it get ya, kid. Galan's a bigger bum than Ducky. Anyway, Medwick'll play tomorrow when the left-handers pitch. The bum!"

Medwick played in the Sunday doubleheader, getting three hits in eight bats against southpaws Max Lanier and Ernie White. Again we sat behind the man with the big cigar and he turned around when Medwick was announced. ("Number seven, playing left field . . .")

"I told ya, kid. There's your bum." He winked at George McDonald, who laughed out loud. Medwick came up in the second inning with nobody on and hit the first pitch off the center-field fence for a double. I shook the shoulders of the cigar smoker, yelling, "See. *See!*"

"Ah," he said. "He was lucky. Musial would've had a triple easy."

That weekend at Ebbets Field had been a long time ago, early in World War II, and I smiled, thinking about it. Now, on this sunny March day at the training camp in St. Petersburg under a domed blue sky, I finally closed in on Muscles and introduced myself.

"I heard you were coming," he said. "I know what you're trying to do." He looked me straight in the eyes. "I'm not going to talk to you about the Gashouse Gang."

I have the world's worst poker face. It starts falling inside me, right behind the eyes, slides to the heart, then the liver, finally, plummeting so that my chin strikes my knees. It must be a God-awful sight to behold; sometimes I look like a man about to have apoplexy. That's the way it must have struck Medwick, for he grasped my arm to steady me.

"I don't mean to be rude," he said. "A book like that makes a lot of money. I might do it myself someday. I'm not going to talk about those days unless I'm paid. I want fifteen hundred dollars or I won't answer questions."

$1,500! $$$$$#*!@$SSS

My face hadn't recovered from its knee-high descent. Now it might never climb back to its proper place. I am empathetic, compassionate, God-fearing, enlightened—BUT GODDAMN IT—$$$$—1,500 *dollars!*

Looking at Medwick, clearly there were dollar signs embossed on his eyeballs. How could he have ever hit all those savage line drives looking through green bills? The beautiful blue sky, the sun, the gentle breeze—all vanished in my mind to be replaced by a terrible blackness.

Standing in the lovely Florida sunlight beneath the postcard sky, I listened to my old hero.

He was chattering about everything but the Gashouse Gang. He talked about modern players, about their huge salaries, even about their meal money (much too high; nobody could eat that much). He discussed his records, his golf game, even the Cardinals' great training camp. Mostly, he talked about the fine art of hitting a baseball. This depressed me. *God*, Joe, I thought—your tips are thirty years too late to help me.

He demonstrated his grip, showing the proper way to hold a bat. His hands caught my attention. I stared at them, not believing my eyes. Those hands that slashed out 2,471 lifetime big-league hits, that established the National League season record for most doubles (sixty-four), that gave him a lifetime batting average of .324, that swung him into the Baseball Hall of Fame—those hands were too small. Mentally, I held up my right hand against his right hand. My hand was small, but his must be smaller. His fingers were short and stubby, reminding me of Casey Stengel's remark about Japanese baseball players: They can't possibly play the game with those little fingers. Yet they did and Medwick led the National League in just about every batting department in 1937. How could he have done that with those stubby fingers?

Medwick finished his lecture on batting and was moving off with a wave of his arm—a friendly wave?—accompanied by several young players. As minor-league batting coach of the Cardinals, he tutored youngsters all spring, every day, hour after hour. Although I wasn't invited, I tagged along behind the imperial Medwick and his entourage, standing in the doorway of the nearby shed which housed two batting machines in parallel lanes. Medwick sat in a chair with his back against the wall, calling out instructions in a clipped voice: "Bunt two and rip away. There's a man on second and nobody out. Get him over to third now, at least. Hit it to right field. Let's see daylight between your arms and body. Don't cock your bat against your head, Number eight."

It must be painful for the old batting champ to watch inept hitting day after day, I thought, feeling sorry for him, but my pity was watered down by the studious way he ignored me. Then there was the barrier between us: 1,500-dollar-bills high, much too high for me to scale without help. I retreated from the lovely field, upon which great writing careers are made or broken, and found my way back to the motel to plan my strategy, but mainly to lick my wounds.

I pondered the problem of Joseph Michael Medwick, the Hammerin' Hungarian with the small hands, both of them outstretched toward me, palms upward. It was not my first experience with money-crazed baseball players. As a writer and editor, I had dealt with a number of them who suffered from a type of lockjaw curable only by a large check. I knew that baseball players, coaches, managers, and others were supposed to cooperate free of charge to promote that game we all love. Most of them do cooperate, out of enlightened self-interest if nothing else. Some of them refuse. Usually these are the so-called superstars at the peak of their careers—stars whose names dominate the sports pages. Medwick's name had not been in the news for many years, yet he still felt entitled to big money. He was one of the do-nots and will-nots. His slogan as a young star had been "Base hits and *buckerinos*," and while he made a lot of the former he never seemed to get enough of the latter.

He had been the pride of New Jersey and St. Louis. He had played in two World Series and married a beautiful girl from a fine family. After leaving baseball, he had been in an automobile agency and then in the insurance

202 **The Gas House Gang**

business. He must have money, I thought. Why *must* he? Maybe most of it slipped through his fingers. After all, it had happened to a lot of famous players who got involved in business without adequate knowledge and without the ability to acquire it. That was it. He actually needed the money, but was too proud to admit it. So the key to his heart was in my wallet. But $1,500!

It was simply a matter of negotiation. The dickering took up the better part of three days. Finally, for $250 Medwick agreed to an interview. In addition, I promised him the free-lance commission I was to receive for a newspaper photo taken during spring training. It turned out to be a lowly $20, which I mailed to him later that year.

One sunny morning I was back at the minor-league field, ready and eager to chat with Joseph Michael Medwick, alias Mickey, Muscles, and Ducky-Wucky. We sat in an observation booth on the second floor of a small building that was the hub of the training complex. Below, two St. Louis farm teams were playing a practice game, which we watched while chatting. During that session, and one on the following day, Medwick was cooperative but touchy, sensitive to any suggestion of criticism.

His career had been melodramatic. He was born in November 1911. His parents had been Hungarians who settled in Carteret, New Jersey, and became U.S. citizens. "They were from the old school," Medwick said. "One came from Buda and one came from Pest." Both are dead now, but his two sisters and a brother are still living. As a boy, Medwick was a tremendously gifted athlete—the one-in-a-million kind.

"I participated in every sport," Medwick said. "I was a four-letter man even in my freshman year in high school." He was all-state in football, basketball, and baseball, a legend in New Jersey before he ever played professional baseball. In football, he played fullback and then quarterback. He could kick a football fifty-five or sixty yards, and pass an equal distance with ease. He was the team's punter and passer and key runner. "I was a triple-threat man," he said. "You played every minute, too. My parents wanted me to play baseball. But my mother didn't want for me to play football, because she thought I might get injured and not play baseball."

While still in high school, Medwick tried out with the Newark Bears, a farm team of the New York Yankees. Tris Speaker was the manager; Jocko Conlon, the old National League umpire, was the center fielder; Wally Pipp, ex-Yankee, was first baseman. A pitcher named Carl Fischer was throwing batting practice. "He knocked me down," Medwick said. "And Wally Pipp hollered at him: 'Give the kid a chance.' He knocked me down in batting practice. Deliberately."

Medwick's voice rose and his eyes flashed as he remembered the incident.

"I got angry and hit a few balls out of the park. Then Fischer really got angry. He wanted to show me up, because I was a good hitter."

Medwick hit a ball out of every part of the park, but after the workout manager Speaker told him he was too young. The finest prospect ever to come out of New Jersey slipped through the fingers of the New York Yankees. Medwick might have been playing on those great Yankee teams of the 1930s, alongside Joe DiMaggio. Instead he went on to become one of the Gashouse Gang. Before settling on a baseball career, Medwick weighed numerous offers for college scholarships, most notably from Notre Dame, which was anxious to add him to its football squad. But the young Medwick lacked one and a half credits for admission, and was reluctant to attend prep school to acquire them.

Shortly after graduating from high school in 1930, he was playing for Scottsdale, Pa., in the Middle Atlantic League. He used the name Mickey King to protect his amateur status in case he changed his mind about a college education. He batted .419 with 100 RBIs in only seventy-five games, an astonishing performance for an eighteen-year-old. This led to his promotion in 1931 to Houston in the Texas League, where he became a big favorite with fans. He led the league in home runs and runs batted in that year and picked up the name "Ducky" when a fan compared his walk to that of a duck. The comparison did not please him, but the creation of a candy bar in his name, the "Ducky-Wucky" candy bar, did, especially since he shared in the proceeds. Medwick played in the city until late August 1932, when the Cardinals called him up to St. Louis. His last game was one of those dramatic performances that had dotted his colorful career.

When he swaggered to the plate for his last at bat of the game, his many fans rose as one to pay him tribute. The noise was thunderous as he tipped his cap and planted himself, his bat cocked and ready. The first pitch was low, but he swung at it and missed. The crowd groaned. The next pitch was a high inside fast ball, a hard pitch to hit. But, according to the *Houston Post*, "Medwick tied into the ball with all the power in his stocky body and the ball sailed over the left-field fence. When the second game was ended, Medwick was surrounded by several hundred kids all anxious to shake his hand."

A glorious way to leave town, a big bouquet for the departing hero? Not exactly. According to Medwick's recollection, there were thorns among the roses. "I was so damn angry," he said. "They used to give you a traveling bag or some damn thing when you leave the city. They didn't give me nothing. And then the fellow who had the candy bars wanted me to leave them there and I said 'Hell, no!' And they had to take all the wrappings off the bars. We had an agreement if I left [Houston] they couldn't sell them."

The comical picture of all those "Ducky-Wucky" bars without wrappings made me want to laugh out loud, but I knew better than to test the Medwick temper. A resentment that smolders for more than forty years is too deadly to challenge.

After each burst of anger Medwick recalled another dramatic triumph followed by a blister of resentment followed by triumph, each canceling out the other. The Houston experience is typical. Over a decade and a half after he left all those naked candy bars, he returned, an aging veteran on the brink of retirement, to help Houston manager Johnny Keane get into the playoffs.

In August 1948, Joe Medwick led off the second inning, his first time at bat since leaving sixteen years before. The fans began shrieking, "Hit it over the wall, Joe. Hit it over the wall." Ken Sterling, the opposing pitcher, ran the count to Medwick to three balls and one strike. Then Medwick lashed the ball high and far toward left field. "It's a home run!" the crowd yelled. The ball was hit in the same spot as the one he hit in his last at bat in 1932.

"I was on my way out in 1948," Medwick recalled. "And they said I was going to get the Houston ball club to manage. So I went down there, but they changed their mind and I didn't get it."

When Joe Medwick joined the Cardinals in September 1932, he was only twenty years of age, and had played less than three full seasons of professional baseball. But he was ready. He was a major-league hitter, who swung at anything and hit it hard. Pitches at his feet. Over his head. Pitches off the bill of his cap. He attacked them all furiously, batting .349 in the last month of the season.

"He was one of the finest right-hand hitters I saw in my day," Tex Carleton said. "He could hit the ball to all fields and hit it hard. It was murder to throw him a change of pace. It looked like you would get him with his stance and stride—the way he jumped at that ball. But he would recock the bat and restep and hit the ball to right or right center for extra bases, even home runs. He was the only man I ever saw who could hit the change of pace for extra bases. *Hard!* I saw some good change-of-pace hitters, but they all would just lay it out there with their hands and arms. Their body was gone from the swing. But Medwick would do a double shuffle up there, recock, and hit the ball against or over the fence."

Carleton considered himself a benefactor of the young slugger from Carteret. The tall Texan had played with him at Houston and knew what a great prospect he was and how much he could help a ball club. "It wasn't easy to come up to the majors in those days," Carleton said. Older players didn't lay out welcome mats for rookies. As Carleton put it, "You kind of had to fight your way in."

In 1933, several of the players thought Medwick was too pushy. "They gave him a hard time," teammate Pat Crawford remembered. "The veterans rode him viciously. They wanted him put in his place, not to be too much of a take-charge guy. Right from the start, Joe wanted to be a big star. If he wasn't getting that publicity, he'd gripe about it."

In those days, Crawford pointed out, rookies were "to be seen and not heard." Medwick was treated roughly in '33, too roughly, some of the Cardinals felt. The savage riding might break his spirit. Tex Carleton took his part. "I almost had a fight defending him," he recalled.

By 1934, the hazing was over. Medwick was a proven player, having hit .306 and batted in ninety-eight runs the year before, the kind of performance veterans respected. Men such as Frankie Frisch and Pepper Martin, who had been in World Series and appreciated money and glory and prestige, saw that Jersey Joe could help the team to a pennant. Achievement was Medwick's passport to acceptance.

Forty years later, sitting in the spring sunlight in St. Petersburg, Medwick played down his hard times as a rookie and his later reputation as a tough guy. It was just part of the game.

"They used to haze a rookie. They were jealous of a young fellow. A young fellow had to learn how to protect himself. If he didn't they'd run you out of the batter's box."

Nobody ever ran Medwick out of a batting box, although in 1934 his old friend, Tex Carleton, tried to. Medwick loved to get as much batting practice as possible to sharpen his skills. "Tex was one of the guys who tried to stop me one day. Did he tell you that story?" Medwick asked me.

"Tell it again," I asked.

"I had gone to Frisch and said: 'Frank, I wanna go out and hit.' This was fifteen minutes before the pitchers hit. So I started to go into the batting cage, and Carleton said: 'Where are you going?'

"I said, 'I'm going in the batting cage.'

" 'I don't think so,' Carleton said.

" 'I think so,' I said. And I hit him, right there, that was it. They never stopped me again."

Medwick's version of the famous fight doesn't square with that of Carleton's. Carleton had said: "The pitchers always hit first on a team, and Medwick was always trying to bust in there. This day he did and we had some words and he called me a name and I whacked him and he whacked me around a little bit. But—hell!—it wasn't serious. We became friends within fifteen minutes and remain friends to this day."

Both of these versions are dramatic and violent but, according to Paul

Dean, neither is accurate. "There was no fight," he told me on the telephone. "No punches were thrown."

Bill Hallahan has *another* version of the episode. "What actually happened," Hallahan recalled, "was that Medwick was scheduled to pose for photographs and to be paid for this by a national magazine. We all knew about it, except Tex Carleton. When Joe jumped into the cage, Tex said, 'Where the hell do you think you're going?' Medwick hit Tex with a right cross on *top* of his head. Not on his jaw or face. On the top of his head. This stunned Tex."

Later, Carleton exclaimed, "Damn, why didn't you guys tell me Joe had arranged a special deal."

This episode marked the beginning of Medwick's fighting career. "After that," Hallahan said, "Joe was quick with his fists."

His renown as a one-punch artist stems partially from Dizzy Dean's comment: "Durndest man I ever seen. Before you even get to do enough talking and get mad enough to fight, Joe whops you and the fight's over."

One of Joe's victims was a pitcher named Ed Heusser, who was nicknamed "The Wild Elk of the Wasatch." The big pitcher accused Medwick of loafing on a fly ball and permitting a run to score. Muscles knocked the Wild Elk unconscious with one punch, right on the steps of the dugout in the Polo Grounds. Frisch had to rush in a pitcher from the bullpen.

Dizzy Dean and Ducky feuded on and off during the '30s. Once in Pittsburgh, three runs scored on a drive to left field that Dean thought Medwick should have handled, and told him so in the dugout. When Diz and brother Paul made a threatening move toward the left-fielder, Muscles picked up a bat.

"Come on," he snarled. "I'll break up this brother act here and now."

Later in the game, Medwick came to bat with three Cardinals on base, and hit one far over the left-field wall. Returning to the dugout, he filled his mouth with water, walked over to Diz—and spit on his shoes. "There's your three runs and one to spare," he snapped. "Now, let's see if you can hold the lead."

Another of Medwick's adversaries was Rip Collins, with whom he had exchanged punches in 1934. Two years later, Muscles wanted to take Rip apart, limb by limb.

"I had tied the National League record with ten straight hits in ten times up," Medwick recalled. "I was going for a new record. When I wasn't looking, Collins borrowed my favorite bat and broke it in practice."

There was murder in Medwick's voice as he recounted the incident. "He didn't have to do that. He had his own bats. When I found out about it, I was going to kill him. But Frisch stopped me."

If he had committed murder, no jury would have convicted the fiery left-fielder. I wondered if Joe knew that Collins had a fence made of broken bats at his home in upstate New York. I was afraid to ask him *that.*

As a young major-leaguer, Medwick had been a clean-living, well-conditioned athlete. He did not drink or smoke and there was a strong strain of Puritanism in him. He admired Jesse "Pop" Haines.

"If you ever saw a perfect man it was Jesse. I think the only two perfect men I ever saw in my life were Freddy Fitzsimmons and him. Hedy Lamarr could be sitting right there bare-assed"—Medwick slapped the table hard—"and it wouldn't make no difference. I never heard him cuss. I never saw him smoke. I never saw him drink. Freddy Fitzsimmons was the same way."

He respected Frankie Frisch, whom he considered a "good man, very fair. He liked to play. He liked to fool around, but when that bell rang, he was all business. He expected you to play baseball. I liked Frank. To me, he was one of the greatest managers in baseball."

"One of the Gashouse Gang told me Leo Durocher was the brains behind that team," I said.

"That wasn't true," Medwick said. "Frankie Frisch was. Leo had knowledge and he went on to become a pretty good manager. Frankie was a great manager. He never gave up. He was a good teacher. He never bothered you. When you made a mistake, he'd take you aside and talk to you. He never showed you up, which was a great thing. And the way I always felt was: When I made a mistake I wanted the manager to tell me, not the other players. A player's got enough to take care of his own position and his own job. And I would *not* allow anybody to tell me," Medwick's voice rose, "that *I* had made a mistake. Frankie Frisch, my manager, would tell me."

In our interviews Joe Medwick tried to follow the old-fashioned rule: If you don't have anything good to say about somebody, don't say anything at all.

"Any playboys on the '34 team?" I asked.

"I don't like to go into that," he said.

"I won't put it on the tape recorder," I said.

"I'm not *even* going to say it," he snapped. "I don't think it's fair. When we're talking about me, fine. But about anybody else's personal life, I don't want to get into it."

One of his favorite Gashouse stories *is* critical of Dizzy Dean.

"We're playing the World Series," he recalled, "and Hank Greenberg is up. Bill DeLancey is giving the sign, and Diz refused to take it. Finally, Frisch called time.

" 'What's the matter?' he asked Diz at the mound. 'You won't take the sign, Diz? What's Greenberg's power? Don't give him anything up high.' Frisch motioned.

"Diz went back to the mound, Frisch went back to second and DeLancey behind the plate. He kept giving the sign and Diz wouldn't take it. So DeLancey says, 'You throw it and I'll catch it.'

"Greenberg hit one up on top of the roof in Sportsman's Park. As he's running around the bases, Diz is right with him. 'I'm going to strike you out three times after this,' he says. And he did it," Medwick said with an annoyed look on his face. "Here in 1934 if we don't win—shit!—I'm in the red, you know, because we only got about $5,400 at that time. But it was a lot of money. Here we're playing our hearts out and he's screwing around out there. Of course, he and Paul, they win all the four games. Diz wins two and Paul wins two."

Before the World Series, the Cardinals were holding a meeting. "Diz gets up," Medwick went on, "and says:

" 'Frank, what are you having a meeting for? I'm going to pitch the first game and if I get in trouble, Paul will help me. Tomorrow Paul will start. If he gets in trouble, I'll help him. We don't need the rest of these bums!'

"And they win the four," Medwick said. "At that time, Diz could throw the ball, you know. He was a great pitcher, no question. But he got a lot of runs, too. For example, he'd get eight or nine runs. Hallahan would get nothing, Jesse Haines would get nothing."

The 1930s, America's dark decade, were bright and shiny for Ducky Medwick. He married the beautiful Isabelle Heutel in 1936. He was named most valuable player in the league in 1937, when he won the Triple Crown, leading the National League in homers, runs batted in, batting average, and in nine other batting departments. He considered the Triple Crown a wedding-anniversary present for his wife. He led the league in runs batted in for three consecutive years ('36, '37, and '38), tying a major-league record. He established the National League season record for most doubles in 1936. From 1932 through 1939, his batting average was a brilliant .337.

He was a celebrity in St. Louis, a hero to the knothole gang but a hard man to get along with. He used to hit line drives back through the pitcher's box in practice, deliberately trying to knock down a young Cardinal employee named Bing Devine. Now general manager of St. Louis, at that time Devine was a very junior executive in the public-relations department. He dreamed of a career as a major-league player.

"One day," Devine recalled, many years later, "I was heading for the field when Medwick grabbed me by the arm."

" 'Well, whadda you know,' Joe said. 'We've got the Goddamn college boy for batting practice again today.' "

Devine was on the spot. Directly challenged by Medwick, the young man felt he couldn't back down, yet he knew Muscles could knock him cold. Young Devine might also get fired for brawling with the star.

"I didn't know what to do," he said. Fortunately, center fielder Terry Moore came by and shoved Joe toward the field.

"Come on, Muscles," Moore said. "You're holding up the parade."

The Cardinal center fielder winked at Bing Devine as he passed by. (Thirty years later, the same Bing Devine hired Medwick as his minor-league batting coach.)

By 1940, Medwick's popularity was declining in St. Louis. He argued with fans at Sportsman's Park. They booed him. Then, in June of that year, in one of the biggest trades of that era, Medwick was sent to Brooklyn to play for his old pal, Leo Durocher. It was a deal that nearly ended his career.

On June 19, 1940, the Dodgers faced the St. Louis Cardinals in the second game of a series at Ebbets Field. There was special tension in the air. The world was exploding. The Nazis were cutting deeply into France and charging through Holland and Belgium. The British were retreating to a dark rendezvous at Dunkirk. And in Brooklyn, the Dodgers had just dropped four straight games and the fans were furious. The Cardinals had won the day before, holding their ex-teammate hitless, and knocking Brooklyn out of first place. They also had needled Ducky Joe sharply.

I remember the game to this day. My father and I were huddled around the Philco, listening to Red Barber, and we were ecstatic when Walker, Lavagetto, and Vosmik hit safely in the first inning. Bob Bowman, the Cardinal pitcher, was in the middle of a torn-up pea patch and Ducky Medwick was in the cat-bird seat. But not for long. Bowman's first pitch sailed high and tight and Medwick was hit behind the ear. He fell to the ground as though shot in the head. Thirty-four years later, on that balmy Florida day, I asked him what had happened.

"What did you do, lose the ball?"

"No," he said. "He threw the ball behind me. I couldn't get out of the way."

"He threw the ball *behind* you?"

"That's the way you hit a batter. If they want to hit you, they throw behind you: Your natural reaction is to fall backwards."

"Fall right into it?"

"That's right," Medwick said.

The beaning of old Muscles caused a riot on the field, charges and counter-charges off the field, even an investigation by William O'Dwyer, then district attorney in Brooklyn. Bowman was absolved of all charges, but the incident did accelerate the development of the batting helmet.

After the beaning, while he was lying in a hospital bed, Medwick received the kind of telephone call you could only get in Brooklyn. Medwick remembered it this way:

"Do you want his arm?" the guy asked.

"No, it was just one of those things," said Medwick.

Then the guy said, "I'll get Bowman's arm for you and send it to you."

Now Medwick shook his head in wonder. "That was Brooklyn. They were rough then."

Although suffering from a concussion, earaches, and blurred vision, Medwick had returned to the lineup in a few days and battled his way though the season. Baseball people felt he was plate-shy after the beaning and that he didn't attack the baseball with his former fury. Whatever the cause, fear or the failure of reflexes, he never again was the great hitter he had been in St. Louis, although he averaged .300 or better for the next three years.

Traded to the Giants in 1943, he remained with them until 1945, when he was sent to the Boston Braves. Like many fading stars, Medwick was bouncing from team to team. In 1946, he was back with the Dodgers for their stretch against the Cardinals, who won the pennant in a playoff. In the spring of 1947, he went to camp with the New York Yankees, and when they released him, he figured his playing days were over. But one more dramatic appearance was called for.

Sam Breadon phoned him at a golf course where Muscles was about to tee off. The Cardinal owner asked him to rejoin the team, which could use his help as a pinch hitter and part-time player. Medwick rushed back to his home, picked up glove and shoes, and headed for Sportsman's Park. Eddie Dyer, who had been his first manager way back in 1930 at Scottsdale, was managing the Cardinals.

"What are you doing here?" he asked.

"I've just joined the club," Medwick said.

The Cards were playing the Pirates a doubleheader, and Medwick watched the first game from the bench. It was a sunny, beautiful day in May. In the fifth inning of the second game, with St. Louis trailing 2–0, the Cardinals got a man on first and Manager Dyer looked down the bench at Medwick: "You're the hitter," he said.

Medwick broke out in a sweat, feeling fear for perhaps the first time in his life. He went to the bat rack, picked up the first bat that came to hand, and walked out of the dugout. He was wearing number 21 and the fans didn't recognize him, for he had always worn 7 in St. Louis. But when the PA announcer said, "Joe Medwick, now batting for Jim Hearn," the entire stadium rose and cheered. Medwick felt shivers run down his spine. The old left-hander, Fritz Ostermueller, was on the mound for Pittsburgh, and he ran the count two and one on Ducky. The next pitch was high and outside, but Medwick reached out and lined the ball toward the fence in right center field. It hit the number 5 in the 354-foot sign, narrowly missing a home run. Medwick chugged into second with a double that scored the Cardinals' only run. When he left the field for a pinch runner, the crowd gave him an ovation. Tears flowed from his eyes as he ran into the dugout.

Medwick played out the 1947 season, and then appeared in a few games in 1948 before going to Houston for his dramatic farewell in that city. He was a playing manager in the minors for three seasons and retired from baseball in 1952, returning to St. Louis to live with his wife and son and daughter. He became a businessman and suburbanite. He was a first-rate golfer, the champion of his country club; he dabbled in local politics; he sold cars and insurance; he coached some baseball at St. Louis University. And he campaigned hard and furiously over the years to make baseball's Hall of Fame. He button-holed sportswriters, wrote letters, made telephone calls. Much to the annoyance of the writers who disliked him in his heyday, Medwick blew his horn, year after year, until in 1968, perhaps weary of the trumpeting, they voted him in. It was an honor he richly deserved, as he had been telling the world for many years. The Medwick scowl turned into a grin that lit up St. Louis. He even made a wisecrack which was widely quoted: "It was the longest slump I ever had," he said in reference to the twenty years since he left the majors. "I've been oh-for-twenty, but not oh-for-twenty years."

1968. It was a triumphant year for Ducky Medwick. In addition to his induction at Cooperstown, N.Y., he appeared as a TV commentator during the World Series and was the featured speaker at the annual meeting of the Illinois Associated Press editors. It was time to take a bow and to play a mellow, gracious role. According to newspaper reports, he basked in the applause and the spotlight. Such recognition should come to all great players while they are alive to enjoy it. It was good and proper that he celebrate, for pain and suffering lay ahead like a Biblical echo from Ecclesiastes: "To every thing there is a season . . . A time to weep and a time to laugh; a time to mourn and a time to dance."

In April 1969, Joe Medwick entered the Deaconess Hospital in St. Louis, where he stayed for eighteen days. It was his first operation on a hip that had been causing pain and cutting down on his activity. He would require a second operation. It took place in October 1973 at Barnes Hospital, St. Louis, and was performed by Dr. Fred C. Reynolds, a distinguished orthopedic surgeon. Medwick got a complete artificial hip.

"Joe's second surgery was a miracle, just a blessing." Mrs. Medwick told me during a telephone interview. "He hadn't played golf for years, from a year or two before his first surgery. Now he plays golf and is doing just beautifully."

If it weren't for this operation, Medwick could have wound up in a wheelchair and from there, when pain intensified, to a bed flat on his back, a vegetable waiting for the end. A great athlete was spared a hellish ordeal. Of course, instead of par golf he would have to settle for a bogey game, which is a level of golf most people never reach on two healthy legs. To shoot 90 playing on an artificial hip is a splendid achievement, one only a great and stubborn athlete could reach. Several times during our Florida talks Medwick spoke with pride of his new golf game. But never once did he mention any suffering involved in his experiences, and he never discussed the pain connected with his beanings. In fact, he never spoke of any physical pain. Were pain and suffering beneath contempt? Unworthy of a star's acknowledgment? An indication of imperfection? Of human vulnerability?

Joe Medwick certainly wasn't a stoic in other respects. He often felt put upon—by players, management, fans, and sportswriters. Every example of his resentment bears in on one point: the failure of others to acknowledge his athletic greatness. He never felt he got his due, whether it was money for an interview or a suitcase as a going-away gift.

Joe Medwick died on March 21, 1975, exactly a year after our meeting. The news reached me in Clearwater, at the minor-league base of the Philadelphia Phillies. It was a beautiful sunny day and several of us had been an audience for batting-coach Wally Moses, one of baseball's most delightful talkers.

"Paul Waner used to bring a bottle of beer back to his room," Moses was saying. "He'd uncap it and let it stand all night. Then he'd drink it in the morning. He swore it was a sure cure for a hangover. Ain't that right, Elmer?"

Wally turned to coach Elmer Valo, his friend and occasional straight man. "That's right, Wally." Valo, a husky man with the head of an old lion, had played twenty years in the majors. He had been a good player, but his claim to uniqueness had been that he was the only big-leaguer born in Czechoslovakia.

"Waner was real loose at the plate," Moses continued. "He kept his bat on his shoulder until he was ready to hit."

"Drunk or sober," Valo chipped in.

"He had this saying," Moses went on, not paying any attention to his pal Elmer. "Waner'd look at the pitcher and say: 'You show me your ass and I'll show you mine.'"

Moses fell into his familiar sit-down batting stance, demonstrating how "Big Poison" used to turn his right hip when the pitcher went into his motion. Just then a long black car drove up and a large man with a leathery tan stepped out.

"You-all hear what happened to Joe Medwick?"

There was total silence around the batting cage.

"He died this morning. Heart attack." Without another word, the man climbed back into his car and drove off.

It had been a massive attack and the sixty-three-year-old slugger had passed away a few hours after the first chest pains. My instant thought was: *God, I wish I could have given him that $1,500.* Anyway, he didn't linger and suffer, I thought, standing mute as Wally Moses paid tribute to Ducky's batting ferocity.

"Pitches off his shoe tops, pitches over his head. They all looked good to Joe," Wally said. "He hit nothing but frozen ropes."

Muscles was the finest bad-ball hitter of them all, and the meanest, toughest player on the Gashouse Gang, the team that taught me courage when I was a runt growing up in a tough coal town. I'll always see Ducky Joe in my imagination, strutting to the plate as the crowd roars. The public address system blares, "Number seven, now batting for the Cardinals . . ." He stands at the plate with that big brown bat cocked, his muscular arms glowing and a savage look in his eyes. The pitcher winds up, the ball hurtles in, and then—*crash*—a white streak orbits toward the billboards in right center. Runners dash around the bases and, in a cloud of dust, Muscles slides in.

He jumps to his feet, tipping his cap to the ovation of the fans.

The game is over.

Chris Von der Ahe, the first beer baron to bring championship baseball to St. Louis. *Courtesy of the* Sporting News.

Curt Welch, famous in baseball history for his "$15,000 slide." *From* The National Game.

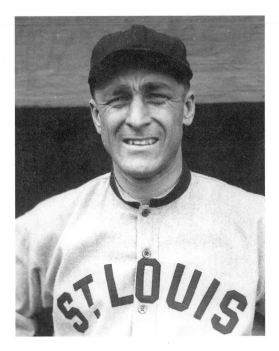

Branch Rickey in his days as manager of the St. Louis Browns. *Courtesy of the* Sporting News.

George Sisler, the greatest player to wear a Browns uniform. *Courtesy of the* Sporting News.

Rogers Hornsby, player-manager of the Cardinals'
first World Championship team in 1926.
Courtesy of the Sporting News.

Jesse "Pop" Haines, winner of the deciding
game in the 1926 World Series.
Courtesy of the Sporting News.

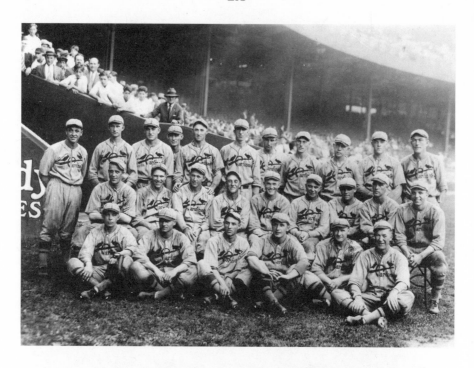

Team photograph of the 1931 World Champion St. Louis
Cardinals.
Copyright: the Sporting News / *Zuma.*

(Opposite)

Team photograph of the 1926 St. Louis Cardinals.
Copyright: the Sporting News / *Zuma.*

Charles Lindbergh shakes hands with Grover Cleveland Alexander,
with player-manager Bob O'Farrell to Alexander's immediate right.
Copyright: the Sporting News / *Zuma.*

Pepper Martin, hero of the 1931
World Series.
Copyright: the Sporting News /
Zuma.

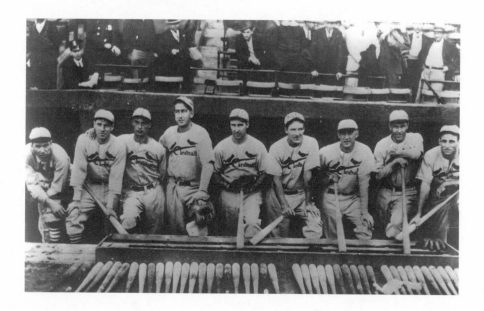

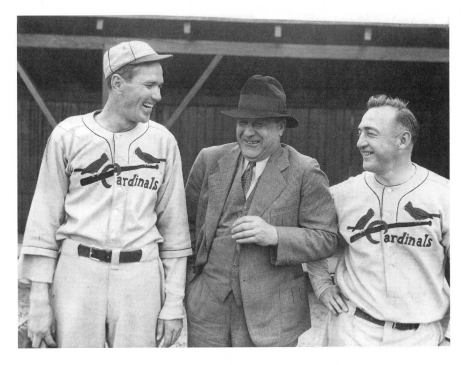

Dizzy Dean, Branch Rickey, and Frankie Frisch share a laugh.
Copyright: the Sporting News / *Zuma.*

(Opposite)

The Gas House Gang starting lineup for the first game of the 1934 World
Series. The batting order (right to left): Pepper Martin, Jack Rothrock,
Frankie Frisch, Joe Medwick, Ripper Collins, Bill DeLancey, Ernie Orsatti,
Leo Durocher, Dizzy Dean.
Copyright: the Sporting News / *Zuma.*

Mort Cooper and his trademark number 13.
Copyright: the Sporting News / *Zuma.*

Enos Slaughter, hero of the 1946 World Series, with
teammate Johnny Beazley and manager Eddie Dyer.
Copyright: the Sporting News / *Zuma.*

Stan "The Man" Musial, the most
popular player in Cardinals' history.
Copyright: the Sporting News /
Zuma.

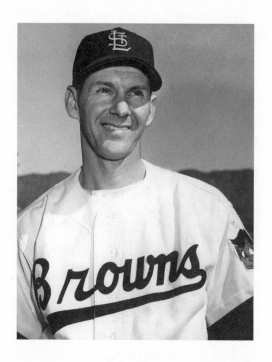

The mighty Eddie Gaedel at the bat.
Copyright: the Sporting News / *Zuma.*

(Opposite)

Marty Marion, the Cardinals' National League Most Valuable
Player in 1944, as Browns manager in 1952.
Copyright: the Sporting News / *Zuma.*

Bill Veeck with Satchel Paige.
Copyright: the Sporting News / *Zuma.*

Hall of Fame broadcasters Harry Caray and
Jack Buck with newcomer Joe Garagiola.
Copyright: the Sporting News / *Zuma.*

(Opposite)

Bob Gibson, greatest pitcher in Cardinals' history.
Copyright: the Sporting News / *Zuma.*

Curt Flood dazzles in the friendly confines of Wrigley Field.
Copyright: the Sporting News / *Zuma.*

Red Schoendienst,
Cardinals manager
for twelve seasons.
*Courtesy of Richard
A. Lawson.*

Lou Brock, the Cardinals'
greatest steal.
*Courtesy of Richard
A. Lawson.*

Whitey Herzog whittles an umpire down to size. *Copyright: the* Sporting News / *Zuma.*

Sportsman's Park, home of the Browns and the Cardinals.
Copyright: the Sporting News / *Zuma.*

(Opposite)

Willie McGee, the 1985 National League MVP,
and fielding wizard Ozzie Smith.
Copyright: the Sporting News / *Zuma.*

Mark McGwire shatters Roger Maris's single-
season home run record in 1998.
Copyright: the Sporting News / *Zuma.*

The last section of the old stadium before its demolition, with
the partially constructed new Busch Stadium behind it.
Courtesy of Steven Gietschier.

(Opposite)

Busch Stadium, home of the Cardinals from
1966 to 2005.
Copyright: the Sporting News / *Zuma.*

The last game at old Busch Stadium.
Courtesy of Steven Gietschier.

St. Louis Swifties
and the Streetcar Series

After winning three pennants and two world championships in the early years of the Great Depression, the St. Louis Cardinals duplicated their feat in the early 1940s. Under the leadership of Billy Southworth, who had briefly managed the team in 1929, the wartime Cardinals won the National League pennant in 1942 in a close, exciting race with the Dodgers and, after losing the first game of the World Series against the Yankees, went on to four straight wins and the world championship. They also won pennants in 1943 and 1944 and, after losing to the Yankees in the 1943 World Series, defeated the St. Louis Browns in the 1944 Streetcar Series.

E. G. Fischer, longtime official historian of the St. Louis Cardinals, wrote this article on the 1942 St. Louis Swifties for the Society of American Baseball Research publication on St. Louis baseball. He describes the coming of age of Stan Musial, Whitey Kurowski, and Johnny Beasley after their schooling in Branch Rickey's farm system, the clutch play of Enos Slaughter, Terry Moore, Marty Marion, and Walker Cooper, and the brilliant pitching of Mort Cooper, who won the National League Most Valuable Player Award with a record of 22–7 and ten shutouts.

Billy Southworth's St. Louis Swifties
E. G. Fischer ————————————————————————

New York World-Telegram cartoonist Willard Mullin labeled Billy Southworth's Cardinals the "St. Louis Swifties." They were a young and determined ball club utilizing speed, great defense, and good pitching to stage one of the greatest pennant drives of all time, winning 43 of their last 51 games in August and September to clinch the pennant on the last day of the season to beat out a talented Brooklyn Dodgers team.

Although they stole only 71 bases, the 1942 Cardinals ran with a purpose, routinely stretching singles into doubles, doubles into triples. They hustled from first to third or scored from second base on most base hits and tagged up and scored from third on almost every fly ball. Casey Stengel, Boston Braves manager, called them a "track team that ran like uncaged rabbits."

Shortstop Marty Marion cemented an air-tight defense in the infield and Terry Moore, their captain and team leader along with two future Hall of Famers, Stan Musial and Enos Slaughter, closed the gaps in the outfield with acrobatic catches. A pitching staff that included two twenty-game winners, Mort Cooper and rookie Johnny Beazley, held opponents to only 3.1 runs per game, fewest in the National League.

The 1942 Cardinals displayed an "esprit de corps" resulting from the fact that virtually every one of the players had been schooled in and risen from Branch Rickey's innovative and productive farm system. They were also one of the youngest teams to win a pennant, averaging only 26 years of age. Terry Moore was the oldest regular at the age of 30.

Experts had picked the Brooklyn Dodgers and St. Louis Cardinals as co-favorites for the National League pennant in 1942. The 1941 Cardinals, plagued with key injuries to Terry Moore (beaned), Enos Slaughter (fractured collar bone), Walker Cooper (fractured shoulder blade), Mort Cooper (surgery for elbow chips), Johnny Mize (broken finger) and Jimmy Brown (fractured hand) had waged a constant battle with the Brooklyn Dodgers from April through September. For almost the entire 1941 season, the teams were within two games of each other, until the Dodgers eventually clinched the pennant three days before the end of the season. The Dodgers finished the season 100–54, 2½ games ahead of the Cardinals, who finished with a record of 97–56.

While their near miss in 1941 was disappointing to the Cardinals, they did call up three players from their farm system in September who would make key contributions in the 1942 pennant race. The new players joining the Cardinals in September of 1941 were outfielder Stan Musial, third baseman George Kurowski, and pitcher Johnny Beazley. Musial batted .426 in 12 games. Kurowski appeared in five games for the Cardinals, batting .333 (three hits in nine appearances), and Beazley made his major league debut as a starting pitcher on September 28, 1941, and pitched a nine-inning complete game victory, allowing only one run.

The Cardinals would make one other key move, this one after the 1941 season. Ray Sanders was another young prospect of the Cardinals' farm system, a first baseman. He was asked to report to the Cardinals in spring training in 1942. In order to make way for him, on December 11, 1941, the Cardinals traded their slugging first baseman Johnny Mize to the New York Giants for cash and three players, catcher Ken O'Dea, pitcher Bill Lohrman, and reserve first baseman Johnny McCarthy.

The opening day line-up for Billy Southworth's 1942 Cardinals included Ray Sanders 1B, Frank Crespi 2B, Marty Marion SS, Jimmy Brown 3B, Stan Musial LF, Terry Moore CF, Enos Slaughter RF, Walker Cooper C, and Mort Cooper P. They lost on opening day, before a good crowd at Sportsman's Park, to the Chicago Cubs, 5–4. They continued to struggle, being shut out in five of their first twenty-four games, and were only at .500, winning 15 and losing 15 after their first thirty games, while the Dodgers led the league from the first week of the season. The Cardinals did move into second place in late May by winning four games in a row and then proceeded to win seven in a row in early June before starting to sputter again. By late June, Billy Southworth revamped his lineup, making several changes in the starting infield. Marty Marion would be the only infielder keeping the same job all season. Southworth moved George Kurowski in as the regular third baseman, he shifted Jimmy Brown to second base replacing Frank Crespi, and he had Johnny Hopp replace Ray Sanders at first base.

The Dodgers continued rolling up victories, winning four out of five games from the Cardinals at Ebbets Field. The Dodgers ended the first half of the schedule with a record of 55–22, building up an eight-game lead on the Cardinals, whose record at the halfway point of the season was 47–30.

While the Dodgers had built up a 10-game lead on August 5, 1942, the Cardinals were starting to catch fire. They were to lose two games in a row once during the second half of the season, and had begun their August-September record drive of winning 43 of their last 51 games.

The Cardinals had won nine of their last ten before the Dodgers came to St. Louis for a key four-game series, August 24–27. "Pass the Biscuits Mirandy" had become the Cardinals' fight song to be played constantly in the club house. Mort Cooper, who defied superstitions by wearing uniform #13, was wearing uniforms from his teammates to coincide with whichever victory number he was seeking.

The Dodgers came to town leading by 7½ games, but the Cardinals won three of the four games. Lefty Max Lanier beat Larry French and the Dodgers 7–1 in the opener. Mort Cooper and Whitlow Wyatt engaged in a twelve-inning scoreless pitching duel the next evening. Both the Dodgers and Cardinals scored a run in the thirteenth inning. Mort Cooper became the winner as the Cardinals scored a run in the bottom of the fourteenth inning to beat the Dodgers 2–1. The following day, Johnny Beazley beat the Dodgers 2–1 in a ten-inning game. Max Lanier came back and attempted to start the final game with only two days' rest, but was defeated by Curt Davis and the Dodgers 4–1. The Dodgers lead was reduced to 5½ games with 30 games left to play.

The Cardinals continued their winning ways. By their next showdown with the Dodgers on September 11 and 12 at Ebbets Field, the Brooklyn lead was down to 2 games. Mort Cooper was again paired against Whitlow Wyatt for the opener of the two-game series. Cooper went on to pitch a three-hit shutout, beating the Dodgers 3–0 for his 20th victory of the season. Max Lanier won the next day against the Dodgers 2–1 on Whitey Kurowski's two-run home run. The Cardinals, having defeated the Dodgers in five of the last six games played between the two clubs, had tied the Dodgers in the standings with 14 games to play.

On Sunday, September 13, 1942, the Cardinals captured first place all to themselves. The Dodgers lost a doubleheader to the Cincinnati Reds, while the Cardinals split a doubleheader with the Philadelphia Phillies.

The Cardinals maintained first place. They went on to win eleven of their final twelve games, including seven in a row, and had a record of 21–4 for the month of September. Going into the final day of the season, the Cardinals had a record of 104–48, holding a 1½ game lead over the Dodgers, who had a record of 103–50. The Cardinals were scheduled to play the Cubs in a double-header, while the Dodgers would be playing the Phillies in a single game. The Dodgers would have to win and the Cardinals would have to lose the double-header for Brooklyn to tie St. Louis. The Cardinals clinched the pennant at home. Ernie White beat the Cubs 9–2 in the first game and Johnny Beazley achieved his 21st victory, beating the Cubs in the second game for good measure.

The Cardinals ended up with the most wins (106), the fewest losses (48) and best winning percentage (.688) of any Cardinal team. Their 106 wins in 1942 were the most wins by a National League pennant winner until 1975 when the Cincinnati Reds won 108 games (in a 162-game season).

Enos Slaughter led the team in batting with a .318 average (second in the league to Ernie Lombardi's .330). Slaughter led the National League in base hits (188), triples (17), was second in runs scored (100), third in runs batted in (98), and third in slugging average (.494). Marty Marion led the National League in doubles (38). Stan Musial, after a slow start in his first full season in the majors, ended up batting .315 to finish right behind Slaughter.

Mort Cooper, who would be voted the NL's MVP in 1942, went 22–7, led the league in wins, ERA (1.77), starts (35), and shutouts (10). Johnny Beazley finished second in the National League in wins (21) and second in ERA (2.13). Max Lanier finished with a record of 13–8, ERA of 2.96, and was 5–2 against the Dodgers. Mort Cooper was 5–1 against the Dodgers. The Cardinals' pitching staff led the National League with the best ERA (2.55).

As a team, the Cardinals topped the National League in batting (.268), hits (1,454), doubles (282), triples (69), runs scored (755), slugging average (.379), and total bases (2,054).

Even though they would lose the first game of the 1942 World Series, the Cardinals would regain their momentum to beat a heavily favored New York Yankees team that had won its sixth pennant in seven years. Red Ruffing beat Mort Cooper and the Cardinals in the opening game at Sportsman's Park 7–4. Ruffing had a no-hitter for seven innings, before Terry Moore singled to right. The Yankees led 7–0 going into the bottom of the ninth. The Cardinals came up with a spirited ninth-inning rally, scoring four runs and still had the bases loaded with two outs and Stan Musial at bat for the second time in the inning. As the first batter leading off the bottom of the ninth, Musial had fouled out to catcher Bill Dickey. For one of the rare times in his career, Musial would account for two outs in an inning by grounding out to Buddy Hassett.

However, the Cardinals had thrown a scare into the Yankees and gained the confidence to keep their momentum going. Johnny Beazley beat the Yankees and Ernie Bonham 4–3 in Game Two. As the series moved back to Yankee Stadium, Ernie White shut the Yankees and Spud Chandler out 3–0 in Game Three. Ernie White was supported by two outstanding defensive catches in the seventh inning, one by left fielder Stan Musial taking a home run away from Joe Gordon with a leaping catch, and the other by right fielder Enos Slaughter robbing Charlie Keller of a home run with a spectacular leap and catch. The Cardinals won Game Four in a slugfest 9–6, Max Lanier receiving the win with three scoreless innings of relief.

The "St. Louis Swifties" topped off their fabulous 1942 season with a 4–2 victory over the New York Yankees in Game Five to become World Champions. Whitey Kurowski hit a two-run home run off of Red Ruffing in the top of the ninth to provide Johnny Beazley with his second complete-game victory in the World Series. The Cardinals celebrated their upset triumph over the New York Yankees with a rendition of "Pass the Biscuits Mirandy" in their victorious clubhouse celebration.

After a dismal financial year in 1941 despite the St. Louis Browns' best won-lost record since the late 1920s, owner Donald Barnes decided to move his desperate franchise to Los Angeles for the 1942 season. But Pearl Harbor prevented the Browns from moving to the West Coast, and Barnes kept the team in St. Louis, where they won their first and only American League pennant in 1944.

In his article for the Society of American Baseball Research, Bill Borst, co-founder of the St. Louis Browns fan club in 1984, describes the dramatic turn-around of the Browns in 1942 when the team finished in third place with a record of 82–69, their third-best record in franchise history. Manager Luke Sewell had taken a no-name team of unwanted misfits and discarded veterans and molded them into a first-division team. Two years later, Sewell's Browns would confound the baseball world by wresting the American League flag from a Yankee team that had won three straight pennants.

A St. Louis Harbinger: The 1942 Browns
Bill Borst ————————————————————————————

They're making me feel famous and I love it!
—Chet Laabs in July

After suffering through one of the most dismal decades in baseball history in the 1930s, the St. Louis Browns began to turn things around in the early 1940s. In 1940 they bounced back from their worst year ever to finish in sixth place, and in 1941 they improved to their best won-lost record since the 1920s. But it was the 1942 season that brought the real breakthrough: the club's first over-.500, first-division season since 1929 and its best winning percentage since 1922. Although the team fell back to sixth place in 1943, the seeds had been sown for the Browns' one surpassing triumph, the 1944 pennant. For St. Louis Browns fans, 1942 was a harbinger of better things ahead.

Unfortunately for the Browns, Branch Rickey's St. Louis Cardinals grabbed all the headlines in St. Louis in the summer of 1942. The Cardinals experienced a bumper crop as their farm system paid off handsome dividends. A 21-year-old former pitcher named Stan Musial made his impact felt with a .426 average in the waning days of the 1941 season. In '42 he gave evidence of a Hall of Fame career in the making by hitting .315.

The cash register rang with a melody that was sweet music to Rickey's ears as fans poured into Sportsman's Park when the National League teams came to town to play the "St. Louis Swifties." Though the Cardinals lost a dogfight with Brooklyn in 1941, nearly 650,000 laid down their money to see the team, and when they overcame a big Dodger lead to win the pennant in '42, Red Bird attendance was over 550,000.

The Browns, on the other hand, usually played before family and a few loyal diehards who showed up to cheer their team on no matter how poorly they played. Crowds of 500 were not unusual, while crowds of 4,000 to 6,000 were more the exception than the rule. Despite an improvement on the field, the Browns' bottom line had been disappointing in 1941, as only 176,000 had paid to see the Browns play. The team ran a $100,000 deficit, minuscule by 1992 standards but enough to put a team in severe trouble just before the nation entered World War II. To save money, the club dropped five of its minor league franchises. And the American League, which had contributed to the deficit by limiting the Browns to just seven night games in 1941, was forced to chip in with $25,000 to get them over the hump. The constant losing had taken its toll on owner Donald Barnes' bank account, and Brownie stock that fans had purchased for $5 a share dropped to a mere $2. Furthermore, under the terms of their leases, the Browns and the Cardinals split the ushering and cleanup costs at Sportsman's Park, in effect making the Browns underwrite part of the Cardinals' success.

Barnes had planned to move the team to Los Angeles, but America's entrance into World War II stopped the move. In February of 1942 a white knight rode in to save the day for the Browns. Richard D. Muckerman, an ice magnate and owner of the St. Louis Ice and Fuel Company, had purchased $300,000 worth of new stock and was named vice president of the club. Muckerman's money gave Donald Barnes, the DeWitts, Bill and Charley, and manager Luke Sewell enough financial backing to maintain their policy of keeping their most promising players and acquiring others to fill their key needs, albeit at bargain basement prices.

For the St. Louis Browns, 1942 was thought to be a rebuilding year. Since coming over to the team in June of 1941, Sewell had generated a new spirit of optimism long absent from the franchise. Under his leadership the team had played .500 ball to finish with its best record in a dozen years.

Sewell was unhappy with the keystone combination. The 1941 incumbents, the ever-popular Johnny Berardino and Don Heffner, were not Sewell's kind of ballplayers. To replace them, Sewell had to buck the advice of the Brownie brain trust. Fred Haney, who had become the Toledo Mud Hens' manager after Sewell replaced him in St. Louis, was not impressed with the abilities of his slugging shortstop Vern Stephens, who had impressive statistics as a Mud Hen. According to Haney, "Stephens will never play shortstop in the major leagues as long as he has a hole in his ass." Sewell figured that even without radical reconstructive surgery Stephens would be an improvement. As the pride of Akron put it, "It doesn't take much to be better than the man we got at shortstop." Stephens was brought up and quickly became a key player.

Third baseman Don Gutteridge had been demoted to the minor leagues at age 30 after five mediocre seasons with the Cardinals and had hit .309 and scored 113 runs with the Sacramento Solons in 1941. His 46 stolen bases had led the league, yet he was passed over in the major league draft. Frustrated at the demotion and lack of interest by the big leagues, Gutteridge said he would quit baseball rather than spend another year in the minors. So the Cardinals offered him for sale to the Browns for $7,500 on a contingency basis, Rickey offering the opinion that Gutteridge could not make the switch to second base. The ever-realistic Sewell saw an opportunity since "the man we got can't play second." Gutteridge turned out to be an excellent second sacker and a good leadoff man.

The Browns also picked up another National League discard from the 1941 Sacramento team, pitcher Al "Boots" Hollingsworth, who had been battered around in the National League for a 33–67 record in five years.

Sewell was cleaning house to get rid of those players who did not share his aggressive passion for winning or his distaste for losing. In June, Roy Cullenbine was dispatched to Washington for pitcher Steve Sundra and outfielder-first baseman Mike Chartak. Cullenbine was a great statistical hitter, but DeWitt recalled that the rap on him was that "Cullenbine wouldn't swing the bat! Sewell would give him the hit sign and he'd take, trying to get a base on balls. Laziest human being you ever saw!" In his ten-year major league career, Cullenbine amassed 1,072 hits and 852 walks, an amazing ratio for a player who did not lead off or hit for great power.

Most teams still had their major stars in 1942. The perennial favorite Yankees were as strong as ever. Joe DiMaggio, Charley Keller, Tommy Henrich, Phil Rizzuto, Bill Dickey, Red Ruffing, and Ernie Bonham all suited up to start the season. The Red Sox had Ted Williams, Bobby Doerr, Dom DiMaggio, Jim Tabor, and Tex Hughson. The only big-name stars in the military were Hank Greenberg of the Tigers and the Indians' Bob Feller. Sewell realized he had his work cut out for him if he wanted the Browns to rise in the standings.

Yet the patchwork performed well enough to rank one of the best in Browns' history. Its 82–69 mark (.543) ranked it in a tie with the 1928 team for the third best win total in franchise history behind the 1908 and 1922 team. In many ways the 1942 season served as a prelude to the '44 club which would win the pennant.

The Browns started out on the right foot, winning their first four contests. After slumping badly in the spring, they advanced in the summer, jumping into the first division in July and nosing ahead of Cleveland in August to finish third, their highest standing since 1928. They wound up 19.5 games behind the Yankees and 9 games in back of the Red Sox.

The high point of the season was an eight-game winning streak in July that vaulted the Browns into fourth place. A tall, dark Venezuelan, Alejandro Aparicio Elroy Carrasquel of the Senators, stopped the streak with a 3–0 shutout. Chet Laabs powered the offense with a Ruthian display of punch that had too often been absent from Brownie box scores. He went 16 for 29 during the heart of the streak, personally producing 25 of the team's 46 runs during the skein. In a four-game series in Philadelphia, Laabs poled five homers, including a grand slam. There was talk that the slugger, who had come to the Browns with Mark Christman and others for Bobo Newsom, Red Kress, and Beau Bell in 1939, would be the first Brownie to win the home run title since Kenny Williams had unseated Babe Ruth in 1922. After six seasons of mediocrity, he got hot in July, and Chesty Chet was suddenly mobbed by reporters. He loved all the attention.

When the Browns came home in late July, there was some genuine fan interest. Their largest crowd of the year and second-largest in a dozen years, 20,812 paid, came out for a twi-night doubleheader against the second-place Red Sox. The Sox won the opener, but Laabs' homer in the eleventh inning gave pitcher Johnny Niggeling a 3–1 win in the nightcap. It was Chet's 19th of the season, tying him with Williams temporarily. Niggeling would wind up beating Boston six times in seven decisions, seriously dampening the Red Sox' ability to catch the Yankees.

The Browns suffered a great loss of momentum during a doubleheader loss to the Detroit Tigers on August 9. The team, which had fielded well all season long, fell apart defensively and committed 11 errors in losing 9–3 and 3–1. A total of eight unearned runs crossed the plate for Detroit that day. Seven different players contributed to the fielding breakdown, with the regular infielders (George McQuinn, Don Gutteridge, Vern Stephens, and Harlond Clift) making two miscues each. Johnny Berardino, Frankie Hayes, and Mike Chartak chipped in with one apiece. This display still did not come close to the league record of 16 errors set by Cleveland against Washington in a doubleheader in 1901.

The twin disaster dropped the Browns' record to 56–56, but they played at a .667 (26–13) clip down the stretch to finish at 82–69. But disappointing attendance and sluggish cash flow continued to be vexing problems. The league allowed 14 night games, and the Browns averaged nearly 9,000 per date under the lights. Sunday doubleheaders did even better, but Monday-thru-Saturday day games averaged less than 1,200. The twin disaster against the Tigers drew only 4,842 on a Sunday, while that same day over 48,000 fans filled Comiskey Park in Chicago to watch Satchel Paige lose the Negro East-West All-Star Game. With the Cardinals' late pennant drive diverting the fans, St. Louis fans ignored the Browns in September. When they drew over 8,000 for an exhibition against the Pirates in Council Bluffs, Iowa, on September 23, it was more than any of the games on the homestand they had just finished. Even the Yankees could attract just 2,200 per game. And when the Browns clinched third place with a thrilling 5–4, sixteen-inning win over the A's on September 14, the paying attendance was 256,000, an increase of 45 percent from 1941 and the club's highest since 1929, but it was still far and away the worst in the American League.

The most magnificent individual performance was turned in by Laabs, who finished second in the league with 27 homers and drove in 99 runs. Stephens proved that Haney knew as little about baseball as about anatomy, hitting 14 homers and batting .294 to begin a string of several seasons as the league's premier slugging shortstop. Though there was no official recognition of rookies in 1942, the consensus among American League beat writers was that Stephens was second only to Boston's Johnny Pesky, who hit .331. Center fielder Walter Judnich batted .313 and had 17 homers. He was one of the team's quiet heroes. An outstanding player as well, his .991 fielding average led the league, yet he failed to attract much newspaper attention. The city belonged to Terry Moore, who made one more error than Judnich in four fewer games and handled fewer chances, 284 to Judnich's 337. Even when the Browns were playing solid ball down the stretch, Enos Slaughter's marital problems drew more ink than the Browns' box scores.

The *Sporting News* called Sewell a sorcerer. "His pitching staff is haunted!" wrote J. G. Taylor Spink. "Graybeards like Al Hollingsworth, Elden Aucker, Johnny Niggeling, Denny Galehouse, and George Caster live in a bygone day, but pitch decidedly in the present." The 39-year-old Niggeling was 15–11, submariner Auker was 14–13, Hollingsworth 10–6, Galehouse 12–12, Sundra 8–3, and Caster, pitching in relief, 8–2. Fritz Ostermuller chipped in with a 3–1 mark after his recall from Toledo. He would later make a career out of beating the Cardinals as a member of the Pittsburgh Pirates. It was a very old pitching staff. Of the 16 pitchers who appeared in 1942, 11 of them were over 30 years of age. Niggeling turned 39 in July, and Ostermuller, Caster, and Hollingsworth, heart of the relief corps, were all 34.

Leadoff hitter Gutteridge hit .255 and led the league's second basemen in putouts and assists. Veterans McQuinn and Clift manned the corners well. Laabs and Judnich anchored a productive outfield. The weakest link in the Browns' armament was definitely behind the plate. At age 36, future Hall-of-

Famer Rick Ferrell could muster just a .223 batting mark in 99 games. His backup Frankie Hayes hit .252 in 56 games.

Sewell did a marvelous job in getting his players to play over their heads. A harbinger of the scrapping '44 Browns appeared on August 1 in a game with the Yankees. Manager Sewell was behind the plate in a rare start.

In the first inning, Tommy Henrich attempted to score from second on a hit to right. Chartack came up firing and gunned a strike to Sewell. Henrich elected not to slide, and he bumped the 42-year-old general less than lovingly as the tag was being made, causing Sewell to react with fighting words. The play fired up the Browns, who won easily, 7–3. Sewell also got his only hit of the season in the game. Although the team was only 7–15 against New York in '42, they would sweep the Yankees in a four-game set at the end of the '44 season to get into the only World Series in their history.

Along with Mel Ott's New York Giants, the Browns were the real Cinderella story of baseball in 1942. They moved up three positions in the standings and increased their win total by 12. Despite this big improvement, it was difficult for fans and players alike to get too excited about the progress that the Browns had made. The game's future seemed in jeopardy, despite President Roosevelt's "green light letter" about the importance of baseball as a morale booster. Most owners, players, and fans were resigned to the belief that the total number of regular season games would have to be greatly reduced, maybe even as far as to just 100 games, because of increased demands in manpower that the World War would inevitably put on baseball. Some pessimists envisioned the game being shut down altogether. The real tragedy for St. Louis was that just when the Browns were becoming competitive and had a chance to make some money, the war put baseball's future in doubt.

Decades before Ozzie Smith's fielding acrobatics, Marty Marion was dazzling Cardinal fans with his brilliant play at shortstop. Nicknamed "Slats" because of his long and lean appearance, Marion was so respected for his defensive skills that he was named National League Most Valuable Player in 1944, even though he hit only .267. With the Cardinals, the perennial All-Star played on four pennant-winning teams and three World Series champions. After his playing career was over, he managed the Cardinals in 1951. After being replaced by Eddie Stanky the following year, he went on to manage Bill Veeck's St. Louis Browns in 1952 and 1953.

In this "as told to" piece from My Greatest Day in Baseball, *Marion remembers the thrill of beating Red Ruffing and the Yankees in the seventh game of the 1942 World Series and the dramatic pick-off play in the ninth inning that decided the game and the Series' championship.*

Marty Marion
Lyall Smith

It was a cocky bunch of Cardinals that went into that big barn of a Yankee Stadium on October 7 in the 1942 World Series. We'd found out by this time that we could whip the Yanks. We were on the long end of a 3–1 score in series games by now, but we wanted to do one thing. And that was to beat Red Ruffing.

We knew we could lick him even though he'd won the opener down in St. Louis. He had us nibbling out of his hands for eight innings before we finally got over our chills and teed off on him to knock him out in the last of the ninth. But even though we chased him, Red won that game 7 to 4 and we still wanted to whip him all the way.

We knew he was going to face us in the fifth game when we went out to the park and even though we were anxious to pick on him we still had a few misgivings. For the day was one of those dark, dreary ones in New York with low misty clouds sailing off the ocean.

Captain Terry Moore was standing at the window when I went into the locker room under the stands to dress for the game. He was staring out at the dull skies. "That Ruffing will be hard to hit today," he murmured. "If that fast one is working he'll be tough."

There's no fooling about our being chesty when we went out that day.

None of us was superstitious except Moore and he was really worried. I remember I walked into the dugout with Kurowski and we started talking about what we were going to do with the $6,000 that went to the winners.

"Holy smokes," moaned Terry. "Don't talk like that, you guys. We haven't won it yet." He was really fretting.

Well, we started the game. Jimmy Brown opened with a walk but Ruffing fooled Moore on a third strike and Slaughter banged into a double play. That was the first one we had hit into all through the series and Enos was really talking to himself when he went into the outfield.

It didn't take the Yanks long to score, for Phil Rizzuto, their little shortstop, slammed one of Johnny's fast balls into the stands the first time up and boom . . . just like that we were behind 1–0.

We pecked away at Ruffing in the second when Walker Cooper got a single, and then picked up another hit in the third on a liner by Jimmy Brown.

Came the fourth and Slaughter put us back in the game with a homer off Ruffing that tied it up. We felt better but didn't have long to feel that way for Rolfe opened up the last half of the same inning with a bunt down to Beazley.

Johnny was too anxious and after fielding the ball badly he threw wild to first and Red went on down to second. He got around to third on a long fly by Roy Cullenbine and Joe DiMaggio then socked a single to left on the first pitch to put the Yanks in front again 2–1. It looked bad for a while when powerful Charlie Keller, toughest looking player I ever saw at the plate, hit another one of Beazley's slow curves for another single to put DiMag on third. But Gordon fanned and I threw out Dickey.

We got our fourth hit in the fifth when Beazley broke his bat on a single but nothing came of it and we still trailed as the Yanks came up in their half. Gerry Priddy opened with a smash through the box but I was playing him in the right spot and threw him out on a close play. But Ruffing beat out a tap to Beazley and when Johnny Hopp made a low throw to me on a grounder by Rizzuto I couldn't hold the ball and they had men on second and first with one out. We got jittery for a minute and Jimmy Brown kicked Rolfe's roller to load the bases.

Then Beazley really bore down. He made Cullenbine pop out to me and Kurowski came up with DiMaggio's hot grounder to step on third for the out.

Up we came again. Moore hit Ruffing's first pitch for a single and Slaughter, who was really hungry that day, got another hit on the first pitch. We started whooping it up then and Ruffing looked a little rattled. He got Musial on an infield pop but Walker Cooper socked a fly down the foul line and although Cullenbine caught it, Terry came ripping in from third and tied it all up again.

That made it 2–2 and it stayed that way through the next two innings. Up came the ninth inning. Cooper was the first batter and he brought us off the bench when he reached out those long arms of his and poked a slow curve into right-center. Southworth gave Johnny Hopp the bunt sign and he laid down a beauty to put Walker on second. That brought up Kurowski.

Ruffing stood out there for a few short seconds that seemed like ages while he looked down at Whitey in the batter's box. He fanned him three times in that first game of the series, probably was trying to figure what he threw him those times. He got one strike and one ball on Kurowski and then served him another one. Whitey swung and he really hit it.

"There it goes," screamed Moore. "There it goes." Right into the stands and we had two more runs. I remember tackling him and we mobbed him until he begged us to let go.

Then we sobered down in a hurry for we still knew the Yanks had a punch in those bats of theirs. And they proved it. Joe Gordon led off with a single and we started to worry. Dickey up. He hit a bouncer down to second, the kind that Jimmy had gobbled up all year easy-like. But he muffed this one and Bill was safe at first and Gordon was on second. We stopped to talk things over again with Cooper walking slowly out to the mound to talk to us.

He talked to Beazley for a while and then he looked at me. "Watch it, Marty," he said. "We might try something."

That's all he said but I nodded. I knew. Priddy was at bat and we knew he was going to try to bunt those runners along. Walker called for a high fast one and Beazley sent one down a mile a minute that was right across Priddy's eyes. Quick as I could I cut behind Gordon who had about a 10-foot lead off second base. I dove for the bag and just as I hit it the ball got there too.

Cooper had reared back and thrown it with all the power he had in his big wide shoulders. And that was plenty. It came to me waist high just as I got to the bag. Gordon was on his way back to second and crashed into me. But I held the ball. He rolled over and I went at Umpire George Barr.

I just about jumped out of my shoes. "You're out," he bellowed. We'd picked him off!

Priddy popped out to Brown and Jimmy came right back to make up for his earlier boots by throwing out George Selkirk who hit for Ruffing.

That gave us the World Series. We beat Red Ruffing. We smashed a Yankee hold on the world championship. And my day was complete. I was in the right spot at the right time for a throw.

A throw that I knew was coming just because Walker Cooper, best catcher I ever saw, told me we might try something.

At the end of October, barely weeks after the Cardinals defeated the Yankees in the 1942 World Series, Branch Rickey accepted the joint position of president and general manager for the Brooklyn Dodgers. In Rickey's twenty-five years with the Cardinals, he served as president, vice-president, general manager, and manager. During his tenure, the Cardinals won six National League pennants and four World Series. Rickey, who started his professional career with the St. Louis Browns, had revolutionized baseball with his farm system and would do it again with the Dodgers when he signed Jackie Robinson to a contract in 1945.

J. Roy Stockton's article in the October 29, 1942, St. Louis Post-Dispatch probes the reasons why Rickey decided to leave the Cardinals.

Branch Rickey Is Named President of the Brooklyn Dodgers
J. Roy Stockton ————————————————————————

Branch Rickey, who today was appointed president and general manager of the Brooklyn Dodgers, was father of the chain store or farm system in baseball, and long has been considered one of the most astute figures in the national game.

Moving from the Browns to the Cardinals in 1917, when the club was purchased by a syndicate of business men, he served as president, field manager, and vice-president and general manager. During his regime the Cardinals won six pennants and four world championships and in the most recent triumph, the team's 1942 victory over the fabulous Yankees, virtually every man on the St. Louis squad was a product of the farm system which Rickey conceived and developed.

Rickey's appointment as director of the Brooklyn property terminates the long-lived partnership with Sam Breadon, who has served as president of the Cardinals through the years of their prosperity. During those years, it is estimated, Rickey received more than $1,000,000 in salary and bonus money. His most recent five-year contract, which expires with the end of the year, called for a basic annual salary of $50,000 and a percentage of the profits. For 1941 his share of the profits brought his income from the club to approximately $88,000.

First intimation that a breach had developed in the Rickey-Breadon relations came in the spring of 1941, when the *Post-Dispatch* disclosed exclusively that Rickey had been informed that because of uncertain world economic conditions and the threat of war, the club did not deem it wise to renew his five-year contract.

Coolness Develops

Neither Rickey nor Breadon has ever discussed the causes of the breach, but persons close to the club had noticed a coolness developing between president and general manager in recent years. It was a strange partnership always, with each having always a great respect for the ability of the other, while their personalities, habits, and their views of extra-curricular things were so diametrically opposed that there never was any bond of friendship between the partners.

During the early days of Rickey's association with the Cardinals, the team was so poor that old uniforms had to be patched to clothe the team in the spring, and as there was no money for transportation the athletes even trained in St. Louis one season. Finding it impossible to compete in the open market for players, Rickey conceived the idea of finding prospects when they were young and planting them on minor league clubs, or farms. Rival baseball operators laughed at the idea, but it worked with golden magic.

Players developed on those farm teams helped the club win its first pennant and world championship in 1926 and other pennants were won in 1928, 1930, 1931, 1934, and 1942.

When the Cardinals won the 1942 pennant and defeated the glamorous Yankees in the world series, Rickey said it was the happiest moment of his life, because it was a victory for his boys, young men who with only a few exceptions, were products of the now far-flung chain store system that Branch had fathered and developed.

The same rival baseball operators who laughed at the Rickey farm system, since have paid him the compliment of following his lead and now virtually all major league clubs with the necessary means have established similar connections with minor league clubs.

Rags to Riches

At times the Cardinal organization, under Rickey's direction, included more than two dozen minor league affiliates, some owned outright, others controlled by working agreements. And from a poverty-stricken club in 1917, the Cardinals have grown to an organization appraised in the millions.

Several years ago, Lou Wentz, Oklahoma oil operator, offered and almost purchased the Cardinals for a little more than a million dollars. It is doubtful if that figure would be attractive to Breadon today, if world conditions were normal.

Besides the local property, the Cardinals own the Rochester club in the International League, Columbus in the American Association, Sacramento in the Pacific League, and Houston in the Texas League, each of these more important minor league holdings being worth, in normal times, more than $500,000.

Started as Catcher for Browns, Managed Both St. Louis Clubs

Moving to Brooklyn, where he will succeed the fiery and colorful Larry McPhail, now a lieutenant colonel in the Army and in his early baseball days a protégé of Rickey, Branch will find a set-up drastically different from the one he is leaving in St. Louis. With the Cardinals, in a city of less than a million population, it was customary and allegedly necessary to sell players each year, to balance the budget and put substantial profits on the books. In Brooklyn, under the McPhail regime, it has been the custom to buy players. McPhail, in fact, was one of Rickey's best customers. It was to Brooklyn that Rickey sold Joe Medwick, Curt Davis, Mickey Owen, Don Padgett, and others.

Baseball conditions have changed radically, too, since Rickey found a new idea and turned it into a fortune for Cardinal stockholders. Competition in the farm system has become keen, and especially under war conditions, the scouting business is poor, with the armed forces having first call on the young men who in normal times would be prospects for baseball talent hunters.

Rickey's baseball career in St. Louis started as a catcher with the Browns, who in that year—1906—were known as the Ravens. He returned to the St. Louis American League club in 1913 as secretary and became manager the following season. He was still manager in 1917, when a syndicate, headed by J. C. Jones, purchased the Cardinals, then playing at Robison Field, Vandeventer and Natural Bridge, from Mrs. Helene Hathaway Britton.

With the Cardinals Rickey served as president, and later as manager. In late May of 1925, Breadon appointed Rogers Hornsby to replace Rickey as field manager, and Branch moved to the front office as vice-president and general manager.

In the Cardinals' three consecutive pennant-winning years from 1942–1944, Mort Cooper was the dominant pitcher in the National League, winning more than twenty games each year and compiling a 65 and 22 record overall. Despite his remarkable success during the regular season, Cooper, who wore the number 13 on his uniform, had difficulty winning games in the World Series. In My Greatest Day in Baseball, *Cooper gives his account to John Carmichael of his 4–3 complete-game victory over the Yankees in Game Two of the 1943 World Series, the only game won by the Cardinals in that Series. It was Cooper's first World Series victory in five tries, but it was also a day when he had to overcome personal tragedy to defeat the Yankees.*

Morton Cooper

My biggest, and saddest, baseball day was also the longest day I ever put in and you might know which one it always will be. That day was October 6, 1943, the second game of the last World Series, and it began without warning at 6 o'clock in the morning. My wife and I were asleep in our New York hotel when the phone rang. It was long distance . . . asking for Mr. Cooper. I answered, and you can tell how sound asleep I'd been when I didn't even recognize the voice.

It was my oldest brother, Bob, and I didn't know it. I said: "This is Mort," and the voice said: "Oh, pardon me, I wanted Walker Cooper . . ." and the line went dead. I climbed back to the hay and it wasn't until around 9 o'clock that we went down to breakfast, joining Walker and Johnny Hopp and their wives. There was something wrong with Walker. Then, of course, I didn't know what, but I accused him of being afraid of the Yanks and he just grinned feebly and let it go at that.

We'd just about finished eating when Walker's wife said to me: "You and Walker go on ahead upstairs . . . Billy Southworth wants to see you both in your room." Well, we walked out and left the women folks there and I said to my brother: "Wonder what Billy wants . . . I'll bet he heard from the slack people." (We'd signed with some company that made slacks for advertising purposes you know.) But Walker shook his head. "No it ain't," he answered abruptly. I looked at him funny . . . he seemed too tight lipped and sort of cold looking and he walked straight ahead of me and he never looked around.

We got in the room and I started to flip on the radio, but Walker told me to turn it off. Billy was there and we all sat down and suddenly Walker spoke. I remember that he talked real slow as though the words wouldn't come out. "Mort," he said, "somebody's got to tell you. Dad died today." I sat there. Nobody said a thing for what seemed an hour . . . only it wasn't even a minute. Southworth told me later I said, "No, no"; but I didn't know that I did. But I heard Walker say: "Yes, that's the phone call you got this morning.

"R. J. (that was my older brother) got you by mistake. He didn't want to tell you because he knew you were pitching today. If we only could have kept it quiet until afterward . . . but the newspapers have it . . . " and my brother's voice trailed off. The writers gave me all the credit after that game, but it belonged to Walker. He's the kid who deserved any honor. He not only had the same burden to share that I did, as a brother, but he had to keep me together, too. I had to pitch. Walker had all the grief and me on top of it to shoulder. He was the strong man . . . carrying me along.

Billy (Southworth) sat there quietly and let it sink in and when he spoke it was hardly more than a whisper. "Mort," he told me, "you're my pitcher today. Do you want to go?" That seemed to wake me up. Walker said my voice filled the room. "Yes, sir," I told Billy, "The lid is off now. The worst has already happened to me. Nothing else can hurt and besides you don't think for a minute Dad would want me to miss this game?"

I saw Billy and Walker exchange quick looks and I felt better. So did Walker . . . I could see that. Billy said good-bye and left and in a few minutes the women folk came in. By this time my wife knew what had happened, but they tried to act real casual-like and we all went to the park early. Some of the Yankees had heard about it and when I met them they all stopped to tell me they were sorry. Afterward, when we got home for the funeral, there were only two big sprays of flowers on the casket . . . one at the top from the Cardinals, one at the bottom from the Yankees. Dad would have been pleased.

That's the only game I ever beat the Yankees; the only game I ever licked an American League club in what is it . . . five starts? But somehow it comes back to me sort of piecemeal, even now. I guess because of the circumstances, it was too big for me to appreciate right away. But I remember saying to Walker in our clubhouse meeting: "Bill Dickey's the guy we have to stop, don't forget that. Remember last year?" My brother did. We pitched harder to him than anybody and still couldn't get him out.

He's the hardest man to fool I ever pitched to. You can even cross him up and he'll get a piece of the ball. He's a helluva guy, too . . . don't forget it. When he hit that home run off me in the fifth game, to win the series, I told him: "If I had to lose that way, I don't know anybody I'd rather have beat me" and he came back with: "I hit it off the best pitcher in the league, Mort . . ." and then he invited me to come down bird-hunting with him in Arkansas. I'd rather take a chance with Charley Keller anytime than Dickey . . . yet it was Keller who almost beat me in that second game.

We started the game. I never pitched more carefully in my life. I wasn't in a daze, but I felt all alone out there. Once I caught myself nodding to Walker, down there behind the plate, when he wasn't even giving me a sign. He straightened up and took a couple of steps, but I knew what he meant and I nodded and waved him back. Well, as you know, we got off in front and going into the ninth, the Cards led 4–1. Every time I came by third base to pick up my glove, I'd get thinking about dad and I'd say to myself:

"I can't think of him now . . . the ballgame comes first. He knows that."

That way I went along. Then Bill Johnson doubled in the ninth and Keller hit for three bases. One run was home, another on third. It was my own fault although to people who've asked me from time to time why I threw a fastball to so-and-so or a curve or anything else and let 'em hit me, I always say: "Listen, don't take credit away from me . . . give those fellows some. After all they're good hitters . . . probably as good as I am a pitcher, or better. It's as much their fault as mine."

But in this case I got carried away by the fact that it was the ninth inning. I told myself: "Now I've got you guys, after all this time and I'm going to pour it on." I did. Instead of going along like I had been, I decided to show off. That's what it amounted to. So Johnson hit and Keller hit. You can't throw the ball past those guys and I knew it. They'd hammered me the year before. But in my moment of triumph as I thought, I forgot.

Southworth came running out on the field. Probably everyone thought he was going to yank me because there was nobody down and the tying run was coming to the plate. But he wouldn't have taken me out . . . I know that. "Mort, Mort," he said to me. "Listen. Pitch your natural game. Don't go overboard now. Settle down. You got a two-run lead." I nodded and grinned at him and he wagged a finger and ran back to the bench. The other guys returned to their positions and I looked at the plate. Who was there but Dickey!

I recalled that in the '42 series we pitched him 11 straight curve balls to try and catch him waiting for a fast one and we still didn't get him out. Here he was again, in his own park with that short right-field fence. There was only one thing to do . . . try and make him hit it on the ground. If it got through, only one run scored anyway; if it went anywhere near a fielder, the guy could kick the ball a little and still be able to get Bill, who isn't fast. So I shook Walker off until he called for a screwball. It was as perfect a pitch as I threw all day, knee-high over the outside corner and still he got a hold of it.

What's more he got that bat around so fast he actually pulled the ball between first and second. He smacked it on a line too but right into the hands of

Lou Klein for the first out. Then Nick Etten was at bat. I slowed up on him for the "good pitch" and he grounded to Klein as Keller scored. It was 4–3 with two out and Joe Gordon hitting. He was crouched over the plate, expecting the same kind of outside treatment I'd given the other two. And that's what he was going to get . . . but the pitch slipped . . . !

That was the worst ball I threw in the whole series, both games. Instead of getting it low and away, it boomed in there high and inside, exactly the pitch for a guy like Gordon to belt out of the lot. Walker knew it too . . . and he jumped up and acted like he was going to dash out in front of the plate and head it off. And Gordon? He saw what was coming before it got there and tried desperately to pull back and swing hard. He swung, but he was too close and the ball ticked off the handle of the bat and sailed high to the left of the plate . . . a foul.

I can see Walker and Kurowski going for it yet. My brother got it . . . but it jiggled in his glove just a little, he squeezed it so hard. But I don't think it would have fallen even if it had jumped free. Kurowski would have had it. We won . . . I won . . . Walker won, mostly . . . the Cardinals won. But I guess Dad won, in the long run, because maybe I'd a' got licked again if that hadn't happened to him. I'm not being sentimental when I say that I believe Dad died so that I could win that game.

Baseball writers described the 1944 World Series between the Cardinals and the Browns as a Cinderella story, but there was no "happily-ever-after" ending for the Browns, who lost in six games after taking an early Series lead. The Streetcar Series, as reported by then Marine Sergeants Robert W. Broeg and Robert H. Myers for The Leatherneck, *was a pitchers' affair with a record set for total strikeouts. Unlikely heroes such as Browns pitcher Denny Galehouse and the Cardinals' Blix Donnelly emerged in the early going, but with the Brownies playing the field like Cinderella's ugly stepsisters—they committed ten errors to the Cardinals' one—the Cardinals eventually took control of the Series and won the last three games after trailing 2–1. As Broeg and Myers reported, "This was one fairy tale that didn't come true."*

World Series Review
Sgts. Robert W. Broeg and Robert H. Myers

In reality, the hands on the big timepiece in left field pointed to 6 minutes past 4 on that chilly afternoon of early October, but everyone knows that fairy tales aren't fashioned around such an uneventful, uninspired hour as that. Midnight is the witching hour, so it must—it had to be—that time, just as the storybook said, when the clock struck 12 for the 1944 Cinderella of the sports world, the St. Louis Browns.

Whatever the time, the Cinderella Brownies shed their jewels and gay finery and went back to sackcloth; they changed their coach and eight spanking horses for a ten-cent seat on the trolley; their rent was overdue in the dream castle, so back to their frowzy cellar they went. And, as far as anyone knows, they didn't need even bother to look around for any glass slippers lost in the shuffle. The clock had struck, and the Brownies had struck out. This was one fairy tale that didn't come true.

And now, cooking on the front burner in the international Hot Stove League for the fifth time in eight tries for the world championship, are the St. Louis Cardinals. They won the title fair and square in a six-game series that drew a daily average throng of 34,000 to Sportsman's Park, for a total attendance of 206,708 customers who paid $906,122 in gross receipts. But it is not being unkind to whisper that the moans of grieving Brownie fans throughout the world far exceeded the cheers for the winning Redbirds.

It was a good Series, this first all–St. Louis affair. But there was a sharp contrast in the general public's behavior as compared to other years—years such as 1926, when the Cards won their first National League pennant and clipped the Yankees in the Series, or when the boisterous, hellraising Gas House Gang took the Mound City apart in 1934 and the brothers Dean pitched the Birds to victory over Detroit. Compared to those years, St. Louis was as quiet as the public library. The natives, plus a few thousand out-of-town folks who "happened" to have business here during Series time, were enthusiastic, but somewhat reserved. They ate something like eight miles of hot dogs per day, drank their fill of beer and pop, but their excitement never hit a stage that could be called nerve shaking.

The weather and the Browns had much in common. Luke Sewell's boys were hot when they started off, and so was the sun. Both cooled off, to put the matter briefly.

The Cardinals won the championship because their hometown rivals beat themselves with errors in the second game. Those second-game miscues, giving the Redbirds two unearned runs that loom particularly large in retrospect, typified, too, the main difference between the National and American League entries.

Essentially a superior team in all departments because they had more players of pre-war caliber, the Cards failed early to demonstrate any hitting or pitching edge over a team that was forced to battle to the very last day of the regular 154-game season for its pennant victory and rolled on to win two of the first three Series games. Later, once they regained the momentum that had enabled them to coast to their pennant, the Redbirds showed better punch and pitching than the Browns.

But from start to finish, the Birds showed and maintained a marked supremacy in one department—fielding!

That defensive difference, more than any other factor, tipped the scales in favor of the Cardinals, who took into the World Series a new National League record of .982 for highest team fielding percentage. One error, a harmless outfield juggle of a basehit, marred otherwise perfect Redbird defense play, while the Browns kicked in ten misplays, most of them damaging to the point that where in runs scored the Cards showed 16 to 12 for the American Leaguers, seven of the World Champion's scores were unearned. But none of the Browns' runs were of the unearned variety. The Cards, though slow to find their victory touch, refused to beat themselves . . . or to give the Browns any opportunities—or runs—the easy way.

Thanks to Brownie errors, the Redbirds scored unearned runs in all games except the first and fifth. But none of those gift runs meant so much to the Birds, hurt the Browns so severely, as the two that prolonged the second game into extra innings, at which time the Cards' only earned run of three gave them a victory and evened the Series.

The cold truth is that minus those second-game miscues, the Browns would have won three straight games, for they took the first and the third, and if that situation had existed, the Cardinals would have faced an obstacle no team has overcome in the 44-year history of World Series play. No team, three down, has ever come back to win the championship.

So, though the '44 World Series went to six games, the Browns, a team of destiny throughout the season, lost their golden opportunity in the second game. And particularly when the Cardinals romped off with the fourth game, thereby averting a 1-to-3 short end in games won, a World Series hole from which only the Pittsburgh Pirates of 1925 have been able to emerge victorious, by taking the final three contests from Washington, the outcome was no longer in doubt. The Cardinals had found themselves, period; the Browns, though unawed by the Redbirds' reputation, had found themselves lacking.

Seldom, if ever, since the World Series of 1905, in which the New York Giants won four of five games from the Philadelphia Athletics, a Series in which the losing team was shut out in every game, has pitching so completely prevailed as in the 1944 blue-ribbon, inter-league classic. There was no Christy Mathewson as an outstanding individual hurler to whitewash the opposition three times as he did back in '05. But the general effectiveness of the men on the mound this time was remarkable. Cardinal pitchers held the Browns to an average of 2 runs and 6 hits per game, the Browns' hurlers checked the Redbirds with 2.66 runs and 8.16 hits per contest.

The best indication of the brilliant pitching by both sides, however, was— in an era when strikeouts aren't so numerous—an all-time Series record for S.O.'s (49 by Cardinal hurlers, 43 by Browns) and another mark in the highest number of men left on base (51 Cardinals, 44 Browns).

Relief pitchers, the baseball firemen who cool enemy bats and save games, were especially distinguished. The Series was replete with instances where relief pitchers stepped into the breach and broke up rallies so that the largest single innings were a four-run third inning for the Browns in the third game, and a three-run fourth inning in the last game for the Cardinals, the only inning throughout the series in which the Redbirds scored more than one run.

The world's championship was the Cardinals' second in three years and their fifth all told, more than any other National League team holds. (The Yankees have won eight to lead the A. L.). And it was the National League's 16th world's championship. The American has won 25.

In the language of the baseball dugout, Luke Sewell had "more guts than a burglar" by taking a gamble unequaled in 15 years in the choice of an opening-day selection for a World Series. But a tall, thin man with a high collar and watery blue eyes, sitting less than a hundred feet away from the Browns' bench, could have told him that the risk isn't always as great as it seems.

On the opening game of the 1929 World Series between his Philadelphia Athletics and the Chicago Cubs, patriarchal Connie Mack, the tall thin man with the high collar and watery blue eyes, amazed experts and common garden-variety of fans alike by passing up his pitching aces, Lefty Grove and George Earnshaw, to start a graying veteran who for months had sat around just listening to his arteries harden. That was Howard Ehmke, who hadn't pitched a ball for two months. But with Chicago sluggers trained—physically and mentally—for the blistering fastball of Grove and Earnshaw, the ancient Mack had a hunch that Ehmke's slow curve and half-speed ball would throw the Cubs off stride. He gambled—and won. Ehmke gave up only three hits, struck out 13 batters for a series record that still stands, and beat the puzzled Chicagoans, 3 to 1.

Luke Sewell gambled, too, for the opening game of the 1944 World Series, where his blue-ribbon managerial predecessors since Mack in '29 had feared to do because of the obvious opportunity for grandstand managing and second-guessing if the longshot failed, and started Denny Galehouse, 32-year-old righthander who concluded the regular American League with only nine victories, one less than he lost. Sewell blandly shrugged off the 19 victories of Nelson Potter, the 17 of Jack Kramer, and told quizzical writers, already whetting their literary harpoons, that "I'm going to use Galehouse first if it rains until Christmas before we open."

It rained only until mid-morning of the scheduled day, however, and with a warm sun as critical an observant as the 33,242 shirt-sleeved spectators, Galehouse won as early as the third inning a ball game that was settled actually in the fourth when George McQuinn, lean Brownie first baseman, skipped a home run onto the rightfield roof.

The Cardinals had wasted Stan Musial's first-inning single and Marty Marion's second-inning double by the time Johnny Hopp and Ray Sanders pried open the last half of the third with sharp one-base hits that sent Bob Muncrief and Sig Jackucki into feverish activity in the Browns' bullpen. But Galehouse never flinched, and after Musial sacrificed the runners along and Walker Cooper was intentionally passed, filling the bases, he fanned Whitey Kurowski and forced Danny Litwhiler to tap to the infield. But he was really over the hump when he shook off a signal from his rookie catcher, Myron Hayworth, for the only time during the game and flung a fast third strike past Kurowski, best clutch hitter on the Cardinals.

The Browns, winning 2–1 on McQuinn's homer, which followed Gene

Moore's single, got no other hits in the game, thereby setting a World Series record for a game won on the fewest number of hits—two.

For Mort Cooper, the defeat was a repetition of previous starts against American League teams in inter-league play: a damaging home run ball. But for Sewell and his choice, Galehouse, who threw only thirty-six balls wide of the strike zone in nine innings, the victory represented a gamble that paid off—and as early as the third inning, too, for from that crucial third inning until the ninth, when they merely averted a shutout, the Cardinals never got a hit.

Sylvester Ulysses Donnelly—you can see why they call him "Blix"—could pitch as many years as Lou Diamond has time in the Marine Corps, but neither he nor 35,076 persons who gripped their seats could forget four innings of baseball (and one in particular) he pitched against the Browns in the second game of the 1944 World Series.

Donnelly, at 175 pounds and five-feet, nine-inches tall, physical measurements considered too chunky and too short for a pitcher, held the American League champions scoreless, allowed only two hits and struck out seven batters in that four-inning stretch. And his jug-handle curveball, sweeping so wide it seemed to detour by way of third base in its arc toward the plate, reached an eighth-inning height of perfection when he fanned three successive batters. That inning—the eighth—was the frame which really balanced the scales in favor of the Cardinals, though the game wasn't terminated until the eleventh.

Donnelly had waited a long time for that moment, when, as Max Lanier sagged on the ropes, ready for the knockout, and Mike Kreevich pranced around second, eager to romp home with the run that would break a 2–2 deadlock, Manager Billy Southworth wigwagged to the bullpen for Blix. Donnelly, 29 years old and serving his first full season with the Redbirds, had put in a lengthy minor league apprenticeship that included brilliant records at Springfield, Mo., Sacramento, Cal., and Rochester, N.Y.—and three no-hit games along the way, too. But by the time the Cards moved into the '44 World Series, brown-haired and brown-eyed Blix was still low man on the team's totem pole, for in the regular season he had pitched fewer innings, won fewer games, two, than any pitcher who was with the club all season. Yet, in that eighth-inning crisis Southworth played a hunch—he called it that himself—and, ignoring pitchers who had warmed up for the emergency, chose Donnelly. Sylvester Ulys—oh, hell, let's continue calling him Blix—had hurriedly tossed only a few pitches by the time Kreevich belted Lanier to the showers with an inning-opening double.

The side-armed Donnelly flung that big-breaking hook at Chet Laabs, Vern Stephens, and Mark Christman, heart of the Brownie batting order, and struck out the three of them. And though he condescended to yield an eleventh-inning double to George McQuinn, which Donnelly immediately thereafter nullified with a great fielding play on an intended sacrifice bunt, nipping Mac at third, Blix had blitzed the Browns for good back in the eighth.

Donnelly's work almost was equaled, though, by Nels Potter and Bob Muncrief, who pitched for the losers. Single runs by the Cardinals in the third and fourth innings were unearned, attributable to three of the Browns' four errors (Potter made two of them himself). But after George Moore's single, Red Hayworth's double, and Frank Mancuso's pinch single tied the score on the faltering Lanier, Muncrief seemed destined to fare better than Potter.

Trouble is the Browns didn't reckon with Donnelly or gray-thatched Ken O'Dea, Cardinal pinch-hitter extraordinary, who flushed home the winning run with a base hit in the eleventh, ending the first World Series game to go into extra innings since the fourth and last contest of the 1939 blue-ribbon set, won by the champion Yankees on ten innings from Cincinnati. And with Lanier and Donnelly flashing a strike-out ball, not overlooking the foul flies that spun skyward off Brownie bats, catcher Walker Cooper ended up with 15 putouts for an all-time World Series record for receivers.

The Cardinals caught "lightning in a bottle" in the third inning of the third game of the '44 World Series. The Redbirds understood, probably for the first time, what Lippy Leo Durocher meant when, stunned and bewildered, the garrulous manager of the Brooklyn Dodgers coined the expression as his team stumbled glassy-eyed into their Ebbets Field clubhouse after the next-to-last contest of the 1941 Series.

That was the day, you'll recall, that Brooklyn's beloved Bums, flying the banner of the National League against the world's champion Yankees, seemed about to even the inter-league classic at two games each, for they entered the last of the ninth inning leading 4–3 and husky Hugh Carey quickly retired two batters. But within one out of victory he was never to achieve, Casey threw a game-ending third strike that fooled Tommy Henrich, the hitter, and—more important—fooled Mickey Owen, the Brooklyn catcher. The ball squirted out of Owen's glove, Henrich reached base safely, and the floodgates opened. The Yankees, pardoned at the eleventh hour, quickly slugged Casey for four runs that beat the Dodgers and made them pushovers the next day, too. Brooklyn, Durocher mumbled unbelievingly, had caught "lightning in a bottle."

The imagery found a sequel as Ted Wilks, chunky rookie righthander of the Cardinals, who had won 17 games and lost only four in his freshman major league season (1944), retired the first two batters of the light-hitting Browns in the third inning of this year's third game. Even base-hits that followed off the bats of Gene Moore and Vern Stephens disturbed neither Wilks nor Billy Southworth, who ordered no activity in his bullpen. Only one out to go, and the Cardinals would protect that 1–0 lead gained in the first inning on Stephens' two-base error and Walker Cooper's single.

But Wilks never got that third out. George McQuinn, continuing his timely hitting, sliced a single to left. One run. Al Zarilla lined a hit to center. Two runs. Mark Christman belted a clothesline single over third base. Three runs. And the crowd of 34,737 roared, as head down, Wilks walked the last mile to the showers, and Fred Schmidt, who had warmed up hurriedly too late, came in and before getting that third out he fired a wild pitch. Four runs.

Those five straight hits with two outs, the lightning in the bottle, beat the Cardinals, for apple-cheeked Jack "Pretty Boy" Kramer, discharged Seabee pitching for the Browns, was toughest in the one exciting moment in which he needed to be most effective. And so he didn't need one of those four runs in the fatal third inning or two tallies added in the seventh.

An error gave the Cardinals a second unearned run in their half of the seventh, and though the Redbirds threatened in the eighth, Kramer called on cunning to aid a tiring right arm. Singles by Johnny Hopp and W. Cooper with one out brought up rangy Ray Sanders, slugging Cardinal first baseman, with Whitey Kurowski on deck. Luke Sewell stopped the game at that point to inquire about Kramer's condition, for the Brownie manager had Bob Muncrief and Boots Hollingsworth ready. Catcher Ray Hayworth and Kramer pleaded with him to let the pitcher stay in. Sewell agreed.

He doubted the wisdom of that decision a moment later, however, for firing five fastballs, Kramer ran the count to 3–2 to Sanders and had to bring the payoff pitch in to the long-distance hitter. But, with Sewell and an appreciative crowd squirming, rooting one way or the other, the handsome guy changed to a slow curve. Flatfooted and leaning in for another fastball, Sanders was caught off balance, watched the third strike sail past. And when in the parlance of the baseball trade Kramer "pulled the string" again on Kurowski and forced him to lift a harmless fly to the outfield, the Browns had a 6–2 victory and a temporary lead in the Series.

The fourth game was over on brawny Sig Jakucki's twelfth pitch of the first inning, though you couldn't know at the time that Harry (The Cat) Brecheen, short and wiry southpaw of the Cardinals, could dominate a World Series contest with his limited tools of the pitching trade.

The twelfth pitch that ended the game almost before it began was a fastball that Stan Musial, brilliant young Redbird outfielder, whacked to the roof of the right-field pavillion for a home run, scoring Johnny Hopp ahead of him. The two runs were sufficient. The final score was 5–1.

The two runs were enough because Brecheen, carrying a heavy load, pitched masterfully, particularly in the pinches. The Browns, who won a pennant because they made the most of their infrequent hits, found their season-long asset missing for the first time in the Series. They staked themselves to nine hits, but the ten men they left on base served only to underscore The Cat's excellence in moments of distress. Bud Byerly early, then Blix Donnelly late, labored in the bullpen, just in case a game so important to the Cardinal cause got out of control. But the pair wasted a pleasant afternoon.

Brecheen, though he won 16 games in the National League season, lacks the high hard one, the fastball so desired in the evaluation of a pitcher; and his curve doesn't break sharply. But for a left-hander he has good control, varies his delivery from sidearm to three-quarters overhand, and he mixes the speed of his pitches—medium fast, slow, slower, and slowest.

In the fourth Series game, Brecheen needed help only twice. Mike Kreevich singled in the first inning, and George Moore drove a long fly toward the right centerfield wall, where Johnny Hopp, racing across, made a clutching leap of the ball. In the eighth, Moore's walk and Vern Stephen's single gave the Browns men on first and third, none out, and Chet Laabs, author of already two hits, at the plate. He hit hard again a ground smash close to second base. But Brownie partisans among the 35,455 spectators groaned as the long-legged Marty Marion, a great defensive shortstop, ranged over and speared the ball with his glove, starting a double play on which the American Leaguers' only run crossed the plate.

The Cardinals backed Brecheen with their first solid attack of the Series. They routed Jakucki, who had beat the Yankees in the vital final game of the American League season. The big blond righthander went out for a pinch-hitter after yielding five hits and four runs in three innings; and the National League champions picked up seven more hits and a run off the combined pitching of Boots Hollingsworth and Tex Shirley. Musial added a double and a single to that home run on the twelfth pitch of the game—the drive that tied the Series at two victories each.

Dennis Galehouse, trying for his second victory against the Cardinals, threw only two pitches he regretted, a slider and a fastball, both of which cleared the Sportsman's Park right field barrier for home runs. But even if he hadn't made those two pitching mistakes, Galehouse couldn't have won that day from the big fellow with the baggy pants. Not the Morton Cecil Cooper of the fifth game of the World Series.

Those home runs, Ray Sanders' in the sixth inning on a 3–1 slider and Danny Litwhiler's in the eighth on a first-pitch fastball, came with the bases empty and were the Cardinals' only runs of the game. But the Redbirds won 2 to 0, for the Browns, outhitting the National Leaguers, seven to six, got only one runner around to third base. That fifth game M. Cooper was not the same guy American League players had faced in previous World Series and All-Star games.

American Leaguers knew Cooper as a nice-looking big guy, kind to his mother, who served a fat home-run ball and who had won only one game from them on seven tries. Mort might be some pumpkins in the National League, where he won more than 20 games a season for three consecutive years, but to the American League he was just the big fellow with the baggy pants who foolishly tried to defy superstition with a big No. 13 on the back of his uniform.

Bur M. Cooper had his "inning"—nine of them, in fact—and even though Galehouse pitched excellent baseball, he faced defeat. Home runs or no, the Cardinals would have scored a run sooner or later, anyway, and that fifth game Cooper couldn't be beat—or scored upon. He pitched the best ball game of his career, and in the best traditions of the legendary Dizzy Dean, whom he emulated, rared back and "fogged 'em" past the determined Browns. Fastball, fast curve, slow curve, forkball, and screwball were included in the assortment the six-foot two-inch, 210-pound righthander used to give the Cardinals the edge in victories for the first time in the Series.

Baggy-Pants struck out 12 Brownies, a performance only one shy of the all-time World Series record established by Howard Ehmke of the A's in 1929, and with Galehouse fanning 10 Cardinals the total of 22 in a game bettered by one the old mark set in 1906 (Chicago White Sox vs. Chicago Cubs) and equaled in '29 (Philadelphia Athletics vs. the Cubs).

The Browns troubled Cooper once, but when they did, Mort not only powered the ball past hitters who sought to give him the traditional American League going-over, he also helped himself defensively. Mike Kreevich singled to right field as a starter, and with the game scoreless at that point, Luke Sewell played percentage and ordered a sacrifice bunt by Gene Moore. Moore bunted along the first-base line, but the hulking Cooper, no gazelle and ordinarily no "fifth infielder" on defense, pounced on the ball and caught Kreevich at second with a snap throw. Then, after Vern Stephens singled Moore to third and dangerous George McQuinn walked, Cooper silenced the Browns and their supporters among the 36,568 spectators by fanning Al Zarilla and

Mark Christman. So effective in that pinch was the big fellow with the baggy pants that the third strike on both hitters was called. They couldn't hit or even swing at something they couldn't see.

The Browns switched to pinch-hitters in a desperate ninth-inning effort. Three of them came up—Milt Byrnes, Chet Laabs, and Mike Chartak. Cooper wiped the perspiration from his fat face and fanned the side.

Wild pitches have lost too many ball games, including one in the 1927 World Series when Pittsburgh's John Miljus shot an uncontrolled delivery over his catcher's head to give the Yankees—as if they needed any help—the winning run and a fourth straight victory. But, incongruous as it may seem, a wild pitch won a game for the pitcher who threw it in the sixth and final encounter of this year's blue-ribbon event of baseball.

Max Lanier threw the wild pitch, and the chunky lefthander was credited with his first World Series victory in four starts over a two-year period. But if he hadn't skipped a fastball into the dirt past catcher Walker Cooper in the sixth inning of the sixth game, Lanier and the Cardinals might not have achieved that triumph. In that event, the '44 World Series would have gone the seven-game limit for only the seventh time in 43 years.

The score was 3-to-1, Redbirds, at the time of Lanier's wild pitch. The southpaw had yielded a run in the second inning on Chet Laabs' triple and George McQuinn's single, and in the fourth the Cardinals had staked themselves to three runs, their largest rally of the Series, knocking out Nelson Potter, regular-season No. 1 guy of the Browns' pitching staff. The weak-sisters of the Redbird lineup, Emil Verban, who became the Cards' batting leader, and Lanier, normally an automatic out, delivered the most important hits. But Vern Stephens committed a serious error, characterizing the American League Champions' damaging fielding lapses throughout the post-season play, that contributed to Potter's exit.

Meanwhile, the Browns had failed twice to capitalize on Lanier's wildness. Max bore down to protect his lead. Then came the Americans' sixth and, with one out, Laabs and McQuinn drew the fourth and fifth passes the lefthander had issued. With two righthanded hitters, Mark Christman and Red Hayworth, next at bat, Billy Southworth halted the game to talk to Lanier, who—the Cardinal manager asserted later—assured him he was okay. Max hitched up his belt, with Christman at the plate, and fired a wild pitch—THE wild pitch—that sent Laabs to third, Hayworth to second, and Lanier to the dugout. Southworth rushed out, took the ball from the pitcher's hand and beckoned for Ted Wilks in the leftfield headquarters of the Knights of the Bullpen.

Lanier, angered, threw his glove into the dugout, but that was nothing to what Wilks, batted out in less than three innings in the third game, threw at the Browns. The freshman righthander stopped the Browns without a run, as Luke Sewell ignored the opportunity to call upon his lefthanded pinchhitters. Christman grounded to Whitey Kurowski, whose accurate throw to the plate caught Laabs coming in standing up, and then Hayworth flied to center field.

The Browns had reached Lanier for three hits, but in his three and two-thirds innings, Wilks held them hitless, and when in the ninth he fanned the last two men to face him, the Cardinals were world's champions and the 1944 World Series had featured more strikeouts (92) than any played previously. (The old record was 87, set by the Cardinals and Philadelphia A's in 1931.)

But if Hubert Max Lanier, who has as much stuff as any pitcher in the game, had not wild-pitched in the sixth inning of the sixth game, just after Southworth's first visit to the mound, he might have lasted long enough for Christman or Hayworth, both better hitters against southpaws, to deliver a base-clearing hit. Undoubtedly, he was wobbling.

"I knew," said Southworth amid the Cardinals' celebration in their clubhouse, as 31,630 overcoated fans filed from the park, "that Max was forcing himself. And when he threw that wild pitch, I was damned sure he was."

The first outsider to rush into the dressing room victory celebration of the champions was Manager Luke Sewell of the losing Brownies. He stuck out his hand and congratulated Billy Southworth.

The gesture was symbolic of the clean spirit and good sportsmanship apparent throughout the entire series. There were, with but one exception, no beefs. Neither team engaged in jockeying.

The only fly in the pie was a tiff between Emil Verban, Redbird second baseman, and a Brown man who happens to own the club—Donald P. Barnes. Verban and Barnes had a skirmish over tickets given to Emil's wife, who found herself seated behind a post.

As the final out of the final game, as the other Birds raced to the dugout, slapping each other on the back, Verban stepped hurriedly over to Barnes' box and yelled, "Now you're sitting behind a post." Not a bad crack at that.

Later, in the dressing room of the winners, Barnes congratulated Southworth, and then said flatly, "You've got one louse on your ball club, Verban." That was about all, except while the handshaking went on, the irrepressible Emil hollered to a teammate, "This oughtta cool that Barnes off."

All in all, the verbal set-to rated but a small place in the otherwise harmonious proceedings.

Reminders of the war were everywhere in St. Louis during the 1944 World Series. During the opening game, a bomber cruised over Sportsman's Park several times before banking sharply to give its crew a better view of the game. The Series edition of the Sporting News *featured Marine PFC Bill Veeck, with a picture of Veeck with his GI haircut, "somewhere in the Pacific." But one of the oddest reminders came about over the apartment that managers Bill Southworth and Luke Sewell were able to share during the housing shortage because one of them was always out of town. Hall of Fame Research Director Tim Wiles, writing on the occasion of the 50th anniversary of the Streetcar Series, tells the story of how the managers dealt with their housing situation when their pennant-winning teams put them in St. Louis at the same time.*

Full House
Tim Wiles

Luke Sewell and Billy Southworth had a problem on their hands. The managers of the St. Louis Browns and Cardinals, respectively, had agreed to share an apartment during the 1944 season, never dreaming that the hapless Browns would rebound from their sixth-place finish in 1943 to take the American League pennant on the last day of the season. The Cardinals figured to have a shot at the World Series, as they had split the last two with the Yankees. But the Browns did win the pennant by half a game, and soon the two men were wondering who would get to stay in the apartment at Lindell Towers at 3745 Lindell Blvd.

During the regular season, scheduling practice held that both teams would never be at home—they shared Sportsman's Park—at the same time. Ditto with the apartment. When Sewell's Browns were headed out on the road, he put his wife, Edna, on the train back home to Akron, along with his two teenage daughters, Suzanne and Lois.

When the road trip ended, the Browns returned home to find Sportsman's Park vacated, and the Sewells returned to a clean and empty apartment, as Mabel Southworth and nine-year-old daughter Carol were on their way back to the farm in Columbus, Ohio.

The system worked well for both families, trying to economize during wartime, and also to do their part to ease the resulting housing shortage. The men of the house had a space crunch of their own, sharing the flat as they did with two wives and three daughters. Luke and Billy got one closet to split up between them, with Sewell's clothes on one end and Southworth's on the other.

The novel living arrangement had received brief mention in the local paper as the Browns made their rush toward the pennant, winning 11 of their last 12 games. "Mrs. Sewell would like to meet Mrs. Southworth some day but never has," declared a local paper, "as they are never in town at the same time." What will happen at home, asked the society columnist, if the Browns pull it out and win their first pennant? Mrs. Sewell found it a simple matter, declaring that she and Luke would stay put, and the Southworths would look for a new place.

The space crunch got worse as Luke Sewell, hoping for a Browns victory, had invited his mother from out of state to watch her first World Series. Eight people in one apartment just wouldn't do, and the idea of rival World Series managers trying to share the same living room while they thought out the next day's lineup just didn't seem plausible.

Once the pennant was clinched, the two gentlemen decided to settle the matter the old-fashioned way. They flipped a coin. Sewell won the toss, thus making Edna's confident prediction come true. The Southworths were on their own. Thankfully, another resident of the building stepped forth and offered his apartment to the Southworths, as he would be away on business during the World Series.

Meanwhile, back on the field, Sewell's upstart Browns won two of the first three games, surprising the Cardinals, who'd just gone 105–49 to post three consecutive 100-win seasons. But the Cardinals returned to form and won the Series in six games, ending the Browns' title hopes and sending both the Sewells and the Southworths back to Ohio.

Slaughter's Dash and the Brownies' Flight

The Cardinals won their third National League pennant in four years in 1946, but the powerhouse Boston Red Sox were the heavy favorites in the World Series. The Cardinals struggled against the Dodgers all season before defeating them in a best-of-three playoff after the teams finished in a tie. The Red Sox ran away with the American League pennant, finishing 12 games ahead of the defending champion Detroit Tigers. The 1946 World Series was cast as a showcase for MVPs Stan Musial and Ted Williams, but Harry "the Cat" Brecheen, a .500 pitcher for the season, stole the spotlight by becoming the first left-hander in World Series history to win three games. Brecheen became the Series MVP, but it was Enos "Country" Slaughter who stole the Series in a mad dash around the bases that still has baseball fans debating whether it was Slaughter's daring or Johnny Pesky's mental lapse that made the difference.

Hall of Fame writer Fred Lieb covered the 1946 World Series and wrote this report for the Sporting News. *Nearly thirty years later, another Hall of Fame writer, Bob Broeg, who also covered the 1946 World Series, wrote his account of Slaughter's dash in the* Sporting News *after watching Series highlights on* The Way It Was *PBS series.*

Cards Champs Sixth Time Because of Old Fight
Frederick G. Lieb ——————————————————————————————

The never-give-up Cardinals are on the top roost again. Battling against odds—yes, seven times the bookmakers issued figures and seven times they made the Boston Red Sox favorites—Sam Breadon's Redbirds came from behind to become 1946 champions of the world by beating Tom Yawkey's Millionaires, four games to three. It was the sixth time in nine series since 1926 that baseball's highest honors have gone to the St. Louis Cardinals, directed by Breadon, the former New York bank clerk who in 1902 went west in search of fame and fortune and now, after 44 years, is still gathering both.

In fact, of the eight world's championships won by the National League in the last 21 years, six have been captured by Breadon's colorful Redbirds under five different managers—Rogers Hornsby, Gabby Street, Frankie Frisch, Billy Southworth, and now the 1946 freshman skipper, Eddie Dyer. "I guess now they'll let me play on the Varsity," laughs Dyer.

Following an old Cardinal custom, incidentally a most beneficial one financially to Lucky Sam, the Redbirds won this one by going to the full limit of seven games. It was the fourth time the Cards took a seven-game Series, and as in 1926 and 1934, they did it the hard way, coming from behind to win the sixth and seventh games. It also was the fifth time the Cardinals dropped the first game and still won the Series.

Cut A. L. Advantage to 26 to 17

The victory was the seventeenth for the National League in its 43 post-season Blue Ribbon Series with American League champions, and reduced the lead of the Harridge loop to 26 to 17. It followed up the newly acquired knack of National League champions winning in the even years, as the Cincinnati Reds won in 1940 and the Cardinals in 1942, 1944, and 1946. And for National League men, it was sweet revenge for the humiliating 12 to 0 defeat the senior circuit suffered in the All-Star game at Fenway Park, the home of the defeated Red Sox, on July 9.

Despite the fact that the Red Sox stayed in the Series until the final put-out, the defeat was a bitter one for Joe Cronin and his team. What made it especially painful was that it was the first suffered by a Boston team in a modern World's Series, the Red Sox having won previously in 1903, 1912, 1915, 1916, and 1918 and the Braves in 1914. Winning their pennant in a romp, the Red Sox were supposed to be playing a team tired and frayed from the hot National League race and the subsequent playoff series with Brooklyn. Smart betting commissioners made the Red Sox favorites at odds which now look silly. It was this underdog Cardinal team, considered by many as a World's Series pushover, which smashed the legend of Red Sox World's Series invincibility.

Never Ahead Till Seventh Game

The Cardinals never were ahead until the seventh game, and on the very last play of the game, a force at second, a fraction of a second prevented the Red Sox from scoring the tying run in the ninth. Red Schoendienst slightly fumbled Tom McBride's last grounder; the ball seemed to run up Red's arm like a mouse, but the freckled second baseman managed to get hold of it and toss the ball to Marty Marion for the final out. Had the throw reached Marion a moment later, Paul Campbell, Rudy York's pinch-runner, would have been across the plate with the tying run.

Despite the closeness of the Series, and of the last game, the final averages show that the Cardinals outbatted, outfielded, and outpitched their American League opponents. Eddie Dyer outgeneraled Joe Cronin, and when the final chips were down the Redbirds outfought and outhustled the more famous players on the American League squad.

Helped by the 20-hit game of October 10 at Fenway Park, the National leaguers outbatted the Americans, .259 to .240, and with only four errors to ten for the Red Sox, the Cards had an edge in fielding, .984 to .963. The Red Sox were jittery in the field, especially in the early games, and Johnny Pesky, generally regarded as the shortstop of the year, made as many errors as the entire St. Louis team.

Pesky also had a fatal mental lapse in the eighth inning of the seventh game, when it took him too long to decide what to do with the ball after Slaughter showed his intention of trying to score from first on Harry Walker's double to left center. Most writers in the press box thought Enos was running to sure death. Pesky said he did not expect Country to try to score, and held up a moment deciding where to throw. When he did get off his belated peg to the plate, it was late and too short, and Slaughter scored the run which made the Cardinals World's Champions.

Even with Howie Pollet, their star pitcher during the season, handicapped with a pulled shoulder muscle, the Cardinals also got an edge in hurling, where little Harry Brecheen, a 15–15 pitcher in the National League, with some help from Dickson and Munger, was too much for that famed staff of Tex Hughson, Dave Ferriss, Joe Dobson, and Mickey Harris.

Brecheen entered a new name among the World's Series immortals when he emerged from the Series as the first lefthander to win three games in a modern World's Series and the first pitcher to post three victories in 26 years. After pitching two triumphs, in which he gave up only one run, Brecheen was rushed to Murry Dickson's rescue in the eighth inning of the seventh game after only one day of rest. The Cat's arm was tired; his nerves were frayed; he had a slight fever, but the chips were down and twice Harry turned the Red Sox batting terrors back. George Munger, the fellow who came back from the Army in August, won an important game, though he had that 12-run, 20-hit barrage to make the day easy for him.

Joe Dobson, the least favored of Boston's pitching Big Four, proved Cronin's best pitcher. He turned in one four-hit game and did not give up an earned run in 12 innings. Neither Hughson nor Harris brought in a victory, and after Ferriss pitched a six-hit shutout in his first World's Series effort, the famous Red Sox sophomore, with a 25 and 6 A. L. record, was knocked out when he tried to repeat.

Joe's Mound Aces Jolted

The two most heart-rending games in Cronin's book were when Hughson was jolted off the rubber in the fourth game, and Ferriss in the seventh. Joe had jockeyed his staff so that if the Series went to a seventh game, he would have Boo to send after it. Ferriss failed, but Cronin later came in for plenty of criticism himself, when he pitched Bob Klinger, the N. L. discard, after his team tied the score in the eighth inning of this game.

Next to Brecheen, there were so many Cardinal heroes that it would be impossible to name just a No. 2 standout. There was Harry Walker, who was only a part-time player, but who hit .412 and drove in six runs, more than any other contestant, and Enos Slaughter, who was a "toughie" for the Red Sox all during the Series, though painfully hurt on the right elbow in the fifth game. The two young Cardinal catchers, Joe Garagiola and Del Rice, were magnificent, getting nine hits between them, in sharp contrast to the one lone bingle for Hal Wagner and Roy Partee, the Boston receivers. While Stan Musial hit below expectations, five of his six hits were for extra bases, and Terry Moore put on a center field display such as only the St. Louis home bred can give it.

Highlighting the Red Sox were Rudy York, the big first baseman, who won Boston's first two games with home runs, and Bobby Doerr, second baseman, who hit .409, and played brilliantly in the field.

The goat of the Series unquestionably was Ted Williams, fabulous left fielder of the Red Sox, who hit a poor .200 with only five singles and one run driven in for the seven games.

Enos's Dash to Destiny Revived
Bob Broeg

If nostalgia is golden, shake hands with a millionaire.

I've just seen an episode in the delightful *The Way It Was* series offered by some 250 Public Broadcasting Service television stations, which is another way to say that educational TV has discovered sports.

The event I saw recaptured on film and recapped in conversation was the 1946 World Series, the one in which Enos Slaughter scored from first on a king-sized single to give the Cardinals, a 7–20 underdog, a seven-game upset victory over the powerful Red Sox.

To serve as window-dressing Curt Gowdy had Slaughter, Stan Musial, and Harry Walker of the '46 Cardinals, as well as Joe Cronin, Bobby Doerr, and Johnny Pesky of the Red Sox, as guests.

Additionally, because the program was filmed several months ago, the late Dizzy Dean was there, as big as life, and moreover, Ol' Diz, who broadcast games of both the Cardinals and the old St. Louis Browns in '46, narrated the film clips of a half-hour show that zipped away all too fast.

The '46 Series is etched so indelibly in this memory because (1) I'd worked in Boston just before going into the Marines and (2) with World War II happily in the past, I'd traveled the season with the Cardinals, the first and only time I'd been on the road with a pennant winner in 13 seasons.

First and foremost, the '46 Series will be remembered because of Slaughter's spectacular sprint to win the seventh game. I can remember a cold opening trip of the season in Chicago, where the short, stocky outfield veteran beat out an infield hit, and Jim Gallagher, then general manager of the Cubs, growled from around his cigar:

"That big-rumped baboon goes into the Army, drinks beer for three years and comes out running faster than before."

The season was historic, too, because it produced the first playoff in major-league history. Down the stretch, one night or, more accurately, early morning at the Moravian, a one-man club operated in Philadelphia by the late Herb (Curly) Perry, the poor man's Toots Shor, I was introduced by the effervescent host to a quiet, dignified chap he had pointed out as a big-time gambler.

"I don't care to talk to sportswriters," the man said coldly and before I could tell him where to go, with or without odds, he offered an interesting explanation.

"I don't mean to offend," he said, "but once, years ago, a sportswriter tipped me off how soused he's seen old Pete Alexander the morning of a big game and I plunged heavily against Alex and lost. So I decided to rise and fall on my own judgment, not any newspaper's."

Fair enough but . . .

"So," the gambler went on, "I'll tell you something: If your club wins the pennant, I'm going to take St. Louis. The reason? Because I think Harry Brecheen is a blue-chip, big-game pitcher."

Brecheen was only a 15–15 pitcher in '46, but in view of the fact that The Cat won three games that Series, I often wonder if that insulting so-and-so wise-guy gambler really put his money where his mouth was.

If he did he cleaned up because, as mentioned, the Bosox were favored heavily after having cantered to the pennant. The Red Sox won almost too easily and too soon, creating a problem, as Cronin related on *The Way It Was* rerun 28 years later.

To keep Boston sharp while the National League pennant was decided in the best-of-three series of train travel between St. Louis and New York (Brooklyn), the American League put together an All-Star team that played the Red Sox informally. Unfortunately, a misbehaving knuckleball from Washington's lefthanded Mickey Haefner injured Ted Williams' right elbow.

The Sox tried to downplay the injury, but Williams wasn't himself in the Series, troubled by the elbow and the pinpoint control of St. Louis' lefthanded pitching, especially by Brecheen, who kept his screwball down and in on the slender slugger so that Teddy Ball's best shots were long fouls.

Williams, getting only five singles in the seven games of the World Series in which he played, batted just .200 and took the defeat hard, as captured in an unforgettable photograph showing the handsome curlyhead bowed as he sat slumped before his locker in the visitors' clubhouse at old Sportsman's Park here. With class, Ted contributed his losers' share of $2,140.89 to equipment manager and clubhouse confidante Johnny Orlando.

For the Series, Eddie Dyer, St. Louis's freshman manager, adopted a version of Cleveland Skipper Lou Boudreau's radical shift for Williams, with shortstop Marty Marion the only infielder on the left side of second base.

Just once in the Series, Williams gave in. When he did, a Boston afternoon paper bannered on Page One in 72-point type: "TED BUNTS."

Williams's St. Louis counterpart, Stan Musial, who had hit .365 in the regular season and shifted to first base in a critical mid-season move that won him a Most Valuable Player, batted just .222, but five of The Man's six hits were for extra bases and he drove in four runs to his rival's one.

One of his hits was a triple to center field at Fenway Park, and Terry Moore, the Cardinals' captain then, has rerun his private film of the Series time and again to show the speed with which a young Musial sped around the bases.

The Red Sox won the first game on a tenth-inning homer by Rudy York, 3–2, but the inside story of a tense moment didn't come out until much later. Dyer's pitching protégé, classy 21-game southpaw Howard Pollet, battling a bad back, hung on to a 2–1 lead in the ninth.

With the tying run on second, two out, and righthanded hitting Tommy McBride pinch-batting, Pollet shook off a breaking-ball sign relayed by 20-year-old catcher Joe Garagiola from the bench. Garagiola glanced again at the Cardinals' dugout and Dyer repeated the signal, which the young batterymate relayed to his pitcher.

Pollet, against his better wishes, threw the two-strike curve, and McBride bounced it into the hole between third and short for a game-tying hit.

Dyer, unhappy about having lost without permitting his best pitcher to throw the pitch he wanted, encountered a second problem when Slaughter, a grumbler, groused that he could have scored a precious run earlier if Mike Gonzales, coaching at third base, hadn't held him up.

"All right, all right," said the manager irritated. "If it happens again and you think you can make it, go ahead and I'll back you."

So it came down to the seventh game, even-Stephen. Slaughter, hit painfully in the elbow with a pitch by Joe Dobson in the fifth game, was in right field against Dr. Robert F. Hyland's advice. Old Enos, stubbornly, had a date with destiny.

After Murry Dickson was removed in the eighth inning, leading 3–1, with two on and none out, the little righthander's road roommate, Brecheen, retired two men before Dom DiMaggio hit a game-tying double and then pulled up lame and was forced to leave the lineup.

A miffed Dickson dressed and left the park, driving around to listen on his car radio, as Slaughter singled in the home eighth off Bob Klinger. With two out, the country boy from Carolina was off and running even before Walker sliced what amounted to a long single to left-center.

By the time he reached second base, Slaughter, aware that Leon Culberson had replaced DiMaggio in center field, had made up his mind to score. So he ran through a hand-wringing Gonzales's stop sign at third base, and Pesky, taking the relay at shortstop with the crowd roaring, paused for just a fraction of a second, then threw off balance.

Actually, Slaughter scored easily in advance of the throw that sagged. Look at it again friends: As I've said all along, Slaughter was the hero, but Pesky was no goat.

The Cardinals survived the defection of ace pitcher Max Lanier to the Mexican League in 1946 and went on to win their sixth world championship in twenty years. But a year later, they fell victim to the Dodgers and National League Rookie of the Year Jackie Robinson and finished in second place. The impact of Robinson on the Cardinals' 1947 season has long been a subject of debate, controversy, and denial, but James N. Giglio in Musial: From Stash to Stan the Man *wrote a balanced summary of the Cardinals' reaction, especially among those players from the Deep South. Giglio's account ranges from a threatened Cardinal strike to the infamous Slaughter spiking of Robinson. It was a breakthrough year for baseball, but "a troubling year" for the Cardinals.*

A Troubling Year
James N. Giglio

Once the 1947 season began with Robinson playing first base, general manager Herb Pennock of the Philadelphia Phillies brazenly demanded, however, that Rickey keep Robinson from the road trip to Philadelphia. Robinson also received countless death threats through the mail. Some fans in Philadelphia, Cincinnati, and St. Louis were particularly militant in shouting racial epithets or booing Robinson. Often the enthusiastic cheering of blacks, who now flocked to the ballparks in great numbers, succeeded in drowning out the abuse. In St. Louis record crowds, including many blacks, attended the Cardinals-Dodgers series that spring. One black newspaper, the *St. Louis Argus,* gratuitously admonished blacks "to act like human beings" at the ballpark, "not like a tribe of cannibals."

The greatest challenge Robinson faced came from opposing players, some of whom were blatant racists or afraid that integration might cost them their jobs. Indeed, Robinson encountered strong opposition from his own teammates, especially from the Dixie contingent. The Dodgers probably led the National League in the number of southerners on their roster. Some of them, steered by the popular Dixie Walker, the "people's cherce," initially refused to play with Robinson and asked to be traded. Only after Kentuckian Pee Wee Reese befriended him and he had proved himself on the field did most of the club rally behind Robinson, especially when he faced relentless racist abuse from opposing dugouts. No one carried it to greater extremes than Alabaman Ben Chapman, the manager of the Phillies. He encouraged his club to bombard Robinson with racial venom arguably unequaled in the annals of the game. Chapman justified this by insisting that taunting was common practice against rookies. More than verbal invective, Robinson encountered beanings at the plate and spikings in the field.

Much talk centered on a player strike against Robinson that spring. The reported ringleader, Walker, had contacts on other teams, including brother Harry on the Cardinals prior to his trade to the Phillies. A conspiracy of silence and denial has persisted among the surviving participants, most of whom refuse to admit to any anti-Robinson activity. They have faced the embarrassment of being on the wrong side of history. No club has met greater criticism for its role in a proposed strike than the St. Louis Cardinals.

The focus on the Cardinals seems unfair given the opposition to Robinson on other clubs, including his own. Outfielder Al Gionfriddo, who began the season with Pittsburgh, insisted fifty years later that "every team had voted on whether to play the Dodgers." Gionfriddo also confirmed a planned strike on opening day with Dixie Walker as organizer. The Pirates, according to Gionfriddo, decided to adopt a wait-and-see approach since there was some question as to whether Robinson would make the Dodger club. Evidence exists that the Cubs voted to strike on opening day. Two surviving Cubbies, pitcher Hank Wyse and catcher Dewey Williams, participated in the vote and understood that other teams were balloting too. What prevented the strike from occurring is uncertain. Williams claimed that before the game the team awaited a call from Walker, which never came. Wyse insisted that a telegram came from the league office that said that "anybody that [*sic*] didn't play would be barred for life." Williams remembered team members felt that if "a colored player" must play they wanted it to be Campanella, who was "a lot nicer." Robinson, he said, "was too brash—another [Ed] Stanky" of the Dodgers. Consequently, according to Wyse, Cub starting pitchers had standing instructions to deck Robinson: "Paul Erickson knocked him down four times before [Erickson] came up to hit. . . . We put in another pitcher so they couldn't get back at him," Wyse explained.

The Cardinals' hostility toward Robinson easily matched that of the Dodgers and a few other clubs. Next to the Dodgers, the Redbirds had more players from the Deep South than any other team in the league, including Marty Marion of South Carolina, Terry Moore of Alabama, Enos Slaughter of North Carolina, Harry Walker of Mississippi, Howie Pollet of Louisiana, and Ken Burkhart of Tennessee—the first three the reputed ringleaders. Some, though tough and competitive to the core, were perfectly capable of treating Robinson humanely. This was particularly so of Marion, whom Robinson said "was always nice to me." Robinson remembered one game in which he slid into Marion at second base. Marion picked him up "anxiously" and asked if he were hurt. Even so, most southerners were victims of their culture and responded predictably on issues relating to integration.

Racism, however, ranged far beyond Dixie; in the North it prevented Robinson from staying with teammates in the Ben Franklin Hotel in Philadelphia, misnamed as "the City of Brotherly Love." It had a stronger hold in the Midwest and the upper South. In the St. Louis press, sportswriters expressed, at best, little empathy toward Robinson. The St. Louis-based *Sporting News* had earlier opposed the integration of baseball. The virtual war the Cardinals waged with the Dodgers throughout the 1940s compounded the problem. Not only black, Robinson happened to be Dodger black as well.

Musial had little to say in his autobiography about Robinson. He mentioned elsewhere that he had watched Robinson play on an "all-colored team" after the 1946 season while barnstorming with Bob Feller's squad. Robinson made little impression on him as a ballplayer because of his short, choppy swing and his lack of grace in the field. Upon hearing of Robinson's promotion to the Dodgers, Musial remembered that the atmosphere seemed unready for a "colored" player, an expression often used at that time. Musial later told sportswriter Roger Kahn of the *New York Herald Tribune* that he heard talk among the Cardinals about Robinson: "It was rough and racial." But he never admitted that it went beyond that. In his autobiography, he said only that a strike vote had never occurred.

Other Cardinal players deny any discussion of a strike. Slaughter later implausibly wrote that "we hadn't said one word to each other about the Robinson incident." Red Schoendienst also later claimed that "nobody ever said anything to me about [a strike]," while Marion failed to recall discussion of a strike in the clubhouse. Supposedly the only Cardinal who took the strike talk seriously was Dick Sisler, who told historian Jules Tygiel in the 1970s that "very definitely there was something going on . . . whereby they said they weren't going to play." Sisler contended that the strike planning came from older players.

On May 9, Stanley Woodward, the distinguished sports editor of the *New York Herald Tribune,* first broke the news of a threatened Cardinals player strike against the Dodgers. Woodward received that information from Cecil Rutherford Rennie, a *Herald Tribune* sportswriter, who had heard the story from a concerned Dr. Hyland, the Cardinals' team physician, over a few drinks in early May. Rennie immediately telephoned Woodward, explaining that he could not write the piece because of his relationship with Hyland. Woodward, after checking some of the sources, decided to write it himself.

According to Woodward, Cardinal players, after talking with other National Leaguers that spring, had discussed striking against the Dodgers in Brooklyn on the opening game of the series on May 6. Since the Cardinals would also play the Dodgers in St. Louis on May 20, some thought that a more opportune date to respond. Either way, this action, it was hoped, would set off a general strike involving other National League clubs for the purpose of terminating Robinson's stay.

Breadon, who got wind of the scheme from Hyland, flew to New York. While there he conferred with his players; what he heard disturbed him enough to act. Recognizing that a racial conflict would devalue a franchise he secretly contemplated selling, he went to the New York office of National League president Ford Frick, who through Breadon left the Cardinals with the following message: "If you [strike], you will be suspended from the league. You will find that the friends you think you have in the press box will not support you. You will be outcasts. I do not care if half the league strikes. Those who do it will encounter quick retribution. All will be suspended and I don't care if it wrecks the National League for five years. This is the United States of America and one citizen has as much right to play as another. . . . You will find if you go through with your intention that you have been guilty of complete madness." Never had the wishy-washy Frick acted so forcefully. In a follow-up, Woodward acknowledged that he may have had some of the particulars incorrect, but he stood behind the story. Viewing his exposé as public service, he wagered that "it can now be honestly doubted that the boys from the Hookworm Belt would have the nerve to foist their quaint sectional folklore on the rest of the country." Woodward's story probably stiffened the backbone of club owners, who now leaned on their players to keep playing. For his efforts Woodward received the E. P. Dutton Award for the best sports reporting for 1947.

To the Cardinals and their supporters, Woodward's revelation represented nothing more than "barnyard journalism"—a phrase Broeg later employed. Broeg contended that while a few players were upset, the Cardinals' opposition to Robinson was no different from other teams, and it did not lead to a strike vote. Breadon's trip to New York, he insisted, came because of the poor performance of the ball club, accentuated, Breadon thought, by the Robinson matter. An overreacting Breadon asked Moore and Marion in New York their opinion of manager Dyer and whether they intended to strike. Despite supposed reassurances, he still went to Frick's office, concerned about a possible boycott, Broeg admitted. It was then that Frick warned Breadon of the obvious consequences of the strike. A couple of days later, Breadon telephoned Frick from St. Louis; he called the affair "a tempest in a teapot," nothing more than a few players "letting off a little steam." Later in 1947 Stockton acknowledged the anti-Robinson feeling on the Cards, especially among the southerners. They "muttered in little circles" but reason prevailed, Stockton wrote. He, too, believed that Woodward had exaggerated the incident. Woodward's "foul up," according to St. Louis sportswriters, unfairly singled out the Cardinals as a racist club as well as harmed the careers of several ballplayers. Commenting years later on Woodward and the story, Slaughter contended that "that son of a bitch kept me out of the Hall of Fame for twenty years."

The clash between the St. Louis and New York press over the Robinson issue prevailed into the 1990s, with award-winning journalists Broeg and Kahn firing the major salvos. Kahn remained critical of how the Cardinals had handled the Robinson matter. His major gripe centered on Broeg, who lacked "sensitivity to racial matters" and who he said attacked Woodward, the "greatest sports editor of the century," because Woodward had "scooped" him. Kahn contended that if "Musial were to talk at length about the Woodward scoop he'd be in the uncomfortable position of publicly correcting his Boswell. Dr. Johnson could do that. Stan Musial can't."

In the mid-1990s Musial found himself uncomfortably seated between Broeg and Kahn at a dinner meeting in St. Louis to promote Kahn's book, *The Era: 1947–1957*. The two privately went after one another. While Kahn claimed that racism existed on the 1947 Cardinals, as it did everywhere in America, Broeg, whose signature bow-tie portrait had graced *Post-Dispatch* columns for nearly forty years, responded, "Roger, you're Jewish and you know about conclusion jumping, and you know what you guys have gone through, and yet you automatically want to go black and white when there were a lot of shades of gray." As the two went back and forth, they turned to Musial for affirmation. He seemed oblivious to it all, while cutting up his steak, before kicking Kahn's leg underneath the table to end the discussion.

Musial publicly played down the Cardinals-Robinson controversy. At a Long Island University conference in 1997 honoring the fiftieth anniversary of Robinson's inaugural major-league season, he went beyond his earlier measured denial that a strike vote occurred by insisting that the Cardinals never even talked about a boycott against Robinson's Dodgers. Broeg aside, he undoubtedly had no desire to embarrass former teammates, particularly Slaughter, by revealing confidences.

Musial said more to Kahn in private about his views on race, probably because of Kahn's probing and Musial's respect for the New York writer, the author of *The Boys of Summer* (1973), a fascinating semi-autobiographical account of the Brooklyn Dodgers of the 1950s. Despite the racist feelings of the time, Musial affirmed that he "had no trouble with integration." He reminded Kahn that he "had played with a black kid in high school." (Musial actually played with two—Buddy Griffey and Grant Gray.) He also "knew that integration was overdue." Inexplicably, he claimed that his parents came to America for economic opportunity—seeking, like Jackie Robinson, the

American Dream. (Musial's mother was born in New York.) He neglected to mention that he and his high school basketball teammates had opposed the exclusion of Grant Gray from the Pittsburgh hotel on the eve of the playoffs. It had been Flo Garcia, however—not Musial—who became outspoken on that matter. "I didn't know how to make speeches," Musial confessed in referring to the Robinson question. "Saying it to older players, that was beyond me. Besides," he continued, "I thought the racial talk was just hot air." Musial's passive support for Robinson seems much in character.

There exists, however, an unsubstantiated, unlikely assertion, first published in the St. Louis press soon after the Cardinals' squabble over Robinson, that remains part of the lore. It concerns a supposed clash between Musial and Slaughter over Robinson and the proposed strike on the eve of the Brooklyn road series in early May. In the midst of heated discussion Slaughter—at times an angry, confrontational personality—allegedly hit Musial in the midsection, aggravating his appendicitis and forcing him to seek treatment. No one has admitted to witnessing that incident. Moreover, Slaughter and Musial vehemently denied it. In his autobiography Musial dismissed it by suggesting that Broeg had seen him naked and unmarked in the hotel room prior to an examination for appendicitis by the hotel physician. But a blow to the stomach would not necessarily have left a mark. Musial's and Slaughter's denials prove nothing one way or another. Any Musial admission would have reaffirmed Slaughter's alleged racism and jeopardized an otherwise harmonious relationship—one that became closer in time. The only other "evidence" is hearsay, coming from a longtime St. Louis historian, who had been told of the scuffle by someone close to the team.

One thing is certain: Musial had expressed his support for Robinson in other ways. The best-known instance came in a game against the Dodgers at Ebbets Field on August 20, 1947, when Slaughter spiked Robinson at first base after Slaughter had come close to doing so earlier in the contest. Two days before, Joe Medwick of the Cards had spiked Robinson on the left foot, producing a bloody gash. Slaughter claimed improbably that he "never deliberately spiked anyone in my life." He blamed Robinson for the incident because the inexperienced first sacker had placed his foot hurriedly in the middle of the bag in a play in which Slaughter was actually out by more than ten feet. "The basepaths belong to the runner," Slaughter intoned, "and I don't believe I have to apologize for not making an exception . . . for anyone." Besides, Slaughter asserted, Robinson's injury did not prevent him from staying in the game. Others have defended Slaughter as a hustling player who did no more than play aggressive baseball.

Robinson and the Dodgers viewed Slaughter in a different way. Burt Shotton, the usually mild-mannered manager who had replaced Durocher for the 1947 campaign and again in 1948 at midseason, became so enraged at Slaughter for an attempt to spike Robinson in 1949 that he told a reporter, "Slaughter's a dirty player, and he always has been." In the 1947 incident, Dodger pitcher Rex Barney saw Slaughter jump in Robinson's direction. Right fielder Carl Furillo remembered that Robinson had his foot on the edge of the bag, but Slaughter still got him just below the calf—by all appearances a deliberate intent to do bodily harm. The attack seemed so blatant to second baseman Eddie Stanky that he commented that "I've lost all my respect for [Slaughter]." Ralph Branca, working on a no-hitter, also saw it as deliberate. He went over to Robinson to say, "Don't worry Jackie, I'll get that son of a bitch for you." Robinson retorted, "No, Ralph, just get him out."

Robinson, who singled in the next inning, told Musial at first base that "I don't care what happens, but when I get to second base, I'm gonna kill somebody. I'm gonna knock [the second baseman] into centerfield. I don't care what kind of play it is, he's going down." Musial supposedly whispered, "I don't blame you. You have every right to do so." On another occasion in St. Louis, after several attempted spikings, an exasperated Robinson threatened to cut Musial only because he was at first base. If this bothered Musial, he never said so. Years later Robinson publicly apologized for what he had said. "It was a dumb thing for me to say," he acknowledged, for "Musial always treated me with courtesy."

Durocher also marked Musial for retaliation after Cardinal pitchers threw at Robinson. Rarely did Musial complain; the exception came in early 1948 after a ball hit his bat, leading to a putout, as Musial avoided being hit. Later in the game he approached Durocher on the field, saying, "Hey, Leo, I haven't got the ball out there. I didn't throw at your man." Durocher replied, "Stan, my boy, you'd better tell that man in there to let my man alone. . . . You're the best man I know on the Cardinals. For every time [Robinson] gets one, it looks to me like you're gonna get two." Durocher claimed that he had no more trouble with the Redbirds over Robinson.

Other incidents also arose in 1947. On September 11, Joe Garagiola and Robinson locked horns after Robinson had made it a practice of stealing frequently on the Cardinal catcher. Robinson did not like the St. Louis native because he thought him one of the leading antagonists on the Cardinals. Garagiola, Robinson felt, had previously sought to spike him, and he had heard racial epithets coming from him. On the eleventh at Sportsman's Park, Garagiola stepped on Robinson's heel, forcing him to the bench "for repairs," a deliberate act, the Dodger rookie later wrote. The next inning Robinson and Garagiola nearly came to blows when Robinson came to bat. Plate umpire

Beans Reardon had to separate them as words were exchanged between the two. A *Sporting News* photograph captured Robinson appearing to clap his hands while Reardon focused his attention on Garagiola. For the remainder of the evening, the Dodger bench hounded Garagiola. In later years Garagiola, a famous TV personality, professed not to remember the 1947 spiking and minimized the overall racial conflict.

In contrast, Robinson later had good things to say about manager Eddie Dyer, whom he thought a kind man. He recalled that in his first game in Sportsman's Park, as he walked from the visitor's clubhouse through the Cardinals dugout to reach the playing field, he could feel the players' stares, but then Dyer stopped him and said in front of his team that "he was glad to see me and that he wished me luck"—an unmistakable message to his own club. It was the sort of thing coach James Russell of Donora High School might have said. That kind of sportsmanship also remained with Musial during the 1947 season. It did not make him a public defender of Robinson, but it nevertheless placed him firmly on the humane side of the issue.

But even Musial had grossly underestimated the enormous talent of Robinson, whose quickness, speed, power, and aggressive play soon made the Dodgers the National League's top team. He hit .311 for the Dodgers from 1947 to 1956 and won the National League's Most Valuable Player Award as a second baseman in 1949. He entered the Hall of Fame in 1962. Robinson's 1947 accomplishments, leading to the National League's Rookie of the Year Award, had not completely ended the tensions over the inclusion of blacks in major-league baseball. That matter involved Musial and the Cardinals in conflicts well into the 1950s.

Before departing from the tumultuous conflict over Robinson, some conclusions are warranted regarding player opposition over his integration. At least one club probably voted to strike at the beginning of the 1947 season. Several other teams, including the Cardinals, seriously considered striking before external pressures and reason prevailed. Even though no evidence exists that the Cardinals voted on the issue, Musial, Slaughter, Marion, and others were less than candid in recent years in claiming that Cardinal players had not discussed striking. At the same time, thanks largely to Stanley Woodward's stories, the Cardinal ball club was unduly singled out for its reaction to Robinson.

After winning the American League pennant in 1944, the Browns, with one-armed outfielder Pete Gray in the lineup, fell back into third place in 1945. Financially strapped and forced to sell off their best players, the Browns dropped to seventh in 1946 and finished in last place the following season. In 1951, the once again lowly Browns were sold to the baseball maverick Bill Veeck. The master of the outrageous gimmick, Veeck thought he could drive the Cardinals out of town, but when Anheuser Busch purchased the Cardinals from tax-troubled Fred Saigh, Veeck knew he couldn't compete against the brewery's millions. By 1954, Veeck was out as owner of the Browns and the franchise was in Baltimore. In the "I'm from Missouri—Momentarily" chapter from Veeck As in Wreck, *the Barnum of Baseball tells his story of his early attempt to save the Browns and the antics that turned St. Louis upside down, momentarily.*

I'm from Missouri—Momentarily
Bill Veeck ───────────────────────

My purchase of the Browns in 1951 brought on a quick reaction in my own little world of sports, something like that of a family gathering around a loved one in time of sickness.

Grantland Rice was inspired to new heights of poetic awe:

Stalwarts have hunted the charging lion, deep in the jungle veldt.
Brave men have stood to the tiger's rush seeking his costly pelt.
Hunters have tackled the elephant, never a job for clowns.
This world is packed with its daring deeds—but Veeck has purchased the Browns.

John Lardner wrote in wonder: "Many critics were surprised to know that the Browns could be bought because they didn't know the Browns were owned."

If John had been trying to buy the Browns, that lamentable gap in his education would have been filled in a hurry. The Browns were not only owned, they were the most owned team in captivity. They were owned by the DeWitt brothers plus more than 1,400 odd-lot stockholders, and maybe you don't think that gave us a headache. On July 3, 1951, we finally amassed the amount of stock we needed, although we still had to wait until after the holiday to sign the contracts. I swung right into action on the Fourth, though, heading for the park and the bleachers to introduce myself to the customers and warm up my lungs on the umpires.

Mary Frances was supposed to join me. To my surprise, she didn't show up. On the way to the park her taxi had swerved to avoid hitting a truck, and she had been thrown against the partition and taken home, woozy. Do you suppose somebody was trying to tell me something?

Mary Frances and I got our first chance to work as a team that same night. The Browns owned a promising young outfielder, Frank Saucier, who had perhaps the best minor-league batting record in the country. (Yes, the same Saucier whom Eddie Gaedel batted for.) Saucier was not playing for the Browns though. He was working for an oil company in Okmulgee, Oklahoma. Having signed with the Browns originally for nothing, he felt he was at least as entitled to a bonus as some kid just out of high school who had yet to swing at a pitch in professional anger and would probably never rise above a Class-B league. He was talking down my alley. I had been arguing all along that the money flowing *out of baseball* in the form of bonuses should be going to the care and preservation of the slowly dying minor leagues, with the minor-league club then giving the player a percentage of the purchase price when he was sold to the majors—something I had always done in Milwaukee.

When I returned to the hotel after the game, I put in a call to Okmulgee and was told Frank was gone for the holidays. After tracking him all over the Midwest, we finally found him, at one o'clock in the morning, at his parents' home in Washington, Missouri, only forty miles away.

"Don't go to bed," I told him. "I'll be right over."

"Gee, Bill," he said, "it's kind of late, isn't it. Let's make it tomorrow."

"Stay right where you are," I said. "I'll be right over."

Mary Frances and I rented a car and arrived at 2:30. It wasn't only a question of the bonus at this point. Frank was completely disillusioned with baseball. He was expecting a draft call and he saw little sense in setting up a new home in St. Louis for half a season. I told him if he agreed to come back, he would go on the payroll immediately and could take all the time he needed to go back to Oklahoma and put his affairs in order. I kept talking to Frank. Mary Frances kept talking to his wife. We all kept drinking coffee. At about 4:30, he agreed to sign.

We got back to our own apartment at 7. I had another cup of coffee, soaked my leg, and went down to the bank to sign more papers. From the bank, I toured the park to see what changes were to be made. I didn't get to bed for forty-eight hours, and it was a great feeling. I was back in action.

Because I wanted to get it clear in everybody's mind that the days at the bottom of the slag heap were over and done with, I ran a big canvas streamer across the front of Sportsman's Park announcing: OPEN FOR BUSINESS UNDER NEW OWNERSHIP. To get it up in time to meet the, let-us-hope, thrilled and expectant eyes of the first arrivals at our twi-night doubleheader, we had to hang it wet and unfinished and let the painter put on the final letters while the customers were filing in.

I also had to get the Board of Public Service to convene in special session so they could issue us a fireworks permit. I made it clear that I had no immediate plans for shooting off fireworks, because I wanted to hold to the old formula of never announcing them in advance.

We drew 10,392 people into the park that night, and between the games they were treated to a fireworks display. Just after the second game began, I took the public-address system and announced: "As a tribute to the Browns' future success, let's all have a drink on the house." Grabbing a bucketful of beer, I passed among the customers in the grandstand and had a drink with them myself. Altogether we gave out 7,596 bottles of beer and 6,041 bottles of pop, which would indicate the presence of some 3,000 switch-hitters in the park.

This toast, incidentally, was not the sudden impulse it was written up to be. You cannot distribute 13,000 bottles of anything on impulse. You have to be sure you have an adequate supply on hand and you have to hire extra help.

The rest of the operation was the same as always. The doors came off the offices; our phone numbers were publicized. I brought Ada Ireland, the world's greatest switchboard operator, down from Cleveland. Before you ask what's so important about a telephone operator, remember this: the telephone operator is your only contact with the outside world. Ada, a gray-haired fiftyish matron when we first met, can hear a man's voice once and greet him by name when he calls back again a year later. If you don't think that makes him feel as if we know him, treasure him and want his business, then you're crazy. The first time I met Ada in Cleveland, I told her, "Just call me Bill." She said, "I don't like to be that informal, darling." *Touché.* She always called me "darling" after that.

In Cleveland, Ada had assigned herself the staggering duty of keeping me presentable, if not respectable. "Darling," she would snap, "you look like a bum." She would send me rushing off to an important appointment, and when I got to the address it would turn out to be a barbershop. She sent my clothes out to be cleaned. She kept herself posted on the females in my life and, more important, she kept them apart.

Ada captivated Mary Frances, of course, at first meeting. "You little so-and-so," she said. "You married the only man I ever loved."

As much as I kid about the Browns and St. Louis, there were things about our two and a half years there that were the happiest and most satisfying of my life. My first full year in St. Louis, I will maintain to the end of my life, was the best job of promoting I have ever done. The last year was a prison sentence, compliments of the American League.

One of the things that made the first full year so ideal was that we lived in our own ball-park apartment, something I had dreamed of from my concession days in Chicago. In concessions, the only things that can go stale on you are popcorn and rolls. Uncut rolls you can return, which means that you don't start cutting until you have some idea about the weather and the crowd. Before a big doubleheader, I'd get into the park at 3 a.m. and cut from 30,000 to 35,000 rolls. Well, there wasn't much sense going home from night school when I had to be back at 3 in the morning, so I slept in the firehouse on Waveland Avenue, right across the street. The firehouse was not without its advantages—I had my own quarters, good company was always available, and the taxpayers, as is their custom, picked up the tab. But Bob Dorr, the grounds keeper, had his own little house attached to Wrigley Field, and how I envied him. To me, that was the greatest thing in the world.

Upon first coming to St. Louis, I had moved the Browns' offices from the second floor of Sportsman's Park down to the street where they belonged. That left a lot of room upstairs. Mary Frances had been running around the neighborhood whenever she had any time during the season trying to find a house. With the season at an end, she still hadn't found anything. Now what could be more logical?

"She'll never go for it," Rudie Schaffer said.

"No harm trying," said I. "Boy, wouldn't it be great!"

"Great," Rudie said. "But she'll never go for it."

Normally, Mary Frances and I didn't see very much of each other during the day. We had set up separate speaking schedules in those early days to enable us to cover twice as much territory and, we hoped, work up twice as much interest for the coming season. As soon as we both had a free morning, I invited her to lunch, bringing Rudie along to leap to my support and scoff at her objections.

Well, you've probably guessed it. She had the same idea herself. She had been sneaking up there for weeks, banging on walls and deciding how to break up the maze of partitioned offices into rooms. She even had a preliminary floor plan already drawn up.

It was an odd apartment in many ways, with windows in strange corners and at odd angles. We had giant pillars in places the more classically trained architects would have frowned upon—like in the middle of the kitchen and living room—because they lent a casual atmosphere so fitting to the landscape, and because the park would have fallen down without them. Mary Frances wound spirals of lights and flowerpots around them, and they were the most attractive pillars anybody ever had to live with intimately.

We had a nice little playyard for Mike, too. Just behind the leftfield stands, where the concession area broke from the park itself, there was an odd architectural formation jutting out of the wall. We covered it with ivy and built a green-and-white picket fence around it and Mike—who was about a year old when we moved in—played there quite happily, oblivious to the big beer trucks grinding in and out of the driveway right alongside him.

Actually, life got to be pretty rough on Mary Frances, because she was always entertaining. She had all kinds of special diets tacked to the kitchen door. Red Rolfe was managing at Detroit and she had his special ulcer diet. Anybody who expressed a particular liking for any dish had to be sure he wasn't just being polite because Mary Frances would tack another note to the door and make sure he got it again next time he visited us. The wives of the players and the sportswriters were always telling her what *not* to feed their husbands. "I can't do anything with him at home," they'd say. "But up here they'll all be talking baseball and he's going to eat anything you shove in front of him."

The feeding would sometimes start as early as 5 o'clock if the Yankees or Tigers were in town, because Casey Stengel and Fred Hutchinson liked early dinners. That was followed by the cocktail hour and dinners for the late diners and later arrivers. On a good night the party could continue until 5 a.m. before we broke up. In the morning, the manager and the coaches would be up, along with Rudie and Bob, to have breakfast with me. Our conferences were always held in the bathroom while I sat in the tub soaking my leg. Mary Frances would get there first to leave the breakfast trays and make sure that the window was open. She was afraid that if she waited until everybody was gone and tried to clear out all the cigar smoke (mainly from Rudie and Marty Marion) at once, somebody would turn in a fire alarm.

Between the members of the group, we blanketed a 250-mile radius around St. Louis, covering parts of eight different states. I averaged better than two speeches a day on a year-round basis and once made seven in one day. We developed one new technique, too. We descended in force—in what I liked to call "safaris"—upon small towns within our radius to hold a press conference for the local newspaper and radio people. We would hire the ballroom of the local hotel, throw a banquet and arrive with Mary Frances and myself, our manager, our coaches, Bill Durney, Bob Fishel, and our radio announcer Bud Blattner. As an added starter, we would dragoon Charlie Grimm whenever we were within dragooning distance of his section of Missouri. The safaris were just to let the small towns know that we considered them important to us. And they were. One of the things we were never able to overcome was the Cardinals' vastly superior radio network. They had 83 stations; we had just a handful. Since the population of St. Louis was only 850,000, we had to pull customers in from out of town if we were going to succeed.

The only attraction the Browns had when we came was Ned Garver, who by mid-season had won 11 games, exactly half the team total. Just as we had pushed Feller to the strikeout record in Cleveland, for its peripheral publicity value, we decided to push Garver as hard as possible to help him become the first pitcher to win 20 games with a last-place team. It was easy to do with Ned because he was also the best hitter on the team and there was never any reason to take him out for a pinch hitter in the late innings. There was almost nothing Ned could do to get knocked out of a game, as a matter of fact, short of allowing 10 runs in the first inning. (We'd take him out then so that we could start him again in a day or two.) The Browns lost 102 games, which seemed to be overdoing it a little even for a last-place team, but Garver won his 20.

The team we took over at the halfway point was already 23½ games behind the leader. I couldn't very well go around insulting the intelligence of my audiences by praising them, so I edged in through the back door by talking about the Browns as if they were the worst team that had ever existed. (If your town is destroyed by a hurricane, there's no sense having it *almost* the worst hurricane in history. There's a certain satisfaction in being with a record-breaker.) "I'm not asking you to come out and see the Browns this year," I would say. "In fact, I advise you not to. It hurts. I only go out to see them because I have to. I'm telling you, though, that we'll have a better team next season, one that you won't be ashamed to look at."

"We've got rid of half our players," I'd say fervently, "and we mean to get rid of the rest as soon as possible."

And usually I'd start my speech by saying, "You're going to have to forgive me if I seem nervous. I'm not used to seeing so many people."

Everybody, the players included, took it for what it was: an attempt to get people into the park by playing it for laughs. Our attendance in the second half of that year was double what it had been in the first half. At the end of the season, after being in town only four months, I finished second to Stan Musial in a sportswriters-sportcasters poll to name the city's outstanding sports figure of the year.

Satchel Paige was the first player I brought in. Max Patkin and Jackie Price came back to entertain. Within the first month we had a miniature circus, featuring "Millie the Queen of the Air" sliding down a tightwire that extended from right field to third base.

Five days after we outraged the higher sensibilities and sensitivities of the baseball world by sending a midget to bat, we held a Grandstand Managers' Day in which the fans called all our strategy. It started as a promotional gag, really, for the *Globe-Democrat*. The paper was to print a ballot on which their readers would choose our opening lineup, position by position, for the game.

Everybody who submitted a lineup was mailed a ticket which would entitle him to sit in the special section behind our dugout where the Grandstand Managers would gather to call the plays.

The ballot ran in only one edition before one of the more conservative editors let out a horrified gasp and killed it.

Out of that one edition we received 4,000 ballots. Since this was one of those rare gags which by its nature had to be announced beforehand, I wanted to get Connie Mack in on it. Mr. Mack was still traveling with his team, in his eighty-ninth year, although his mind was beginning to wander and he no longer sat on the bench. Whenever the Athletics came to town, we had a schedule posted in the office to make sure that someone was always assigned to sit with him during the game. I felt very strongly that he deserved that small gesture of respect. Mr. Mack sat with Mary Frances and me in the Grandstand Managers' section for a couple of innings and enjoyed himself tremendously.

The Athletics' general manager, Art Ehlers, had threatened to protest ahead of time on the grounds that we were—and I quote—making a travesty of the game. That was all right with me; it gave me a chance to observe that he was afraid my amateurs would outsmart his experts.

And the funny thing is that they did. Never has a game been called better.

The way it worked, the Grandstand Managers showed their special passes as they entered and were given large white signs with YES printed in green on one side, and NO printed in red on the other. Bob Fishel, standing at the rail just behind our dugout, had a stack of cards to cover every conceivable situation. He held up the indicated card, the managers voted a green YES or a red NO, and a circuit judge standing alongside Bob with a walkie-talkie tabulated the result. The judge relayed the decision to Johnny Berardino, who was standing in the dugout with another walkie-talkie.

Before the first inning began, Jimmy Dykes, the A's manager, informed umpire Bill Summers that he was prepared to protest to league headquarters if all this vote tabulating delayed the game. Jimmy, always a good fellow, was just trying to help the gag along. To make sure everybody knew he was protesting, he kicked up the dirt around the plate and scowled toward my tyros. My tyros scowled right back. They were fit and ready and straining to start thinking. Here again, funny thing, the game took just over two hours, despite all the tabulating, which had to make it one of the fastest games of the year.

As for our regular manager, Zack Taylor, he reclined in a rocking chair on top of the dugout, in civilian clothes and bedroom slippers, and just leaned back and puffed on a long, curved pipe. Summers told him he had to get off the field, not because of the rocking chair or the pipe but because he wasn't in uniform. So we moved Zack, the rocking chair and the pipe into a box just beside our dugout.

The fans were brilliant. To begin with, they had made two changes in our regular lineup, putting Sherm Lollar behind the plate and Hank Arft at first base. Lollar collected three of our nine hits, scored three runs, and drove in three including the game-winning home run. Arft, of course, knocked in the other two runs.

To make it even more dramatic, all the key plays were squeezed into the first three innings. In the first inning, Ned Garver, the almost unanimous choice to pitch, was hit very hard. With three runs already in and runners on first and third, Fishel flashed the sign SHALL WE WARM UP PITCHER?

Well, they voted against even warming up a pitcher, presumably on the theory that Garver's feelings might be hurt. Among the naysayers was my bride, Mary Frances, which caused Mr. Mack and me—who had of course voted YES—to wonder what kind of strategist I had gotten myself involved with.

Fishel then flashed the sign, INFIELD BACK?

The majority voted YES, playing for the double play rather than to cut off the run at the plate, excellent strategy at that point. Pete Suder obligingly grounded into a double play, making my experts right two times on only one play.

We did some scoring ourselves in the first. With one run in, Lollar on first, and a 3–2 count on the batter, the Grandstand Managers voted against having the base runner go with the pitch. Which was fortunate because the batter took a third strike and the slow-moving Lollar would undoubtedly have been doubled up. The next batter doubled, and Hank Arft tied the score with a single.

Arft was then allowed to steal and was thrown out at second, the only bit of strategy that didn't work all day.

We won the game 5–3 to end a four-game losing streak. I retired all my amateur managers with honors, went back to my professional, and lost five of the next six games.

There was another gag I really wanted to try. Before the next season started I had hired Buddy Blattner and Dizzy Dean to broadcast our games. Buddy had retired only a couple of years earlier and he was still in pretty good shape. My plan was to sign him for one game, put a walkie-talkie on his back, and have him broadcast the game for one turn at bat and maybe an inning or two in the field. You know: "Here comes the pitch . . . oooops . . . he caught the outside corner with a curve." Wouldn't that have been great?

Blattner's contract was still owned by the Phillies. I called Carpenter and told him exactly what I wanted to do, and Carpenter said, "Sure."

"OK," I said. "Why don't you give him his unconditional release? I'll sign him for a day and then you can get him back."

"Sure," Carpenter said, "I'll be glad to do it that way for $10,000."

As I was saying, "Here comes the price . . . ooooops, too high. Much, much too high."

Let me state one thing as clearly as possible. I did not buy the Browns with the intention of moving them out of St. Louis. If I did, I put on an awfully good act of working twenty-four hours a day for a year and a half trying to sell them.

I did come into St. Louis—and I'll make this as clear as possible too—knowing perfectly well that the city could support only one team. I had been saying for years that the only cities in the country who could support two teams were Chicago and New York.

That would seem to mean only one thing. That I had come into St. Louis to try to run the Cardinals out of town. Yes. That was precisely what I had in mind. St. Louis had, in fact, been supporting only one team for years. The Cardinals. And understandably. The Cardinals had won more pennants than any team in the previous quarter of a century except the Yankees. The Cardinals still had all the important names: Musial, Schoendienst, Slaughter, Marion. But the Cards were on the downgrade. They were on the downgrade on the field and, just as important from my point of view, they were weak in the front office. The Cardinal owner was Fred Saigh, an attorney. Saigh was wealthier than me, of course, but he did not have unlimited wealth. That meant he could be run out of town. He didn't have unlimited experience in running a baseball team, either; as I saw it, Saigh didn't have the foggiest notion of what he was doing.

I first became convinced I could take him when his radio announcer, Harry Caray, tried to stop me from acquiring the stock I needed to close the deal. It came about in this way: Bill and Charlie DeWitt owned only 56 percent of the Browns' stock. We wanted at least 75 percent. We needed that amount for tax purposes, and I wanted it from my own point of view for, one might say, the principal of it. If you're running a club with 51 percent control, you're working just as hard as if you had 100 percent but you're getting only half the profits.

The Browns had those 1,400-odd stockholders, with anywhere from one to five shares apiece, because one of the earlier owners had once had the bright idea that the team should be citizen-owned. DeWitt, in selling me an option to buy the club, had requested that the other stockholders deposit their certificates with the Mercantile Commerce Bank & Trust before July 3. I was offering $7 a share against the $3 that had been paid. My option allowed me to cancel the whole deal if I couldn't get the 75 percent. (Technically, it would be more accurate to say that my lawyers had bought the option from his lawyers. Bill and I never met after word came to me through—who else?—Louis Jacobs that Bill thought he could get the 75 percent.)

I went to St. Louis myself, wrote letters to the stockholders, and appeared on radio shows to request that they send the certificates in. It was at this point that Harry Caray, on his own nightly sports program, began to implore the stockholders not to sell their stock to this well-known capital-gains hustler, this con man. In case there is any doubt in anybody's mind as to who hires, pays, and fires the guys who broadcast the games for a big-league team, let me clear that up. Directly or indirectly, it is the owner of the team. At the same time, I should say in all fairness that Caray is an excellent announcer. He does as good a job of selling as anybody on the air.

I'm not sure whether I'd have taken the team without that minimum 75 percent. It was a decision I would have had to make at the last moment. While the St. Louis closing wasn't quite the dramatic last-minute dash of Cleveland, it was still a near thing. The stock certificates dribbled into the bank in all sizes, shapes, and colors, and it was not until two days before the deadline that we hit our 75 percent. We ended with 79.9 percent.

As soon as Saigh put his announcer Caray to work on me, I knew I had read my man right. Understanding that, it was just a matter of laying the traps. Poor Saigh walked, ran, or dove into every trap we set. He was such a patsy that it wasn't even much fun.

I began to work on him from Day One. The Cardinals were our tenants at Sportsman's Field at a ridiculously low rent. They had their offices on one side of the field, we had ours on the other. To give Saigh that grim persecuted feeling as quickly as possible, I painted the walls on our side of the park and left his side unwashed, unpainted, and untouched. To drive home the point that he was to look upon me as an enemy, I barred him from using our special press room or our fancy private box when the Cardinals were playing at home.

In decorating the park we put up murals of old St. Louis heroes on the walls behind the concession stands. By coincidence, they were all pictures of old St. Louis Browns players. This was a detail that would have gone completely unnoticed if Saigh had not done exactly what I expected him to. I had prodded him, he had to swing back. As soon as the Cardinals were at home, he covered the murals over with bright cardinal blankets, thereby making himself look petty and ridiculous and calling attention to something nobody had particularly noticed.

One of the first things I did, as always, was to set Saturday as Ladies' Day. The Cards had no Ladies' Day and I didn't want them to have a Ladies' Day.

To guarantee they didn't start now, all I had to do was challenge Saigh to throw the park open to the ladies on Saturday too. I wasn't going to push *him* into anything.

A couple of weeks later, I sent out another challenge. The Browns were in eighth place and the Cardinals were in fourth place, 12 games off the lead but not completely out of it. To cement the good feelings that had been established between us I suggested that since it was obvious that neither St. Louis team was going to be in the World Series that fall, we should immediately schedule a post-season game for the Community Chest. Saigh somehow got the impression that I was trying to tell the people of St. Louis that they could write off the Cardinals' pennant chances.

He had to react, of course. He wrote a letter to the Community Chest—and incidentally to the press—in which he made it clear that he was far from ready to strike his team's colors. His statement read:

> Any time Mr. Veeck gives you a check for $10,000, I will match that with a Cardinal check in addition to our regular contribution. From past history, $20,000 is considerably more than would be netted from any game or post-season series. If Mr. Veeck does have the good of the Chest at heart, he will not care from whence the money came just so it got to you. . . .

This is why I loved Mr. Saigh so dearly. With a chance to take the initiative by laying his $10,000 on the table and casually brushing me aside—which would have forced me to trip over myself in my haste to match it—he had handed the initiative over to me and, to make it even better, made it sound as if he really hoped I wouldn't get up the $10,000 so that he wouldn't have to match it.

I promptly sent the check in and renewed my challenge, expressing my sharp sense of disappointment that Saigh lacked such faith in his team's ability to draw more than a paltry $20,000 in a post-season series. To end the whole incident on a pleasant note, I had Abe Saperstein bring the Harlem Globetrotters into the park at the end of the season for the first outdoor game the Globetrotters ever played. We drew 17,000 people—14,000 of whom undoubtedly came to see the Globetrotters—and we were able to turn gate receipts of better than $20,000 over to the Community Chest.

Saigh had a few rapier thrusts of his own. On the bottom of his scorecards, he printed the slogan: THE CARDINALS, A DIGNIFIED ST. LOUIS INSTITUTION. By implication we were those vulgarians from the other side of the tracks. No one had bothered to let him know, apparently, that the dignified Cardinals had seen their greatest glory as "The Gas House Gang," starring such pillars of dignity and sobriety as Frankie Frisch, Dizzy Dean, Pepper Martin, Leo Durocher, and Rip Collins.

Not that I didn't want to identify with the Cardinals. In order to give Cardinal fans a rooting interest in our team, I grabbed every old Cardinal hero I could find. By the next season I was loaded down with old Cardinals.

Toward the end of the season, Saigh had sent an emissary to sound out Rogers Hornsby about replacing Marty Marion as the Cardinals' manager. His emissary was thoughtful enough to pass the information on to me.

I couldn't allow that to happen. Hornsby, according to the newspaper reports, had been barred from big-league baseball by Judge Landis, although I, to be frank, had never heard of any such ban and I had been around baseball a long time. The point, however, was that the fans believed it to be true, and an untruth that is believed to be a fact has to be treated as a fact. Hornsby was the greatest player the Cardinals had ever had. He had managed them to their first pennant. He would be returning home after what seemed an indecent period of exile. My great handicap in battling the Cards was that they already had all the big names in St. Louis. If they added Hornsby, I would be dead.

On the other hand, here were the makings of a marvelous squeeze. If Saigh wanted to hire Hornsby, it meant he was somehow dissatisfied with Marty Marion, even though Marion had his team up to third place, surely as high as they had any right to be. If I could hire Hornsby out from under Saigh, I'd have the returning hero and I'd also have given Saigh something else to brood upon. If he then fired Marion anyway, I would hire Marion as a player-coach, and have two of the greatest Cardinal names on my roster.

There was no time to fool around. I called Hornsby, and signed him over the phone. Hornsby's main concern seemed to be in getting a three-year contract, an indication he had been trying to get a multi-year contract out of Saigh without success. I gave him exactly what he wanted, a three-year contract at $36,000 a year.

The fact that Hornsby was not only coming back to St. Louis, the scene of his greatest triumph, but that he was being brought back by the son of the man who had fired him in Chicago added an extra fillip to the true-life story of one man's triumph over petty prejudice and adversity.

Now Saigh was stuck with Marion. He wasn't going to give me the satisfaction of firing him right away and letting everybody know I had stolen Hornsby from him. No, he waited awhile. He waited almost two full months and then with his sure sense of public relations, he let Marion go on Thanksgiving Day.

I hired Marty in time to brighten up his Christmas.

Before the season opened, I had another of the great Cardinal stars on my payroll. To seduce and subvert the old Cardinal fans even further, Falstaff Brewery signed Dizzy Dean to do our radio broadcasts. Diz was a good and colorful broadcaster, although I must say that television has cramped his style. One of the great virtues of radio was that the listener could not see what was happening. The game Diz announced, while a good game and an exciting game, was not necessarily in strict accord with the game that was being played on the field. I mean when Diz felt that the drama of the game had reached the point where it was time for a man to "slud" into third base—or do any of the number of things that would call his unique and well-publicized vocabulary into play—the runner was darn well going to come into third base "sludding," even if the throw had really gone to second base and the man who was barely sludding in under a rifle-like throw, in Diz's game, had actually rounded third and gone halfway home. Diz became one of this country's foremost victims of technological obsolescence.

The signing of Dean provoked Saigh to new heights of absurdity. The motion picture of Diz's life had just been completed when he signed with us and it was having its world premiere in St. Louis on the day the Browns and Cardinals played their traditional pre-season game. To publicize the picture, 20th Century-Fox held a pre-game parade from the theatre to the park, where we were to conduct some kind of touching pre-game ceremony. A good publicity gimmick for everybody. The Cardinals were naturally invited to participate.

Saigh, stung that we had hired Hornsby, Marion, and Dean, took his trenchant pen in hand again and wrote the publicity man:

> We do not want to take part in any promotion or any program or parade in which the Browns have a single person. This is not a baseball picture, it is the life of a man who spent his active playing career in the Cardinal organization. We do not feel that anyone else should muscle in.

There was little I could do as a man responsive to civic duty but deplore that kind of dog-in-the-manger attitude since, as I saw it, this was not a matter of partisan bickering between two mere baseball teams but of the city itself paying homage to one of its most beloved heroes. And there was little the fans could do but shake their heads, laugh, and wonder what in the world was eating Saigh.

Now that I had him going, I kept after him by putting in claims for everybody he wanted to send to the minors, for I was sure he would withdraw them rather than give me a chance to get another Cardinal on my roster. At last, to clear a place for one of the pitchers he couldn't get by me, the Cards retired Harry Brecheen, one of the great Cardinal pitchers of the decade and one of the handful of pitchers to have won three games in a single World Series. I learned about it when Brecheen's name came through on the next waiver list with the notation that $1 waivers were being asked on him so that he could become a coach.

This requires a brief explanation. The purpose of the $1 waivers is to permit a 10-year veteran to make the best possible deal for himself. By paying the club who owned him only $1, the team that claims him is able to offer the player the amount they would normally have paid to the club or, at the very least, apply it toward his salary. In this instance, the $1 waivers were just a technicality to permit the Cards to take him off their active list and make him a coach. And yet, technically, it also made him a free agent. If somebody else made Brecheen a better offer than the Cards, he was free to accept it. You *know* who made him a better offer.

I offered Harry a two-year contract as a coach and, if possible, a part-time pitcher, at $20,000 for the first year and $14,000 for the second. Harry already had a $10,000 coaching contract from Saigh in his pocket when he and his wife came to the ball-park apartment to talk to me. Harry was really torn between taking that extra money or remaining with the Cardinals, the only team he had ever played for. I had to run off to make a speech, so I left him with his old roommate, Marty Marion.

Brecheen signed with us as, of course, he had to. OK, so we had signed another of the old Cardinal stars. If we were lucky he might win a few games for us. Since he had always been a smart pitcher he might be able to teach the younger pitchers something. (He turned out to be one of the best pitching coaches in baseball.) It was a matter of no particular consequence. At least, it wouldn't have been if Saigh had been able to leave it alone. But how could Saigh leave it alone? He had to explain to everybody that we hadn't really outbid him. "This is important," he said, "so the public won't get to thinking we're tightwads. Our offer to Harry was as a coach; their offer was as a pitcher. And players get more. I talked to Harry this morning. I can't blame him, of course, but I question the moral aspects of it. It verges on tampering. Verges, I said."

Out of his own mouth, he had used the word "tightwad," a word nobody in the city had even thought of, because Saigh had been giving Brecheen a good-enough deal. He also managed to implant the suspicion, again out of his own mouth, that Harry had talked to him that morning to give him a chance to match our offer.

When I was called upon to comment, I had to point out, in the interests of accuracy, that the whole purpose of the $1 waiver was precisely that: to give the 10-year man the chance to make the best possible deal for himself, not to protect him for the team that wanted to get rid of him. "I suggest the Cardinals read the rules," I said, not unmindful that Saigh was a lawyer. "The whole thing is, they didn't want to pay Brecheen what he could make."

You think Saigh could leave it alone after that? Nope. He had to keep it alive by appealing the whole case to Frick. To make himself completely ridiculous he said he was protesting "in fairness to his team, to the fans or other interested parties who might have wanted to negotiate with him and didn't have a chance to. . . ."

What he was trying to do, of course, was to convince St. Louis fans that it was I who had prevented good old Harry from making as much money as he might have. What he really did, though, was to make it sound, out of his own mouth again, as if he hadn't really been interested in keeping Brecheen in a Cardinal uniform in the first place, thereby throwing away his only real bid for sympathy.

And finally, Saigh turned the whole episode into low burlesque by petitioning the Commissioner to stop me from bothering him any more by claiming players he knew I didn't really want. Everybody was picking on poor Fred Saigh.

I had judged my man right, I felt, and we had him on the run. The year before I came to St. Louis, the Browns had drawn 247,131. In 1952, we drew 518,796, more than the Browns' only pennant winner had drawn in 1944.

We had lifted our attendance almost 300,000, and the Cardinals had dropped 300,000. We had a deal brewing with the local CBS station to carry our games, an unheard-of thing. It was still a local station, of course, but it was powerful enough to reach a far greater area than we had ever reached before.

I would have run the Cardinals out of St. Louis, I'm sure of it, except for one thing. Saigh had gotten himself into income-tax trouble. He had already been indicted by mid-1952, and I had to face the possibility that he might have to sell the team.

What a lousy thing for him to do to me.

As soon as I read the verdict, I began to talk to Milwaukee—and, to a much lesser extent, Los Angeles and Baltimore—about moving my franchise.

And yet, I was only going through the motions of protecting myself. We had done so well and had come up so far and were putting together, it seemed to me, such a good team that all the momentum was with us even if I lost Fred Saigh.

At one point, I almost did have it made. In negotiating to sell his club, Saigh went down to Houston to talk to some Texas millionaires. The Cardinals owned the Houston club in the Texas League, so the association was close. There was no question that the money was there, it was just a matter of making the Houston park acceptable. I came that close.

And then out of nowhere—*out of nowhere*—came Gussie Busch with his full-bodied and well-foamed bankroll. When Elliot Stein, one of our stockholders, first gave me the tip that Busch was negotiating, I put it down as just another one of those rumors. I pushed it completely out of my mind because I didn't want to believe it. A few days later, Elliot called back to tell me that while the sale might not be announced for a few days, it was set.

I wasn't going to run Gussie Busch out of town. And I certainly wasn't going to run Anheuser-Busch Inc. out of town. Busch wasn't buying the club himself, the brewery was buying it.

The brewery could run the club as part of its advertising budget, lose an unlimited amount of money and just write it off the company profits.

By the time I hung up the receiver, I knew I had been knocked out of the box.

Bill Veeck's decision to hire Rogers Hornsby to manage the St. Louis Browns was, by his own admission, the worst he had ever made in baseball. When Veeck fired Hornsby two months into the 1952 season, the players gave the Brownies' new owner a two-foot silver loving cup for releasing them from Hornsby's tyranny. The trophy backfired when J. Roy Stockton, sports editor for the Post-Dispatch, *attacked Veeck and his players for "insulting the greatest right-handed batter the game has ever known."*

Spink Award recipient Frank Graham, writing on the occasion of Hornsby's hiring by Veeck, offers a history of Hornsby's rocky managerial career and a portrait of Hornsby's controversial character. He also expresses the belief that the union of Veeck and Hornsby will be exciting and successful because Veeck is eager to win in St. Louis and will not resort to "comedy stunts" in running the Browns.

Hail The Prodigal Rajah!
Frank Graham

In the spring of 1925, when Rogers Hornsby was a Cardinal player, Branch Rickey, then the St. Louis manager, planted the seed that one day was to grow into the lush and complicated setup of pitching strings, batting tees, running tracks, mechanical batting practice pitchers, and six-man infields at Vero Beach in the time of his stewardship of the Dodgers. He put up a blackboard in the clubhouse and, in the manner of a football coach busy with his chalk, went about diagramming plays for his men. Nothing like it ever had been seen in a big-league clubhouse before and when, in June of that year, Rickey withdrew to the front office and Sam Breadon appointed Hornsby as his successor, it was seen no more. Rog threw it out the nearest window.

"You don't have to draw pictures for these fellows," he said. "Hell, they're ballplayers, ain't they?"

They were. After a bad start under Rickey, they could finish no higher than fourth that year. But in 1926, under Hornsby all the way, they won the pennant and beat the Yankees in the World Series.

The story of Hornsby and the blackboard is as typical of him as any story could be. Usually outspoken, he had offered no criticism of the chalk talks as long as Rickey was in command. But as soon as he took over, out went the board, symbol of all Branch's theories. He had never managed a club before but he had no doubt he would succeed and he wasn't borrowing anything from Rickey—or anybody else.

A companion story concerns an incident at Sarasota, Florida, in 1927. Salary differences between him and Breadon had led to his sale to the Giants, and now he was training with them. Manager John McGraw, who had made him captain of the team, said one day: "I've got to leave camp for a few days. You run the club."

Giant captains before him had been content to let things go as they would when McGraw was away, looking lightly on their temporary authority and believing the manager wanted no innovations on their part when his back was turned. Rog, who believes words were meant to convey meanings and not to disguise them, quietly but quickly impressed the other players with the fact that he was their boss in McGraw's absence. They didn't like the idea.

One day, when he checked Freddy Lindstrom rather sharply for the way in which he had made a play, and told him how to make it the next time it came up, Lindstrom said: "I made it the way the Old Man wants us to make it."

"I don't care what he wants," Hornsby said. "You make it my way."

"You think you know more than the Old Man, eh?" Lindstrom said.

"No," Hornsby said. "But when he's here, you do what he tells you to do. When he's away, you'll do as I tell you."

That's the way Hornsby was, is, and always will be. He learned to command by first learning to obey when he was a busher breaking in under Miller Huggins in St. Louis back in 1915. Although at times he questioned the judgment of those set over him, he never questioned their right to tell him what to do, nor argued with them over their decisions. He said some things, sometimes, about his managers, not caring who heard them, things that would have been better left unsaid and that caused him some of the troubles he has had. But no manager can say he ever refused to take orders from him or let personal feelings affect his play.

You may have heard another version of Hornsby's ups and downs in baseball. I have heard it, too, that because of his strong likes and dislikes and his blunt language, he is hard to get along with. That, as a player, he often was a disturbing figure on a ball club. That no manager's job was safe when he was around.

Having known him for a very long while, or since he first entered the major leagues, I can't go along with that one. Actually, my notion is that he likes many people in baseball, has few active dislikes, and is completely indifferent to the others. In his book, Miller Huggins was the greatest manager and the greatest man who ever lived. In his estimation, all other managers, including McGraw and Joe McCarthy, suffered by comparison with the Little Miller. If he was critical of the others, he merely was expressing a professional opinion. If they didn't like what he said, they could lump it. He bore no ill will toward

McCarthy, for instance, although McCarthy disliked him cordially for years. Rog could see no reason why they couldn't be friends—as, by the way, they are now. Strictly a loner as a player, he never sought to influence his teammates in any way. Few of them, indeed, ever saw him away from the ball park, even when the team was on the road.

As a manager, he has demanded of his players only that they obey his orders, keep in shape, and play to the best of their ability. None of them ever has been close to him and, while all have respected him, not all of them have liked him. Whether they like him or not doesn't interest him in the least.

Back in 1928, when he was managing the Braves, a friend of Hornsby said to him: "I read in the Boston papers that your players think you're a so-and-so."

"Is that right?" he asked. "I don't care what they think of me. I'm running a ball club, not a popularity contest."

As a manager, he has brooked no interference from his employers, or anybody else. Even Kenesaw Mountain Landis, once attempting to enforce his will on him in a questionable matter, had a bruising experience with him. That was during the 1926 World Series. The Judge, having declared the New York Central the "official" route between New York and St. Louis for the teams, the umpires, and all others connected with the Series, was nettled when he heard that Hornsby had arranged to have his heroes hauled by the Pennsylvania Railroad.

Summoning Hornsby to his hotel suite, he said: "I am informed that you planned to use the Pennsylvania."

"That's right," Hornsby said.

"Are you not aware," the Judge asked, sternly, "that I have designated the New York Central as the official route?"

"I heard something about it," Rog said, "but that don't make any difference. Your job is to run the World Series and not to tell the ballplayers how to travel. If the Yankees want to take the New York Central, it's all right with me. We're taking the Pennsylvania."

Since the Judge's powers, as defined by his contract, were unlimited, he might have dashed off a rule right there to fit the case. But he didn't. He realized he had acted thoughtlessly in the first place and that, if he accepted Hornsby's challenge, he might run head on into some embarrassing involvements. So he backed off. But he never liked Hornsby after that, which was all right with Rog. He didn't like the Judge, either. He didn't need any encouragement to bet on the horses but I think he got an added pleasure from his hobby because he knew it annoyed the Judge.

He always figured, though, the Judge got even with him. Rightly or not, he believed that, following his release by the Browns in 1937, Landis kept him out of the major leagues.

"It's no accident I can't get a job up here," he said once during a league meeting. "They're so desperate for managers they're hiring a lot of humpty-dumpties, but they're not hiring me. Landis is the one that's behind it and you can't tell me different."

Pride kept him from going to Landis. It must have been pride. It couldn't have been fear, for he's never been afraid of anybody or anything in his life. He wouldn't ask the Judge for quarter. He was taking it now, as once he had dished it out.

It is curious that, after 14 years of wandering through the minor leagues, he should return to the majors in St. Louis, for if Phil Ball had lived, he might never have left there. Hornsby and Ball, you could almost say, were destined for each other. Ball, a self-made millionaire, was hard-handed, tough-minded, and tough-talking. He had come into baseball by purchasing the St. Louis club of the so-called outlaw Federal League in 1913, and, as one of the terms of the peace treaty between the Feds and the National and American Leagues in the winter of 1915–16, he had been allowed to buy the Browns. As an outlaw, he had fought Ban Johnson, the president of the league. Now he became Ban's friend and fought for him. He opposed Landis, whom Ban hated, looking on the Judge as an interloper who had been put in power by his enemies. He fought with newspapermen, with umpires and, on occasion, with his own players. Most of those who came within his range of fire were in awe of him. Then along came Hornsby.

That was in 1933. Released as manager of the Cubs in the fall of 1932, Rog was signed as a player with the Cardinals by his old friend, Branch Rickey. When Ball fired Bill Killefer, who had managed the Browns, Rickey persuaded him to take Hornsby. It was amusing to hear them together. Each having recognized the other for what he was, and mutual respect having been established, they got along splendidly, although, listening to them, a stranger would have thought they were about to start throwing punches.

Their beautiful friendship, which promised so much for the welfare of the club, since Ball was willing to do anything Hornsby asked of him, was brief because Ball died within a few months. Under a new regime, Hornsby was thwarted and he slogged along, unhappily, in the second division until he was let out in 1937.

The joining of Hornsby and Bill Veeck is a happy one. Veeck, like Hornsby and Ball, has few inhibitions. He is eager to repeat in St. Louis the success he had in Cleveland and, in furtherance of his ambition, will spend money as though he had it. Hornsby already has informed him that comedy stunts no longer will have a place on the program at Sportsman's Park. In spite of his flair for fun, Veeck is glad to go along. Basically, he is a baseball man from away back, too. Between them, he and Rog will stir up a lot of excitement and, maybe, win a pennant one of these days.

Meanwhile, Rog is back in the big time, which, it says here, he never should have been allowed to leave.

During his first year as owner of the St. Louis Browns, Veeck signed two of the most memorable characters in baseball history. Veeck's first signing was the ageless Satchel Paige. While critics complained that the signing was a publicity stunt, it turned out well for the Browns. When Paige wasn't sitting in his contour chair in the bullpen, he was leading the Browns pitching staff. In 1952, he was the only Brown player in the All-Star game. He ended the season with 46 appearances, one less than the league leader, and a 12–10 record. In this excerpt from the autobiographical Maybe I'll Pitch Forever, *Paige remembers his days pitching and showboating in a Browns' uniform.*

Veeck's other signing, clearly a publicity stunt, created the most memorable story in St. Louis Browns history when Eddie Gaedel, at 3'8", walked up to home plate and announced himself as a pinch hitter. In his foreword on the Browns for the Putnam team history reprint, Bob Broeg, one of the few people who knew about the stunt in advance, tells the complete story of Eddie Gaedel, from the moment number "1/8" popped out of a birthday cake to his stroll down to first base after walking on four straight pitches.

The Day Veeck Played a Midget
Bob Broeg

Over the years, Veeck loved doing the unexpected. He had the unique notion that everybody should enjoy a ballgame, win or lose. Oh, now and then Veeck would announce a giveaway of an orchid to each woman who attended, but preferably, he liked surprises, like a baseball lottery for a spanking new automobile. Or he would have a crate of cackling chickens delivered to a "lucky" fan or have a 100-pound cake of ice deposited at a customer's seat on a hot night. Or if he was going to provide a can of fruit or vegetables to all, he would have the wrappers removed. If you loved peaches, you might end up with a can of peas.

But back to the day that Veeck played a midget. The occasion was the St. Louis 50th anniversary of the American League. Veeck caught up to me after the Sunday paper had gone to press. He wondered what I thought. I was indignant. I wouldn't spoil it, but I was glad he told me. At my suggestion, *PD* photographer Jack January kneeled down on what would be the first base batting circle. As a result, he got one of the most precious pictures in sports history. By the way, photographers, along with the players' scattered gloves, were allowed on the field until 1954, and this was 1951.

Veeck, by game time, had told only the necessary few about his *piece de resistance.* The Cecil B. DeMille of the diamond had gone up to the rooftop of the grandstand to direct the between-games show, with one admonition. Earlier, he had seen the little guy swinging a toy bat and he said, "If you so much as swing at a pitch I'll shoot you—and I was an expert rifleman in the Marines." From the rooftop, Veeck waved on an eight-piece roving band dressed in uniforms of the Naughty Nineties. Aerial bombs exploded, casting miniature flags onto the field. A hand balancer performed at first base, trampoline artists tumbled at second, and a juggler juggled at third. A four-piece band of Brownie players walked onto the middle of the field—Satchel Paige on the drums, Al Widmar with a bull fiddle, Ed Redys with an accordion, and Johnny Berardino maneuvering the maracas.

Suddenly a giant papier-mache cake was wheeled onto the field. The band played "Happy Birthday" and up and out through the top layer popped a little guy with a fractional number on his back. Quickly, he ran off into the home team's third-base dugout. The crowd laughed happily.

After the Browns lost the first game as usual, manager Zack Taylor visited little Eddie Gaedel, the midget holed up in the empty Cardinals clubhouse. He was wearing a miniature Browns uniform worn by the former owner's son, Billy DeWitt, then age six, and now president of the St. Louis Cardinals. Gaedel's confidence was wavering. It shook further when Taylor tied Gaedel's miniature baseball shoes and said, with a touch of truth as well as humor, "I think you'll be all right kid. I don't think they'll throw *at* you."

The nervous little kid jumped to his feet, ready to grab his fashionable little duds and head back to Chicago, but looming in the doorway was the Browns' traveling secretary.

"Listen, kid, if you don't do what you've been told and when, I'll pinch your head," said secretary Bill Durney, feigning anger, "and you heard Bill Veeck. He'll be on the rooftop with a high-powered rifle."

After Detroit failed to score in the first inning, field announcer Bernie Ebert droned, "For the Browns, number 1/8, Eddie Gaedel, batting for Frank Saucier . . ."

I held my breath. The crowd gasped as the cute little man came out, vigorously swinging miniature bats. Would Ed Hurley, the hot-tempered Boston Irishman umpiring behind the plate, spoil the show?

Arms folded firmly across his chest, staring straight ahead, Hurley merely wiggled fingers at his right hand toward the third-base dugout, Taylor get your butt out here to home plate. And out came Taylor, tugging characteristically with one hand at his knee-length baseball bloomers and waving a telegraph approval contract in the other. Glancing at the contract, Hurley didn't flinch. He shrugged, motioned Gaedel to the plate, and beckoned to the pitcher, Bob Cain, age twenty-six, the same age as the midget.

Catcher Bob Swift went out to Cain. The left-hander wondered if he could throw the ball underhanded—as in softball? No, the catcher told him, Hurley wouldn't permit that. Maybe, Swift suggested, he could go back and lie down behind the plate? No, this time if the pitcher threw cold water, the umpire would really get into a huff. Swift nodded and retreated behind the plate.

Small became smaller as the midget crouched. Cain could not get the ball low enough, lobbing it, and Gaedel dutifully did not swing. At ball four, Eddie triumphantly threw aside his bat and dashed to first base. Quickly, Jim Delsing, who would replace Saucier in right field and is still identified as "the man who ran for the midget," came out to replace Gaedel. Little Eddie, relieved to be alive, grandly patted Delsing on the fanny and disappeared into the dugout.

I wondered aloud to the Browns' PR chief, Robert O. Fishel, later assistant president of the American League, how long Gaedel would remain in the park? Minutes later, just before catching a plane, Fishel introduced us, and I picked up the little man and sat him on the press-box table top. His attire is still fresh in my mind's eye. He wore light tan slacks, a yellow sports shirt, neatly draped by a chocolate sports coat.

He swung his feet merrily from the tabletop and said excitedly, "I feel like Babe Ruth."

"You know, Eddie, you little S.O.B., you're now what I always wanted to be."

"What's that?" he asked me.

"An ex-big leaguer."

The significance of the day sank in. Gaedel straightened, puffed out his chest with obvious pride, smiled, and leaped off the counter and stalked off with a cheery good-bye.

Three nights later in Cincinnati, little Eddie Gaedel was arrested for abusing a cop. Ten years later the little man with a big league thirst was beaten up outside a bar. He crawled to a home he shared with his mother, got upstairs, and died in bed. The Cook County coroner's jury ruled a heart attack, not homicide. When the littlest man was buried, only one baseball man appeared. He was Bob Cain, who coincidentally was traded to the Browns the following spring where he pitched a record double one-hitter victory over Cleveland's Bob Feller.

Years later I wondered why Cain made the effort to come from Cleveland where he made a living as a goodwill ambassador for Kraft Foods. Cain smiled, "I guess I'm a religious sort, but mainly I believe the Gaedel story is probably the best story I tell."

Mine, too!

Maybe I'll Pitch Forever
LeRoy (Satchel) Paige ————————————————————

I might have had troubles with other folks, but I always got along with the Browns real good. They were a fine bunch, even if they were last-placers. There were a lot of boys on that club that hadn't been around too much and they sure liked listening to Ol' Satch.

'Course, I confused some of them. I just sort of got in the habit of giving them a different answer to the same old questions every time they asked them.

That's because I had a lot of answers for them. A man who's been all over like I had picks up a lot of news even if he hasn't had a whole lot of schooling.

Those Brownies'd gather around me and just listen and ask and listen.

What most of them was asking about was pitching. I didn't push myself on them with advice, but if they came to me I had some for them.

The best one for coming for advice was Ned Garver.

When I got to the Browns, Ned was on his way to winning twenty games. I could tell he thought I was just one of those overpowering pitchers because in practice I only threw that fast ball.

But it didn't take many games for me to show him different.

After a couple of them, he came up to me and said, "Satch, I was wrong about you. You know more about pitching than most pitchers could ever fathom. Man, you're in a class by yourself when it comes to know-how."

But I didn't know everything and whenever I needed help, Ned was right there. I used to go ask him about Mickey Vernon, the first baseman. Now I've faced the best in the whole world just about, but I never could get Mickey out. He almost killed me every time he hit against me. Before every game I pitched against him, when he was playing for Washington, I used to go up to Ned to see if he'd heard anything new about Mickey.

"What should I throw him?" I asked Ned.

"Maybe you ought to try keeping the ball away from him."

"I did that the last time. It didn't work. You know what, if Washington gets the bases loaded against me and I got a two-run lead, I think I'll just walk that man and save myself a lot of headaches."

The best thing about being back in the majors was those long, fine trips on the trains, not bumping along on the buses or in a car. What I really liked was that hop on the Wabash from St. Louis to Chicago. They had a dome car on that train and I used to climb up there and all the other boys'd climb up there after me, asking about how it'd been when I was playing on a first-place team. When you're sitting down there in last place, you sure get wet in the mouth thinking and asking about how the uptown folks are living.

On most of those trips I sat with Ned Garver, talking pitching. Ned was a real student.

Next to me, Ned knew more baseball than just about any pitcher in the American League.

Those first few weeks he told me about all the new guys in the league and what they hit and what they didn't. He was right.

"Ned, there's only one thing keepin' you from being the best pitcher in the league," I told him one day after all the stuff he'd told me about pitching to those other teams turned out right.

"What's that?" he asked.

"You don't have that one strikeout pitch, that one thing to get a man when you got him three and two. You need a good fast ball or a real sharp curve."

Ned just sat there a minute, thinking real careful like he always did.

"You're right, Satch," he finally said. "If I had that real good fast ball of yours—the one you got now, not the one you used to have even—I'd be sitting pretty."

And that's all Ned needed. But even with that slow stuff of his, he did right well all along, just using his head.

I didn't joke with Ned too much. He was a real serious boy. But one day I got him to bite good.

We were just talking and Ned asked me what my best relief job was. Now I've had a lot of great ones, but that boy was so serious I just couldn't resist that old temptation.

"That was before I got into pro ball," I told him. "We was in the ninth and was leadin', one to nothin'. The first man up topped the ball and beat the throw. The second man bunted and it looked like it was going foul, but it didn't. Then the third man up walked. Our pitcher had the fourth guy three balls and two strikes and my manager called on me."

"What happened?" Ned asked, real serious.

"Well, I had a ball with me in the dugout and I just dropped it in my pocket. Then I got the game ball from the pitcher I was relieving. When I went back to the resin bag I got that other ball out of my pocket and had me two of them then."

"Yeah? What'd you do then?"

"I just threw those two balls at the same time, one to first and one to third. I picked off both runners and my motion was so good the batter fanned. That was three outs."

Ned wouldn't talk to me for a whole day after that.

That 1951 season was a real picnic for me. When I first got in the majors in 1948, I had to fight all those people who said my being up there was a publicity stunt. But when you win ten and lose only eight in your first two years, that's no publicity stunt.

When I got back with the Browns, people knew I was there because I could pitch. That let me do a little more showboating than I did before. You got to think of the fans if you want to be big in the majors.

'Course, some of that showboating ain't meant just to tickle the fans. Sometimes you use it to win. That's what I did with Larry Doby, my old Cleveland teammate, the second time around that I pitched against him.

The first time he got a couple of hits off me that about cost me a game. I was laying for him the next time. That was in St. Louis and Cleveland came in to play us.

Larry'd been on a real hot streak and before the game he was posing for all kinds of pictures.

I walked over and watched a minute.

"You'd better get all those pictures taken now, Larry," I yelled over at him, "because when the game starts you won't be able to have any taken. You'll be flat on your back."

Now I don't throw at anybody too often. I was always afraid that fast ball'd kill them if it hit them. But with Larry riding that hot hand I knew we had to slow him down.

On the first pitch to him that night, I fired one high and hard and inside, close enough to scare him but not close enough to hit him.

It did what I wanted. He ended up flat on his back, just like I told him he'd be. He was so shook up he didn't cause any trouble that night.

Pitchers have to do things like that. When a batter comes up to the plate, you got to know how you want to get him out and then be able to do it.

If you don't, you don't win any games.

That's why sometimes I'd throw three straight balls to a batter and then act real nervous, like I couldn't get the ball over the plate. That'd get the batter careless. Then I'd fire my trouble ball right by him for three strikes.

But you had to be able to throw the ball as hard as the best in the league to do that. And you'd better have that fine control before you tried something like that.

Whenever I got the chance those days, I'd clown a little. That's what the fans expected.

I remember one game when there were two on and two out and the ball was hit back to me.

I fielded it and started walking toward third base, not even looking at the runner or my first baseman. The crowd went crazy. Then I flipped it back-hand to first without even looking at Hank Arft standing over there and got the runner out. I wasn't taking any chances. I'd practiced that for a long time.

That clowning kept a lot of folks happy, but it was mainly my pitching that kept the Browns happy.

It was that pitching that made guys like Ned Garver come up to me and say, "Satch, you deserve being in the Hall of Fame, just from the ability you've shown me here. And if that's not enough of a reason, you ought to get in for the way you promoted baseball all over the country."

I hadn't set any world records pitching in 1951, but I'd done all right and I didn't have any worries about where I was going to be working in 1952.

And with my stomach troubles behind me and with spring training to get ready in, I was hoping for a pretty fair year.

I got a call from Bill Veeck in February and went to St. Louis February 9 to sign my 1952 contract.

They made a big show of it, just like they'd always done before.

"This contract is just as good as the one LeRoy signed in 1948 when we were with the Cleveland Indians," Mr. Veeck told the reporters.

"How old are you now, Satchel?" one of the reporters asked me. "The Browns' record book says you were born in 1892."

"Oh, no. Not that," I said. "I'm only forty-three. I was born in 1908."

That wasn't true, but I figured if my pitching was getting livelier, I ought to be getting younger.

"LeRoy just drops his age two or three years each season," Mr. Veeck said and laughed. "Today's my birthday, too," he said.

"How old are you, Bill?" somebody asked.

"I'm thirty-eight and there's no arguing about it."

While Mr. Veeck was talking, I was thumbing through the Browns' statistic book.

"Hey, they don't have any of my kids listed in here," I said.

"You a father, Satch?" a reporter asked.

"That's right. I got a wife and three kids. One's three, the other's two, and I got a baby three months old. If they weren't listed before, you'd better change it. I want to get some money back from the tax people."

"What are you aiming for in 1952?" another reporter asked.

"I just want to hit .290."

After I signed my fourth contract with Mr. Veeck, the Browns came out with their new record book. I'd told them I was born in 1908, but that didn't make any difference to anybody. They made a big game out of how old I was and in the record book, under my birthday, they wrote:

"September 11, 1892—Z, 1896—Z, 1900—Z, 1904—Z."

At the end of the pitcher's list they had another line: "Z—Take your pick."

The Gibson Sixties

The decade of the 1950s, with the exception of Stan Musial's four batting ti-
tles, was a roller-coaster ride for the Cardinals, who finished in the first division
five times and in the second division five times. It was also the first decade since
the 1920s that the Cardinals failed to win a world championship. All that
changed in the 1960s, thanks in large part to the brilliant and dominating pitch-
ing of Bob Gibson. Leading the Cardinals to three more National League
pennants and two World Series championships, Gibson had four of his five
twenty-game winning seasons in the 1960s. In 1968, Gibson won the National
League MVP award by winning 22 games and posting a 1.12 ERA, the lowest in
baseball since 1914. He was also masterful in the World Series, winning seven
consecutive games and striking out 17 batters in a single game, both World Series
records.

Roger Angell, generally regarded as baseball's most eloquent commentator,
began writing baseball essays for the New Yorker *in the early 1960s. In "Dis-*
tance," he captures the inner character of a Cardinal pitcher who stood so proud
and aloof on the mound.

Distance
Roger Angell

On the afternoon of October 2, 1968—a warm, sun-shiny day in St. Louis—Mickey Stanley, the Detroit Tiger shortstop, singled to center field to lead off the top of the ninth inning of the opening game of the 1968 World Series. It was only the fifth hit of the game for the Tigers, who by this time were trailing the National League Champion St. Louis Cardinals by a score of 4–0, so there were only minimal sounds of anxiety among the 54,692 specta-tors—home-town rooters, for the most part—in the stands at Busch Sta-dium. The next batter, the dangerous Al Kaline, worked the count to two and two and then fanned, swinging away at a fastball, to an accompanying roar from the crowd. A moment later, there was a second enormous cheer, louder and more sustained than the first. The Cardinal catcher, Tim McCarver, who had straightened up to throw the ball back to his pitcher, now hesitated. The pitcher, Bob Gibson, a notoriously swift worker on the mound, motioned to his battery mate to return the ball. Instead, McCarver pointed with his gloved hand at something behind Gibson's head. Gibson, staring uncomprehend-ingly at his catcher, yelled, "Throw the goddam ball back, will you! C'mon, c'mon, let's *go!*" Still holding the ball, McCarver pointed again, and Gibson, turning around, read the illuminated message on the centerfield scoreboard, which perhaps only he in the ballpark had not seen until that moment: "Gibson's fifteenth strikeout in one game ties the all-time World Series record held by Sandy Koufax." Gibson, at the center of a great tureen of noise, dug at the dirt of the mound with his spikes and then uneasily doffed his cap. ("I *hate* that sort of thing," he said later.) With the ball retrieved at last, he went to work on the next Tiger, Norm Cash, a left-handed batter, who ran the count to two and two, fouled off several pitches, and then struck out, swinging at a slider. Gibson, a long-legged, powerfully built right-hander, whose habitual aura of glowering intensity on the mound seemed to deepen toward rancor whenever his club was ahead in the late stages of a game, now swiftly attacked the next Detroit hitter, Willie Horton. Again the count went to two and two and stuck there while Horton fouled off two or three pitches. Gibson stretched and threw again, and Horton, a righty batter, flinched away from the pitch, which seemed headed for his rib cage, but the ball, another slider, broke abruptly away under his fists and caught the inside corner of the plate. Tom Gorman, the home-plate umpire, threw up his right hand, and the game was over. McCarver, talking about this moment not long ago (he is now a radio and television broadcaster with the Phillies), said, "I can still see that last pitch, and I'll bet Willie Horton thinks to this day that the ball hit him—that's how much it broke. Talk about a batter *shuddering!*"

Bob Gibson's one-game World Series record of seventeen strikeouts stands intact, and so do my memories of that famous afternoon. In recent weeks, I have firmed up my recollections by consulting the box score and the inning-by-inning recapitulations of the game, by watching filmed highlights of the play, and by talking to a number of participants, including Gibson himself. (He had had no idea, he told me, that he was close to a record that afternoon. "You're concentrating so hard out there that you don't think of those things," he said.) Gibson seemed to take absolute charge of that game in the second inning, when he struck out the side on eleven pitches. By the end of four innings, he had run off eight strikeouts. Not until I reexamined the box score, however, did I realize that there had been only two ground-ball outs by the Tigers in the course of nine innings. This, too, must be a record (baseball statistics, for once, don't tell us), but the phenomenally low figure, when taken along with the seventeen strikeouts, suggests what kind of pitching the Tiger batters were up against that afternoon. Most National League batters in the nineteen-sixties believed that Gibson's fastball compared only with the blazers thrown by the Dodgers' Sandy Koufax (who retired in 1966 with an arthritic elbow) and by the Reds' Jim Maloney. Gibson's pitch flashed through the strike zone with a unique, upward-moving, right-to-left sail that snatched it away from a right-handed batter or caused it to jump up and in at a left-handed swinger—a natural break of six to eight inches—and hitters who didn't miss the ball altogether usually fouled it off or nudged it harmlessly into the air. The pitch, which was delivered with a driving, downward flick of Gibson's long forefinger and middle finger (what pitchers call "cutting the ball"), very much resembled an inhumanly fast slider, and was often taken for such by batters who were unfamiliar with his stuff. Joe Pepitone, of the Yankees, concluded the All-Star Game of 1965 by fanning on three successive Gibson fastballs and then shook his head and called out to the pitcher, "Throw me that slider one more time!" Gibson, to be sure, did have a slider—a superior breaking pitch that arrived, disconcertingly, at about three-quarters of the speed of the fastball and, most of the time, with exquisite control. Tim Mc-Carver, who caught Gibson longer than anyone else, says that Gibson became a great pitcher during the summer of 1966 (his sixth full season in the majors), when he achieved absolute mastery of the outside corner of the plate while pitching to right-handed batters and—it was the same pitch, of course—the inside corner to left-handed batters. He could hit this sliver of air with his fastball or his slider with equal consistency, and he worked the opposite edge of the plate as well. "He *lived* on the corners," McCarver said. A third Gibson delivery was a fastball that broke downward instead of up and away; for this pitch, he held the ball with his fingers parallel to the seams (instead of across the seams, as was the case with the sailer), and he twisted his wrist counterclockwise as he threw—"turning it over," in mound parlance. He also had a curveball, adequate but unextraordinary, that he threw mostly to left-handers and mostly for balls, to set up an ensuing fastball. But it was the combination of the devastating slider and the famous fastball (plus some other, less tangible assets that we shall get to in time) that made Gibson almost untouchable at his best, just as Sandy Koufax's down-diving curveball worked in such terrible (to hitters) concert with his illustrious upriding fastball.

"Hitting is rhythm," McCarver said to me, "and if you allow major-league hitters to see only one pitch—to swing repeatedly through a certain area of the plate—eventually they'll get to you and begin to hit it, even if it's a great fastball. But anybody who can control and switch off between two first-class pitches will make the hitters start reaching, either in or out, and then the game belongs to the pitcher. Besides all that, Bob had such great stuff and was so intimidating out there that he'd make the batter open up his front shoulder just a fraction too fast, no matter what the count was. The other key to good hitting, of course, is keeping that shoulder—the left shoulder for a right-handed batter, I mean, and vice versa—in place, and the most common flaw is pulling it back. Gibson had guys pulling back that shoulder who normally wouldn't be caught dead doing it. Their ass was in the dugout, as we say."

Mike Shannon, who played third base behind Gibson in the 1968 Series opening game (he didn't handle the ball once), remembers feeling pity for the

Detroit batters that afternoon. "Most of them had never seen Gibby before," he said, "and they had no *idea* what they were up against." Shannon, who is now a television announcer with the Cards, told me that he encounters some of the 1968 Tigers from time to time in the course of his baseball travels, and that they almost compulsively want to talk about the game. "It's as if they can't believe it to this day," he said. "But neither can I. I've never seen major-league hitters overmatched that way. It was like watching a big-league pitcher against Little League batters. It was frightening."

Gibson, of course, was already a celebrated winning pitcher by 1968. Like many other fans, I had first become aware of his fastball and his unique pitching mannerisms and his burning intensity on the mound when he won two out of the three games he pitched against the Yankees in the 1964 World Series, including a tense, exhausting victory in the clinching seventh game. Then, in 1967, I had watched him capture three of the Cardinals' four October victories over the Red Sox, again including the seventh game—a feat that won him the Most Valuable Player award for that Series. I had also seen him work eight or ten regular-season games over the previous five years or more. Although he was of only moderate size for a pitcher—six feet one and about a hundred and eighty-five pounds—Gibson always appeared to take up a lot of space on the mound, and the sense of intimidation that McCarver mentioned had something to do with his sombre, almost funereal demeanor as he stared in at his catcher, with his cap pulled low over his black face and strong jaw, and with the ball held behind his right hip (he always wore a sweatshirt under his uniform, with the long, Cardinals-red sleeves extending all the way down to his wrists), and with his glove cocked on his left hip, parallel to the ground. Everything about him looked mean and loose—arms, elbows, shoulders, even his legs—as, with a quick little shrug, he launched into his delivery. When there was no one on base, he had an old-fashioned full crank-up, with the right foot turning in mid-motion to slip into its lot in front of the mound and his long arms coming together over his head before his backward lean, which was deep enough to require him to peer over his left shoulder at his catcher while his upraised left leg crooked and kicked. The ensuing sustained forward drive was made up of a medium-sized stride of that leg and a blurrily fast, slinglike motion of the right arm, which came over at about three-quarters height and then snapped down and (with the fastball and the slider) across his left knee. It was not a long drop-down delivery like Tom Seaver's (for contrast), or a tight, brisk, body-opening motion like Whitey Ford's.

The pitch, as I have said, shot across the plate with a notable amount of right-to-left (from Gibson's vantage point) action, and his catchers sometimes gave the curious impression that they were cutting off a ball that was headed on a much longer journey—a one-hundred-foot fastball. But with Gibson pitching you were always a little distracted from the plate and the batter, because his delivery continued so extravagantly after the ball was released that you almost felt that the pitch was incidental to the whole affair. The follow-through sometimes suggested a far-out basketball move—a fast downcourt feint. His right leg, which was up and twisted to the right in the air as the ball was let go (all normal enough for a right-handed pitcher), now continued forward in a sudden sidewise rush, crossing his planted left leg, actually stepping over it, and he finished with a full running step toward the right-field foul line, which wrenched his body in the same direction, so that he now had to follow the flight of the ball by peering over his *right* shoulder. Both his arms whirled in the air to help him keep his balance during this acrobatic maneuver, but the key to his overpowering speed and stuff was not the strength of his pitching arm—it was the powerful, driving thrust of his legs, culminating in that final extra step, which brought his right foot clomping down on the sloping left-hand side of the mound, with the full weight of his body slamming and twisting behind it. (Gibson's arm never gave him undue trouble, but he had serious difficulties with his knees in the latter stages of his career, and eventually had to have a torn cartilage removed from the right knee, which had pushed off to start all the tens of thousands of his pitches over the years and had then had to withstand the punishing force of the last stage of his unique delivery.) All in all, the pitch and its extended amplifications made it look as if Gibson were leaping at the batter, with hostile intent. He always looked much closer to the plate at the end than any other pitcher; he made pitching seem unfair.

The players in the Detroit clubhouse after Gibson's seventeen-strikeout game had none of the aggrieved, blustery manner of batters on a losing team who wish to suggest that only bad luck or their own bad play kept them from putting away a pitcher who has just beaten them. Denny McLain, the starting Tiger pitcher, who had won thirty-one games that summer but had lasted only five innings in the Series opener, said, "I was awed. I was *awed*," and Dick McAuliffe, the Detroit second baseman, said that he could think of no one he had ever faced with whom Gibson could be compared. "He doesn't remind me of anybody," he said. "He's all by himself."

I was awed, too, of course, but nothing I had seen on the field at Busch Stadium that afternoon startled me as much as Gibson's postgame comportment in the clubhouse. In October of 1964 and again in 1967, I had noticed that Bob Gibson often appeared to be less elated than his teammates in the noisy, jam-packed overexuberant World Series locker rooms—a man at a little distance from the crowd. But somehow I must have expected that his astounding performance here in the 1968 opener would change him—that his record-breaking turn on the mound would make him more lighthearted and accommodating; he would be smiling and modest and self-depreciating, but also joyful about his feat, and this would diminish that almost immeasurable distance he had just established, out on the field, between himself and the rest of us. He would seem boyish, in short, and we, the grown-up watchers of the game, would then be able to call him by his first name (even if we didn't know him), and forgive him for what he had done, and thus to love him, as is the ancient custom in these high sporting dramas. But Gibson was unchanged. Talking to the sportswriters gathered in a thick, uncomfortable crowd around his locker, he looked at each reporter who asked him a question (Gibson is an exceptionally handsome man, with small ears, very dark skin, and a strikingly direct gaze) and then answered it gravely and briefly. When one writer asked him if he had always been as competitive as he had seemed on this day, he said yes, and he added that he had played several hundred games of ticktacktoe against one of his young daughters and that she had yet to win a game from him. He said this with a little smile, but it seemed to me that he meant it: he couldn't let himself lose to anyone. Then someone asked him if he had been surprised by what he had just done on the field, and Gibson said, "I'm never surprised by anything I do."

The shock of this went out across the ten-deep bank of writer faces like a seismic wave, and the returning, murmurous counterwaves of reaction were made up of uneasy laughter and whispers of *"What* did he say?" and some ripples of disbelieving silence and (it seemed to me) a considerable, almost visible wave of dislike, or perhaps hatred. This occasion, it should be remembered, was before the time when players' enormous salaries and their accompanying television-bred notoriety had given birth to a kind of athlete who could choose to become famous for his sullenness and foul temper, just as another might be identified by his gentle smile and unvarying sweetness of disposition. In 1968, ballplayers, particularly black ballplayers in near-Southern cities like St. Louis, did not talk outrageously to the press. Bob Gibson, however, was not projecting an image but telling us a fact about himself. He was beyond us, it seemed, but the truth of the matter is that no one at Busch Stadium should have been much surprised by his achievement that afternoon, for it was only a continuation of the kind of pitching he had sustained all through that summer of 1968—a season in which he won twenty-two games for the Cardinals while losing nine, and also compiled an earned-run average of 1.12 runs per game; the best pitching performance, by that measurement, in the history of modern baseball.

When Bob Gibson retired, at the age of thirty-nine, at the end of the 1975 season, after seventeen summers with the Cardinals, he had won 251 games, and his record of 3,117 strikeouts was second only to Walter Johnson's 3,508. Last year, however, Gaylord Perry, who is still going strong at the age of forty-two, passed Gibson on the lifetime-strikeout list (Perry is now with the Yankees and has 3,267 whiffs to his credit at this writing), while three other active pitchers—Nolan Ryan, Tom Seaver, and Steve Carlton—may surpass Gibson's mark next summer.* This kind of erosion of the game's most famous fixed numbers—the landmarks of the pastime—by swirling tides of newcomers is always happening, of course; it is the process that makes baseball statistics seem alive and urgent to the true fan. But Gibson's displacement unsettled me, and when I read in the sports pages last spring that he was among the players who would become eligible for election to baseball's Hall of Fame at the end of this season, after the obligatory five-year post-retirement waiting period (the qualifications for official immortality are established by the Baseball Writers Association of America, whose three hundred-odd members conduct a Hall of Fame balloting in the off-season each year), I sensed that Gibson might be about to slip away into the quiet corridors of baseball history. It is always a discomfiting moment for a long-term follower of the game when a favorite player, whose every feat and gesture on the field still retain clarity and color, is declared for embronzement, but the possibility of Bob Gibson's imminent apotheosis at Cooperstown came as a shock to me. He seemed too impatient, too large, and too restless a figure to be stilled and put away in this particular fashion; somehow, he would shrug off the speeches and honorifics when they came, just as he had busied himself unhappily on the mound when the crowd stopped the rush of the game to cheer him at Busch Stadium that afternoon in 1968. For me, at least, Bob Gibson was still burning to pitch to the next batter. But in another, oddly opposite sense it seemed wrong to think of Gibson as a participant in the soft, sweet rituals with which newly elected baseball immortals are inducted into the Hall of Fame at the ceremonial in Cooperstown each August—the reading of the players' records and their official citations; their speeches of acceptance and gratitude; the obligatory picture-taking, with the still-young heroes, in civilian clothes, holding up their plaques and standing among the smaller, white-haired, earlier great figures who have come back for the occasion: old gents at a reunion, blinking in the hot upstate sunlight—because baseball up to now

---

*By the end of the 1981 season, Gaylord Perry had accounted for 3,336 lifetime strikeouts, while Ryan stood at 3,249, Carlton at 3,148, and Seaver at 3,075. Steve Carlton's total is a new National League record, eclipsing Gibson's old mark, because unlike Perry and Ryan, he has pitched only in that league.

has never quite known what to make of Bob Gibson, and has slightly but persistently failed to pay him his full due as a player and as a man. With this conviction in mind, I determined early this summer to look up Gibson and try to get to know him a little better. I wanted to see how he was faring now that he could no longer stare down at the batters of the world from the height of the pitcher's mound. I knew that he was still living in Omaha, his hometown, and when I reached him there by telephone he told me to come on out if I wanted to. Not a warm invitation, but not a wary one, either. In the next week or two, I mentioned my forthcoming trip to some friends of mine—good baseball fans, all of them—and noticed that many of them seemed to have forgotten Bob Gibson's eminence and élan, if, indeed, they had ever been aware of them. In the history of the game, it seemed, as in his playing days, he already stood at a little distance from the crowd, a little beyond us all. But then I talked about Gibson with some players—old teammates or opponents of his—and they responded more warmly.

Pete Rose, who talks in the same runaway-taxi style in which he runs bases, said, "I'm always afraid I'll forget some pitcher when I start rating them, because I've faced so many of them. I started out against people like Warren Spahn, you know. But the best pitcher I ever batted against was Juan Marichal, because he threw so many goddam different kinds of good pitches against you. The hardest thrower of them all was Sandy Koufax, and the greatest competitor was Bob Gibson. He worked so fast out there, and he always had the hood up. He always wanted to close his own deal. He wasn't no badman, but he never talked to you, because he was battling you so hard. I sure as hell don't miss batting against him, but I miss him in the game."

Billy Williams, now a coach for the Cubs, who hit 426 home runs during his sixteen years with that team and two years with the Oakland A's, told me, "Bob Gibson always got *on* with it. He didn't stand around out there and look around the park, you know. You always got the same message from him: 'Look, I'm goin' to throw this pitch and either you hit it or I get your ass out.' You like a guy like that. The infielders were never on their heels out there behind him. Everyone's on their toes, and it's a better game for everybody. I used to love the afternoon games at Wrigley Field when Gibby pitched against our Fergie Jenkins, because you could always plan something early for that evening. They *hurried.* Gibby was as serious as anybody you ever saw, and you had to be ready at all times. There was hitters that tried to step out on him, to break his pace, but if you did that too often he'd knock you down. He let you know who was out there on the mound. Made himself felt. He never let up, even on the hottest days there in St. Louis, which is the hottest place in the world. Just walked out there in the heat and threw the ball past people."

Tim McCarver said, "He was an intimidating, arrogant-looking athlete. The arrogance he projected toward batters was fearsome. There was no guile to his pitching, just him glaring down at that batter. He wanted the game played on his own terms. He worked very fast, and that pace was part of his personality on the mound, part of the way he dominated the game. One of the things he couldn't stand was a catcher coming out there to talk to him. In my first full year with the Cardinals, when I was only twenty-one years old, our manager was Johnny Keane, who was a fanatic about having a catcher establish communications with his pitcher. So I'd get a signal from Keane that meant 'Go on out there and settle him down,' but then I'd look out and see Hoot glaring in at me." McCarver laughed, and shook his head. "Well, sometimes I'd walk out halfway, to try to appease both parties!"

McCarver is an intimate friend of Bob Gibson's and he told me that Gibson was much the same off the field as on the mound. "Bob is relatively shy," he said. "He's a nice man, but he's quiet. He doesn't enjoy small talk. He doesn't like to waste his time with anything that's weak or offhand. He wants to deal from strength all the time. That's why he projects this uppity-black-man figure that so many people in baseball seem to hate. He's very proud, you know, and he had a ghetto upbringing, so you could understand why he was so sensitive to bigotry—up to a point. But we have a great relationship—me, a kid from Memphis, Tennessee, and him, an elegant black man from Omaha. Any relationship you get into with Bob is going to be intense. He's a strong man, with strong feelings."

Joe Torre, the manager of the New York Mets, who played with Gibson from 1969 to 1974, is also a close friend. When I called on him late in June, in the clubhouse at Shea Stadium, and told him I was about to go west to visit Gibson, he beckoned me over to a framed photograph on one wall of his office. The picture shows the three friends posing beside a batting cage in their Cardinals uniforms. Torre, a heavy-faced man with dark eyebrows and a falsely menacing appearance, and McCarver, who has a cheerful, snub-nosed Irish look to him, are both grinning at the photographer, with their arms around the shoulders of Bob Gibson, who is between them; it's impossible to tell if Gibson is smiling, though, because his back is turned to the camera. "That says it all," Torre said. "He alienated a lot of people—most of all the press, who didn't always know what to make of him. He has this great confidence in himself: 'Hey, I'm me. Take me or leave me.' There was never any selling of Bob Gibson. He's an admirable man. On the mound, he had very tangible intangibles. He had that hunger, that killer instinct. He threw at a lot of batters but not nearly as many as you've heard. But he'd never deny it if you asked him. I think this is great. There's no other sport except boxing that has such a hard one-on-one confrontation as you get when a pitcher and a hitter go up against each other. Any edge you can get on the hitter, any doubt you can put in his mind, you use. And Bob Gibson would never give up that edge. He was your enemy out there. I try to teach this to our pitchers. The more coldness, the more mystery about you, the more chance you have of getting them out.

"I played against him before I played with him, and either way he never talked to you. Never. I was on some All-Star teams with him, and even then he didn't talk to you. There was the one in Minnesota, when I was catching him and we were ahead 6–5, I think, in the ninth. I'm catching, and Tony Oliva, a great hitter, is leading off, and Gibby goes strike one, strike two. Now I want a fastball up and in, I think to myself, and maybe I should go out there and tell him this—tell him, whatever he does, not to throw it down and in to Oliva. So I go out and tell him, and Gibby just gives me that look of his. Doesn't say a word. I go back and squat down and give him the signal—fastball up and in—and he throws it *down* and in, and Oliva hits it for a double to left center. To this day, I think Gibby did it on purpose. He didn't want to be told *anything*. So then there's an infield out, and then he strikes out the last two batters, of course, and we win. In the shower I say, 'Nice pitching,' and he still doesn't say anything to me. Ask him about it."

Torre lit a long cigar, and said, "Quite a man. He can seem distant and uncaring to some people, but he's not the cold person he's been described as. There are no areas between us where he's withdrawn. Things go deep with him. I miss talking to him during the season, and it's my fault, because I'm always so damn busy. He doesn't call me, because he never wants to make himself a pain in the ass to a friend. But he is my friend. The other day, I got a photograph of himself he'd sent me, and he'd signed it 'Love, Bob.' How many other ballplayers are going to do that? How many other friends."

Most ballplayers who are discussing a past rival or a teammate go directly to the man's craft—what pitches he could hit, his arm, his range afield, or (with pitchers) his stuff and what he threw when the count was against him. But I had begun to notice that the baseball people talking about Bob Gibson all seemed anxious to get at something deeper; Gibson the man was even more vivid and interesting to them than Gibson the great pitcher. Bill White, the well-known TV and radio announcer with the Yankees, played first base behind Gibson with the Cards for seven years, and was then traded to the Phillies and had to play against him. "He was tough and uncompromising," White told me. "Koufax and Don Drysdale were just the same, with variations for their personalities—they had that same hard state of mind. But I think a great black athlete is sometimes tougher in a game, because every black has had it tough on the way up. Any black player who has a sense of himself, who wants to make something of himself, has something of Bob Gibson's attitude. Gibson had a chip on his shoulder out there—which was good. He was mean enough. He had no remorse. I remember when he hit Jim Ray Hart on the shoulder—he was bending away from a pitch—and broke his collarbone. Bob didn't say anything to him. I'd been his roomie for a while on the Cards, but the first time I batted against him, when I went over to the Phillies, he hit me in the arm. It didn't surprise me at all."

And, once again, Mike Shannon: "I think every superior athlete has some special motivation. With Bob Gibson, it wasn't that he wanted to win so much as that he didn't want to lose. He *hated* to lose. He just wouldn't accept it."

It was ninety-seven degrees at the Omaha airport when I landed there early one evening in July, and when I called Bob Gibson from my motel he invited me to come on out and cool off with a dip in his pool. He picked me up in his car—a black 1972 Mercedes SEL, lovingly kept up, with CB equipment (his call signal is Redbird) and terse "BG" license plates. Gibson looked well kept up himself, in tailored jeans, a white polo shirt, thin gold spectacles, a gold bracelet on his left wrist, a World Series ring, and a necklace with a pendant "45" in gold—his old uniform number. He is forty-four years old, but only his glasses spoiled the impression that he was perfectly capable of working nine tough innings the next afternoon. I asked him what he did for exercise these days, and he said, "Nothing." I expressed surprise, and he said, "I played sports hard for thirty years, which is enough. Now I'm tired of all that." No apology, no accompanying smile or joke: no small talk. He spoke pleasantly enough, though, in a light, almost boyish voice, and when he did laugh—a little later, after we were more used to each other—the sound of it made me realize that only in the world of sports would he be considered anything but a young man. There were some quiet spells in the car during our longish drive out to his house, in Bellevue, a comfortable suburban district on the south side of town, but by the time we got there I had lost any sense of foreboding that I might have had about imposing myself on such a famously private man.

Bob Gibson has done well for himself in Omaha. He was born and grew up there in the black North Side ghetto; his mother was a laundress, and his father died before he was born. He was the youngest of seven children—his three sisters and three brothers are all still living—and at the time of his birth the family lived in a four-room shack. When he was an infant there, he was bitten on the ear by a rat. By the end of his playing days, Gibson was earning more than a hundred and fifty thousand dollars a year, which made him one of the two or three best-paid players of his time, and he invested his money with care. Today, he is the chairman of the board—an interracial board—of the Community Bank of Nebraska, which he helped get started seven years ago, and which does most of its business in the black community of Omaha. He is also the co-owner and the active, day-to-day manager of a new and successful medium-sized bar-restaurant called Gibby's, a couple of blocks away from Creighton University, which Gibson entered as a freshman on a basketball scholarship in 1954. Much of Gibson's life these days seems new. Gibby's opened in late 1978, and last November he was married to Wendy Nelson, whom I met at their home, to the accompaniment of frenzied barking from their four-month-old miniature schnauzer, Mia. ("Kill, Mia!" Gibson said delightedly. "Kill, girl!") Wendy Gibson, a composed, striking-looking blonde woman in her late twenties, is in the financial division of the local telephone company, where she works, by preference, on the very early shift, driving to work each day shortly after dawn in the family's *other* Mercedes. (Gibson's previous marriage, to Charline Johnson, ended in divorce some years ago; their children, Renee and Annette, are grown up and have moved away from Omaha. A captivating oil portrait of the two girls and their father—all of them much younger then—hangs in Gibson's study in his new house; the artist is an old friend and teammate, Curt Flood.) Wendy and Bob Gibson moved into their house last May. It is a spacious, comfortably furnished and carpeted three-story contemporary wooden structure, with a sundeck that looks over a steep hillside and a thick green growth of oaks and cottonwoods. A flight of steps leads down from the deck to a big swimming pool, which had had its inaugural only a week before my arrival. Bob Gibson is handy. He helped design the new house, and he put in the deck stairs and built a raised wooden patio beside the pool, and also did most of the landscape work on the grounds, laying in some old railroad ties to form a rose garden and planting shrubs and young trees everywhere. The pool was built to Gibson's design; its sides and bottom are painted black—a da Vinci-like idea of his, meant to help the water hold the heat of the sun in the spring and fall. Somehow, though, he had not remembered the warmish mid-summer Nebraska sunshine, and when he and I slipped into the inky waves, the water temperature stood at ninety-two degrees—only a fraction cooler than the steamy, locust-loud night air. "Another mistake," Gibson said mildly. Swimming was a bit like sloshing through black-bean soup, but after a couple of turns up and down the pool he and I settled ourselves comfortably enough on the top steps at the shallow end, with our legs dangling in the water, and while Mia sniffed and circled me warily we talked a little baseball.

I asked Gibson if he recalled the low-and-inside pitch he had thrown to Tony Oliva in that All-Star game, against Joe Torre's signals.

"Well, I never really liked being on the All-Star team," he said. "I liked the honor of it, being voted one of the best, but I couldn't get used to the idea of playing with people from other teams in the league—guys who I'd have to go out and try to beat just a couple of days later. I didn't even like having Joe catch me—he was with the Braves then—because I figured he'd learn how to hit me. In that same game, he came out and told me not to throw the high fastball to Harmon Killebrew, because the word was that he ate up that pitch." Gibson's voice was almost incredulous as he said this. "Well, hell. I struck him out with three high fastballs. But in any of the All-Star games where I got to pitch early"—Gibson was voted onto the National League All-Star squad eight times—"I'd always dress right away and get out of there in a hurry, before the other players got done and came into the clubhouse. I didn't want to hang around and make friends. I don't think there's any place in the game for a pitcher smiling and joking with the hitters. I was all business on the mound—it *is* a business, isn't it?—and I think some of the writers used to call me cold or arrogant because of that. I didn't want to be friends with anybody on the other side, except perhaps with Willie Stargell—how could you not talk to that guy? None of this was meant to scare guys, or anything. It was just the way I felt. When Orlando Cepeda was with us, I used to watch him and Marichal laughing and fooling around before a game. They'd been on the Giants together, you know. But then Cepeda would go out and *kill* Marichal at the plate—one of the best pitchers I ever saw—and when it was over they'd go to dinner together and laugh some more. It just made me shake my head. I didn't understand it."

I had been wondering how to bring up the business of his knocking down his old roommate Bill White, but now Gibson offered the story of his own accord. "Even before Bill was traded, I used to tell him that if he ever dived across the plate to swing at an outside pitch, the way he liked to, I'd have to hit him," he said. "And then, the very first time, he went for a pitch that was *this* far outside and swung at it, and so I hit him on the elbow with the next pitch. [Some years earlier, Gibson hit Duke Snider after similar provocation, and broke his elbow.] Bill saw it coming, and he yelled 'Yaah!' even before it got him. And I yelled over to him, 'You son of a bitch, you went for that outside ball! That pitch, that part of the plate, belongs to *me!* If I make a mistake inside, all right, but the outside is mine and don't you forget it.' He said, 'You're crazy,' but he understood me."

I mentioned a famous moment when Gibson had hit Tommie Agee, of the Mets, on the batting helmet with the very first pitch of the first inning of the first Cardinals spring-training game in 1968. Agee had come over from the Chicago White Sox and the American League in the previous winter, and when Gibson's first swallow of the spring conked him, several Gibson students among the Mets and Cardinals baseball writers in the press box at Al Lang Field called out, "Welcome to the National League, Tommie!" (Agee went to the hospital for observation, but was found not to have suffered serious injury.)

Gibson was silent for a moment, and then he said, "It's very easy to hit a batter in the body with a pitch. There's nothing to it. It's a lot harder to hit him in the head. Any time you hit him in the head, it's really his own fault. Anyway, that was just spring training."

Joe Torre had told me that the Agee-plunking was an accident, but I noted now that Gibson had not quite denied intention in the affair. He had put doubt in my mind, just as Torre had told me he would. He still wanted that edge.

"I did throw at John Milner in spring training once," Gibson went on, paddling his legs in the water. "Because of that swing of his—that dive at the ball." Milner, an outfielder then with the Mets and now with the Pirates, invariably takes a full-scale, left-handed downtown swing at the ball, as if he meant to pull every pitch into the right-field stands. "I don't like batters taking that big cut, with their hats falling off and their buttons popping and every goddam thing like that. It doesn't show any respect for the pitcher. That batter's not doing any thinking up there, so I'm going to *make* him think. The next time, he won't look so fancy out there. He'll be a better-looking hitter. So I got Milner that once, and then, months later, at Shea Stadium, Tom Seaver began to pitch me up and inside, knocking me down, and it took me a minute to realize that it must have been to pay me back for something *in spring training*. I couldn't believe that."

There was a little silence at poolside while I digested this. Gibson sounded almost like a veteran samurai warrior recalling an ancient code of pain and honor. I suggested that there must be days when he still badly missed being out there on the mound, back in the thick of things.

"No, I have no desire to get out and throw the fastball again," he said quietly. "Even if I wanted to, I couldn't."

I had noticed that Gibson limped slightly as he walked around the pool, and the accounts of some of his baseball injuries and how he had reacted to them at the time came back to me. In July of 1967, while pitching against the Pirates in St. Louis, he was struck just above his right ankle by a line drive off the bat of Roberto Clemente. He went down in a heap, but after the Cardinals trainer had treated the injury with a pain-deadening spray, Gibson insisted on staying in the game. He walked Willie Stargell, retired Bill Mazeroski on a pop-up, and then, firing a three-two pitch to Donn Clendenon, came down hard on the right leg with his characteristic spinning follow-through and snapped the already cracked bone. Dal Maxvill, then a Cardinals shortstop and now a Cardinals coach, said to me recently, "That was the most extraordinary thing I ever saw in baseball—Gibby pitching to those batters with a broken leg. Everyone who was there that day remembered it afterward, for always, and every young pitcher who came onto our club while Gibson was still with us was told about it. We didn't have too many pitchers turning up with upset stomachs or hangnails on our team after that."

Gibson came back to win three games against the Red Sox in the World Series that fall, but his next serious injury, in midseason of 1973, took a heavier toll. Leading off first base in a game against the Mets at Shea Stadium, he made a sudden dive back toward the base after an infield line drive was caught, but collapsed when his right knee buckled. The trainer and the team doctor came out to succor him, but Gibson cried, "Don't touch it! Don't touch it!" and again refused to be taken out of the game. When the inning ended, he walked to the mound and began his warmup tosses and fell heavily to the ground. The surgeon—Dr. Stan London—who performed the cartilage operation the next day said afterward that Gibson had the knees of an eighty-year-old man. Gibson recovered in time to pitch and win a game that September, and he continued for two more full seasons on the mound, although, as he told me now, he sometimes had to sit in the clubhouse for two hours after a game before he felt able to head for the showers. "I'd had the left knee drained about seventeen times, too," he said. "I'd sit like this"—he hung his head and arms like a broken puppet—"and I'd think, *Why do I put up with this? Why, why?*" He laughed now, mocking himself. "I just couldn't give it up," he said. "Couldn't let go."

I asked if he'd become a different kind of pitcher then, using change-ups and slip pitches, the way many older hurlers do in their final seasons.

"No, I always threw hard," he said. "They didn't use me much in my final season, after I'd announced I was going to retire—I never did understand that. But once, when I hadn't pitched in three weeks, they brought me into a game against Houston in extra innings—I was the last pitcher we had—and I struck out the side on nine pitches that were nothing but fastballs. So I still had something left, even at the end. I always had pretty good control, you know, so it wasn't like I didn't know what I was doing out there. But later that season I gave up a grand-slam home run to Pete LaCock, of the Cubs, and that told me it was about time for me to get off the mound for good." Gibson spoke lightly enough, but at the time this home run was an almost insupportable blow to his pride. A pitcher who was with the Cubs that year told me that as LaCock (who is not exactly famous as a slugger) circled the bases, Gibson stalked after him around the base paths, reviling him for what he had done.

"Pitching is about ninety percent thinking," Gibson went on. "I threw hard when I was younger, but I didn't know how to get people out. I don't care how hard you throw, somebody's going to hit it if you don't think out there. It's not all that detailed—you don't think three or four pitches ahead. But one pitch might set up the next two you throw—it depends what the guy does with it. You know. If he misses a fastball by a foot, then he'll see another one. If he fouls it off or *just* misses it, he'll probably get a breaking ball next. It isn't exactly scientific, or anything."

Gibson suddenly laughed in the darkness beside me. "But not everybody understands what a pitcher *does*," he said. "About his control, I mean. I remember when Mike Shannon was moved in from the outfield and began playing third base for us—back in the middle sixties, it was. He was really nervous over there. He kept asking me where I wanted him to play—up or back, near the line or away. He wanted instructions. I always told him I didn't give a damn where he played unless there was a right-handed batter coming up with a man on first and less than two out, but then he should be ready, because he'd be getting a ground ball, right to him or around his area. And I'd throw a sinker down and in, and the batter would hit it on the ground to Mike, to start the double play, and when we came in off the field Mike would look at me with his mouth open, and he'd say, "But how did you *know*?" He didn't have the faintest idea that when I threw that pitch to the batter he *had* to hit it to him there! He didn't know what pitching was all about."

To go back a little, Gibson also won his second start in the 1968 Cardinals-Tigers World Series—a 10–1 decision in the fourth game, during which he fanned ten batters and whacked a home run. It was Gibson's seventh straight World Series victory—an all-time record. The Tigers, however, captured the Series, rallying in stimulating fashion after trailing by three games to one, and beating Gibson in the memorable finale, when Detroit outfielder Jim Northrup, batting with two out and two on in the seventh inning of the scoreless game, smashed a long drive that was misjudged by Curt Flood in center field, who then slipped on the turf and allowed the ball to go over his head for a triple. The Tigers won the game by 4–1, and the Most Valuable Player award for the Series went to Mickey Lolich, a portly left-handed sinkerball specialist, who won the second, fifth, and seventh games. Gibson, however, had established a Series record of thirty-five strikeouts (still standing), and a few weeks later he was named the Most Valuable Player of the National League for 1968 and became the unanimous winner of the Cy Young Award as the league's best pitcher. The following year, 1969, Gibson compiled a 20–13 record, with an earned-run average of 2.18, and in 1970 his 23–7 won-lost mark and 3.12

ERA won him the Cy Young again. Injuries began to gnaw him after that, but he declined only stubbornly, throwing a no-hitter against the Pirates in 1971 and running off eleven straight victories in the course of a 19–11 season in 1972. His lifetime earned-run average of 2.91 runs per game is the ninth-best in baseball history. (Walter Johnson's 2.37 leads all comers, while Tom Seaver, at 2.62, and Jim Palmer, at 2.73, stand third and fourth on the all-time list at this writing.)

Many observers (including this one) believe that Gibson's 1.12 earned-run average in 1968 is one of the Everests of the game, ranking with Joe DiMaggio's fifty-six-consecutive-game hitting streak in 1941 and Hack Wilson's 190 runs batted in in 1930. Gibson's record, however, was not much noted or celebrated in its time, partly because it was achieved in a summer during which the pitchers in both leagues established a mesmerizing dominance over the batters. The leagues' combined batting average fell to an all-time low of .237, and twenty-one percent of all games played were shutouts. Many pitchers came up with startling performances that summer. Gaylord Perry, of the Giants, and Ray Washburn, of the Cardinals, threw no-hit games on successive days at Candlestick Park; Jerry Koosman, a rookie, won nineteen games for the Mets; Denny McLain, as I have noted, won thirty-one games for the Tigers; and Don Drysdale, of the Dodgers, ran off fifty-eight and two-thirds consecutive shutout innings—a record that still stands. At the end of the year, the baseball fathers studied these figures and determined to rebalance the game by shaving five inches off the height of the mound (reducing it to ten inches), and by closing up the upper and lower limits of the strike zone. Gibson's golden season may always appear a mite tarnished by these circumstances, but even a brief rundown of his 1968 summer outings suggests that in that single season he came as close to some ideal of pitching as most of us are ever likely to witness or wish for. Younger fans may argue for Ron Guidry's marvelous 25–3 season for the Yankees in 1978, when he threw nine shutouts and wound up with a 1.74 earned-run average. Others will cite Steve Carlton's one-man-band performance in 1972, when he finished with an earned-run average of 1.97 and a record of 27–10—all this for a frightful last-place Phillies team that won only fifty-nine games in all—while geezers may bring up Carl Hubbell's 23–12 and 1.66 earned-run mark for the Giants in 1933. But no matter: these great case studies of the game are forever moot.

On May 28, 1968, Bob Gibson lost to the Giants, 3–1, and saw his record for the year decline to three victories and five defeats. Surprisingly, however, his earned run average of 1.52 for the young season was fifth in the National League at this point—an oddity explicable by the fact that his teammates had supplied him with a total of four runs in the five games he lost: starvation fare.

On June 2, Gibson pitched the Cardinals into first place (this was before the leagues had been subdivided into East and West sectors) with a 6–3 victory over the Mets; the final Mets run—a homer by Ed Charles—came in the seventh inning. It was also the final run that Gibson surrendered in the month of June, for he threw shutout games in his next five outings. Only the last of these brought him much attention from the national press, and that came because reporters had noticed that his next appearance, on July 1, would be against the Dodgers in Los Angeles, and that his mound opponent there would be Don Drysdale, whose record shutout skein of fifty-eight and two-thirds innings had been set over a span of six games in late May and early June. A matchup between the two seemed exciting indeed, for Drysdale, who was six feet five and threw almost sidearm, had a hostile scowl, a devastating fastball, and a reputation for knocking down batters he didn't care for: another intimidator. Gibson by now had forty-eight scoreless innings to his credit, but the tension of the famous confrontation vanished in the very first inning, when two Dodgers singled and Gibson, while pitching to Ron Fairly, let go a wild pitch that allowed Len Gabrielson to score from third base. Gibson had lost the duel with Drysdale and a shot at his record, but he won the game, by 5–1. He then pitched a shutout against the Giants, beat Houston by 8–1, and afterward shut out the Mets and the Phillies in succession. On July 30, once again facing the Mets, Gibson surrendered a run with two out in the fourth inning, when Ed Charles scored on a double by Eddie Kranepool—the same Ed Charles who had homered against him on June 2. In that span—from June 2 to July 30—Gibson had given up two earned runs (and two runs in toto) in ninety-six and two-thirds innings.

Gibson won that Mets game, and he did not lose a game, in fact, until August 24, when he fanned fifteen Pirates but lost, 6–4, after giving up a three-run homer to Willie Stargell. Between May 28 and August 24, Gibson had won fifteen straight games, ten of them shutouts. He threw two more shutouts in his next two outings, and somebody figured out that in the course of three straight games in August, Gibson's infielders had to make only eight assists. (His shortstop, Dal Maxvill, told a reporter, "It's like having a night off out there when he's pitching.") Possibly tired by now—or perhaps a bit understimulated, since his club had run away with the league by this point, having established a fourteen-and-a-half-game lead over the second-place Reds by August 1—Gibson lost three games in September, one of them to the no-hitter by Gaylord Perry. His final victory, on September 27, was a 1–0 decision over the Astros—his thirteenth shutout. His season was over; the World Series and the Tigers were just ahead.

A further thin cement of statistics will finish the monument. Gibson completed twenty-eight of the thirty-four games he started in 1968, and was never removed in the middle of an inning—never knocked out of the box. His 1.12 earned-run average is second only to the all-time low of 1.01, established by the Red Sox' Hub Leonard in 1914, and it eclipsed the old National League mark of 1.22, set by Grover Cleveland Alexander in 1915. Gibson's thirteen shutouts are second only to the sixteen that Alexander achieved the following summer. But those very low early figures, it should be understood, must be slightly discounted, for they were established in the sludgy, Pleistocene era of the game, when aces like Leonard and Alexander and Walter Johnson and the White Sox' Red Faber regularly ran off season-long earned-run averages of two runs or less per game, thanks to the dead ball then in use. The lively ball, which came into the game in 1921, when the owners began to notice how much the fans seemed to enjoy watching a young outfielder (and former pitcher) named George Herman Ruth hit towering drives into the bleachers, put an end to the pitchers' hold over the game, and none of the four worthies I have cited ever pitched consistently in the less-than-three-runs-per-game level after 1922. Bob Gibson, we may conclude, was the man most responsible for the *next* major change in the dimensions of the sport—the lowering of the mound and the shrinkage of the strike zone that came along in 1969. Gibson, like all pitchers, complained bitterly when these new rules were announced, but Bob Broeg, the sports editor of the *St. Louis Post-Dispatch* and the dean of Cardinals sportswriters, told him he had only himself to blame. "I said, 'Goddam it, Gib, you're changing the game!'" Broeg told me not long ago. "'It isn't fun anymore. You're making it like hockey.'"

On another day, Omaha slowly came to a broil under a glazy white sun while Gibson and I ran some early-morning errands in his car—a visit to his bank, a stop at the drive-in window of another bank, where he picked up the payroll checks for Gibby's—and wound up at the restaurant, where the daytime help greeted the boss cheerfully. Gibson seemed in an easy frame of mind, and he looked younger than ever. I recalled that many of his teammates had told me what good company he was in the dugout and on road trips—on days when he wasn't pitching. He was a comical, shrill-voiced bench jockey, and a grouchy but lighthearted clubhouse agitator, who was sometimes known to bang a bat repeatedly and horribly on the metal locker of a teammate who was seen to be suffering the aftereffects of too many ice-cream sodas the previous evening. While he drove, Gibson, with a little urging, recalled how he had pitched to some of the prime hitters of his day—inside fastballs to Willie Mays (who feasted on breaking pitches), belt-high inside deliveries to Eddie Mathews, low and away to Roberto Clemente, and so on.

He said that Frank Robinson used to deceive pitchers with his plate-crowding (Robinson was a right-handed slugger of fearsome power, whose customary stance at the plate was that of an impatient subway traveler leaning over the edge of the platform and peering down the tracks for the D train), because they took it to mean that he was eager for an inside pitch. "Besides," he said, "they'd be afraid of hitting him and putting him on base. So they'd work him outside, and he'd hit the shit out of the ball. I always tried him inside, and I got him out there—sometimes. He was like Willie Mays—if you got the ball outside to Willie at all, he'd just *kill* you. The same with Clemente. I could throw him a fastball knee-high on the outside corner seventeen times in a row, but if I ever got it two inches up, he'd hit it out of sight. That's the mark of a good hitter—the tiniest mistake and he'll punish you. Other batters—well, somebody like Joe Adcock was just a guess hitter. You'd pitch him up and in, and he'd swing and miss every time. He just didn't give a damn. I don't know what's the matter with so many hitters—it's like their brains small up." He shook his head and laughed softly. "Me, too. I got beat by Tommy Davis twice the same way. In one game, I'd struck him out three times on sliders away. But I saw that he'd been inching up and inching up toward that part of the plate, so I decided to fool him and come inside, and he hit a homer and beat me, one-oh. And then, in another game, I did exactly the same thing. I tried to outthink him, and he hit the inside pitch for a homer and it was one-oh all over again. So I could get dumb, too."

I said that he didn't seem to have made too many mistakes in the summer of '68. Gibson thought for a moment or two and said, "You can't say it was a fluke, although some people *have* said that. Just say it was totally unusual. Everything I threw that year seemed to go where I wanted it. Everything was down, all year. I was never that good again, because they went and changed the rules on me. The next year was a terrific struggle. I had a good season, but I never worked so hard in my life, because so many of my breaking pitches were up. I'll never know, but I doubt very seriously I'd have had another one-point-one-two E.R.A., even if they'd left the mound where it was. I'd like to think I'd really perfected my pitching to that point, but I'll never know."

The talk shifted to pitchers, and Gibson (echoing Pete Rose) said that he thought that Juan Marichal had been the best hurler of their time, because of his absolute control. "I had a better fastball and a better slider, but he was a better pitcher than me or Koufax," he said. Among contemporary pitchers, he had warm things to say about the Phillies' Steve Carlton, once a young teammate of his on the Cards. "He's always had a great arm," he said. "And if you have a good arm and you're in the game long enough, you're going to learn how to pitch. He sure knows how now. What makes a player great to me is longevity."

I named some other mound stars of the sixties and seventies, and Gibson shrugged and shook his head. "I guess I was never much in awe of anybody," he said. "I think you have to have that attitude if you're going to go far in this game. People have always said that I was too confident, but I think you'll find that most guys who can play are pretty cocky." The locution "He can play"— as in "Carl Yastrzemski can play a little"—is a throwaway line, the professionals' designation for star-quality athletes. "They're not sitting around worrying about who they're going to pitch against or bat against the next day. You hear a lot of talk about the pressure of the game, but I think most of that comes from the media. Most guys don't let things worry them. Pressure comes when you're not doing well. I've always thought that you only really enjoy baseball when you're good at it. For someone who isn't at the top of the game—who's just hanging on somewhere on down the totem pole—it's a real tough job, every day. But when I was playing I never wished I was doing anything else. I think being a professional athlete is the finest thing a man can do."

I asked about the source of his great confidence in himself, and he said, "I've always been that way. After all, I was playing basketball with grown men when I was thirteen years old. I always thought I was good enough to play with anyone. I don't know where that came from."

When Gibson was playing baseball, he was considered one of the two or three very best athletes in the game. His early basketball experience had come when he was a water boy with an itinerant black basketball team, the Y Travellers (named for Omaha's North Branch YMCA), which was coached by his grown-up oldest brother, Josh; whenever the Travellers ran up a comfortable lead over some local Nebraska or Iowa all-star club, Josh would send his kid brother into the game, just to rub things in a little. Bob Gibson won city and statewide basketball honors at Technical High School, in Omaha, and a few in baseball, too (he was a catcher in the beginning), and he broke every basketball record at Creighton, where he was the first black student to be given a basketball scholarship—and, for that matter, to play on the team. After leaving Creighton, he played for the Harlem Globetrotters during the 1957–58 season, after he had signed on as a pitcher with the Cardinals organization. "It was all right being with the Trotters," Gibson told me, "but I hated that clowning around. I wanted to play all the time—I mean, I wanted to play to win."

In spite of Gibson's spinning, staggering pitching motion, which certainly did not leave him in the squared-away, weight-on-both-feet attitude that coaches recommend as the proper post-delivery fielding stance for the position, he was agile enough out there to win the Gold Glove award as the best defensive pitcher in his league every season from 1965 through 1973. Fans and writers and players still talk about some of his fielding plays in the same awestruck tones they use for the seventeen-strikeout Series game. In one play (I can still see it) in the 1964 World Series, he scampered over and plucked up a hard-hit ball struck by Joe Pepitone that had nailed him on the hip and caromed halfway to third base; Gibson leaped and turned 180 degrees in midair and made an overhead throw to first—a basketball one-handed fall-away jumper—that nipped Pepitone at the bag. There was also a nationally televised game in which he ran down a ball that a Giants batter had bounced over his head out on the mound; Gibson caught up with it while running full tilt away from the plate and toward second base, and he flipped it, underhand and right-handed and away from his body (try it), to first for the out. Tim McCarver, who weighs a solid 190 pounds, told me that one day when he and Gibson were horsing around on the field, Bob had suddenly seized him and lifted him above his head at arm's length, holding him aloft like some Olympic weight lifter at the end of a clean and jerk. "The man is somewhat startling," McCarver said.

Gibby's is a welcoming sort of place—a squared-off, three-sided bar downstairs, with strips of stained-glass decoration on the far wall and a short flight of steps up to the sun-filled upper level, where there are some comfortable wooden-backed dining booths and hanging plants everywhere. On a busy night—on Saturdays, for instance, when a jazz group comes in to play—Gibby's has room for about 130 diners and 20 more customers at the bar. I was not surprised to learn that Gibson had had a hand in the restaurant's design and construction. He is there every day, starting at eight in the morning, when he turns up to check the books for the previous night's business, to inspect the incoming meat and produce (the menu is modest, and is built around steaks and shrimp and delicious hamburgers), and generally to keep an eye on things. "I want to make sure nobody is throwing out the forks with the garbage," he said lightly. He went to bartenders' school for three months before Gibby's opened—not so much to learn how to mix cocktails, although he can now whip up eighty different drinks, as to learn how veteran waiters and bartenders can fleece a rookie owner. "What I *should* have done was to become an accountant," he said. "About ninety percent of the job is damned paperwork." Gibby's clientele is an interesting mixture of races and ages and sexes—a "neat crowd," according to the owner ("neat" is a favorite word), and perhaps the only such cosmopolitan mixture in Omaha. The waiters are mostly young black men, and the bartenders mostly young black women. Gibson is a calm and approachable boss; the staff seems to care about him, and vice versa. When a small, very young waitress began putting coins into a cigarette machine near us, Bob said reprovingly, "Those aren't for *you*, are they?" (They weren't.) Later on, he let slip that the previous week he had taken the four-year-old daughter of one of his female bartenders out to his new pool for the afternoon when her mother couldn't find a babysitter. At the last moment, he also asked the daughter of one of his regular customers to come along, too. "I used to have little girls myself," he said to me. A lot of the arriving diners and drinkers at Gibby's say hello to him in an easy, friendly way, but there isn't much hearty bar chatter with the host. Not many people would feel impelled to buddy up to Bob Gibson. I suggested that he must be exposed to a good deal of barside baseball expertise at his place of work, and he said, "Who wants to talk to fans? They always know so much, to hear them tell it, and they always think baseball is so easy. You hear them say, 'Oh, I was a pretty good ballplayer myself back when I was in school, but then I got this injury. . . .' Some cabdriver gave me that one day, and I said, 'Oh, really? That's funny, because when *I* was young I really wanted to be a cabdriver, only I had this little problem with my eyes, so I never made it.' He thought I was serious. It went right over his head."

Gibson's impatience with trifling or intrusive strangers accounted for considerable coolness between him and the media during his playing days—a mistrust that may even keep him out of the Hall of Fame for a year or two, since some members of the Baseball Writers Association have been known to allow personal pique to influence their judgment. (Each writer selects up to ten names of eligible former players he thinks worthy of the Hall of Fame, and a player must be named on seventy-five percent of the ballots in order to be immortalized.) A couple of years ago, when Willie Mays first came up for election, twenty-three members of the B.W.A. resolutely omitted him from their ballots. A good many St. Louis reporters still recall the time in 1967 when Gibson had the cast removed from his broken leg and then, annoyed by their clubhouse importunings and questions, taped a sheet of paper to his shirtfront on which he had written "1. Yes, it's off; 2. No, it doesn't hurt; 3. I don't know how much longer"; and so on. The club was in a pennant race, of course, and Gibson's condition was a matter of daily concern to Cardinals fans everywhere, so his broadside was not taken in good part.

"I don't like all this personal contact with the press," Gibson told me. "The press expects everyone to be congenial. Everyone's *not* congenial! They want to put every athlete in the same category as every other athlete. It's as if they thought they owned you." I had been told of a St. Louis television reporter who had once done something to offend one of Gibson's teammates and had then tried to reassure Gibson about their relationship. "You know I'll never do anything to hurt *you*, Bob," he said. Gibson looked at him incredulously and said, "Why, hell, the only way you could ever hurt me is if you happened to be a pretty good fastball hitter!" One longtime Cardinals writer said to me, "Bob was a thorny, obdurate personality, and there weren't too many people who were crazy about him. If he'd had a little more give to him, he could have owned this city. If he'd had Lou Brock's personality, he'd still be working for the Cardinals somewhere."

There is a standoff here. The price of Bob Gibson's owning St. Louis seems to be his agreeing—in his mind, at least—to let the press own him. I have considerable sympathy for any writer who had to ask Bob Gibson some sharp, news-producing questions two or three times a week over the span of a decade or more, but wanting Gibson with a sunny, less obdurate temperament would be to want him a less difficult, less dangerous man on the mound—not quite a Bob Gibson, not quite a great pitcher. The man is indivisible, and it is the wonder of him. It is my own suspicion that both sportswriters and fans are increasingly resentful of the fame and adulation and immense wealth that are now bestowed so swiftly upon so many young professional athletes, and are envious of their privileged and apparently carefree style of living. The resentment is a half-conscious appreciation of the fact that they themselves—the fans and the media people, that is—have to a great degree created these golden youths, and because of that there is indeed a wish to own them; to demand ceaseless, inhumanly repeated dazzling performances from them on the field, and to require absolute access to their private lives as well. Most athletes, who are very young when they first come to prominence and, for the most part, have a very limited experience of the world, respond to these demands either with a convulsive, wholly artificial public "image" of affability, or (more often, of late) with surliness or angry silence. Bob Gibson did neither. Somehow, he has always kept his distance and his strangeness, and there is something upright and old-fashioned about such stubborn propriety. He is there if anyone really wants to close that space—the whole man, and not a piece of him or an image of him—but many of us may prefer not to do so, because at a distance (from sixty feet six inches away, perhaps) he stands whole and undiminished, and beyond our envy: the athlete incarnate, the player.

Gibson had allowed me to close this space a little by his willingness to talk about himself, and I had begun to sense the intensity of relationships with him that Tim McCarver had told me about, and the absence of any withdrawn places in him that Joe Torre had mentioned. There is reason to believe that he has allowed himself to become more approachable since he left the game. Bob Broeg, who covered Gibson from his first day in spring training as a rookie, in 1958, to his retirement at the end of the 1975 season, said to me, "Bob didn't know how his personality worked against him. I don't think I wrote many things about him over the years that weren't appreciative of his great skills—he and Dizzy Dean were the two best pitchers I ever saw here—but he was always indifferent to me. One day, late in his career, I was in the clubhouse with him, and he was as closed off as ever, and I finally said, 'You've never said a kind or personal word to me in the years I've known you.' I walked away, and he chased me all the way across the room to ask what I meant. I'd pinked him, and he was extremely upset. He just didn't realize how cold he could be in everyday relationships."

But other intimates of Gibson's from his Cardinals days have a very different view of him. Gene Gieselmann, the team's trainer—he is thirty-three years old but looks much younger—counts Gibson among his closest and warmest friends. "My memories of baseball are all shiny where he's concerned," he said. "I cherish him. I think his problems with people go back to his never having had a father. He never knew him, you know. He dearly loved his mother, but I don't think he was very close to anyone else in his family. So when somebody, especially a white person"—Gieselmann is white—"showed him over a long period of time that he could be more than just a trainer or more than just another ballplayer, and that there could be something deeper in their relationship—well, that meant a lot to him, and then he showed how sensitive and generous he really was."

Gibson is a compulsive truthteller, and he appears to have a wry understanding of the burdens of that self-imposed role. At one point, he was talking with me about the difference between himself and Joe Torre when it came to dealing with writers and other strangers, and he said, "Joe knows everybody, and he recognizes them right away. I don't. I always had a hard time remembering people's names and recognizing their faces." There was a moment of silence, and then he added, "That's only half of it. I didn't *care*. And if I think somebody's wrong I'm going to say it."

I suddenly recalled an incident some years ago involving Gibson and another player, a well-known American League infielder, who were members of a small troupe of ballplayers making a postseason tour of military bases in the Pacific. Gibson's roommate on the trip was a public-relations man with one of the major-league teams, who was acting as an escort and travel agent for the group. Early in the trip, the infielder let drop some plainly anti-Semitic remarks about the P.R. man, who was Jewish, and Gibson stopped him in mid-sentence and advised him to keep his distance and not to talk to him for the remainder of the trip. "And if I ever pitch against you," Gibson said levelly, "I'm going to hit you on the coconut with my first pitch." Fortunately (or perhaps *un*fortunately), the two never did play against each other.

Gibson told me that racism had been easy to find when he came into baseball.

When he first reported to the Cards' spring-training camp, in St. Petersburg, in 1958, he presented himself at the Bainbridge Hotel, where the club was quartered, and asked for his room, but he was guided out a side door, where a taxi picked him up and drove him to the house of a black family on the other side of town; the same arrangement had been made for all the team's black players. (Three years later, the entire club moved to a different, unsegregated hotel in St. Pete.) Earlier, when he was an eighteen-year-old sophomore at Creighton, Gibson and the rest of the college's basketball team had gone to Oklahoma by train for a game against the University of Tulsa, and on the way Gibson was told that he wouldn't be able to eat or sleep with his teammates there. "I cried when I was told that," Gibson said to me. "I wouldn't have gone if I'd known. I wasn't ready for that."

At one point, I said to Gibson that when I had seen him play I had always been very much aware of the fact that he was a black athlete; somehow, his race had always appeared to be a considerable part of what he brought to the mound when he went to work out there.

He didn't respond—he simply said nothing at all—and I understood that my remark was not a question that anyone could easily respond to; it was not a question at all. But a little later he mentioned the many times he had been harassed by semi-official white people—hotel clerks and traffic cops and the like—who later began fawning on him when they learned that he was *the* Bob Gibson, the famous pitcher. "It's nice to get attention and favors," he said, "but I can never forget the fact that if I were an ordinary black person I'd be in the shithouse, like millions of others." He paused a moment, and then added, "I'm happy I'm *not* ordinary, though."

All this was said without surface bitterness or cynicism but with an intensity that went beyond his words. Some days later, Bill White, who is also black, commented on this tone of Gibson's. "He was always so proud," he said to me. "You could see it in his face and in the way he met people and talked to them. He never dropped it. I used to tell him, 'You can't be as tough on people as you are—it hurts you.' And he would say, 'You can do that, take all that, but I can't.' We didn't agree. But, of course, you never know what it's been like for another person. Some people have the ability to forget these things, but Bob Gibson always had the ability to make everybody remember what he had been through."

Gibson and I spent that afternoon at the restaurant, and he and Wendy had me to dinner at their house that night: steaks and mustard greens, prepared by the Gibsons together, and a Cabernet Sauvignon. (He is a demanding, accomplished cook; when he was playing, he invariably got his own meals at home when he returned from road trips and road cooking.) It was our last evening. Bob showed me some of the nineteenth-century American antiques he collects—a delicate bevelled-glass-front walnut secretary, an immense Barbary Coast–style sideboard, and so on—and took me into a basement room where he keeps his HO-gauge model-railroad set: an entire railhead in miniature, with yards and sidings and a downtown terminal, complete with surrounding streets and buildings. He said he didn't use the trains much anymore. The three of us took another swim in the pool, and Bob and I played a little noisy one-o'-cat with Mia in the living room with an old tennis ball. Gibson was relaxed and playful, but, as always, there was a silence about him: an air not of something held back but of a space within him that is not quite filled. At one point, I asked him if he liked Omaha, and he said, "Not all that much. It's all right. It's what I know." Then I asked if he liked the restaurant business, and in the same brusque way he said, "It isn't much, but it sure is better than doing nothing."

I knew that Gibson had had a brief career in sports television with the American Broadcasting Company, shortly after his retirement as a player. He was a "color man" with ABC's *Monday Night Baseball,* and on one occasion he conducted an impromptu, nationally televised interview with the Pittsburgh Pirates' John Candelaria, just after Candelaria had pitched a no-hit game. Gibson's questions centered on the future financial rewards of Candelaria's gem, but this insidey banter between co-professionals was evidently not a line of sports talk that the network brass approved of, and Gibson's media career declined after that, although he has since done some baseball broadcasts with the HBO cable network. It was a disappointment to him.

When Gibson was out of the room for a moment, I said to Wendy that I sensed something missing or incomplete in Bob, and she said, "Yes, he's still looking for something, and I don't know if the right thing for him will ever come along. It's sad."

Last winter, Gibson made inquiries with the Cardinals and the Royals and the Mets and the Giants in the hope of landing a job as a pitching coach; interest was expressed, but nothing quite worked out. One difficulty may be the very modest salaries of big-league coaches, but when I talked to Bob about his joining some team in this capacity I got the feeling that he might be willing to make a considerable financial sacrifice in order to get back into the game. Several of Gibson's old friends and teammates told me later that they had heard of his wish to get back into baseball, and without exception they hoped he would. They said that the game would be better off with a man of Gibson's character back in uniform. But some of them went on to express their doubt that he would be satisfied with a job of such limited rewards as that of a pitching coach. "It won't be enough for him," one man said. "Nothing will ever be enough for him now."

"I don't miss pitching," Gibson said to me on that last evening, "but I can't say that I don't miss the game. I miss it a *little*. There's a lot I don't want to get back to. I don't want the fame or the money or all that attention. I always hated all the waiting around a pitcher has to do. I used to wish I could press a button the minute I'd finished a game and make the next four days just disappear. I sure as hell don't miss the traveling. I think it's the life I miss—all the activity that's around baseball. I don't miss playing baseball but I miss . . . baseball. *Baseball.* Does that sound like a crazy man?"

For the first time in our long talks, he seemed a bit uncertain. He did not sound crazy but only a man who could no longer find work or a challenge that was nearly difficult enough to nurture his extraordinarily demanding inner requirements. Maybe there was no such work, outside of pitching. Baseball is the most individual and the most difficult of all team sports, and the handful of young men who can play it superbly must sense, however glimmeringly, that there will be some long-lasting future payment exacted for the privileges and satisfactions they have won for themselves. Like other team sports, baseball cannot be played in middle age; there is no cheerful, companionable afternoon to the game, as there is for old golfers and tennis players and the like. A lot of ex-ballplayers become sentimental, self-pitying, garrulous bores when they are cut off from the game. Some of them, including some great stars, go to pieces.

Thinking of what Wendy had said, I told Bob Gibson that I was sometimes aware of a sadness in him.

"Sad?" he said uncomprehendingly. "No, I'm not sad. I just think I've been spoiled. When you've been an athlete, there's no place for you to go. You're much harder to please. But where I am right now is where the average person has been all along. I'm like millions of others now, and I'm finding out what that's like. I don't think the ordinary person ever gets to do anything they enjoy nearly as much as I enjoyed playing ball. I haven't found my niche now that that's over—or maybe I have found it and I don't know it. Maybe I'll still find something I like as much as I liked pitching, but I don't know if I will. I sure hope so."

Maybe he will. Athletes illuminate our imagination and raise our hopes for ourselves to such an extent that we often want the best of them to become models for us in every area of life—an unfair and childish expectation. But Bob Gibson is a tough and resolute man, and the unique blend of independence and pride and self-imposed isolation in his character—the distance again—will continue to serve him in the new and even more difficult contest he is engaged in. Those who know him best will look to him for something brilliant and special now, just as they have always done. Even those of us who have not been spoiled by any athletic triumphs of our own and the fulfillment of the wild expectations of our early youth are aware of a humdrum, twilight quality to all of our doings of middle life, however successful they may prove to be. There is a loss of light and ease and early joy, and we look to other exemplars—mentors and philosophers: grown men—to sustain us in that loss. A few athletes, a rare handful, have gone on, once their day out on the field was done, to join that number, and it is possible—the expectation will not quite go away—that Bob Gibson may be among them someday. Nothing he ever does will surprise me.

In 1964, the Cardinals were no longer the brainchild of Branch Rickey, even though Rickey had returned as an adviser to owner Gussie Busch. Bob Gibson, Ken Boyer, Tim McCarver, and Mike Shannon were products of the Cardinal farm system, but other key players such as Curt Flood, Julian Javier, Bill White, Curt Simmons, Lou Brock, and Dick Groat were acquired through trades made by Bing Devine. The irony of Devine's success is that he was fired late in the 1964 season by Busch, who was clearly influenced in the decision by Rickey.

In We Played the Game, *Dick Groat recalls the shock of being traded by the Pirates to the Cardinals for the 1963 season and the good fortune that followed the trade. In 1963, Groat batted second in front of Stan Musial, who was in his last year as a Cardinal player, and joined White, Javier, and Boyer in an all-Cardinal starting infield at the All-Star game. In 1964, after Devine traded for Lou Brock, the Cardinals surged past the collapsing Phillies, won the National League pennant, and defeated the Yankees in the World Series.*

Dick Groat
Danny Peary

Because the Cardinals needed a shortstop, I had the good fortune to play for the finest organization in all professional sports. The Cardinals treated players better, they treated your kids and family better, they paid you better, they made travel better. The Cardinals were a fairly close team when I got there and became very close. Guys like Bill White, Ken Boyer, Curt Flood, Tim McCarver, Bob Gibson, and I were tremendous competitors. White, Flood, and I hit over .300; Boyer and White each hit around 25 home runs and drove in over 100 runs; White, Javier, Boyer, Flood, and McCarver were superb defensively. Bob Gibson and Ernie Broglio each won 18 games and Curt Simmons won 15. And we had Stan Musial. This was a solid team.

I went to St. Louis with the intention of showing Pirates general manager Joe Brown that he made a very bad mistake trading me. And in 1963 I had the best year of my career, a better year than in 1960. I hit the ball with more authority. I was leading the league in batting average when Don Drysdale hit me on the thumb in Dodger Stadium. I couldn't hold the bat, but the ballclub was going pretty good and I kept on playing. I went 0 for 28. Still I finished at .319, tying Henry Aaron for third in the batting race behind Tommy Davis and Bobby Clemente. I led the league with 43 doubles, drove in a career-high 73 runs, and had a career-high 201 hits. I was the biggest vote-getter in either league for the All-Star Game, and I finished second to Sandy Koufax in the MVP voting. This was after Joe Brown had said, "We could never win another pennant with Dick Groat in there." It was a matter of pride.

Ken Boyer, Julian Javier, Bill White, and I were the starting infield for the National League. It was the only time that four players from one team made up the infield. We were really proud of that because we were chosen by our peers, not the fans. The game was played in Cleveland and Willie Mays had a big game, scoring two runs, driving in two runs, and making a great catch. That was Stan Musial's 24th and last All-Star game.

Playing between Boyer and Javier was as good as playing between Don Hoak and Bill Mazeroski at Pittsburgh. After Maz, Javier was the best-fielding second baseman in baseball. Boyer was the captain of the Cardinals and everyone looked up to him on the field and off. He looked after his team-mates. In fact, Kenny found a home for my wife and me. After that we would socialize a great deal with Kenny and his wife, Kathleen, and on the road, Kenny and I palled around.

Bill White could do it all. He was a marvelous left-handed batter who hit for power and average and was the best fielding first baseman in the league. I never saw a player work so hard, which he had to do to compensate for in-juries. He was a very special person, an intelligent, sentimental guy.

White and Boyer were our leaders. But there were many guys with strong personalities on that team, who either motivated the others or led by exam-ple. For instance, we all looked up to Stan Musial.

Curt Flood was a super guy with the greatest sense of humor. I loved being around him. We were both very superstitious, so we warmed up together be-fore every game. We were both having good years, so we didn't want to leave each other. Curt could flat out play centerfield and could really handle a bat. He changed his style and became a truly great hitter. He would pay me one of the greatest compliments in his book when he said I helped teach him how to hit. He was already a .300 hitter, so I guess what I taught him is that you could make sacrifices at the plate for the team and still bat .300. (Curt was a fantas-tic artist. In fact he did it professionally in the off-season. He had an art shop in St. Louis. At the time, I wouldn't have thought Curt would be the type to challenge the reserve clause. None of us then really thought about free agency—personally, I had no bitches. But Curt had ties to the city and ballclub and wouldn't want to leave in a trade.)

Flood was the leadoff hitter and I batted second, in front of Stan Musial. I can't say enough about Musial. He was the Cardinals. The team had a family picnic every year at Grant's Farm, which was owned by the Busches. It was great for our kids because they could swim in a pond and see all kinds of wild animals—buffaloes, elk, deer—by riding around in a train. In 1963 the picnic was held on an unbelievably hot day in August. We were waiting for the big outdoor cookout to begin when several television trucks started coming in. I knew something was going to happen. It was then that Stan Musial announced that he would retire at the end of the season, after 22 years. At the time we were in sixth place. All of a sudden Musial turned on the blowers. I couldn't believe how hard he hit the ball until the end of the season. He was unreal.

Don Cardwell hit me in the ribs in Pittsburgh and I was out for three games. Don Drysdale once hit me on top of the helmet, and Juan Marichal once hit me on the back of the helmet, but Cardwell was the only guy I felt hit me on purpose. I had been traded for him, and I guess the media got to him about how good I was going while the Pirates had dropped way down in the standings. I missed the rest of the series, and when we got back to St. Louis on a Sunday night, they started shooting cortisone into me. I got up the next day and got another shot. I went out to the ballpark and felt pretty good. I discovered I could field grounders, throw, and swing the bat, so I told Johnny Keane, "I'm ready to play again." I'll never forget this as long as I live. The only thing I hadn't done was run. I didn't have any idea that it was going to hurt that much. Glen Hobbie started against us. With one out in the first, I doubled down the right-field line. When I started, I said, "Oh, Jesus!" I just got to second base, trying to get that thing straightened around. Then, on the first pitch, Musial drilled a liner up the middle for a base hit. So I had to run again and come around to score. The next time up, I singled, and just as I got to first base, Musial hit a frozen rope to right field. I'm running like hell. I was never so happy to see an umpire wave his hand that I could come around to score. I never saw a man hit the ball like Musial did after he announced his retirement. He was 42 at the time. Musial sparked our team to a terrific streak. We almost won the pennant and gave the Dodgers a good scare.

Bob Gibson was a great pitcher, on the same level as Sandy Koufax. In terms of longevity, Warren Spahn was the greatest pitcher of my era, but the best pitchers I saw were Gibson and Koufax, who were a bit ahead of Juan Marichal, Jim Maloney, and Don Drysdale. Bob was a great athlete who had played basketball with the Harlem Globetrotters. Not only could he pitch, but he was a terrific hitter and a fast runner. Gibby had some games where I'd just stand at shortstop and be awed. He could be completely overpowering. He'd devise a game plan and pitch exactly that way. Gibby always had a great sense of humor and he and I were real good friends. Gibby and I both loved bridge and were always partners. We took on anybody, only the more we played, the better we got, and it was hard to get anybody to play with us. The meanness of

Bob Gibson? I never saw it. Never. In fact, in those days, he didn't want to knock down batters. He threw so hard, he didn't need to pitch that way.

My former Pirates buddy Bob Skinner joined the Cards in the middle of the '64 season. I roomed with Skins, and at other times he, Boyer, and I roomed together. Everybody got along just great. The guys were as funny as they were competitive, and we had constant fun on the buses and planes and in the clubhouse. So many guys had great senses of humor: Tim McCarver, Ray Sadecki, Bob Gibson, Curt Flood. Of course, Bob Uecker was incredibly funny. That's why it was such an enjoyable season.

Uecker joined the team in 1964 from the Braves and backed up Tim Mc-Carver. On the buses, everybody would be talking, and then one by one we noticed that he was in the back doing some impersonation. And it got quieter and quieter until all you could hear was Ueck doing Harry Caray. He'd do Caray's familiar voice and then add a smart remark and everybody would be roaring with laughter. He'd make Harry livid.

We improved a big notch when we got Lou Brock in a mid-season trade with the Cubs. I already knew he had a great set of legs and blinding speed, and I now noticed that he had a great, strong body, with large shoulders and thin waist. One day I backed into left to catch a pop fly and just as I caught it, he ran into me. It was like standing in front of a Mack truck. I was lucky that I was so relaxed, because I was able to walk away without any problems. Lou was a super guy and a tremendous competitor, but I hadn't realized what a great offensive player he was because he was just a kid. He hit almost .350 with us and finished with 200 hits and over 40 stolen bases. What a lift he gave us.

We had some great competitors on this team. Nobody wanted a rest. You couldn't get Curt Flood out of the lineup despite a badly swollen ankle that he'd have to tape up. He played 162 games and led the league in at-bats and hits. Ken Boyer, who was voted MVP in the league, also played every game, leading the league in RBIs. Bill White played 160 games and I missed only one game. Bill had a shoulder so bad that he couldn't lift it, but he wouldn't take time off and still hit .300 and drove in 100 runs. Brock ground it out every day and was tremendous. Javier missed only a handful of games and had a fine year at the plate and at second base. McCarver caught almost every game in hot St. Louis, yet hit close to .290. Gibson, Simmons, and Sadecki took the ball every fourth day and were extremely effective: Bob won 19, Curt 18, and Ray was a 20-game winner. In long careers neither Curt nor Ray ever won that many games in a season.

As Simmons used to say, "You gotta have a closer." You have to have somebody to close the deal. Barney Schultz was the ace of the Cardinal bullpen and he came through down the stretch. He didn't come up until late in the season, but then he was magnificent. He gave batters fits with his knuckleball.

Mike Shannon came up and did a good job for us in right field, switching off with Charlie James. He was goofy and you didn't know what he was going to do. When he first came up, someone hit a ball down the right-field line. He could have caught it but instead played it off the wall, thinking he was going to throw the batter out at second base with his great arm. But the guy slid in safely. "Hey, Mike, play the game straight. No tricks. Just get the ball. Don't be baiting guys in the major leagues. They know how to run bases." All those kids. You could tell them anything when they came up and they would listen to you. And they all became great players.

Johnny Keane pretty much let us play. However, he was the only manager—or coach—I had any problems with in my career. We just differed on how the game should be played. But he never benched me or took me out of a game because of our differences.

I got off to a bad start in 1964 but I still came back and hit .294. I was the starting shortstop in the All-Star Game. Bill White and Ken Boyer also started. The game was played at Shea Stadium, the new home of the Mets. Don Drysdale started against the Angels' Dean Chance, and it was an exciting game. Billy Williams and Boyer homered for us, but we trailed 4–3 going into the bottom of the ninth. Then Mays singled, stole second, and scored on Orlando Cepeda's blooper to tie the game. Then Johnny Callison of the Phillies hit a three-run homer off Dick Radatz and we won 7–4. So I was on the National League squad that started the long winning streak against the American League. And I took pride in that. (To be honest, seeing All-Star games is what makes me the most nostalgic. They were very special to me, especially since the players were the ones who voted me onto those teams. It was a great experience.)

I thought the 1964 Cardinals were a carbon copy of the 1960 Pirates. We were contact hitters, line-drive hitters. We scrambled, every game. We employed the hit-and-run, moved men on second to third when there were no outs, went from first to third on singles. We knew when to bunt, we knew when to take a strike, we knew which base to throw to. We had many players who didn't need managers because they were managerial material themselves. We were a competitive team that made few mistakes. We were also a very close team. If anything, because of Brock and Flood, the Cardinals had more speed than the 1960 Pirates.

Everybody talked about the collapse of the Phillies in 1964, and I agree that there was at least a semicollapse. But don't forget how good we played down the stretch. The Phillies must have thought they were entitled to lose a game now and then, but every time they lost, we won. And they lost a lot. The pennant drive was filled with pressure. We had a tough time getting the coffee and eggs down in the morning, there was so much tension. We swept the Pirates five in a row in Pittsburgh and had moved to just 1½ games behind the Phillies with 6 games left. They were coming to play us at Busch Stadium Monday, Tuesday, and Wednesday. We were all happy after the Pirates series and the plane trip home was very lighthearted. The minute we landed at Lambert Field in St. Louis, we saw that the place was packed with Cardinals fans. That's the first time everybody reacted: "Oh, shit! We are in this up to our asses."

About ten or twelve of us stayed at the Bel-Aire Hotel during the Phillies series. Most of our wives had gone home to put the children in school. I was rooming with Bob Skinner. Tim McCarver and seven or eight other guys were on the same floor. We're playing the Phillies Monday night. Baseball players are notorious for not getting up in the morning. But on Monday morning I got up to go to the bathroom and saw that it was about quarter to six. When I came out of the bathroom, Skinner was sitting there. I asked, "What are you doing up?" He said, "Well, I wanted to get coffee. See if they're out in the hallway with coffee yet." I opened the door and about four or five doors opened at the same time and out stepped the other Cardinals to get coffee. We were running on nervous energy. A week before, those doors wouldn't have opened until ten or eleven o'clock.

Chris Short, who started the first game, was the Phillies pitcher we were scared to death of. Chris was a tough lefty and we were primarily a left-hand hitting team with Brock, White, and McCarver. Short gave us fits earlier in the year. When we beat him we felt we had a chance to sweep them. I think we beat Dennis Bennett the next night. In the final game, Jim Bunning was dazzling everybody and struck out three of the first four batters he faced. I singled to right and then McCarver, who wore out Bunning, hit his first offering over the wall. We went on to get the sweep. Then there were three games left, and now they were behind us by 1½ games. Then the Mets came in and they were the team we figured to beat, that we had better beat. But little Al Jackson beat Gibson, 1–0. Then they won the next game. We realized there were no shortcuts, even if we played the Mets. Fortunately, we won the final game with Gibson in relief and took the pennant by a game over the Phillies and the Reds.

When Pulitzer Prize–winning author David Halberstam searched for a year that was both a turning point for baseball and the country, he selected 1964. In his critically acclaimed October 1964, *he portrays the Yankees as an aging baseball franchise, trapped by their Ruthian culture and slow to integrate their roster. He sees the Cardinals, on the other hand, after overcoming their early resistance to Jackie Robinson, as a young, dynamic, fully integrated ball club at a time when America was beginning a civil rights revolution. In this excerpt from* October 1964, *Halberstam examines the seventh game of the 1964 World Series and the social implications of Gibson's victory over the Yankees.*

October 1964
David Halberstam ————————————————

The sixth game was in some ways a repeat of the third, with Jim Bouton again pitching against Curt Simmons. For the first seven innings, it was a tight, well-pitched game. For the Yankees it provided a last World Series hurrah for the home-run tandem of Maris and Mantle, when they and Joe Pepitone flashed a demonstration of the vaunted Yankee power. Simmons did not feel he pitched that well; he preferred the cold, in which he had worked earlier at the Stadium, and he had sensed that his breaking ball was not sharp on this day. As for Bouton, he was delighted to be getting his second shot in this Series. Far more than most baseball players, he was an adrenaline player, and he liked pitching under this kind of pressure. He had pitched exceptionally well in the third game of the 1963 World Series, which he had lost to Don Drysdale, 1–0, a game in which both teams got a total of only seven hits; he had given up one run and six hits in the third game of this Series, and his combined World Series earned run average for his three starts after this day was 1.48.

Bouton was puzzled by the behavior of the Yankee ownership on the morning of the sixth game. The players had been told to pack their suitcases and check out of the St. Louis hotel before they left for the ball park. If they lost, they would leave for New York right after the game; if they won, they would return to the hotel and check back in. Management clearly did not want to be charged for an extra day in St. Louis if they were going to lose the game and the Series. That stunned Bouton: in the past the Yankees had always been both arrogant and parsimonious, but this was the first time he could ever remember their parsimoniousness outweighing their arrogance. It was, he thought, the work of people with a loser's mentality. But Bouton felt good on this day; he loved being the center of attention and being given the ball in a game this big.

The Cardinals scored in the first inning. Curt Flood opened the game with a single to left, then went to third on Lou Brock's single to center. Flood scored when Bill White hit into a double play. The Yankees tied it in the fifth; Tom Tresh, who had hit the Cardinal pitching hard all week, lined a ground-rule double down the left-field line, moved to third when Clete Boyer grounded out, and scored when Bouton himself singled to left-center. In the sixth the Yankees nailed Simmons. Richardson, the team's leading hitter in the Series, popped up. Up came Maris, who had been a notoriously poor hitter in this and previous World Series games. Simmons hung a curve to Maris and Maris jumped on it, hitting it up on the roof in right, the ball landing just fair. Then Mantle came up and Simmons threw him a fastball; Mantle batting righty, hit it on a line to the roof in right field. This gave the Yankees a 3–1 lead. Then, in the eighth, with Simmons out of the game and first Barney Schultz, then Gordon Richardson, on the mound for the Cardinals, the Yankees scored five more times, including four runs on a Joe Pepitone grand-slam home run. The final score was 8–3, and the Yankees had to check back into their St. Louis hotel.

In the seventh game Bob Gibson took the ball. There was a time, only recently past, when that would have surprised people, a black pitcher getting the call in a decisive seventh game of the World Series, for it had long been part of the myth of white America that blacks were not mentally as tough as whites and therefore could not be counted on in the clutch: it was the performances of such athletes as Gibson that destroyed that particularly scabrous fiction. In a way Gibson's very presence on the mound in so big a game showed how much baseball had changed in its ethnic makeup in so short a time. Only fifteen years earlier, in the final regular-season American League game that would decide the pennant, neither team had a black player on its roster, and when the Yankees took the field, four of the nine players, DiMaggio, Rizzuto, Berra, and Raschi, were Italian-American. Now four of the nine Cardinal starters were black, and if Julian Javier had not been injured, the total would have been five black or Hispanic players. The only black starter for the Yankees was Ellie Howard. Now Gibson, starting the seventh game of the World Series for the Cardinals, was a long, long way from the moment seven years earlier, when he had been pitching for Columbus in the Sally League, a brief unhappy stint lasting only eight games, and someone had yelled out at him, "Alligator bait! Gibson, you're nothing but alligator bait!" *Alligator bait,* he thought, *what the hell is that?* for he had no idea at all what it meant. Later he was told it was an old Deep South expression, and it recalled the good old days when the good old boys went into the swamps in search of alligators and tied a rope around a black man, or so they claimed, and threw him in the water as bait.

In the seventh game Bob Gibson was battling his own fatigue as well as the New York Yankees. He was determined not to give in to it. Most pitchers as tired as Gibson was on this day, with only two days' rest, slowed down their rhythm so that they could rest between pitches. Not Gibson. If anything he sped up his pace so the Yankees would not know that he was tired. He did not want to show even the slightest hint of weakness, and so he set a blistering pace. Gibby was struggling, Tim McCarver, who was catching him, thought. He was sure that Gibson was more tired than he had been when he pitched against the Mets in the final game of the season. Then, McCarver had been able to see the fatigue in his face, but on this day he could see it even more clearly in Gibson's pitches. Against the Mets his breaking ball had been a little flat, but now, in his third World Series start in a week, it was not only his breaking ball that was flat, it was his fastball as well. It did not explode in the strike zone the way a Gibson fastball normally did.

And yet even with all that, he had the Yankees off balance. Gibson was still a very fast, very smart pitcher, and even more, a great competitor. The Yankees might be a great fastball-hitting team, but that did not mean that hitting Bob Gibson was going to be easy. When the Cardinals played against Koufax or Maloney or Bob Veale, Gibson used to tease his teammates: "Okay, all you fastball hitters, there he is, now just go out there and have a field day." It was like telling a kid who liked ice cream to eat a gallon of it at one sitting, McCarver thought. Gibson was going to do that on this day; he was going to make the Yankees earn every hit.

In baseball, thought McCarver, players admired the ability of a pitcher who could reach back and find something extra. More than anyone he had ever played with, Bob Gibson could do that. He might be exhausted, but he seemed to understand even on the worst day that he would be finished in two and half hours. That allowed him to force his body to do things it did not want to do. It was a triumph of the spirit over body; since he refused to be defeated, he was not defeated. He would walk off the mound after one of those games, his arm aching, and he would sit in the locker room icing his arm, saying that he was going to quit, that it was not worth it, that the pain was too great. The constant use of his slider had literally bent his arm out of shape. When Gibson and McCarver went to the tailor together, the tailor would tell Gibson to drop both his arms straight down so that he could measure their length; the left arm dropped normally, but the right arm remained bent just slightly. "Let your arm hang straight, Bob," the tailor would say, and Gibson would say, "It *is* hanging straight." That was as good as he could do. The slider had done it to him. He always knew the price he was paying for the success he sought.

Normally, the day after he pitched his arm was all right, and then on the second day, it ached terribly, and on the third day the ache began to go away. It was not the rest of his body that was tired, only his arm. In those days he, like other pitchers, took Darvon to kill the pain. Gibson thought he had rather good stuff early in the game, and he struck out three batters in the first two innings, including Mickey Mantle.

The Yankees went with Mel Stottlemyre, who had gone, in a few brief weeks, from ingenue to rookie sensation to ace of the staff. Yogi Berra and the coaches came to him and asked if he could pitch on two days' rest. The other possibilities were Ralph Terry, whom they had not used much late in the season and who had not had a good year, and Al Downing, about whom they clearly were uncertain. So Stottlemyre said yes, and he felt reasonably good when he went to the mound. He thought he was pitching fairly well, although his slider had less bite on it and his ball had less movement than usual. But the Cardinals were hitting the ball on the ground.

But in the fourth inning the Yankees self-destructed. They had fielded poorly throughout the Series, and though when it was over they were charged with nine errors to the Cardinals' four, in reality their fielding had been far worse than that. There had been numerous bad throws and bonehead plays, which were not counted as errors but which cost them dearly, just as their poor baserunning had cost them on offense. Ken Boyer started the home fourth with a single to center. Dick Groat walked on four pitches. Then Tim McCarver hit a bouncer to Pepitone that looked like a double-play ball. Pepitone made a good pickup and threw to Linz at second for the force on Groat. Stottlemyre covered first for the return throw, but the throw from Linz, which should have beaten McCarver easily, was wide of first and rolled to the stands. Backing up the play, Bobby Richardson picked up the ball and threw home, but Boyer scored for the first run of the game. Mike Shannon's single sent McCarver to third. So far in the Series, the Cardinals had been relatively cautious in their baserunning, but they decided in this game that they would challenge Howard and the Yankees, and they tried the double steal. Shannon broke for second, and behind the plate Ellie Howard double-pumped; then Howard bit and threw to second, but his throw was high and to the right, and Shannon slid in safely. When Howard threw, McCarver raced for home, and he scored when Richardson's throw was in the dirt and went through Howard. Dal Maxvill singled to right, and Mantle got to the ball quickly. A good throw from Mantle might have caught Shannon, but Mantle threw wide and Howard dove for Shannon and missed. The Cardinals had three runs on only one Yankee error, but four bad Yankee throws. The once-great Yankees, wrote Dick Young, "had looked more like the Mets than the Mets. Linz made a bad play. Howard made a bad play. Richardson made a bad play. Mantle made a bad throw and up went three ragged runs for St. Louis and the Yankees were never in the ball game again."

Worse, Stottlemyre jammed his shoulder diving for the ball from Linz, and it quickly stiffened on him. The Yankees sent up a pinch hitter for him in the fifth, and then sent Al Downing to the mound in the bottom of the fifth. Brock greeted Downing with a four-hundred-foot drive to the pavilion roof in right-center. Then Bill White singled to center and Boyer doubled to right, sending White to third. That was it for Downing, and Roland Sheldon came in to pitch. Groat grounded to Richardson, who had to throw to first and had no chance to get White, who scored. Boyer went to third. That made it 5–0. Then McCarver hit a soft fly to right and Boyer beat Mantle's throw, which skidded through Howard again. That made it 6–0.

In the top of the sixth the Yankees began to struggle back. Richardson beat out a slow roller to Ken Boyer at third. Maris hit a ground single to right, with Richardson stopping at second. All during the Series Gibson had pitched Mantle outside, going against the book. McCarver had thought the scouting reports were right, but Gibson was Gibson—he did not like coming inside on power hitters; he believed the outside of the plate belonged to him, and he was not a man easily argued out of anything. So far his strategy had worked. Mantle had been 1–10 against him in the Series. But now Gibson was really beginning to tire and he came outside, and Mantle hit the ball into the left center field bleachers to make the score 6–3. It was Mantle's third home run of the Series and his record eighteenth in World Series competition.

But even then the Yankees could not hold the Cardinals. Ken Boyer hit a solo home run off Steve Hamilton in the home seventh. By the seventh inning Gibson knew he was tiring, but Johnny Keane left him in, in part because he had a four-run lead, in part out of respect for Gibson as a competitor, and in part because of his anxiety about his own bullpen. Gibson hated to come out for a relief pitcher in any circumstance, and he most certainly did not want to come out of this game. But by the seventh inning he was finding it harder and harder to put the ball where he wanted. He had to put more effort into getting extra break on the ball, and as he did that, he lost location. There was a danger at a moment like this, he well knew, of slipping, of pushing rather than firing the ball, of losing both location and speed, and then of beginning to fall behind the hitters. The other danger, he thought, was that it was easy to become lazy without knowing it, to give in to your body and stop reaching back. So he spent those last three innings talking to himself on the mound, trying to keep himself alert: *Let's go asshole, don't quit now. . . . This is where you've always wanted to be, the seventh game of the World Series with you pitching for everything against the New York Yankees . . . this is not the time to get lazy and get soft.* Out on the mound his throat was dry because every time he threw, he grunted from the effort.

In the seventh the Yankees hit the ball relatively hard on him. With two out Richardson singled to center, and Maris hit a line shot to right field, but directly at Mike Shannon for the third out. The eighth was easier. Mantle flied to center. Ellie Howard struck out, which was a relief for it showed Gibson still had some pop on the ball. Then Pepitone popped up to Maxvill. The Cardinals did not score in the bottom of the eighth. Now it was time for the top half of the ninth. Rarely had Bob Gibson wanted anything so badly as to finish this game. When it was time to go out on the mound for the ninth, Johnny Keane, *who knew he was tired and knew he was wearing down,* came over to Gibson and told him he was going to stay with him, and reminded him that he had a four-run lead. "Bob, I'm going with you in the ninth. Just throw it over the plate," he said. "Don't be cute. Don't go for the corners. Just get it over. They're not going to hit four home runs off you." What Gibson had always wanted was the confidence of his manager, and on this day he had it more than any pitcher could ever ask for. He did not want to betray that trust in the ninth.

He struck out Tom Tresh, the first batter. Then Clete Boyer came up and hit a home run into the left-field bleachers. *That's one home run,* Gibson thought to himself. Johnny Blanchard batted for Pete Mikkelsen and struck out. Two outs now, both strikeouts. Then Phil Linz came up, and he hit the ball into the left-field bleachers, making it 7–5. *That's two home runs,* Gibson thought. *Maybe Keane is wrong.* Up came Bobby Richardson, who already had thirteen hits in the Series. Out in the bullpen, Ray Sadecki was warming up. Aware that he had not pitched well in the Series, and that Johnny Keane was down on him, he wondered whether Keane would go to him if Richardson got on. Until then Keane said he never thought of lifting Gibson. But if Richardson had gotten on, he would have gone to Sadecki. Keane went out to the mound to talk with his pitcher for a moment. McCarver did not go all the way out because he knew Gibson hated it when the catcher came out, and besides, there was nothing to say. The count was 1–1. Richardson liked the ball high and out over the plate, and Gibson made a very good pitch to him, a fastball that moved in on him at the last instant. Richardson popped it up, and Dal Maxvill gathered it in a second.

Afterward Gibson realized for the first time how hard he had fought against his fatigue and how much his arm hurt. It would hurt on and off for an entire month, but it was a month in which he did not have to pitch. He had struck out nine men, which gave him a total of thirty-one for the Series, a Series record, which he would soon break. He was voted the Most Valuable Player in the World Series, just ahead of McCarver. After the game, when reporters crowded around Johnny Keane, they asked the manager why he had left Gibson in during the ninth when he was so obviously tiring. Keane answered with one of the nicest things a manager ever said about a baseball player: "I had a commitment to his heart."

Johnny Keane shocked the baseball world by resigning as Cardinal manager just one day after his team won the 1964 World Series. While Keane headed to the Yankees to replace the fired Yogi Berra, the Cardinals moved quickly to replace Keane. They decided to fall back on tradition by hiring Red Schoendienst, one of the most popular players in Cardinal history.

Globe-Democrat *sports editor Bob Burnes, reporting here for the* Sporting News *from spring training, gives some historical background to the Cardinal managerial change, the second time in team history that the franchise had to replace a manager after a world championship season, and offers a review of Schoendienst's temperament and approach just before the beginning of the 1965 season.*

Redhead Cool Operator on Redbird Hot Seat
Bob Burnes

If new Cardinal Manager Red Schoendienst has more than normal concern about the task in front of him, he has not shown it outwardly at any time since he was appointed pilot last October.

His job—top a miracle, do better than the best.

The Cardinals came from behind in one of their traditional storybook finishes in 1964, won the pennant, then capped it by beating the Yankees in the World Series. No manager can do more than that.

Johnny Keane resigned the day after it was all over and shortly afterward became Yankee manager. The job of filling Keane's shoes in St. Louis was handed to Cardinal coach Schoendienst.

It was a popular decision, one that may be a determining factor in 1965. The redhead, as second baseman and captain of the Redbirds and later a coach, is one of the most popular figures in St. Louis baseball history. Because of this and because of the circumstances surrounding the whole change, Cardinal fans are expected to be patient in 1965.

Only One Similar Case

Only once in baseball history has the same thing happened—a managerial change after a club won a pennant and world championship. That was back in 1926, also in St. Louis, when Rogers Hornsby was traded to the Giants after leading the Redbirds to their first pennant and world title. A contract dispute between Hornsby and Owner Sam Breadon forced the trade.

Catcher Bob O'Farrell was named Hornsby's successor and lasted one year. The Redbirds finished second in 1927, but might have won had not shortstop Tommy Thevenow, a key figure the year before, suffered a broken leg in mid-June.

There was a difference in the 1926 and 1964 situations. Hornsby could have run for mayor in St. Louis and been elected in a landslide. Keane, while generally well liked by Cardinal fans, was not nearly as well known nor as popular as Hornsby.

Thoughts of this situation, and the change at Brooklyn after Charley Dressen won a pennant in 1953 and was ousted, plus the changes with the Yankees involving Casey Stengel, Ralph Houk, and Yogi Berra after pennant-winning years, all had to go through Schoendienst's mind when he took over the job of leading the Redbirds in 1965.

If those thoughts have worried him, he hasn't shown it.

Red Earns Respect

In fact, everybody who has watched Red operate through his first five months in office is convinced that he is equal to the task. He has surprised even his closest friends with his down-to-earth approach to the job.

No one can recall that Red ever spoke loudly of his desire to manage a major league club, but it is obvious that he has been preparing for it for a long time. Such preparations went into high gear in late 1958 when he was hospitalized with tuberculosis after helping the Braves to two pennants.

"I had a chance to do a lot of thinking that year," he has said, "and I've watched how other managers have handled clubs. I've played under a lot of managers and I think I've learned from all of them."

The one Red admittedly admires the most and from whom he has borrowed many ideas was the Braves' pilot in those pennant-winning years, Fred Haney, now general manager of the Angels.

"Fred did a great job of keeping up morale as well as running the show," Red said. "He handled his players like men."

What have been some specific examples of Red's preparations for the job?

Example No. 1—His coaches. Joe Schultz, a holdover and Red's roommate last season, is his top assistant. Bob Milliken has moved up to a coaching job from batting practice pitcher.

To replace Vern Benson and Howard Pollet, Red obtained Joe Becker and Mickey Vernon.

Pilot Withstood Pressure

Before they were hired, and this is especially true in the case of Vernon, Schoendienst was exposed to considerable pressure in St. Louis to appoint any one of several former Cardinals now residing locally.

The lobbying was terrific but Red was unmoved.

"I just want one thing in my coaches," he said. "I want men who aren't afraid to work. I was never on the same team with Joe Becker or Mickey Vernon, but I saw a lot of them and I was always impressed by how hard they worked. That's what I want."

Example No. 2—The trades. The Cardinals dealt three times during the winter. They obtained Bob Purkey from the Reds, Tracy Stallard from the Mets, and Tito Francona from the Indians. Red was particularly active in the Purkey deal. He had told General Manager Bob Howsam that if there was any possibility of a deal for Purkey, he'd like to make it.

Howsam called him at home one day and said, "I just got your pitcher for you." Schoendienst immediately flew to Pittsburgh for a personal visit with Purkey.

"Bob's a great competitor," Red said, in explanation. "He'll battle you all the way. I just wanted to find out how he felt about joining us, to tell him that we had started negotiations because we wanted him. Bob told me he was delighted to be with us, that his arm was sound, that he preferred starting but that if I needed him in the bull pen, he'd be out there."

Stallard Admires Setup

Example No. 3—His training camp. Pitcher Stallard, who has been with the Red Sox and Mets, said, "This is the best organized camp I've ever been in. There's no lost motion."

Veteran Dick Groat paid an even greater compliment. "This is the first time in all the years I've been going to training camp," he said, "that I had all the batting practice I could stand. I batted against four different pitchers for 15 minutes each and then I went out and worked some more against the pitching machine. The pitchers weren't tired when they got to me."

Schoendienst and Howsam agreed in advance of camp that there would be 20 players in search of much batting practice. They felt there should be one pitcher available for every hitter. There were 18 pitchers on the roster; Dick Egan and Earl Francis, on the Jacksonville (International) roster, were added to bring it to 20.

"I want my pitchers throwing and my batters hitting," Red said. "We spent some time in getting everybody's legs in shape and I'm all for that. But players have to strengthen the weapons they're going to use all summer. That's why I wanted as much concentration as possible on the throwing and hitting."

Simple Set of Rules

Example No. 4—His rules. The first day in camp, Schoendienst gave out simple regulations governing general conduct. But he had answered the question back in October when he took over the club.

"Managers," he said, "don't make rules on major league clubs. The players do. If the players show that they need to have a lot of regulations, I'll issue those regulations. From what I've seen, though, most players don't need a lot of tough restrictions."

This latter point brings up one of the two questions which have been raised most often about Schoendienst. Can he be tough enough to ride herd on a major league club? Red has long been known as one of baseball's most pleasant personalities.

One of his closest friends, his long-time roommate, Stan Musial, answered that one.

"That would be one of the least of my worries about Red," Stan, now a Cardinal vice-president and the first to recommend Red for the job, said. "He's down to earth about baseball. He knows how the game is played, he knows what he wants and he can say so. He won't have any problems with discipline."

Schoendienst himself has said: "If I were just coming out of the playing ranks, I'd be more worried about it. But I have been a coach the last few years, a bit removed from real close association with the players."

The other question. He has never managed before. Will he be able to make decisions?

"I've been on the bench and watched other managers make decisions," he said. "Sometimes I thought they were making the right move and sometimes I didn't. Sometimes I was right and sometimes I was wrong. But I think I've had the background experience.

"Managers, especially Johnny Keane, consulted with me at times before making a move, just as I'll consult with Joe Schultz. But the idea of having to make decisions in every game doesn't scare me. That's what the manager is paid to do. If I didn't think I could do it, I never would have taken the job in the first place."

Schoendienst is engaged in a job this spring for which he has prepared himself for a long time. Card fans have indicated they are in his corner.

During their first two seasons under Red Schoendienst, the Cardinals finished in the second division and began to reshuffle the team. By 1967, Dick Groat, Bill White, and National League MVP Ken Boyer were gone in trades. With Orlando Cepeda, acquired from the Giants in 1966, leading the way, the Cardinals, despite the loss of Bob Gibson for several weeks, coasted to their eleventh National League pennant and defeated the Boston Red Sox for their eighth world title in a contentious seven-game World Series.

In their coverage of the deciding game of the 1967 World Series Bob Burnes and Ed Wilk describe the "vicious desire" of Bob Gibson, who came back from his broken leg to dominate the Boston Red Sox and win the MVP award.

Gibson Pitches Three-Hitter in 7–2 Finale
Robert L. Burnes

Bob Gibson carried the Cardinals home Thursday—on his arm, on his bat, on his legs, and on his dead game courage.

The strong-armed 31-year-old right hander did it all in the seventh game of the World Series, pitching and helping bat the Red Birds to a convincing 7–2 victory over the Red Sox who went down fighting before 35,188 of their faithful fans at Fenway Park.

Thus the Cardinals won their eighth world championship in 11 trips to the Series post and retained their record of never losing a seven-game competition.

In the game for all the marbles, it was Gibson all the way as he wrote his way into the record book of the World Series alongside the names of some of the game's immortals.

Three Victories

He pitched three victories in the Series, the first, fourth, and seventh games. In the process he allowed just 14 hits, matching a record set by Christy Mathewson for the Giants 62 years ago. In the finale, although obviously bone-tired and arm weary at the finish, he allowed only three hits.

His three victories without defeat also tied him with six others—Mathewson, Jack Coombs of the A's in 1910, Babe Adams of the Pirates in 1909, Stanley Covelski of the Indians in 1920, Harry Brecheen of the Cardinals (against the same Red Sox) in 1946, and Lew Burdette for the Braves in 1957.

Matching his two complete game victories in the fifth and seventh contests in 1964, Gibson tied Hall-of-Famer Red Ruffing of the Yankees for most consecutive complete game triumphs in Series competition.

Gibson now owns more World Series victories, five, than any other Cardinal pitcher in history, breaking a tie with Brecheen.

A Tremendous Athlete

A tremendous athlete, Gibson also hammered a home run in the fifth inning to pad a previous 2–0 lead. It was only the second homer in history by a Cardinal pitcher. Jesse Haines supplied the other one in a 4–0 victory over the Yankees in the third game of the 1926 series.

Did Gibson do it alone? Not quite. He carried the big burden but Cardinal bats came alive in this last game of the Series.

Finally stung by some of the taunts and gibes of the rabid Boston press and ghost-writing members of the Red Sox, the Cardinals came out fighting and played in the finale the kind of baseball they displayed all summer.

Lou Brock set record after record, wound up the top hitter in the Series with 12 safeties, one short of the record. He stole seven bases, three in the finale, and his seven swipes erased a mark set by Honus Wagner in 1909.

Julian Javier smashed a three-run homer that made the score 7–1 in the sixth and took the game out of contention. He wound up with nine hits, Roger Maris with 10.

Everybody had a hand in this one except forlorn slump-ridden Orlando Cepeda and Captain Tim McCarver was the first to speak a loyal word in behalf of Cha-Cha in the clubhouse afterwards.

"Orlando carried us all summer," Tim said. "Don't forget that if he hadn't been great all year, we wouldn't be here now."

Dream Battle

This was billed as a dream battle between Gibson and Jim Lonborg, who had been brilliant in two victories for the Red Sox, but it wound up a nightmare for Gentleman Jim.

He had practically nothing left in the clincher, working on just two days rest.

The Cardinals nibbled at him without success in the first two innings but the first ominous warning came from an unexpected source in the third.

Dal Maxvill lashed a 400-foot line drive off the wall in dead center. Courageously, Lonborg almost worked out of the jam, getting Gibson on a liner to Joe Foy at third and Brock on a pop fly.

But Curt Flood, as he has done so often, picked up the thread with a single to center and the Cardinals were out in front, 1–0. This was important. The team that scored first in each game went on to win it.

Maris sent Flood to third with a single to right and Curt scored a moment later on a wild pitch by Lonborg. Lonborg made it through the fourth, but was tagged again in the fifth.

Towering Drive

With one out, Gibson belted his towering drive against the wall [behind the fence] in deep left center, a 390-foot homer. Brock singled to left, stole both second and third with ridiculous ease, and came home on Maris's sacrifice fly to right. That was Maris' seventh RBI of the Series, the best on either side.

The roof fell in on Lonborg in the sixth and, completely weary, he was allowed to tarry too long. McCarver broke out of his slump with a double to right, Ken Harrelson missing a diving try. Mike Shannon slashed one which Foy juggled at third for a questionable error.

Manager Dick Williams came out to talk to Lonborg at this point but let him stay in. On a 1–2 pitch, Javier climaxed his tremendous series with a home run high into the screen in left center and you knew it was all over.

Lonborg finished the inning and was given a standing ovation by the crowd as he trudged wearily into the dugout, knowing he was leaving for a pinch hitter.

"I wish I could have spared Lonborg that inning," Williams said later. "He carried us as far as he could and just ran out of gas. We thought Javier was going to bunt in that situation and Jim begged to stay in. I can't say enough for what he did."

It was about that time that the Red Sox started to make a few threatening gestures against Gibson.

The Cardinal pitcher started haltingly in the first, walking Foy who moved up on Mike Andrews' sacrifice. But Carl Yastrzemski, who took a nap instead of batting practice, popped out, and Ken Harrelson fanned.

9 Strikeouts

Gibson blew down the next nine batters and had seven of his nine strikeouts in the first four innings. Then in the fifth, George Scott lined a triple to dead center and scored on Javier's over-throw at third. Gibson retired the next six, walked Yastrzemski leading off the seventh, then cut down three more.

Only in the eighth did he start to give real signs of weariness and Nelson Briles and Steve Carlton started throwing in the bullpen.

Rico Petrocelli doubled to left, pinch batter Dalton Jones walked, and two force outs brought in a run, but Gibson pounced on Andrews' tap for a good play to end the inning.

Real Satisfaction

There was one gasp left. Yastrzemski singled for the third Boston hit. But Harrelson bounced into a double play smartly started by Maxvill, and Scott ended it by striking out weakly.

That was a point of real satisfaction to Gibson and the Cardinals. Of all the taunts hurled in their direction, the one that dug them the most was one by Scott.

"We'll finish Gibson in five innings," he had jeered in one of the newspapers.

The bench and the bullpen gang, poised at the starting gate, poured out to join the wild melee near the mound. Mike Shannon and Tim McCarver were the first to reach Gibson as they pounded him and congratulated him. Manager Red Schoendienst was almost blocked out of the play but still got his hand to Gibby before they reached the dugout.

One youngster grabbed Ed Spiezio's cap but Eddie got it back with a quick swipe. Another youngster grabbed Cepeda's cap and knocked him down in the process. Orlando started after the boy but was restrained by Maxvill. The youngster ran a brilliant open field sortie until tackled by police in the right field corner. He wasn't allowed to keep his prize.

In the clubhouse, Gibson admitted he was tired.

"I could feel myself weakening but Red came out and kidded me a little. He asked me if I wanted to go out. I told him I wanted to stay in and finish. Red said he knew I did and gave me a pat on the back. The rest helped."

'Proud of Them'

Manager Schoendienst, weary but proud, said, "These guys answered every challenge all year and they did it again today. I'm proud of them. Give Gibby a lot of credit and give those guys who started every game some credit too. I'll bet you this is the first time in Series history eight guys started every game in the same place in the lineup."

It wound up a brilliant year for Gibson who missed seven weeks because of a broken ankle, came back in time to pitch the pennant clincher in Philadelphia on Sept. 18. Then he wrote his name into the World Series record book on page after page.

He also won the automobile awarded the outstanding player, just as he did in 1964. But he promised to let Lou Brock, only a step behind him in brilliant performance, drive it now and again.

Tim Hails 'Vicious Desire' by Hoot
Ed Wilks ──

Timmy probably said it best.

Tim McCarver took a swig of champagne and said, "Listen, Gibson's got some kind of vicious desire, hasn't he? Tenacious. That's what he is. Tenacious.

"He pitches on guts. You can see it. He challenges anybody. Hell, he'd challenge Michael the Archangel, if he had to."

Gibby challenged everybody who came down the pike yesterday, and he beat 'em into the ground. Carl Yastrzemski, George Scott, and . . . well, on the Boston Red Sox, baby, there ain't nobody else to challenge. When you mention Yaz and Big George you've said it all.

McCarver was talking in the cramped, crowded quarters allotted to the visiting club at Fenway Park in Boston. The Cardinals were world champions for the second time in four years by then and McCarver and Gibson were enjoying it.

The first writer in the clubhouse rushed up to Gibson and asked, "How's your arm?"

Gibby gave him sort of a half grin and he said, "I wish I could take it off and hang it up somewhere."

Gib's like that. He'd just tied Red Ruffing's record of five consecutive complete-game victories in World Series play, and Gibby tells you he's pooped.

He could have been. Gibson, sidelined with a leg bone fracture July 15, hadn't pitched this season with only three days of rest until Sunday, when he blanked the Red Sox, 6–0.

He had won the Series opener, 2–1, and yesterday he was back at the old stand—pitching when the Cardinals needed pitching the most. And winning with a three-hitter in the seventh game of the Series.

Roger Maris has been around. He's been in World Series before, with the New York Yankees in 1960 and 1961 and 1962 and 1963 and 1964.

"I'm just as glad I'm playing with him instead of against him," said Maris of Gibson. Roger was on a loser against two-game winner Gibson in '64.

"Playing behind Gibson is like playing behind Whitey Ford," said Maris, an old hand at playing behind past Yankee ace Ford. "They're the same type of guys. You know they've got to win if you get them some runs."

The Bostons, in on a pass to the seventh game, didn't have a hit off Gibson for four innings. Then Scott got a hit and a half. He sent a Gibson fast ball off the green wall in center. The ball bounced away from Curt Flood, who ran it down but had a tough time picking it up before firing into the infield.

Second base Julian Javier was the relay man. And his throw was into the Cardinal dugout, permitting Scott to score from third on the error.

"Scott hit a pretty good pitch, I thought," said Gibson. "It was down and away. When he hit it, though, I thought it was gone."

McCarver thought the hit by Scott might have been his fault.

"Gibby's best pitch was his slider, and I might have messed up a bit. With a four-run lead, I stayed with his fastball."

This was no breeze for Gibson. He had walked leadoff hitter Joe Foy in the first inning in his one-for-the-money duel with two-time Series winner Jim Lonborg.

"I was throwing too hard on the walk to Foy," said Gibson, who pitched the Boston third baseman ball, foul, ball, ball, ball. "But I just try to throw as hard as I can as long as I can, with the idea that I can go nine innings, of course.

"I feel that if I can go five or six innings, I ought to be able to finesse them a couple of innings, anyway."

Gibby's as full of finesse as a club over the head. Which is, by the way, just what he handed the Red Sox. He tapped Lonborg for a one-out homer in the fifth, when the Cards built a 4–0 lead.

Funny thing, but Gibson hit a fast ball and Gibson said he wasn't a fast-ball hitter. Before the game, Gibby had said he could hit the ball far, but hadn't lately.

The hit by Scott was no worrisome thing for Gibson, even if it did break up his no-hitter.

"I'll never pitch a no-hitter," said Gib. "I'm a high-ball pitcher, and a high-ball pitcher makes mistakes. That's the ball guys hit: the ball that's high."

Standing inside a crescent of writers after the game, Gibson clutched a bottle of champagne in his right hand and considered the question when writers, who don't know Gibby, asked if he had "had the jitters before the game."

Gibson, winner of the seventh game in '64, too, passed up a curt reply. "Jitters? I never have jitters," said Gibson. "The only thing that makes me nervous is my wife."

His wife, Charline, had been nervous before the game. She knew that Gib hadn't had anything to eat for breakfast, because of a breakdown in service at the Cardinals' motel. When she got to Fenway Park, she stood behind the Cardinal dugout trying to catch Gibby's eye.

She caught it. "Have you had something to eat?" she asked in sign language to Robert, as she calls him, out near the batting cage.

Gibson gestured that he had, and Charline went to her seat in the stands.

What Gibby had to eat was one ham and egg sandwich, delivered by *Post-Dispatch* sports editor Bob Broeg, who filled Gibby's request en route to the park.

The ham and egger Gibby ate before the game was dry. The other one, which he consumed after the game, was washed down with champagne.

Cardinal coach Dick Sisler poured champagne on the head of telecaster Joe Garagiola, a hitting hero of the Redbirds' 1946 Series victory over the Red Sox. Sisler did it on camera at pal Joey's request.

That's show biz.

In 1968, the "Year of the Pitcher," Bob Gibson and the Tigers' Denny McClain won both the Cy Young and the Most Valuable Player awards and led their teams to easy pennants. The 1968 World Series was another pitcher's showcase for Bob Gibson after his brilliant season and great past performances in the 1964 and 1967 World Series, but it was roly-poly Mickey Lolich, not 31-game winner Denny McClain, who stole the show from Gibson by defeating him in the seventh and deciding game.

Lowell Reidenbaugh, writing for the Sporting News, *and Bob Broeg, in the* St. Louis Post-Dispatch, *give their accounts of the twists and turns of a World Series that had its share of historical landmarks, but also had so many unlikely heroes and goats that Broeg described it as the "Silly Series."*

Untamed Tigers Savor Sweet, Sweet Victory
Lowell Reidenbaugh ——————————————————————————————

Through the tunnel they came, Mayo Smith leading the way and shouting, "Be careful! Don't anyone get hurt!"

Out of the visitors' dugout at Busch Memorial Stadium, through two walls of policemen and newsmen, they charged into their clubhouse and the blinding glare of television lights.

It was 3:10 p.m., October 10, and these were the Detroit Tigers, freshly crowned kings of baseball. Laughing, shouting, shoving, they jostled into their steamy quarters and an orgiastic celebration customarily reserved for World Series winners. Particularly those clubs that wait 23 years for such an opportunity to celebrate.

In the sauna-like clubhouse climate, bedlam reigned unchallenged. Owner John Fetzer and General Manager Jim Campbell shouted their "thanks" to well-wishers above the hail of champagne corks.

Kaline Accepts Plaudits

Al Kaline, hero of countless Tiger triumphs in his 16 years as a pro, quietly, almost shyly, accepted congratulations.

Jim Northrup, big gun of the final two games, explained patiently about his seventh-inning triple that clinched the final contest, just as his third-inning grand slam had put the sixth game beyond the reach of the National League champion Cardinals.

Mickey Lolich, the eighth pitcher to win three games in one Series, and winner of a sports car from a national magazine as the outstanding performer, discussed his assortment of pitches that had held the Redbirds to five hits.

And almost everywhere, it seemed, was Denny McLain, the free spirit who won 31 games during the regular season and one out of three decisions in the Series.

One moment, Denny was dousing visitors with champagne, the next he was shooting it from his hip like a deranged tommy-gunner.

The Tigers, alive and roaring, were not to be confused with the scrawny, gasping pack of jungle cats from three days earlier.

On October 7, the Tigers were just eight outs away from total blackout. With one out in the seventh inning of Game No. 5, they trailed the Cardinals on the scoreboard, 3–2, and in games, three to one.

Back from the Depths

Then, as if through some miracle potion, they clawed back for a 5–3 victory and the chance to fight another day, and still a third day that carried them to their newest eminence.

For the baseball buff who likes everything, the 1968 classic was tailor-made.

There was record hitting:

Lou Brock's 13 hits, equaling Bobby Richardson's total for the Yankees in 1964; Jim Northrup's grand-slam homer, which had been accomplished ten times previously, and Bob Gibson's second Series homer, making him the first pitcher to perform that feat. He had turned the trick in 1967 also.

And lack of hitting:

Dal Maxvill going hitless in 22 at-bats, breaking the mark of 21 fruitless attempts, tied last by Gil Hodges in 1952.

There was record pitching:

Gibson fanning 17 batters in the first game, shattering Sandy Koufax' old standard of 15, and Lolich winning three games, a tie with many other hurlers.

And lack of pitching:

The Cardinals tied a record by employing four pitchers in the Tigers' ten-run third inning of the sixth game.

There was base-stealing:

Lou Brock swiping seven bases to match his total of the 1967 Series and raising his career total to 14, matching the record set by Eddie Collins.

And there was a tinge of controversy, resulting from a play at the plate in the fifth game.

Brock, attempting to score from second base on Julian Javier's single to left field, approached the plate standing up and was called out by umpire Doug Harvey on Willie Horton's throw to Bill Freehan.

Fuel for Second-Guessers

If Brock had slid, the grandstand managers argued, he would have been safe, making the score 4–2, Cardinals. There would have been only one out and additional scoring was a distinct possibility.

And Mayo Smith, the argument followed, could not have afforded to let Lolich bat with one out in the seventh inning. Lolich singled and opened the way for a three-run rally that gave the Tigers a new lease on life.

But, right or wrong, Brock emerged as the hitting star of the 65th Series. His .469 batting average gave him a career mark for Series competition of .391, surpassing the record of .363 set by J. Franklin (Home Run) Baker with the Athletics of 1910, '11, '13 and '14 and the Yankees of 1921 and '22.

The Series also will be remembered as the one in which Smith took a calculated gamble, shifting center fielder Mickey Stanley to shortstop, and getting away with it.

The Tiger manager arched a host of eyebrows with his daring maneuver, aimed at getting Kaline's big bat into the Tiger line-up. Stanley's experience at the position was limited to the tail end of the season, starting September 23, but he did nothing at the strange post to make Smith regret the move.

The youngster handled 31 of 33 chances and neither of his two errors damaged the Detroit cause.

A Special Anniversary

By coincidence, the biggest scoring day of the Series, October 9, when the Tigers mauled the Birds, 13–1, marked the 34th anniversary of a dark day in Tiger history. On the corresponding day in 1934, the Cardinals humiliated the Bengals, 11–0, in the deciding game of the classic at the Detroit park.

This year it was a complete turnabout. With their ten-run explosion, matching the Philadelphia Athletics' rally against the Chicago Cubs in the fourth game of the 1929 Series, the Tigers deadlocked the '68 classic at three wins apiece.

With that, the stage was set for the grand finale—Gibson seeking his eighth consecutive victory for the Cardinals and his second consecutive three-win Series, against Lolich, pitching with two days of rest for the first time in 1968.

Additionally, the Cardinals had never lost a seven-game Series, winning in 1926 (Yankees), 1931 (Athletics), 1934 (Tigers), 1946 (Red Sox), 1964 (Yankees), and 1967 (Red Sox).

With Gibson on the hill, the Cardinals were 17–10 favorites on the Las Vegas line to capture their ninth world championship. But the Tigers knew something the bookmakers didn't.

A turf made soggy by the previous rain betrayed Curt Flood when he attempted to retrace his steps on Jim Northrup's seventh-inning liner into center. The ball fell for a two-run triple and with it fell the Cardinals' chances of repeating as world champions. Had they pulled it off successfully they would have been the first National League club to defend its title since the Giants of 1921 and '22.

Third World Crown

The Tigers, however, were record-conscious, too. By coming all the way back, after trailing by three games to one, they duplicated a feat performed by the Pittsburgh Pirates against the Washington Senators in 1925 and the New York Yankees against the Milwaukee Braves in 1958.

The world championship was the third for the Tigers, who beat the Cubs in 1935 and again in 1945.

When the city last celebrated a World Series victory, Manager Smith was a 30-year-old outfielder with the Philadelphia A's, hitting .212, Al Kaline was a ten-year-old schoolboy in Baltimore, Mickey Lolich was a five-year-old in Portland, Ore., and Denny McLain was an 18-month-old toddler in Chicago.

Twenty-three years and a lot of heartaches later, the wheel of fortune came full cycle and, like more than a few expressed it, the winning was well worth the wait.

The 'Silly' Series: Heroes, Goats, Turning Points, Tears
Bob Broeg

When Jim Northrup came up with two on and two out in the seventh, the first inning in which Detroit had as much as hinted it might score against Bob Gibson yesterday, the guy in the next pressbox chair gave off what sounded like a dry gurgle.

"Gee, this is odd," he said. "Before the Series, the NBC computer forecast that Northrup would win it with a three-run homer."

Would the electronic brain settle for a tainted two-run triple?

Northrup did win the Series, thanks to Curt Flood's $100,000 slip of the feet. And, somehow, with complete compassion for Curt, a complete ball player, it seemed to sum up a silly Series when the Cardinals lost because their best defensive performer couldn't make what for him would have been little more than a routine chance.

If Curt had caught Northrup's ball, chances are that Gibson and Mickey Lolich still might be pitching because it's silver dollars to sugar doughnuts that the Tigers wouldn't have added that extra run in the ninth if the duel in the sun had been scoreless.

And with a sweeping bow of respect to Lolich, it's unlikely that Mike Shannon would have been favored with a pitch that could be hit for a homer if the game had been even in the home ninth.

The Tigers really slipped the Cardinals a Mickey in Lolich. Over the regular season, the Redbirds had a rousing 35–12 record against lefthanders, but in the World Series they lost three times in a week to the jelly-belly motorbike rider.

Sampling the Turning Points

Until Lolich became not only a three-game winner, but also the first foe ever to come away with a seventh-game victory over the Cardinals, Lou Brock had a seat in the new automobile given annually by *Sport* Magazine to the outstanding player in the Series.

For the second straight year, however, Brock wound up with the hubcaps. A year ago, Gibson drove off while Lou wasn't looking in the seventh game at Boston, and it's just possible that Gibby, if he'd won a third game this Series and his eighth straight, might have beaten Brock to the keys again.

But Lou had the steering wheel in his hands firmly when voting was taken midway through the fifth game, at a time it looked as if the Cardinals would win their easiest World Series since their dazzling young 1942 team upset the New York Yankees in five.

Did the turning point come as early as the third inning of that fifth game when Bill Freehan finally threw out Brock trying to steal? Did it arrive in the fifth when Lou didn't slide and was declared out at the plate on the most controversial, perhaps biggest and, yet, not the worst call of a poorly officiated Series?

Was the moment the momentum changed the instant an inning earlier, as Red Schoendienst thought, when Northrup bad-hopped a single over Julian

Javier's head, giving Nelson Briles only a one-run lead to wet-nurse through the final rounds?

Or was that turning point, as pragmatist Mayo Smith put it, simply the seventh inning of that fifth game when the Tigers rallied for three runs, taking the lead on Al Kaline's clutch single in the game they had to have to stay alive?

Of Brock, Kaline—and Gibby

Brock was the best hitter in the Series, as witness a .464 average and a record-tying 13 hits, and he was the most spectacular performer, too, even though Detroit clipped his wings on the bases at the finish.

The best player, however, was the veteran Kaline, getting his first Series chance after a wait of 16 years and knowing exactly what to do with it.

Smith's decision to play his center fielder, Mickey Stanley, at shortstop so that he could get the one more big bat in the lineup, meaning Kaline's, was a courageous move that paid off handsomely.

The best pitcher, again with full appreciation of Lolich's efforts, was the great Gibson, who from his first pitch in April until his last one in October was the most consistent these four eyes ever have seen.

Following up that remarkable 1.12 earned-run average in the regular season, Gibson walked only four and struck out 35 in 27 Series innings, in which he gave up 18 hits. And if good friend Flood hadn't proved he's human, too, Gibby might have allowed only one run, Northrup's homer last Sunday.

After the Series yesterday, Detroit's vice president, Rick Ferrell, the long-time American League catching star of yesteryear, said he'd believed after scouting the Cardinals that the Tigers had only one chance.

"I felt we had to beat Gibson once," said Ferrell, "and I knew it would take some doing. Maybe with the kind of break we finally got. But, you know, I was impressed even more with him in the Series than I'd been before.

"By what he said almost as much as what he did. As a man, I mean, even as much as a pitcher. He never belittled us when he won and he didn't complain when he lost."

A Pitching Letdown

It would be easy to stand off and throw rocks at the Cardinals because they lost, but that wouldn't be fair to either the Redbirds or Tigers, especially the Detroit ball club that wouldn't quit.

Maybe the Cardinals took it too matter-of-factly in the clubhouse yesterday.

Perhaps, though, that's the ultra-professional view, or is it merely the inability to grieve when a team is well-fed and well-paid?

Chances are, however, the hurt will be deeper today when the realization soaks in that for the first time in two seasons they've lost a game they had to win.

They became, therefore, the first Redbird team ever to lose in a seven-game Series and missed the chance to become the first National League club in 46 years to succeed itself as world champion.

The feeling existed, recently, that the club was leaning increasingly on Gibson, putting the monkey on the meal ticket's back, relying too much on good ol' Gibby. Trouble is, there comes a time when there is no margin for error, for the rub of the green on which Flood slipped.

No, the Cardinals didn't hit with authority this season, especially the last couple of months, but despite their difficulty in three of the four Series games here, they scored reasonably well in the Series—reasonably well for them, that is.

It's comforting that Bing Devine, who never let the grass grow beneath his feet even before he heard of AstroTurf, already has made arrangements to add Vada Pinson to the Redbird lineup, but more of that another day.

The Cardinals got where they were this season primarily because of pitching, as Sandy Koufax observed yesterday with Jay Randolph on KSD-TV's pre-game program. And that pitching, which diminished down the stretch, just before and after the pennant was clinched, was skimpy in the Series.

Or is that being too unfair to the muscle in the Detroit line-up?

Through the fall, winter, and spring, from the snows of Fujiyama to the sands of St. Petersburg, the Cardinals will replay the Series and the what-might-have-been, the surprising, apparent five-game breeze that became a disappointing and shocking seven-game setback.

If the Redbirds want to do anything about it other than just talk about it, they'll have to hope they can become the first National League team in a quarter-century to win a third straight pennant. And they'll have to hope, too, that the Tigers won't trip over their tails trying to repeat in the American League, now as well-balanced as the National.

After the Cardinals failed to win their third consecutive pennant, they traded popular Curt Flood and Tim McCarver to the Phillies for power-hitting Richie Allen. Winner of seven Gold Glove awards, Curt Flood was an outstanding center fielder, but he earned his place in baseball history when he refused to accept the trade and declared himself a free agent. In a December 24, 1969, letter to Commissioner Bowie Kuhn, Flood wrote, "After twelve years in the major leagues, I do not feel I am a piece of property to be bought and sold irrespective of my wishes." In 1972, the Supreme Court ruled against Flood, but his actions set in motion the events leading to free agency in baseball just a few years later.

In his essay on Curt Flood, Pulitzer Prize–winning writer George F. Will places Flood's action within a tide of civil rights that began with the case of Dred Scott.

Dred Scott in Spikes
George F. Will

Curt Flood, a 165-pound whippet of a center fielder, could outrun most fly balls but it took him twenty-four years to catch up to his 1969 Gold Glove award. His story is rich with lessons about courage, freedom, and the conceit that we can predict freedom's consequences.

He had a career batting average of .293 in fifteen seasons, twelve with the Cardinals. But nothing so became him in baseball as his manner in leaving it. Although he played thirteen games with the 1971 Senators, he really left after the 1969 season when the Cardinals traded him to Philadelphia and he said hell no, I won't go.

Black ballplayers have done much to move freedom forward. In 1944, eleven years before Rosa Parks refused to move to the back of a bus in Montgomery, Alabama, a lieutenant in Texas faced a court-martial for a similar refusal on an Army bus: Lieutenant Jackie Robinson. A similar spiritedness made Flood help win for players the elemental right to negotiate with their employers their terms of employment.

He was born in Houston in 1938 and played his way up through minor leagues in the South in the 1950s, before public accommodations were desegregated. He received food at the back door of restaurants that served his white teammates and he relieved himself behind the bus on the shoulder of the highway.

In the 1950s and 1960s pitchers were driven to distraction by black players such as Hank Aaron and Frank Robinson who played with an implacable intensity that suggested the controlled venting of indignation stored up during many minor league and spring training experiences in a South in transition. The Cardinals of the 1960s were fueled partly by the fierce pride of four black men who were taking out their anger on the ball and on opponents—Flood, Bill White (who would become president of the National League) and two Hall of Famers, Lou Brock and Bob Gibson, the take-no-prisoners pitcher who once drilled the ribs of a rookie (Steve Garvey) who had the impertinence to hit a loud foul off him.

In the 1950s there was a lot of social learning going on in major league clubhouses, as whites and blacks, often in advance of the rest of the country, got used to getting along. There was, for example, the day a white teammate, who was Curt Flood's friend, and Bob Gibson's friend, said to Gibson as he was about to leave the clubhouse, "There's a colored guy waiting for you."

"Oh," said Gibson, dryly, "which color is he?"

There was poetry and portent in the fact that Curt Flood's career blossomed in St. Louis, the city where Dred Scott had taken his case to court. In 1966 the Cardinals moved to a new stadium that is located just a long fungo from the courthouse where Scott, a slave, argued that he had lived on free soil and therefore should be free.

Talk about lighting a long fuse. That one led straight to four years of Civil War. Scott's case went all the way to the United States Supreme Court, which ruled against him and thereby against the strong-running tide of history. It was not the last time that the Supreme Court would blunder when asked whether a man can be treated like someone's property.

That is the question Curt Flood posed when the Cardinals tried to trade him. It had always been so, and always would be. He said, well, we'll just see about that. He rose in rebellion against the reserve clause that denied baseball players the fundamental right to negotiate terms of employment with whomever they choose. He lost the 1970 season and lost in the Supreme Court, but he had lit a fuse.

Six years later—too late to benefit him—his cause prevailed. The national pastime is clearly better because of that. But more important, so is the nation, because it has learned one more lesson about the foolishness of fearing freedom.

In 1975 the clause was overturned by an arbitrator. Loud were the lamentations predicting the end of baseball's competitive balance and a decline of attendance. Well.

The decade 1978–87 was the first time in baseball history in which ten different teams won the World Series. Until 1990 there had been no "worst-to-first" volatility in this century—no team won a pennant the year after finishing last. The Twins and the Braves did in 1991 and the Phillies did in

1993. The 1993 A's were the first team since 1915—the A's Philadelphia ancestors—to finish alone in last place the year after finishing first.

In 1993 the team with the worst attendance—the Padres with 1,375,432— drew more fans than the St. Louis Browns drew in the entire 1930s (1,184,076). The Orioles' lowest attendance for two consecutive regularly scheduled games was 83,307—more than the Browns (who became the Orioles in 1954) drew in all of 1935. ·

In 1954, the year Jacques Barzun wrote that anyone who would know America must know baseball, the average attendance was 13,000. This year the Padres averaged 17,191 and the major league average was 31,337. The Rockies drew 4,483,350, more people than live in Minnesota or thirty-one other states. Major league attendance was 70,257,938, more than the combined population of thirty-two states.

But no one last year bought a ticket to see an owner. Because of what Flood started, the players, who largely create baseball value, now receive their share of that value. In 1969 the players' average salary was $24,909. In 1993 it was $1.1 million, much more than Flood earned in his entire career.

It would be a disservice to Curt Flood's memory to honor him exclusively for what he did off the field. The lyrics of John Fogerty's song say, "Look at me. I can be, centerfield." Centerfield is not for the shrinking violets. It is a big place, a big responsibility; and when you run out of room, you run into walls. And what was once said of another player could have been said of Curt Flood: Two-thirds of the earth is covered by water and the rest was covered by Curt.

Beneath the strife and the turmoil of the baseball business, the game—the craft—abides. It is a beautiful thing, the most elegant team sport. And few have ever matched the grace and craftsmanship Curt Flood brought to it as a player. However, none has matched what he did for the game as a citizen.

Rawlings Gold Gloves are awarded annually to the nine players in each league voted best defensively at their positions. Flood won in 1969, but in the turbulence of his rebellion he never collected his glove. He got it here last week at this year's award ceremony.

He once said, "I am pleased that God made my skin black, but I wish He had made it thicker." Friends of baseball, and of freedom, are pleased that He didn't.

Whitey Ball and a Big Mac Attack

At the end of the 1976 season, Red Schoendienst was fired by the Cardinals after a twelve-year tenure as manager, the longest in team history. The Cardinals had finished the season with a 72–90 record, their poorest since 1955, and had not won a pennant since 1968. The popular "Redhead" was shocked and disappointed, but, after a brief coaching stint with the Oakland A's, he returned to the Cardinals as a coach in 1979 and served as interim manager in 1980 and 1990.

In the October 5, 1976, St. Louis Post-Dispatch, Bob Broeg gives a balanced account of the circumstances surrounding the dismissal and a concise summary of Schoendienst's distinguished career that would eventually lead to his induction into the Baseball Hall of Fame in 1989.

Cardinals Fire Schoendienst; Coaches Also Are Dismissed
Bob Broeg

Albert F. (Red) Schoendienst, manager of the Cardinals longer than any other man in the baseball club's 100-year history, was dismissed today. He took the job in 1965.

In a terse statement issued before entering the Redbirds' annual autumn organization meeting, club president August A. Busch Jr. said, "We simply felt that a change was in order."

Schoendienst, notified of the decision reached this morning by Busch, said he was "sort of disappointed. I thought I did a good job with all the young kids. I played the young guys when they brought them up. I was kind of looking forward to being with them next year."

A Cardinal spokesman said later today that the Cardinals' remaining three coaches also have been dismissed. However, the spokesman said that the coaches, Fred Koenig, pitching coach Bob Milliken, and first-base coach Johnny Lewis, have been offered unspecified jobs in the Cardinals' organization.

Third-base coach Preston Gomez had announced earlier that he was leaving the club.

Schoendienst, who said that he was not offered another job in the organization, said he was given no indication as to why he was dismissed other than that "they said they just wanted to make a change. I was kind of wondering why it was taking so long one way or the other. Devine finally decided it would be better if I went." He was referring to club General Manager Bing Devine.

Devine, said Schoendienst, told him this morning, that "We're going to make a change and I want to make the change."

"He's the general manager," Schoendienst said. "I guess that's his privilege."

Schoendienst said that he would begin looking for a job, hoping for a managerial post. "I'll be trying to latch on with some ball club."

Asked if he would consider the Pittsburgh Pirates' managerial job, vacated by Danny Murtaugh's recent retirement, Schoendienst, said, "Yes, I'd sure like it. It's a contending club. I'd sure like to be considered for it."

Busch, before entering the annual meeting for appraisal of the Cardinals' major and minor league players, issued a statement praising Schoendienst:

"I look back with pride at his many accomplishments and look forward to a healthy and rewarding future for a good friend and a great sportsman."

The statement said: "We simply felt a change was in order," after Busch explained, "This move was discussed carefully within our organization, and the decision was based on the recommendations of several people, including the general manager."

Devine was rehired last Thursday with a two-year contract.

Busch's statement continued:

"As indicated during the past several weeks, all phases of the Cardinal organization are being reviewed. It is our consensus that there is a need for a change at the managerial level.

"There are times, regardless of one's capabilities, when a different perspective is in order. Red Schoendienst's distinguished career as both a player and manager are in the record books for all to see."

The Cardinals finished fifth in the six-team Eastern Division of the National League this year with a 72–90 won-lost record. It was the club's poorest record since a seventh-place finish in 1955, when Eddie Stanky was relieved as manager in late May and replaced by Harry Walker.

Schoendienst, 53 years old, was born in Germantown, Ill. He was a popular second baseman who starred on the Redbirds' 1946 world championship team and with the 1957 Milwaukee champions and 1958 Milwaukee pennant winners of the National League.

He was a Cardinal coach before he succeeded Johnny Keane as manager of the St. Louis club after Keane walked away from the 1964 world champions. Schoendienst won the world championship in 1967 and a pennant in 1968.

He managed the Cardinals for 12 seasons, shattering the club mark for longevity of six-plus seasons held by Branch Rickey, later the team's prominent general manager.

Schoendienst was a shortstop in the minors.

When he came out of military service in 1945, Marty Marion was at shortstop for the Cardinals and Schoendienst played left field.

He moved to second base in 1946, prompting the trading of Emil Verban to Philadelphia and Lou Klein's jumping to the Mexican League.

Schoendienst was an outstanding fielder and a .289 lifetime hitter. His average dwindled with fatigue every September.

Shortly after the 1958 season it was learned that he had tuberculosis. He underwent surgery and missed virtually all of the 1959 season. He returned to the Cardinals in 1961.

A wave of protest mail greeted Schoendienst's trade to the New York Giants in June 1956 by then-general manager Frank Lane.

The outcry was reported to have been exceeded only by that which followed the deal that sent Enos Slaughter to the New York Yankees just before the 1954 season.

Schoendienst's managerial record of 1,010 victories and 925 defeats included these finishes:

1965, seventh place; 1966, sixth; 1967, first; 1968, first; 1969 (division play), fourth, 1970, fourth; 1971, second; 1972, fourth; 1973, second; 1974, second; 1975, third, and 1976, fifth.

Schoendienst is married to the former Mary Eileen O'Reilly. They have four children, Colleen, 25, Cathleen, 24, Eileen, 19, and Kevin, 17.

*The Cardinals were a disappointment in the 1970s, but their failure to finish
in first place in the first full decade of division play was certainly not the fault of
Lou Brock. If it were possible to steal a championship, Brock would have done it
for the Cardinals. In 1974, he stole 118 bases and shattered Maury Wills's single-
season record by fourteen thefts. In 1977, he eclipsed Ty Cobb's career stolen base
total of 892 and he finished his own career with 938. In 1979, Brock's last year
before his retirement, he recorded his 3,000th major-league hit. He was elected to
the Hall of Fame in 1985 in his first year of eligibility.*

In his "Larcenous Lou" article for the Sporting News, *Neal Russo discusses
Brock's brilliant career as he was closing in on Ty Cobb's career record for stolen
bases.*

Larcenous Lou Laughs Off Pressure
Neal Russo ————————————————————————————————

Pressure? You might expect lots of it to be felt by the man as he closed in on
another of his many achievements—the No. 1 base stealer in the major
leagues under modern base-running rules.

The great Ty Cobb had held that distinction for 49 years with his career theft
total of 892. Lou Brock began the 1977 season just 27 short of the Georgia
Peach's mark. It was just a matter of time before the Cardinals' Larcenous Lou
would become the new king of the base paths. On August 28, Lou had 891.

Pressure? If Louis Clark Brock really felt a lot of it, he probably would not
even have approached Cobb's distant mark. Nor would he have set the modern single-season standard of 118 thefts in 1974, when he eclipsed Maury
Wills' record by 14.

And if the pressure had gotten to Brock, he most likely never would have
strung together a record 12 straight campaigns in which he swiped at least 50
bases.

If pressure had affected Lou too much, how could one have expected him
to set more marks by stealing seven bases in each of two World Series? Or, for
that matter, to bat a resounding .391 for his three chances to play in the October classic?

One could go on and on about all the ways that Brock might have let the
pressure prevent him from many great achievements. But he actually shifted
the pressure around. He placed the pressure especially on the opposing
pitcher, and on the rival catcher and on their infield teammates, plus their
manager.

If you had followed Brock around in this year that he was to become the Super Czar of Base Stealers, you would have had to be in great shape.

We are in an era in which more and more athletes seem too sensitive around media personnel. Not so with Brock. He seems, even at the ripe age of 38, to revel in the attention given to him and his chase of various records.

As Brock kept closing in on Cobb's career mark for stolen bases, the media, as expected, kept tailing him in larger and larger droves.

Some reporters were shocked to see Brock, after a long, hard night game, get up early and go through what was becoming almost a daily ritual.

There were interviews upon interviews, for newspapers, magazines, radio, and television. It seemed that every time you looked up, there was someone sticking a mike under Lou's nose.

But Brock typically found time for everybody, from the top network reporter to the kid trying to break in right for a local low-watt radio station.

And there were visits with mayors and governors and other officials—plus keys to the city and proclamations and so on. Lou loved it all, hamming it up often with wife Virgie along.

Brock, who also has his eyes on cracking the rather exclusive 3,000-hit club, still wanted to play every day or night despite all the distractions.

You almost have to feel that Brock feeds on all the adulation and commotion, no matter what city he is in.

Besides his great smiling personality, he has obviously been blessed with a tremendous body and mind to be able to cope with all the pressures he's faced for so many years.

Lou doesn't give you all those fancy wintertime routines for getting in shape. He just plain stays in shape, so that he really doesn't have to get in shape. Moderate living habits are mostly the answer.

Typical of a great athlete is the pride that has kept Brock going at an age when a lot of other stars have figured that enough is enough, especially when they have it made financially, as Lou apparently has.

But here is a man who, past his 38th birthday, complained because he wasn't being played every day, no matter the oppressive heat in St. Louis and other cities.

As in the case of other baseball greats with much longevity, such as Stan Musial, Cobb, Hank Aaron, and Al Kaline, the ability to avoid serious injuries has been a big plus for Brock. Ted Williams stuck around but he had more than his share of injuries.

Not that Lou has not served as a human pincushion at times. How would you like to have your shoulder battered by one of Sandy Koufax' bullet fast balls? Or have your valuable legs used as targets by some pitchers?

But Brock avoided many of the bruises and other hurts suffered by Wills and others in the risky business of stealing bases by perfecting his famous pop-up slide and taking a $3\frac{1}{2}$-step lead off first base instead of the $5\frac{1}{2}$-stepper employed by Wills and others.

By averting many of the dangerous slides into second base and the wild swiping of gloves and elbows by fielders, and by not having to keep diving back to first base, Brock obviously added to his productive years.

Brock always regarded base stealing on a wholesale basis as a work of art. And now he looks upon the career theft crown as the masterpiece he has long coveted.

It took more than God-given speed for Brock to achieve so many honors in stealing. He became an expert on the study of pitchers' habits and deliveries on the mound. He laughs when you ask him if he really kept a black book on each pitcher in the league.

"No way—that's impossible," said a howling Brock.

Instead, Lou has been able to lump the various pitchers in a few categories depending on their leg and arm and head habits, to name a few.

The arrival of Brock as a base-stealing wizard signaled something of a revolution by the thieves of baseball. The theft totals began to zoom in both leagues.

A's Owner Charlie Finley even went to the extreme of employing specialists just for swiping bases. Why keep depending on the home run when you could steal your way to victory? Charley reasoned.

Ah, as in warfare, it seems that every time a new offense is devised, the defenders hurry to the drawing board to come up with a counter balancing move. Such has been the case with the pitchers' union in combating the thievery.

"You won't be seeing so many guys stealing 80 or 90 bases now that some pitchers have altered their motions so much that they can flag down a lot of would-be stealers," said Brock.

The biggest hopes to succeed Brock as King of the Base Burglars would include the Dodgers' Davey Lopes, Frank Taveras of the Pirates, and perhaps Billy North of the Athletics.

But Lopes is a case in point in Brock's noting that burglars must stay healthy as well as get on base a lot. Lopes was sidelined during much of the early part of the season.

Some of the catchers also have been refining their techniques for shooting down would-be base stealers. Among the best receivers in this category are the Reds' Johnny Bench, the Mets' Jerry Grote, and Steve Yeager of the Dodgers.

Brock himself, after being slowed a bit by age, has had to make some special adjustments to keep his steal total decent. Despite these changes this year, he had trouble building up a high ratio of steals to times caught. In fact, he was sinking to a point near the .500 level.

Obviously, that is not good. Going into this season, Brock owned a lofty success percentage of .765 in the art of thievery. His top was .829 against the Padres, followed by .800 against the Mets, .798 against the Astros, .795 against the Reds, .791 against his former club, the Cubs, and .785 against the Giants.

Lou was no lower than .700 against anyone. In fact, that was his figure against the Dodgers, with the Expos next at .701.

Going into the '77 campaign, Brock had swiped two bases in a game 126 times, three in a game 19 times, and four in a game three times.

Urged on by chants of "Lou! Lou!" Brock in his record-breaking year of 1974 moved all the way from ninth to second on the all-time steal list.

Of course, when you talk about big steals, you have to put Cardinal General Manager Bing Devine high on the list. He's the one who "stole" Lou from the Cubs in a June 15, 1964, deal. The Redbirds also got pitchers Jack Spring and Paul Toth and gave up pitchers Ernie Broglio and Bobby Shantz as well as outfielder Doug Clemens.

In Brock's only minor season, with St. Cloud in the Northern League in 1961, he swiped 38 bases in 501 at-bats. He stole 16 for the Cubs in 1962, 24 in 1963, and 10 in '64 before the big deal. Lou went on to swipe 33 more in '64 for the Cardinals. He batted .348 in helping them grab their first pennant in 18 years. The next season, '65, it was 63 steals for Lou.

Brock really did not plan to emphasize thievery until Johnny Keane, managing the Cardinals in 1964, informed him that he wanted Lou to steal bases, not just use his speed in plain running the bases.

It boggles the mind to contemplate how many steals Brock might have had if he had been more of a singles hitter instead of a guy who entered the present season with more than 700 extra-base hits. And imagine how many more thefts Lou might have amassed had he not become the victim of so many strikeouts—1,584 going into 1977?

But who can cry about being in the neighborhood of 900 steals with a chance to add a fair amount to that figure before he finally calls it quits?

By the way, Lou isn't even the top stealer among the Brock clan this year. While Lou was in the low 20s, his cousin, Dale Brock, already had collected 29 thefts as a Cardinal farmhand.

Under managers Vern Rapp and Ken Boyer, the Cardinals, despite a number of individual achievements, continued their uneven play as they entered the 1980s. It wasn't until the hiring of Whitey Herzog, who had won three divisional titles with the Kansas City Royals, in midseason 1980 that the Cardinals began to play championship baseball again. With Herzog serving as manager and general manager in 1981, the Cardinals surged to their best record since divisional play began in 1969. In 1982, with Herzog as manager, the Cardinals, playing "Whitey Ball," won their first divisional title, swept the Braves in the playoffs, and defeated the Milwaukee Brewers in the World Series.

Writing in the St. Louis Post-Dispatch, *Rick Hummel and Kevin Horrigan wrap up the Cardinals' come-from-behind World Series victory, the ninth in team history, after they trailed 3–2 in games. It was a World Series with many Cardinal heroes.*

World Champs: Cardinals Wrap It Up
Rick Hummel ————————————————————————————————————

The last time the Cardinals won the world championship of baseball, Lyndon B. Johnson was president, the split-fingered fastball hadn't been invented, and most baseball teams still played on God's green earth instead of that artificial stuff. The year was 1967, and some of the heroes were Bob Gibson, Lou Brock, Tim McCarver, Orlando Cepeda, and Mike Shannon.

At 10:17 p.m. Wednesday, Joaquin Andujar, Bruce Sutter, Keith Hernandez, Darrell Porter, Tom Herr, a couple of guys named Smith, and a varied cast of achievers, overachievers, and good company men assumed their own spots in Cardinals World Series lore. It was then that Sutter, the art's leading practitioner of split-fingered pitching, blew a non-split-fingered fastball past the swing of a startled Gorman Thomas and the Cardinals closed out a 6–3 victory over the Milwaukee Brewers in the seventh game of the 1982 World Series.

The Cardinals had trailed the Brewers, three games to two, when they returned to Busch Stadium after having lost two of three games in Wisconsin last weekend. But the Redbirds pounded out 27 hits here the last two nights, including 15 Wednesday night when they overcame a 3–1 Milwaukee lead with a three-run rally in the sixth inning.

Only three of their number—Gene Tenace, George Hendrick, and Lonnie Smith—ever had experienced the euphoria of the moment. As champagne was sprayed and the sponsor's product was consumed in large quantities, most of the Cardinals said they wouldn't really know the true essence until several days later, but they knew the feeling was a powerful one.

"The only thing that would compare to it," said Herr, "was being in the delivery room the day that our son, Aaron, was born. That was an awesome feeling."

Catcher Darrell Porter, named the series' Most Valuable Player, said the thrill of this victory ranked somewhere behind sobriety, God, his marriage, and the birth of his daughter, but "it was flat-out fun."

The city was plunged into a nightlong celebration that was to continue today with a downtown parade. The Cardinals have won nine world championships, but 15 years had been a long time to wait.

For Gussie Busch, the Cardinals owner, it indeed was the "one more championship for the great fans of St. Louis" that he had hoped for. "I've never been happier in my whole life," said Busch in a madhouse locker room. "I was sure this team could win it, and it didn't let me down."

It was the first world championship for his manager, Whitey Herzog, who had three division winners as manager of the Kansas City Royals. "I feel about as good as you can feel," said Herzog. "I'm happy for Mr. Busch, the greatest man in the world."

It didn't come easily.

Former Cardinal Pete Vuckovich, having stranded nine runners through the first five innings, nursed a 3–1 Milwaukee lead into the bottom of the sixth inning. With one out, Ozzie Smith stroked a single to left and Lonnie Smith doubled down the third-base line, past a diving Paul Molitor.

Milwaukee Manager Harvey Kuenn, slow to pull his pitchers earlier in the Series, yanked Vuckovich at that point for lefthander Bob McClure, who had earned saves in Game Four and Game Five. For the fourth time in the Series, Herzog pulled lefthanded-hitting Ken Oberkfell for righthanded-hitting Gene Tenace, who had gone nothing for three against McClure and had been three for 48 since late August.

But this time, Tenace, who has drawn more than 100 walks in a season several times in his career, drew another one, loading the bases. Keith Hernandez, a former grade-school teammate of McClure in the San Francisco area, then drilled a two-run single to right center on a 3–1 pitch, tying the score.

"I was trying to protect the plate," said Hernandez. "I was vulnerable inside. I was looking fastball and I thought he might make a fat one. But he made a nasty pitch on the inside corner. I don't know how I hit it, but I did."

The next hitter, Hendrick, hit a slow chopper toward third and third baseman Molitor threw home ahead of the nose-first dive of pinch-runner Mike Ramsey, but home-plate umpire Lee Weyer ruled that the ball was foul. Hendrick then singled to right field for the go-ahead run.

Milwaukee had a righthander, Moose Haas, available to pitch to Hendrick, but Kuenn said: "They had two lefthanded hitters coming up behind George. I thought Bobby could get him out."

The Cardinals added two insurance runs in the eighth, again keyed by a Lonnie Smith double. With Haas pitching, Hernandez was walked intentionally with one out, and Hendrick flied to center. But Porter, whose last two weeks of play erased the last two years of frustration, in fans' minds, singled off lefthander Mike Caldwell, scoring Smith. Then Steve Braun, the Cardinals' third designated hitter of the game, drove in the sixth run with a single.

Braun, who rarely has batted against lefthanders in his specialist's role this season, said, "I haven't seen a lefthander since Huggins-Stengel Field at 10 o'clock in the morning." Huggins-Stengel Field in St. Petersburg, Florida, is where the Cardinals and New York Mets play "B" games in spring training.

Sutter, who had 36 saves and nine victories during the regular season and two victories and two saves in postseason play, dispatched the last six Milwaukee batters.

"Now I can say I'm just like Tug McGraw and Rollie Fingers," he said.

The reference was to two other relief aces—McGraw, here on a television assignment, was sitting to his left. Both McGraw and Fingers had been on World Series winners previously, although Fingers' inability to pitch in this Series for the Brewers gave the Cardinals a huge bullpen advantage.

Andujar, pitching on a sore leg after being hit by a line drive last week, pitched four scoreless innings before Ben Oglivie ripped a first-pitch, 400-foot homer in leading off the fifth inning, tying the score at 1–1. Lonnie Smith's infield single had driven in Willie McGee with the Cardinals' first run the inning before.

In the sixth, Andujar's own fielding misadventures helped the Brewers gain a 3–1 lead. Jim Gantner got his third hit in four appearances against Andujar, a double to right, and then Molitor bunted down the third-base line. Third baseman Oberkfell moved toward the ball and so did Andujar, who caught the ball near the foul line and fired toward first.

But Herr, covering the bag, couldn't get the ball because Molitor obscured his vision and hindered his reach. The throw sailed wide for an error, and Gantner scored.

Robin Yount, the next hitter, bounced a high hopper toward Herr at second. With first baseman Hernandez having moved toward the ball, too, Herr looked toward Andujar to cover first, but Andujar had turned spectator and didn't cover. Yount was safe, and then Cecil Cooper's sacrifice fly scored Molitor.

Andujar pitched a scoreless seventh inning before Herzog removed him in favor of Sutter. One reason was that Herzog felt Andujar might be out of control after a shouting match with Gantner after Gantner had grounded to the mound for the last out of the inning. Hulking umpire Lee Weyer held Andujar back as he tried to charge Gantner.

"Joaquin sometimes gets a little high-strung in those spots," said Herzog.

"But I had told Hub [pitching coach Hub Kittle] that after the inning I was going to use Sutter, anyway.

"Once he [Andujar] got us to the seventh inning, we've got the best relief pitcher in baseball. We pay him an awful big amount of money. I figured we'd better use him."

Sutter does not like being called the million-dollar reliever, but he performed that way Wednesday night, as he had most of the season. "To be very honest," said Herzog, "Bruce Sutter is the guy who turned this thing around."

The Cardinals are not really champions of the world, because a large part of the world doesn't play baseball. But they are champions of the world of baseball. Nineteen eighty-two was a very good year.

Clutch Base Hits Came in Bunches
Kevin Horrigan ————————————————————————————

Keith Hernandez got what he wanted for his 29th birthday—a World Series ring.

"This is it, baby," he yelled across the chaos of the Cardinals clubhouse to Tom Herr, his partner on the right side of the Cardinals infield. He held up his right hand, ring finger forward.

The word for Keith Hernandez is smooth. Smooth fielding, smooth talking, smooth stroke. Mr. Smooth. Some of the ballplayers call him "Hondo," which is Spanish for slingshot, and which is what the Boston Celtics used to call John Havlicek, who knew something about smooth himself.

Keith Hernandez deserved this world championship as much as any player in the Cardinals clubhouse. After going nothing for 15 in the first four games of the Series, his bat got hot. He went seven for 12 in the last three games, including two doubles and a homer. He knocked in eight of the 23 runs the Birds scored in the last three games.

"I pride myself on being an RBI man," said Hernandez. "I'd better be if I'm hitting third."

He was on base four out of five times Wednesday night, with two singles and two walks. His single in the sixth inning knocked in Ozzie Smith and Lonnie Smith and tied the game at 3–3.

"When I went up, it was in my mind to get a hit," he said. "I knew a sacrifice fly would only get one run home and still leave us a run behind."

He's also known as a glove man—he's won four straight Gold Gloves at first base. And his two errors in the first three Series games bothered him more than his sick bat. "I felt a lot more pressure in the field," he said. "I knew I was going to hit."

Well, almost. He knew after Game Four that he was going to hit. Though he went nothing for four in that 7–5 loss to the Milwaukee Brewers, he hit three shots, and that built his confidence. He also began making the plays around first base that Cardinals fans have come to take for granted, scooping out low throws, turning the 3–6–3 double play, and picking off the tricky hops. Nobody does it better.

"If I hadn't hit, I would've been hell to live with," he joked. "Sue [his wife] would have had to hide."

Luckily for Sue and the Cardinals, Hernandez came out swinging in Game Five. So valuable did Hernandez become in the last three games of the Series that there was serious talk of his being the Series' MVP. He demurred.

"Darrell deserved it," he said of catcher Darrell Porter, who won the award. "Here's a man who'd hit rock bottom and then turned his whole life around. I think it's only fitting."

It could have been fitting for Hernandez, too. Here's a man who's seen the worst of the Cardinals' recent times, the dog days of the middle and late '70s. He's played for four Cardinals managers, slogging through one mediocre season after another—though always enjoying good seasons personally. In 1979, of course, he was co-winner of the National League's Most Valuable Player award. He hit only .344 that year.

"When I hit, I'm an animal," Hernandez said. "A wounded animal."

He "dipped" to .321 in 1980 and .306 in 1981, though in both years he should be credited with dozens of "saves" for shagging the scattershot throws of former Redbirds shortstop Garry Templeton. He hit .299 for the 1982 season, exactly matching his career batting record.

"This year, for the first time, I played with 25 guys where there were no big egos, no one or two or four people who always wanted headlines. Whitey deserves the credit for that. We have six or seven guys who'll take the lead, and 25 guys who'll sacrifice for 25 guys."

Hernandez said he didn't watch the World Series, on television last year or the year before. "It hurt too much," he said. "All that work for naught."

And still, he wondered how he would perform under the pressure of the Series. He found out, and it was worth the wait.

"Yes, it was," he said. "It was better than I thought it would be. I get to wear that ring."

Just before spring training in 1982, when St. Louis swapped their unpre-dictable, but talented, shortstop Gary Templeton for the Padres' great-field, no-hit shortstop Ozzie Smith, it looked like one of the worst trades in Cardinal history. But, for the Cardinals, it turned out to be their greatest steal since they traded Ernie Broglio to the Cubs for Lou Brock. With Smith at shortstop, the Cardinals won three pennants in the 1980s and their ninth World Series title. Called "The Wizard" because of his magical defensive skills, Smith won Gold Gloves in each of his seasons from 1980 to 1992, but he was also a clutch hitter, whose game-winning home run against the Dodgers in the 1985 division play-offs became one of the most memorable moments in St. Louis baseball history.

In his July 20, 1983, column in the Los Angeles Times, *Spink Award winner Jim Murray celebrates the fielding wizardry that turned the left side of the infield into Ozzie Smith's "yellow brick road."*

St Louis's Wizard of Ozzie

Jim Murray ————————————————————————————

Last July 6, Osborne Earl Smith of the St. Louis Cardinals was the starting shortstop on the National League All-Star team with a batting average of .205, after spending most of the season under .200. And when I tell you that, I have told you all you may need to know about Osborne E. Smith as a ballplayer.

Ozzie Smith is paid to make outs. No one cares if he makes them with his bat, so long as he makes about 1,000 a year with his glove. He's the best in the long history of baseball at that. He has made the ground single to the outfield in left extinct. The turf between second and third on any diamond he plays becomes the Land of Oz. Other guys play shortstop. Ozzie plays over the rain-bow. It's his yellow brick road.

Ozzie could play shortstop on a field of fresh ranch eggs without breaking a one. He rarely lights. He's like a hummingbird with a glove. He's airborne so much of the time he could probably cross the Mississippi without getting his feet wet. Bojangles in cleats. There are people who don't recognize him unless he's prone, stabbing for a ball. In the field, he usually manages to look like a guy leaping through a skylight.

In another age or on another continent, Ozzie Smith would probably have been in the circus. It has long been the contention of this department that, for sheer agility, dexterity, and body control, there is a troupe of touring jugglers and acrobats someplace in the Balkans who could make the All-Star outfield look clumsy. They could catch balls with their feet if you wanted them to.

Ozzie Smith beefs up this argument. He is of this blessed company. He could probably play the game balancing a ham sandwich on his nose. He can't believe his good luck that they let him stand in one place with rubber shoes and all he has to do for a million bucks a year is pick up this little rolling ball and throw it someplace not far away. I mean, he doesn't have to do a somersault first, he doesn't have to pick up five balls, juggle them, wait for the orchestra to pick up, and then throw one of them behind his back to first. He doesn't have to do back flips before catching the ball.

The way Ozzie plays shortstop, they should have five judges holding up cards with points on them as if it was Comaneci on the uneven bars. So many of Ozzie's plays are perfect 10s. It's a shame to waste them just on an out.

The big leagues are easy for Ozzie, anyway. They give him this great big mitt. They let him play with his eyes open. Some plays he can make without even stooping.

It wasn't always this way. When Ozzie was a kid he used to take the ball, lie on his back with his eyes closed—then throw the ball up in the air and catch it without opening his eyes. Then he would go out and throw the ball by the hour against the garage door—and do a somersault before it bounced back to him and he caught it. That was a distance of 10 feet. In the big leagues, Ozzie gets, oh, 125 feet or so. He gets a glove as big as a peach basket, the ball is nice and white and easy to see and is not out of round. It's almost like being retired.

"With Ozzie out there, you don't need a third baseman," says World Series Manager Harvey Kuenn, a former shortstop. In 1980 Ozzie set an all-time record for shortstop assists, 621, breaking a 56-year-old record. What was interesting was that Ozzie finished with 307 more chances accepted than the nearest competitor. This translates out that many or all of those 300 unhandled hits went for one or two-base hits or more.

Of course, the thing that keeps major league infields from being filled with Yugoslav jugglers is that many of them can't hit the curveball. People with the reflexes to keep plates spinning on thin reeds can't always handle the spinning baseball.

Ozzie himself is hardly Babe Ruth. But baseball, computing the 200 hits the opposition doesn't get, reasons that if you add those to Ozzie's stats you got Rogers Hornsby. Pitchers love him. "I don't care if he never comes to bat," relief pitcher Bruce Sutter has been quoted. "What's the lowest he could bat and still make the club and stay in the big leagues?" his manager, Whitey Herzog, was asked. "How about .003?" Whitey wondered.

Ozzie is batting higher than Herzog's minimum. But he brought something more precious than a .300 average to the Cardinals—the pennant. "I talked to George Hendrick before agreeing to the trade (from San Diego to St. Louis)," Smith recalled before a game the other day. "And George told me, 'You are the missing link. With you we could win the pennant.' Whitey Herzog was even more positive. 'Come over and we will win the pennant,' he said."

Ozzie is just glad baseball can see this, that it's the hits you don't get that decide pennants. He's glad to be around to demonstrate it. He's also glad they let him play with his eyes open and feet on the ground and that they don't declare him unfair and make him play while keeping three Indian clubs, two oranges, and a raw egg in the air at the same time. Or decide that, if he's going to make like Houdini, he has to play out of a locked trunk, wrapped in chains and under water. With the wizardry of Oz, he'd probably still turn the double play.

After off-years in 1983 and 1984, the Cardinals, led by National League MVP Willie McGee and Rookie of the Year Vince Coleman, bounced back in 1985 to win their second division title under Whitey Herzog. They defeated the Dodgers in the National League Championship Series and went on to play the Kansas City Royals, Herzog's old team, in the World Series.

In the "Signatures" chapter from You're Missin' a Great Game, *Herzog discusses in detail the play that he and Cardinal fans will always believe cost the team the 1985 World Series. Now known as "The Call," it came in the bottom of the ninth of Game Six with the Cardinals leading 1–0 and just three outs away from their tenth world championship. The notorious call opened the door for a Kansas City rally and victory in Game Six that evened the Series. The Royals then went on to defeat the demoralized Cardinals in Game Seven, their fifth World Series loss in team history.*

Signatures
Whitey Herzog ———————————————————————

Over here, across the room, are two jerseys under glass: one from the Royals, another bearing my uniform number, 24, in bright Cardinals red. I don't just think of the double-knit they're made of, the miracle fabric that freed us all from the heat and suffering of them old wool flannels. I remember that I managed both big-league clubs in my adopted home state, which nobody's done before or since. But mostly, they take me back to 1985, when the two towns squared off in the first all-Missouri World Series since 1944, when the Cards beat the Brownies.

It was nice to feel at home in both places. But there was nothing cozy about how the I–70 Series turned out. It'll always be part of White Rat lore.

Writers from both coasts took off before we ever got started. We'd knocked off the Mets during the season and the Dodgers in the playoffs, and there were no Yankees in sight, so as far as they were concerned, there wasn't going to *be* no World Series. Well, screw 'em; they missed one of the greatest Series ever. Had it not been for one horseshit call, the Cardinals would have won a best-of-seven championship in six while scoring only fourteen runs.

The pitching and defense were outstanding. Danny Cox, one of my starters and the toughest player I ever managed, would have been MVP. I'd have had one more scalp on the wall, and I might have gotten a charge out of beating the Royals, a team I'd parted with five years earlier on lousy terms.

But you saw the play.

Todd Worrell, my flame-throwing reliever, is in to close down Game Six. We're up three games to two, ready to finish 'em off. It's the ninth; we lead 1–0 and stand three outs away. We've ridden a six-month rollercoaster to get here. We'd lost our stopper, Bruce Sutter, and his team-record 45 saves in the off-season. I went to spring training with a bullpen in shambles. One writer picked me as the first manager to get fired. Yet we hadn't blown one lead in the eighth inning or later all year. My makeshift bullpen-by-committee has racked up 44 saves. Willie McGee has had an MVP year, hitting .353. We're on the brink of a second title in four years.

Well, their leadoff hitter, Jorge Orta, opens the last inning with a high chopper to the right side. Jack Clark, my first baseman, gloves it; Worrell covers the bag perfect. Clark tosses it to Todd. He stomps on the base. Orta's out by a long, long stride, and we have that all-important first one down. But for no earthly reason anybody's ever figured out, Don Denkinger—a fine American League umpire, a man I've always respected, a guy I even *like*—stands right there by the bag, in plain, Show-Me state view, sees the same play the rest of America saw, and waves that runner safe.

Now, most people don't realize that in baseball, the leadoff man is the most important hitter. A team that gets its first batter to first base scores a run in that inning between 50 and 60 percent of the time—in baseball, *huge* percentages. If that man makes an out, the odds drop to about 10 percent. In a one-run game in the ninth, that first man is big. In Game Six of the World Series, he's huge. That was trouble and a half. I shot straight out onto the field.

I didn't know what the damn problem was. I could see from the dugout that the throw beat Orta by a full stride, so I knew *that* wasn't it. I thought maybe Worrell's foot came off the bag. So as the fans went into their I–70 uproar, I got in Denkinger's face and said, "Don, what's the deal? Did Todd miss the bag?" "No," he says, "the runner beat the throw." And I thought, *did I hear this sonofagun right? He beat the throw?*

I said, "Man, are you shittin' me? I *know* he didn't beat the throw; I could see that from the dugout. I thought maybe he missed the bag." "No, the runner beat it." "Damn, Donnie," I hollered, "I can call it from the dugout better than that!" And right there on the field, Denkinger gave me a look that told me everything.

It was a kind of helpless, "oh-well" shrug along with a pained little smile. Now, I know umpires, and he might as well have said it out loud: "Hey, Whitey, sorry; shoulda got it right, but that's baseball, huh?" Don Denkinger was telling me he knew he'd booted the call.

I stared at him. He knew he'd blown it, but I guess he was hoping it'd just even out and go away. We argued. He wouldn't back down. And with a strange, dark feeling, I headed back to the dugout, took a seat, and watched a scene unfold that will stay with me for the rest of my life.

You know what happened. Guys did things they hadn't done all year. Darrell Porter, my catcher, missed a pitch for a passed ball. Clark misjudged a pop foul. We fell apart. The Royals scored two to win the game. We were so shocked about taking it up the rear we got stomped 11–0 the next day. My players lost a World Series they deserved to win.

What an ending: That one damn call might keep me out of the Hall of Fame, and Don Denkinger became famous for the gaffe that made the Royals champions.

In Missouri, we had Quantrill's Raiders and Wild Bill Anderson tearing up the ground all through the Civil War, but the fans' arguments over that call *still* make them psychopaths look tame. To the west, Royals fans: "The Cards should have shrugged it off and won!" To the east, Cardinal fans: "There wouldn't have been no self-destruction if not for that SOB ump!" The play went down as The Call, and you still see framed pictures of it in bars from Jeff City to Joplin.

What they're fighting about is a question as old as the game: What's more important, getting it correct, or following the idea that the ump's always right, no matter how far his head's gone up his ass?

Well, I've had fourteen years to think about this. And here's what I've decided: We blew Game 7 bad—I got kicked out, along with Mr. Andujar—but that wasn't the biggest chance we booted.

Let's go back to the field. I'm jawing with Denkinger. We're on national TV, 200 million people are watching, the call's on instant replay, and *everybody* can see the man is wrong. What would have happened if I'd said, "That's it, Don; I want to talk to the commissioner. Get him down here." And I'd have gotten Peter Ueberroth, who was right behind the Royals' dugout, down from his seat, and said, "Pete, let me ask you something. This game is 1–0. We should have a man out at first with nobody on, two outs from a championship. Instead, we got a runner on first with *nobody* out. The ump admits he missed the call. Everybody in the world knows he missed the call. And *you* know he missed the call. Now, if you don't change that, and that man ain't out, I'm giving you the game. I'm taking my team off the field."

What would have happened?

Pete would have said, "Whitey, we can't do that." And I'd have said, "The hell you can't. Then we ain't playing, because every sonofabitch in the world knows that guy is out. This is the World *Series,* man, let's get it *right!*" I'd have waved my hand from the dugout, my team would have jogged in and left the field, and 50,000 fans and announcers and reporters would've been running around raising all kinds of hell. I'd have been fined, suspended, maybe had my ass run out of baseball.

In other words, it would've been everything my game needed to kick it in the rear. If I had it to do over again, that's just the way I'd play it.

There was precedent. One century before, almost to the day, in Game Two of a postseason series against the Chicago White Stockings, the Browns' manager, Charlie Comiskey, pulled his team to protest the umpiring. God knows what kind of calls *he* had to put up with. It caused a hell of a row, boy, and the series ended up being declared a 3–3–1 tie. Did *he* do right? Did he screw up?

The questions go to the heart of baseball. When should a bad call really be part of the game? When should it *not* be? If the ump blows one in June, you go out there, kick some dirt, cuss a little; and if the ump admits he booted it, hey—you've got half the season to make it up. But can you look me in the eye and tell me it'd be the same thing if you were two outs from the world's championship?

If I'd pulled the vanishing act, maybe we'd have instant replay in the World Series by now. Bad calls at the bases, and along the foul lines, can be fixed in two seconds with a look at video. You'd have to put some limits on it, but that's what we ought to do. Like I said, this is for the championship—let's get it *right*.

Well, I'm not God; I ain't even the commissioner. I'm only an ex–manager. The thing is, only the Pastime could be fiendish enough to pick a guy like me, point its finger and say, "All right, buddy, you've got sixty seconds, 200 million people are watching, and I ain't asking you again: What's your answer?" It's that trick pitch you've never seen, coming in at 98 mph, and by the time you get set, *whap!* It's in the mitt. The hell of it is, once you've figured out what that pitch was, you may never see it again.

Over there, above the sofa, is one of my favorite photos, a color shot of me with the smartest boss I ever had, the old eagle, Gussie Busch. It was taken right after we won the '82 Series. Gussie's looking sharp in a Cardinal red blazer, a scarlet cowboy hat, and a black string tie, and he and I are having a laugh and a taste of the company product, chilled to perfection.

I'll tell you one reason I love that picture. It's not just that he and I were hard-headed, Braunschweiger-chomping Germans who knew each other like brothers. It's not just that great players like Ozzie, McGee, Sutter, and Lonnie Smith got their moment in the sun that night, or that I did, too. No, that Series gave me the best chance I ever had to think about what winning means.

The test of greatness is how often you keep your team in the hunt. Bud Grant, who lost three Super Bowls for the Minnesota Vikings, and Marv Levy, who lost four for the Buffalo Bills, had to be two of the greatest NFL coaches in history just to be in the position *not* to win. Hell, I'll never forget, right after we lost the '85 Series in Kansas City, one of the Anheuser-Busch people came up to me, put his hand on my shoulder and said, "We'll do better next year." *Better?* If you told a guy like that you'd take losing in Game Seven of the World Series any year of your life, he'd send out for a straitjacket.

In golf, when you're putting, you choose your line, stroke the ball, and hope that sonofagun rolls in. If it doesn't, you still know you did it the best you could. Now, I'm a very confident, optimistic person, but by 1982, I was starting to wonder. What happens if you keep on stroking it just right, putt after putt, and then one day you realize, *Hey, that sonofagun's* never *dropped in the hole?* What happens if you *become* Bud Grant?

All my life, I've been good enough to get my teams close. That was true when I was a kid, and it was truer still when I coached and managed. But the strangest things would happen once I got there. You'd have made money betting on Herzog teams over the long haul. But if you'd put your money on some horrible break happening at the last minute, you could've retired early.

It started when I was young. At New Athens High, a tiny school with less than 100 kids in it, our basketball players knew each other so well we almost never lost. Between halves, our coach always gave us the same pep talk: "Boys, remember—this half, shoot at the other basket!" That's all he had to say. My senior year we got to the state quarterfinals, knocking off school after school that were five times our size. But in our last regional game, we played in a gym with glass backboards. We'd never seen those. I was a good foul shooter, but I kept seeing those fans waving their arms through the glass. I missed all six of my free throws. We lost by a point.

Same thing with our baseball team. We went deep in the playoffs but had to play our final game under lights—something *else* we'd never seen. Out in center, I got blinded on a long flyball, it caromed into a cornfield, and we lost by a run.

It stalked me to Kansas City. I managed my ass off for the Royals for five years, and we played great ball there. All three times we won the division, we faced the rich, mighty Yankees in the ALCS. But one year, one of my starting players kicks two balls in the deciding game; I heard later he was up all night using drugs. Another year, a first-game injury to Amos Otis, one of my stars, forces me to shuffle my lineup. I move Al Cowens, my 6–2 rightfielder, to center, and replace him with 5–8 Hal McRae. Well, we're tied in Game Five, a trip to the World Series on the line, when New York's Chris Chambliss hits a fly deep to right center. It goes over McRae's glove—and the wall—by six inches. Cowens could have made that catch. Season over.

In 1985, not only did The Call stomp all over us, but the fastest ballplayer in history—our offensive catalyst that year, the base thief Vince Coleman—got run over by a two-mile-an-hour mechanical tarp before the Series began. Two years later, we played the Twins in the Series. Two guys, Clark and Terry Pendleton, accounted for most of our offensive production that year, but both went down with late-season injuries. We lost.

Fluke plays happen, and no good baseball man uses them as an excuse. But if your tombstone read "He came awful damn close," would *you* be satisfied? When Gussie and I hoisted those Buds and our trophy in this picture, it was a monkey off my back. I'm relieved I never had to face the biggest question of all.

Fifty-some years ago, Joe DiMaggio took the time to sign me that autograph. Twenty-five years after that, his playing days were over and he was a consultant for the Oakland A's. And he called me one day to offer me a job: He wanted me to be their manager.

I was tempted, boy. I'd coached most of those players myself, before the team moved away from Kansas City. I'd hit 'em grounders and fungoes and drilled 'em on fielding and hitting. I got half the pay the other coaches got and did twice the work. I'd driven 'em hard. I knew it was a hell of a group, and I knew they were going to win.

But I also knew that the A's owner, Charles O. Finley, was a meddler of the worst kind. He took credit where it wasn't due; he thought he knew the game. If you were his manager, he'd do everything but fill out your lineup card. Charlie was a good guy—he'd buy you a scotch and soda any day of the week if he met you on a train—but if you worked for him, he thought he owned you. I turned the offer down.

Do I regret it? Those A's teams won three World Series in a row and went down in history as a dynasty. I might have been their Casey Stengel. But Charlie didn't understand something that Joe D. showed me just by the way he carried himself: that in this game, it's the people who count.

What do you value in baseball? Is it how much you win? Is it how famous you get, how they remember you, how much money you make? What kind of signature will you leave? Nowadays, it's hard to know what people think. But when the last inning is played, every man has to answer for himself.

After failing to make the postseason playoffs in 1986, the Cardinals finished in first place in their division for the third time in six years. They came back from a 3–2 deficit in games to defeat the Giants in the National League Championship Series for their fifteenth pennant, then went on to play the Minnesota Twins in the World Series. Even with key injuries to Terry Pendleton and Jack Clark, the Cardinals took a 3–2 lead in games, but, after losing Game Six, they were bested by World Series MVP Frank Viola in the seventh and deciding game.

In his cover story for the St. Louis Post-Dispatch, *Rick Hummel describes the events that led to the World Series defeat of Whitey Herzog's "overachieving" Cardinals. It was the Cardinals' second World Series lost in three years and their sixth in team history.*

Twins Are Champs
Rick Hummel ————————————————————————

Before the seventh game of the World Series, Cardinals manager Whitey Herzog said, "If I've ever had a club that overachieved this one did it."

The Cardinals may have overachieved, but they couldn't overcome Sunday night. They lost the feature game of this World Series to the Minnesota Twins 4–2.

Minnesota, in winning its first world championship, became the first team in Series history to win four games at home. Never had there been a team in Series history to win four games at home. Never had there been a Series in which all seven games were won by the home team.

Though he will be criticized, Herzog lost with his best.

When starter Joe Magrane allowed an infield hit on a disputed call with one out in the fifth inning, Herzog went to righthander Danny Cox, who had won a start just three days earlier and was generally considered the Cardinals' Mr. October. But Cox gave up a game-tying double to Kirby Puckett on his first pitch.

The Twins lost two runners later in the fifth, but in the sixth Cox walked the first two batters, Tom Brunansky and Kent Hrbek. Cox was taken out of the game—and also ejected from the game because of what he said as he walked past home-plate umpire Dave Phillips.

Todd Worrell relieved, and, after Tim Laudner failed to bunt, Laudner fouled to first baseman Jim Lindeman. Worrell then walked pinch-hitter Roy Smalley on a full-count pitch.

Worrell struck out Dan Gladden, but Greg Gagne sent a shot down the third-base line. Tom Lawless backhanded the ball, but after he scrambled to his feet, his one-hop throw was too late to catch Gagne as Brunansky scored what proved to be the winning run.

The Twins scored another run in the eighth on a single by Laudner and a double by Gladden, who was the only player to hit safely in every game of the Series.

Relay man Tom Herr's throw skipped past catcher Steve Lake, who otherwise had a brilliant game, tagging out two runners on throws from left fielder Vince Coleman and throwing out another runner at third.

The Cardinals, after scoring twice against Frank Viola in the second inning, were helpless against the lefthander, who was named Most Valuable Player in the Series. They had just two hits after the second inning against Viola, who left after eight innings.

Jeff Reardon pitched a perfect ninth to preserve Viola's victory, his 13th in 16 games at the Metrodome.

"Viola just pitched a strong game," said Herzog, who again was without Jack Clark and Terry Pendleton, who had combined for 47 homers and 202 runs batted in this season.

Herzog, whose team led 3–2 after five games, said: "We had a pretty good shot at it. I don't know if we deserved to be here, but we got here. We overcame a lot of things.

"I don't mind losing the seventh game. I guess I'd like to lose the seventh game of the World Series for the next ten years. We've been in three World Series in the last six years, and I'd like to be 3–0."

Instead, the Cardinals have tasted the bitterness of seventh-game losses in two of the last three years. They lost to the Kansas City Royals in 1985 after leading that series three games to one.

Herzog's game plan was for Magrane to pitch until the middle of the game and then turn the ball over to Cox.

"Joe pitched a pretty good game," Herzog said. "I thought he'd get us to the fifth inning, and then Danny could get us to the seventh. But Danny couldn't get us there."

Magrane, pitching in and out of trouble, needed a couple of good defensive plays in the first inning.

First baseman Lindeman sprawled to his left to stop Gladden's lead-off smash and then flipped to Magrane for the out.

After Gagne struck out, Puckett got an infield hit on a chopper toward third, although television replays indicated he was out. Right fielder Jose Oquendo then dashed into right field center to make a shoe-top grab of Gary Gaetti's liner.

The Cardinals bunched four singles for their two runs off Viola in the second. Lindeman blooped a single to center and stopped at second on Willie McGee's 10th hit of the World Series. Designated hitter Tony Pena, after just missing a home run to left, got his eighth Series hit to score Lindeman. After Oquendo popped up, McGee went to third on Lawless' long fly to right center.

Lake, batting for the first time in the World Series, lined a single to left to score McGee. Coleman then popped up.

During the inning, righthander Bert Blyleven was warming up for the Twins as the Cardinals peppered Viola.

The Cardinals got a couple of breaks in the bottom half of the second as the Twins scored a run.

Magrane hit Don Baylor on the leg with a 1–2 pitch and Brunansky singled to left. Hrbek struck out on a 3–2 pitch, but Laudner singled to left. Though there was only one out, third-base coach Rich Renick waved Baylor home. Lake fielded Coleman's short-hop throw and tagged Baylor. Umpire Dave Phillips called Baylor out, although replays indicated that Baylor's right foot crossed the plate before he was tagged on the leg.

Minnesota then scored when Steve Lombardozzi got his fourth hit in his last five at bats, a single to center. Gladden popped up to end the inning.

McGee saved an extra-base hit when he leaped to backhand Puckett's drive to straightaway center in the third. McGee jumped several feet in front of the fence and then banged into the plastic covering after catching the ball.

Viola, meanwhile, was cranking into top form. He struck out four men in a row, all swinging, as he worked a perfect third and fourth. In the fifth he also had a 1–2–3 inning, something Magrane didn't have in any of the first four innings. Coleman was Viola's sixth strikeout on a high fastball.

As the Twins' fifth started, Cox, who had been up in the bullpen for the Cardinals in the second, began warming up again.

With one out, Gagne hit a chopper between first and second. Both second baseman Herr and Lindeman hesitated before Lindeman fielded the ball. Lindeman threw a bit behind Magrane, who was late covering. Magrane missed the base with his right foot but appeared to drag his left foot across it in front of Gagne, but umpire Lee Weyer ruled that Gagne was safe.

Cox entered the game and Puckett rifled his first pitch into right-center field for a double, scoring Gagne.

Gaetti walked, but then the Twins lost two runners in rapid-fire fashion.

A Cox pitch eluded Lake, and the Cardinals' catcher couldn't find it briefly. Too briefly for Puckett, who tried for third and was thrown out by Lake.

Gaetti went to second on the play, and then Baylor lined a single to left. Coleman threw a one-hop throw to the plate, and Lake took on Gaetti's hard shoulder block and held onto the ball—barely—in his mitt for the third out. Lake was limping as he went back to the dugout.

"Give Coleman credit," said Minnesota manager Tom Kelly. "He had the guts to play shallow twice."

After Viola retired 11 men in succession, Herr singled with one out in the sixth. But, on a 3–2 pitch to Lindeman, Herr was caught off first by Viola.

Hrbek, taking the throw, fired to second baseman Lombardozzi, who ran Herr back to first. Herr tried to push Hrbek out of the way as Lombardozzi threw to Viola covering. Herr's slide appeared to beat Viola's tag, but Weyer, probably missing his third call of the game, ruled Herr out. Herr protested, as did Herzog.

Cox, pitching on two days' rest, apparently was too tired. He walked both Brunansky and Hrbek to open the sixth and was replaced by Worrell, who hadn't come into a game that early in the last two seasons.

After Worrell allowed the game-winning hit to Gagne, he struck out Puckett and the Cardinals were still alive.

Pena doubled off the right-field fence with one out in the seventh. But Oquendo struck out. Pena stole third, although if Laudner hadn't thrown low, he would have been out. Lawless then flied to center.

Pena was to be the Cardinals' last baserunner.

The Cardinals' epitaph is that they lost three decisions to lefthanded pitchers in the Series, two to Viola.

Clark, who wasn't on the roster, and Pendleton didn't have any at bats against the left-handers. Other than McGee, who was six for 11 against left-handers, Cardinals switch-hitters were three for 39 righthanded, including 0 for 11 by Coleman and 0 for nine by Ozzie Smith.

In June 1990, Tom Boswell of the Washington Post, *one of baseball's most respected commentators, wrote "Our Casey" in celebration of Whitey Herzog as "the best manager in baseball or else the first name mentioned on a very short list." At the time Herzog, in nearly twenty years of managing, including more than ten with the Cardinals, had won six division titles, three pennants, and one world championship. In "Our Casey," Boswell portrays Herzog as a self-taught, self-assured, fun-loving individual, who, as a baseball man, is shrewd, cocky, and respectful of the game and his players.*

Shortly after Boswell wrote his essay, Herzog, one of the most popular managers in St. Louis baseball history, resigned from the Cardinals because the team that had so often overachieved for the "White Rat" was now underachieving and floundering in last place. The manager who loved his job because it was fun was no longer having fun managing the Cardinals.

Our Casey
Tom Boswell

June 1990—Everybody in baseball says the same three things about Whitey Herzog: He's the best manager in baseball or else the first name mentioned on a very short list. He's the most abrasively self-confident and outspoken executive in the sport. And, whether he's in the middle of a controversy or a pennant race, he seems to have a better time than everybody else.

Once, between the fifth and the sixth game of the World Series, Herzog was asked if he'd be available for interviews during the off day. No, he said. Not unless you're in a fishing boat or on a golf course.

Which would it be? Fish or play golf?

"Both," said Herzog. Fish first, then golf. Maybe 36 holes if the sun stayed up long enough.

Herzog's life is one long extra-inning game. When you need only five hours' sleep a night, when the U.S. Army says you have an IQ of 140, when everything about the world fascinates you, when you're the kind of man who laid every one of the 18,000 bricks in his first home with his own hands, when you just naturally can't sleep much later than 5:30 a.m. Why sleep when being awake can be such a kick? Herzog can always sit in that big, quiet house he designed for himself and read until Mary Lou, his wife, wakes up.

"Mary Lou bought that game Trivial Pursuit for Christmas," says Herzog. "We got the family around. But we had to stop playing. I knew all the answers. Every damn question."

Herzog barely graduated from high school. He preferred skipping so he could hitch rides with truckers, hang out in burlesque houses, and watch the St. Louis Browns. But Dorrel Norman Elvert Herzog—a man in search of a nickname since birth—shocks people with his knowledge. Even Mary Lou, who has known him since they were kids, was impressed by his prowess. "She was amazed," he says, grinning. "She said, 'Where'd you learn all that stuff?' I told her, 'Whaddaya think I been doing down here all those years while you've been sleepin'? I read everything.'"

"Whitey has a special place in our game, like Casey Stengel once did," says Frank Cashen, general manager of the New York Mets and Herzog's archrival. "A few of our prominent citizens can, shall we say, scratch themselves at inopportune times and get away with it. Whitey can."

And Whitey does. Herzog the manager is revolutionary enough—preaching such heresies as "Relief pitching is more important than starting pitching" and "Speed beats power." But it's Herzog the cocky, self-reliant White Rat who fascinates people most.

Nobody else seems able to survive managing. Earl Weaver, Gene Mauch, and Dick Williams, recent managers who resemble Herzog the most, have all retired—none contentedly. Cheerful Sparky Anderson ended up in a hospital with "total exhaustion." Billy Martin flamed out, too.

By contrast, Herzog, the St. Louis Cardinals manager, is in beaming health and bumptious spirits. "Talk about a man who enjoys life," says Royals public relations director Dean Vogelaar. "I've never seen anybody who can go as hard, twenty-four hours a day, as Whitey."

And talking every step of the way.

Since Weaver retired, Herzog has become baseball's annual best bet to add a quotation to *Bartlett's*. He once called the Oakland Coliseum "a graveyard with lights" and still refers to Candlestick Park as "a toilet with the lid up." A hint of what he says in private after a few beers may be gleaned from what he says in public. "I'm not going to second-guess Dallas Green. All I'm going to say is that he just traded his best pitcher for a sack of garbage." He deliberately got thrown out of the seventh game of the 1985 World Series, telling umpire Don Denkinger, "We wouldn't even be here if you hadn't missed the fucking call last night."

"Whitey doesn't care whether people like what he says or not," says Milwaukee general manager Harry Dalton, chuckling. "With him, it's 'I think it; therefore, I say it.'"

Herzog has built contenders for fifteen years with raw materials that other teams discard—mediocre pitchers who are lucky to go six innings and swift glove men who can't hit a ball to the warning track.

"You look at the Cards year after year and say, 'They're not that good.' But damn if they don't keep grinding it out for Whitey," says Cleveland general manager Hank Peters, a forty-year front-office veteran who first hired Herzog for a nonplaying baseball job in 1963. "He has the confidence to evaluate and the courage to act."

Herzog's St. Louis teams hit the fewest home runs in baseball. And his starting pitching staffs have been almost pathetic. How on earth did he win three National League pennants in the '80s? Except for a couple of legendary bad breaks—Denkinger's blown call in 1985 and Jack Clark's ankle injury in 1987—he would probably have won three world titles in the past eight years.

Nobody knows exactly how Herzog got the better of the New York Mets in the '80s. They had the talent. He got the rings. No wonder Peters says, "Whitey Herzog is the best judge of talent I've ever seen."

No setback seems to outflank Herzog's capacity for personnel improvisation. That's why 1990 may be a typical Herzog season. He has lost his All-Star catcher (Tony Pena) to free agency, and his bullpen star (Todd Worrell) isn't expected back from elbow surgery until mid-season. In a situation where most managers would be expected to fail, it's assumed that Herzog, until proven otherwise, will find some ridiculous way to succeed.

Herzog creates the impression that he can bully, finesse, or laugh his way through anything. On the first day of spring training this past March, after the thirty-two-day lockout, every team scrambled to work out at the earliest date. Except the Cards, who began a day later than everybody else. The three-week spring was wonderful, said Whitey, far superior to seven weeks. "Shit, we just come down here in February so the general managers can play golf."

Herzog is the only man in baseball history who has held every significant job in the game—big-league player, third-base coach ("I was the best ever"), head scout, farm director, general manager, and manager. He may know more baseball—firsthand and at more levels—than any man who has ever lived. Whether he does or not, he acts like it. One former colleague says, "He's one of my favorite people. But you just have to understand that his ego is bigger than the stadium."

"I'm not as stubborn now as I was," says Herzog. "I had a lot of Dutch in me. But when I *know* I'm right and someone disagrees with me, that's when I have a problem with him. Because when I know I'm right, I almost always *am* right."

Backing up that confidence is a commanding ballpark presence. His white burr-cut hair might as well be a rooster's comb, announcing his arrival. His hands are enormous. He also has the comfortable belly that he wants. He has had that thumbs-at-the-waist farmer hip cock mastered for years. But you need some heft, some ballast to pull off the look. Friendly, solid, but daunting.

The man has been a ham, a hot dog, a dude ever since his mother started sticking him in amateur hours to sing. He loves to play a role to the hilt, hiding behind it all the time. Check out those old '50s black-and-whites from his playing days; nobody in *Damn Yankees* dressed that sharply, not even the devil. Although his eight-year playing career was mediocre, he could run and throw with the best and got more money than Mickey Mantle coming out of high school. Ted Williams even said that Herzog had one of the best swings he had ever seen. Too bad he couldn't hit a slow curve with a canoe paddle.

Back then, Satchel Paige nicknamed Herzog "Wild Child." Now his style is shameless middle-class gothic. That's as it should be. He has boxed the compass and returned to his origins, as few men even dream of doing. Today, he lives just forty miles from the small town of New Athens, Illinois, where he was born and raised.

"My bedroom is now bigger than the whole house I grew up in," he says, not so much proud of now, or ashamed of then, as surprised at how little difference it seems to make to him. The house is big and comfortable, with a confident, sweeping progression to the rooms, all of which are underrated by jock standards. The memorabilia and awards are there, the signs of wealth and celebrity, yet the overall impression is unpretentious.

Herzog has an enormous sense of self, but not an enormous sense of self-importance. He may be a showman and a shoot-from-the-lip go-to-hell guy, but he also respects and enjoys other people. And he doesn't think baseball is the whole world.

Perhaps that's because he has seen so much of it. "My family didn't have much money. They had to scratch," says Herzog. "My Mom had to be a house cleaner." Some boys have a paper route. "My route was the whole town." He didn't just work in a funeral home; he dug the graves, then drove the hearse. Whether mopping the brewery, mowing lawns, or fixing water pipes when it was ten degrees below zero, no job was too hard for him. Nothing was as bad as taking a pick into the mines, as his forebears had. New Athens had two lumberyards, a foundry, a brewery, a shoe factory, thirteen grocery stores, "and sixteen taverns, to make it all bearable," according to Herzog, who remembers his father as a good-hearted man who drank a lot, never took care of himself, and died when he was forty-eight. "I never asked my dad for a dime."

In those days, Herzog lived to play sports. And to get out of New Athens. Both of Herzog's brothers spent most of their lives in their hometown. That suited them but not Whitey. Four years after he left to play in the minors, Herzog passed through New Athens on a team bus. He told his teammates who'd be sitting where on the street, who'd be sitting on which stools in which bars.

"Every one of 'em was right where I said they'd be," recalls Herzog. "Still are unless they're dead."

When one of Herzog's teams has a bad year—and his Cards have followed all three of their pennants with losing seasons—his response is unique in baseball. He shrugs, fishes a little more, and starts planning for next year. Why make everybody miserable?

"I really enjoy managing. In July of 1979, the Royals lost fourteen out of fifteen. Our pitching fell apart. In two weeks, I gave only two signs, because we were always behind by five or six runs so fast. The writers brought me a half gallon of scotch with a nice note. They thanked me for not being a jerk. I could've locked the clubhouse, blown up at everybody. I didn't. I managed my ass off that year to keep us in the race until the last week."

Herzog got fired after that season. "It's no big deal. The way to make more money is to get fired. The first time I got canned [in Texas], our friends wouldn't come around, because they didn't know how to act. So Mary Lou and I threw a party."

How does Herzog get away with such a laid-back style? For one thing, he's as tough on the inside as his coal-mining and farming ancestors. He may look like a big old kindly bear these days, but nobody has forgotten the Garry Templeton incident in 1981. The shortstop, then considered a future Hall of Famer, gave the finger to the hometown fans who were booing him for jaking. Herzog grabbed him with both hands, dragged him into the dugout, and had to be pried off him by other players.

"Templeton doesn't want to play in St. Louis. He doesn't want to play on turf. He doesn't want to play when we go to Montreal. He doesn't want to play in the Astrodome. He doesn't want to play in the rain," Herzog said the day after the fight. "The other eighty games, he's all right."

Templeton was lucky that Herzog traded him to San Diego instead of Tokyo. Everybody said the Rat's anger had gotten the better of his judgment when he dealt Templeton for Ozzie Smith. Funny thing: Templeton's career withered immediately and it's Smith who will go to the Hall of Fame. Herzog's mystique grew.

The manager has only four rules: Be on time. Bust your butt. Play smart. And have some fun while you're at it, for Chrissakes. Transgress the big four, and you'll hear about it plenty. "People say you've never had your ass chewed out until you've been chewed out by me," he says flatly. "I let 'em have it with both barrels. Then it's done. I don't have a doghouse.

"My door is always open. But a lot of guys come in thinking they're gonna tell me off and leave wishing they'd never come in."

Herzog has a way with a harsh word. Asked if Willie McGee reminded him of a young Mickey Rivers, he answered, "Yeah, except Willie doesn't play the horses, he shows up on time, and he can throw." At his first press conference in Texas—never having managed a pro team anywhere—Herzog said, "this is the worst excuse for a big-league ball club I ever saw."

On the other hand, when the players earn Herzog's respect, he reciprocates. He always arrives at the ballpark four hours early so he can post the lineup *before* his players arrive. Then they know where they stand and can prepare properly from the moment they arrive. (Sometimes Billy Martin, when hung over, wouldn't post his lineup until *after* batting practice. His players had to guess who should hit with the regulars.)

As usual, Herzog has sensible ulterior motives for arriving so early. Casey Stengel taught him "to bullshit with the writers" every day. He got the message: they can dig up their own stories or you can write their stories for them.

Patting backs and taping ankles, Whitey fills every notebook every day and doles out off-the-record quotes and background info like a master White House propagandist. Thus, his version of reality dominates the coverage of his team as completely as any other recent manager's. Herzog is one of the few who understands that either the manager controls his team through the media or the media sense a vacuum and gradually take control from the manager.

Herzog even invites reporters into his dugout in spring training. What's to hide?

"You see why I let him hit," crows Herzog when one of his pitchers hits a home run. "I had to talk that man into goin' up there." Next time the pitcher is due up, he snaps, "Sit down. I can't stand to watch you hit another one. It's embarrassing to my other players."

The stars he cajoles and instructs, nagging about technique. "Remember that split-finger right from the ear, like a catcher. Don't reach back." The humpty dumpties, the guys who make a living by sitting, are his buddies. "Whitey handles role players especially well," says Duke Wathan, now the Royals manager but a role player for Herzog in the '70s. "He keeps making small talk, finding out about your family, doing his Casey Stengel imitations, making sure you understand how he plans to use you and where you fit. He's very honest. He never sugar-coats to pacify a guy."

Once, Herzog shocked a scrub, Tito Landrum, by walking up to him in mid-game and apologizing for not having him in the lineup. "The last time we faced this [pitcher], you hit the ball hard three out of four times up," Herzog explained.

"That was two years before," said Landrum. "Even *I* didn't remember."

Herzog, like Earl Weaver in his day, can stay with one team indefinitely, because every clubhouse grievance is aired and then usually forgotten. Very few managers have been smart enough or glib enough to flourish in such an atmosphere of candor. It works only as long as the manager, in a pinch, has the personality to intimidate any of his players.

Also like Weaver, Herzog has little fear of eccentrics or hard-to-manage players. Herzog didn't care if Amos Otis wouldn't talk or Hal McRae dressed like a third world insurgent. He traded for Darrell Porter *after* his cocaine problems became public and won a world title with him as series MVP. Herzog's tolerance finally snapped when he discovered that he had about seven heavy cocaine users. Even then, he didn't get rid of them all and didn't trade Keith Hernandez and Lonnie Smith until he was convinced their play was being hurt.

In trades, he sought out Joaquin Andujar, Jack Clark, and Pedro Guerrero, supposedly the head-case trifecta. To Herzog, they were invigorating. What better way to spend an off day than to have a star player slam on the brakes, pull into a Porsche dealership, point to a $92,000 item, and say, "I'll take two of those. One for me. One for my wife."

"That guy had at least ten cars. Couldn't get out of his own driveway," says Herzog. "He went broke. But a great guy."

Only direct no-shit dealings appeal to Herzog. He once proposed a trade to Harry Dalton by saying, "How'd you like to win the pennant this year?" When they finished swapping players, both the Cards and the Brewers were so vastly improved that they met each other in the next World Series.

"Whitey's one of the few guys who know how to make a trade," says Frank Cashen. "He's very frank, not trying to be sinister like some [executives] who think they're in the CIA. You ask Whitey, he tells you. And you can believe what he says, including what he says about his own players. He's a bright inventive guy who doesn't waste time beating around the bush."

Perhaps the nickname White Rat—given to Herzog in the '50s because he resembled a former player with the same moniker—is unintentionally appropriate. Perhaps it is synonymous in a baseball sense with benevolent dictator. In other words, a rat, yes, but a *white rat*. Sharp teeth and a mean bite? Sure. But this rat, who never pretends to be anything else, is one you laugh with when he steals the cheese—even when he steals it from you.

Put it all together and you have the Autocrat of Astroturf—the man who may be the prototype of a twenty-first century manager. Herzog's success has been predicated on a central guiding idea of a new way to build a modern team. The '80s Cardinals were a concept with several parts—none of them entirely new, all of them the culmination of trends that had been building since the '60s. First came the notion that speed and raw athletic ability are preferred at every position over any other virtue, even at the expense of power or baseball savvy. Herzog didn't invent the bunt, the steal, the hit and run, or taking the extra base at every chance. Ty Cobb did all of that. Also, Herzog didn't conceive the all-out running attack, with six or seven thieves who steal at any time, Chuck Tanner did that in Oakland in 1976. And the Dodgers had five switch hitters in one lineup long before Herzog put six slap-hitting switchers in the same batting order.

But Herzog put in one formula: the Runnin' Redbirds—a team that could lead the major leagues in scoring while being dead last in home runs. He realized that players who aim at the middle to top of the ball, instead of the middle to bottom like power hitters, have the advantage of turning modern pitching theory on its head. "Keep the ball low" has been an adage that has been chiseled in stone since the home run age began. However, a knee-high strike only fuels the Cards' game.

Herzog also realized how team speed in a big park can turn a mediocre starting pitching staff into a good one. His starters allow lots of hits but few walks or home runs. They may not strike out many batters or pitch complete games, but they get lots of double-play grounders.

Herzog claims only one true radical idea of his own: "Start with the closer. Build your bullpen first, then worry about your rotation. . . . I was the first one to look at it that way. My job is to put us in a position to win come nut-cuttin' time."

The old sport of baseball is so afraid of new ideas that few teams have followed any of Herzog's principles. One, however, did—the hopelessly desperate Baltimore Orioles, after they lost 107 games in 1988. "No question about it. I'm a great admirer of Whitey," says O's GM Roland Hemond, who put his fastest and best defensive players at every position, sacrificed power, and put the franchise's best young arm (Gregg Olsen) in the bullpen, not in the rotation. The Orioles broke the major league record for fielding percentage. Great defense rekindled team morale. Hapless pitchers suddenly became mysteriously decent. Olsen was Rookie of the Year. And the Orioles showed the third greatest one-season improvement in the history of baseball (32½ games).

When a manager has such a looming personality, when he is the public focus of the franchise, it tends to diminish the stature of the team's charismatic leaders. In crises, the top dog is in the dugout, not on the field. That can be a slight disadvantage in a playoff or in the Series and may be part of the reason that Weaver and Herzog each have only one world title to their credit. Sparky Anderson and Tommy Lasorda may not be as tactically acute, and their teams do not exceed expectations as consistently. But Anderson and Lasorda teams are not psychologically dominated by good old Sparky and Tommy.

If Herzog has a weakness as a manager, it is that his moods become his players' moods and his fears become theirs, too: Call it the Gene Mauch syndrome. Last season and right into last winter, he seemed fixated on his club's inability to sign either Bruce Hurst or Mike Moore as a free agent in the 1988–89 off-season. As the '90s begin, Herzog has his doubts and, as with everything, does not bother to hide them. True, he was hailed for extracting 86 wins from the Cards last season and keeping them in the pennant race until Labor Day, when injuries to relief ace Todd Worrell and centerfielder Willie McGee caught the team right at the kneecaps.

Still, Herzog has big-picture worries about the shape of his team. The Cards' overall speed isn't what it used to be. "The league is catching up with us. Defense against the running game is better," he says. "Our club doesn't manufacture runs like it used to." Will the Cards be shuffled again?

The White Rat will think of something. He always has. And even if he doesn't, so what? He's already a man who has left more than a mark on his game; he has left a truly personal signature. "I'll retire when it's not fun anymore. Right now, I couldn't be happier. If I get fired here, that'll be the end of it, anyway."

All fates await Herzog with equal promise. He has made his life the way he made that first home—one brick at a time. And that is why it is so solid. He is almost entirely self-created.

When, in his autobiography, *White Rat,* Herzog writes about his own children—smart, educated, normal—he winces, because they remind him of kids in general. "I think we had it better then," he writes of a time when he had nothing. "For kids today, everything is organized. Everybody tells them where to be, what to do.

"One time we built an airplane on the roof of the shed behind my cousin's house. We modeled it after one of those balsawood jobs with the rubber-band motor, only we used an inner tube from a truck tire as a motor. We wound that sucker up, and I jumped in and hollered to let it go. We went right off the shed and I landed on my head. I was lucky I didn't break every bone in my body."

Herzog has been making crazy airplanes ever since, making them his own way, flying them himself as he damn well pleases, and never worrying whether he lands on his head. He takes the chance, he takes the ride, he takes the credit, and he has the laughs.

For all of that, Herzog has never maintained that his dream occupation is a baseball manager. "Perfect job?" he says. "Ski instructor." His only avowed goal on snow is to go in a straight line as fast as possible.

Maybe.

Or maybe Whitey Herzog just wants to see if he can break every bone in his body.

In 1990, George F. Will published his critically acclaimed Men at Work, *a book on baseball excellence that featured Tony La Russa, then manager of the Oakland As, as the perfect example of intelligent baseball thinking. In the same year, La Russa's A's won their third consecutive American League pennant after sweeping the Giants in the 1989 World Series. The Cardinals, after finishing last in their division in 1990, failed to win a division title until 1996, La Russa's first year with the Cardinals. Under La Russa, the Cardinals won consecutive division titles from 2000 though 2002. In 2004, after winning their division and the postseason playoffs, the team advanced to the World Series for the first time under La Russa's leadership.*

In this excerpt from "The Manager" chapter of Men at Work, Will *focuses on the baseball "instincts," the ability "to play the game intelligently," that have made Tony La Russa one of the most successful managers in baseball history.*

The Manager
George F. Will

Managers can do memorable things. On the day in 1944 when the Cubs' Bill Nicholson hit four home runs in a doubleheader against the Giants, Mel Ott, the Giants' manager, ordered Nicholson walked intentionally—with the bases loaded and two outs. Paul Richards (White Sox, 1951–54, 1976; Baltimore, 1955–61) occasionally ordered the pitcher intentionally walked with two outs so the leadoff man would not begin the next inning. But most of the things that managers do that matter do not involve anything particularly noticeable, let alone exotic. For example, writer Leonard Koppett, author of *A Thinking Man's Guide to Baseball,* remembers a routine game in 1965 when, with the score tied with two outs in the bottom of the ninth, the Yankees had a runner on first and the Yankees batter had a 3–1 count. The pitcher had to get the next pitch over the plate, yet Yankee manager Johnny Keane ordered the batter—to his consternation—to take the pitch. It was, not surprisingly, a strike, producing a full count. However, a full count was exactly what Keane wanted. On a full count with two outs, the runner on first would be running with the pitch, so he would be sure to score on a double. And that is exactly what happened. Had the same hit occurred on a 3–1 count, the runner would not have scored. Besides, the pitcher still wanted to get the 3–2 pitch in the strike zone because a walk would have moved the runner into position to score the winning run on a single.

Obviously managers matter. What is not obvious is how much. It is sometimes said that because players' talents are so thoroughly revealed and rewarded over the course of the long season, managers do not win games other than by assembling the team. But that is a *non sequitur*. Talent is the ability to do some things, not all things. So the right player must be in the right place in the right situation. That is very much the result of good managing.

La Russa played professional baseball until he was 32. He says he should have quit when he was 24 because he kept getting worse. He is exaggerating, but not a lot. He was a mediocre player. A lot of excellent managers were marginal players. Which is to say, they made playing careers out of the margin that mind could give them. There have, of course, been great players who were successful managers, even player-managers. Lou Boudreau was one, Joe Cronin another. In 1926 Rogers Hornsby, Ty Cobb, Tris Speaker, Eddie Collins, and George Sisler, all future Hall of Famers, were player-managers. But in modern times, mediocre playing careers have been the preludes to some of the most distinguished managerial careers.

Earl Weaver, who won 1,480 games and had a .583 winning percentage through 17 seasons, never made it to the major leagues as a player. Sparky Anderson, the only manager to win 800 games in each league (863 with the Reds and 895 with the Tigers through the 1989 season), was a .218 hitter in his only year in the major leagues (1959, with the Phillies).

Whitey ("Baseball has been good to me since I quit trying to play it") Herzog, the Cardinals' manager, is now regarded as the National League's Spinoza. In his playing career he drifted through four teams in eight years, compiling a batting average of .257. Gene Mauch managed 3,941 games (the fourth-highest total in major league history) after playing for six teams in nine years and batting .239.

La Russa was born and raised in Tampa. What the Chesapeake Bay is to crabs, Tampa is to baseball talent: a rich breeding ground, known for both quantity and quality. Wade Boggs and Dwight Gooden are just two who were boys in Tampa and now are prospering in the major leagues. La Russa's mother, though born in Tampa, was of Spanish descent, and his father spoke Spanish. La Russa spoke Spanish before he spoke English. Being bilingual is a considerable advantage for a manager in an era when nearly 20 percent of all the players under contract in professional baseball are from Latin America. Managing was far from La Russa's mind when, the night he graduated from high school in 1962, he signed with the Athletics. The team was then in Kansas City and was the toy of Charlie Finley. La Russa got $50,000 for a signing bonus. He was 17 and the world was his oyster. The next year he was in the major leagues for 34 games, 44 at bats, 11 hits. He did not know it at the time, but when the season ended he had already appeared in a quarter of all the major league games of his playing career.

Back in Tampa after the 1963 season, he arrived late for a slow-pitch softball game with some friends from high school. Youth is impetuous; even La Russa was then. At that softball game he went straight to shortstop without warming up. It was filthy luck that in the first inning a ball was hit in the hole. He fielded it, fired to first, and tore a tendon in his arm near the shoulder. He played with a sore arm for 15 more years. Along the way he collected two shoulder separations, a knee injury, and chips in his elbow (probably from throwing awkwardly with a sore arm). In 16 years as a professional player, he had a total of 176 at bats in 132 major league games for the Athletics, Braves, and Cubs. His career batting average was .199. He never hit a home run.

His best season convinced him that his best was not going to be good enough. In 1972 he hit .308 for the Braves' Triple-A Richmond club, but he was not called up to the parent team. Convinced that his playing career had a low ceiling, he turned toward another career. After five off-seasons at Florida State University Law School he had a degree. He was admitted to the bar in 1979. However, by then he was headed for managing.

It is said that the study of law sharpens the mind by narrowing it. But, then, the study of anything narrows the mind in the sense of concentrating attention and excluding much from the field of focus. Besides, a sharp mind, like a straight razor, becomes sharper by being stropped. Tony La Russa is the fifth major league manager to possess a law degree. The four other lawyer-managers (Branch Rickey, Miller Huggins, Hughie Jennings, Monte Ward) are in the Hall of Fame.

La Russa was 34 when, with 54 games remaining in the 1979 season, he became manager of the White Sox. There have been younger managers. Roger Peckinpaugh became the Yankees' manager at 23, and in 1942 the Indians' shortstop, Lou Boudreau, then 24, became the youngest manager to start a season. But by 1989 La Russa was managing in his eleventh season, three more than the 8 Peckinpaugh managed and just five behind Boudreau's 16. If La Russa stays in a major league dugout—and he can if he wants to—until he is 65, he will have managed 31 seasons, more than Walter Alston (23), more than Leo Durocher and Joe McCarthy (24), more than Casey Stengel and Bill McKechnie (25), Gene Mauch (26) and Bucky Harris (29): in fact, more than any other manager except John McGraw (33) and Connie Mack (53).

The rearing elephant sewn on the sleeve of the Oakland Athletics' uniforms has a pedigree involving two of baseball's larger-than-life managers. John Mc-Graw was manager of the Baltimore Orioles in 1901, the American League's first year. McGraw, whose dislikes were many and fierce, disliked the league's president, Ban Johnson, and objected to the admission to the league of the Philadelphia Athletics, a franchise owned and managed by Cornelius McGili-cuddy—Connie Mack. McGraw derided the Athletics as the "white elephants" and Mack, to taunt McGraw, adopted the white elephant as his team's symbol. The Athletics promptly won the pennant in 1902, the year McGraw jumped to the New York Giants. The elephant logo came and went several times during the fluctuating fortunes of the Athletics' franchise. It returned in 1988 for the first time since the Athletics' 13-year sojourn in Kansas City. And in 1989 the two franchises of McGraw and Mack, having followed the course of empire westward, were back at each other, in the World Series.

Connie Mack was born the year after Fort Sumter was fired upon and died the year before Sputnik was launched. He holds one of baseball's most secure records: most seasons as a manager. Mack also holds an unenviable record: most consecutive seasons managing in the same league without a championship (19). Between Mack and La Russa no one managed the Athletics for more than three consecutive years. Longevity isn't as long as it once was.

Today, and in the future, long managerial careers may not occur as easily as they once did. Until relatively recently there was a side of baseball that was not very meritocratic. Baseball served as a haven for some managers and coaches who were not particularly good. This haven existed because baseball people were kind to their pals.

To the familiar classifications of social systems, now add a new category to cover the peculiar governance of baseball. To aristocracy, plutocracy, and democracy add baseball's contribution to government: "palocracy," government by old pals. Baseball has traditionally been run by men whose lives have been intersecting and entwined for decades. They have known one another from the rocky playing fields and spartan offices of the low minor leagues all the way up to the manicured playing fields and well-appointed suites of the major leagues. You do not talk long with a baseball person before you hear the phrase "baseball person." Often it is accompanied by a negative: So-and-so is "not a baseball person." No adjective is required, thank you very much. A baseball person is a good baseball person. A palocracy can make for kinder, gentler governance, but it also can make the world safe for mediocrity. (The prince of managerial mediocrity was Wilbert Robinson. Uncle Robbie of the Dodgers managed for 19 years and produced this record: 1,397 wins, 1,395 losses. It is a shame one of those wins was not a loss.)

Closed systems, such as tenured university faculties or diplomatic corps or military services, are vulnerable to systemic mediocrity. People who have gone to the same schools, climbed the same career ladders, absorbed the same values and assumptions and expectations, become intellectually insular and professionally self-protective. They forgive one another their mistakes, and mediocrity becomes cozy.

As baseball becomes more meritocratic in every aspect it does not need to become bland and (in a gray-flannel sense) managerial. Colorfulness is not incompatible with quality. The most vivid image of a manager in modern times is that of Casey Stengel, who said things like, "What about the shortstop Rizzuto who got nothing but daughters but throws out the left-handed batters in the double play?" Dumb, right? Stengel was dumb like a fox. Few managers are intellectuals but all managers talk a lot. Managing, like politics, is mostly talk, and some smart managers say strange things. Detroit's Sparky Anderson says that Jose Canseco has the body of a "Greek goddess," but you know what Sparky means. Some of the brightest managers—Leo Durocher for one, Earl Weaver for another—had tempers that sometimes made them seem less intelligent than they were. (Weaver was once ejected from a game during the exchange of lineup cards.) Youth is hot and when La Russa became manager at age 34 he had a temper that was too easily detonated. But the best balm is a steady diet of winning. He had only three losing seasons in his first 11 seasons (1979–89) as a major league manager.

La Russa was just 41 when he had the fundamental experience of managing: He was fired. The White Sox fired him in 1986. The Chicago experience "toughened me up pretty well." He certainly is tough enough now. Once when Jose Canseco was a rookie and did not hustle on a play, he returned to the dugout to find La Russa furious. La Russa told him, "Do that again, I'll knock you on your ass."

La Russa never became one of the hard-core unemployed. On July 1, 1986, less than a month after being fired, he was hired by Oakland. The Athletics were in last place, 21 games below .500, which is not easy to be before the All-Star break. The rest of the year they were 45–34. In 1987 they played only .500 ball but in the American League West that was good enough for third place. The 1988 Athletics were the first American League West team to lead the league in wins since the 1983 White Sox, who were managed by La Russa. In 1987 and 1988 the Athletics were 105–63 against the American League East— a thumping 57–27 in 1988.

After the players' strike in 1994 and the cancellation of the World Series, base-ball fans needed a hero to restore their faith in the game. They finally found one in 1998 when Mark McGwire captivated America with his slugging and shat-tered baseball's single-season home run record, asterisk and all. On the night of September 8 at Busch Stadium, McGwire, batting in the fourth inning against the Chicago Cubs, hit a line drive off Steve Trachsel that barely cleared the left-field wall, but was long enough to break Roger Maris's record of 61 home runs. McGwire finished his epic season with a phenomenal 70 home runs.

In Mike Eisenbath's coverage of McGwire's 62nd home run for the St. Louis Post-Dispatch, *he calls the event one of the defining moments in the history of St. Louis, comparable to Lindbergh's flight across the Atlantic and the building of the Gateway Arch, and perhaps "the greatest moment in St. Louis sports history."*

For Mark McGwire, It Was the Culmination of a Season-Long Quest
Mike Eisenbath ——————————————————————

Mark McGwire reached baseball immortality Tuesday night with a line-drive home run at Busch Stadium that shone the spotlight on St. Louis and rejuvenated the national pastime.

McGwire hit his 62nd home run of the season, breaking Roger Maris's single-season standard of 61 home runs—the most hallowed record in baseball.

Maris's record stood for nearly 37 years until 8:18 p.m. Tuesday, Sept. 8, on a balmy evening graced by a nearly full moon. The Chicago Cubs were up 2–0 in the fourth inning when McGwire lashed Cubs pitcher Steve Trachsel's first pitch on a line to left field. The ball began to sink as it neared the eight-foot fence, making it over by less than two feet. It was his shortest home run of the season but touched off the most electric, emotional celebration that possibly could be mustered in the best baseball town in America. The Cardinals went on to beat the Cubs, 6–3.

"Yesterday," McGwire said afterward, "doing what I did for my father, hit-ting my 61st home run on his 61st birthday, I thought what a perfect way to end the home stand, by hitting my 62nd home run for the city of St. Louis and all the great fans. I really and truly wanted to do it here.

"Thank you, St. Louis."

McGwire trotted around the bases with the glee of a 10-year-old, the delib-erate manner of a man wanting to savor each step, the lightness of someone who has just felt a burden lifted from his shoulders.

He had stepped in the batter's box in his trademark manner, relaxed and yet intense. As the flashes of thousands of cameras twinkled around the ballpark, McGwire dug his back foot into the dirt.

The pitch came in low and he sent it on a line over the fence and began a joyous tour of the bases.

"I don't remember anything after that," McGwire said later. "I was numb. I thought, 'I still have to play the game. Oh, my God, I can't believe this.'

"It's such an incredible feeling. I can't believe I did it."

McGwire embraced first-base coach Dave McKay, his batting-practice coach with the Oakland Athletics and now with the Cardinals. Afterward, McKay reminded McGwire to touch the base before making his turn toward second. On the way, Cubs first baseman Mark Grace slapped hands with McGwire. Second baseman Mickey Morandini and shortstop Jose Hernandez each congratulated him with handshakes.

As McGwire approached third base, he saw former Cardinals buddy and Cubs third baseman Gary Gaetti. McGwire paused momentarily and saluted, then ran to hug Gaetti. He rounded third but, before heading for home, gave third-base coach Rene Lachemann a forearm bash and then pointed to the seats behind the plate, where John and Ginger McGwire were applauding proudly for their son.

An enormous welcoming committee awaited 90 feet ahead. In those final few steps, McGwire pointed to the sky.

He hugged Cubs catcher Scott Servais, dealt his familiar smashing-fists, punch-to-the-stomach greeting to teammate Ray Lankford.

Finally, there was Matthew McGwire, St. Louis's favorite batboy. Mark picked up his 10-year-old son and held him aloft.

Red-and-white streamers floated gently into the outfield grass, fireworks boomed overhead. McGwire partied with his teammates, one emotional encounter at a time. He hugged manager Tony La Russa, pitching coach Dave Duncan . . . slowly, he worked through the crowd.

He found Matthew once more and wrapped his huge arms around the boy, hoisted him and planted a kiss smack on his lips.

"I don't know how big the Arch is," McGwire said later, "but the Arch is off my back now."

Moments later, a Cubs player appeared among the sea of Cardinals. Sammy Sosa, who has 58 home runs and has been McGwire's friendly challenger in the chase for Maris's mark all summer, came from his spot in right field.

McGwire hugged Sosa with overwhelming affection.

Soon, McGwire had almost everyone in the place wiping away tears. He ran to the box seats just outside the far end of the Cardinals dugout, climbed over the short wall and engulfed Maris's four sons and a daughter one at a time. Rich and Randy Maris clearly had trouble blinking back their tears. Their father had never known the kind of adulation McGwire was getting. Many Americans considered Maris unworthy when he broke Babe Ruth's home run record on Oct. 1, 1961. McGwire made sure the Marises knew how much he revered their father.

In a flash, McGwire disappeared into the dugout. He emerged holding a microphone and, with a wave of his arm, quieted the crowd of 49,987.

"I dedicate this home run to the whole city of St. Louis and all the fans here," McGwire said. "Thank you for all your support. It's unbelievable. All my family, everybody, my son, Chicago Cubs, Sammy Sosa—unbelievable."

McGwire paused.

"Class," he finished.

President Bill Clinton telephoned McGwire in the Cardinals clubhouse about 90 minutes after the game ended.

McGwire said Clinton told him: "It was outstanding. America is really enjoying this."

McGwire said he appreciated the call. "A really neat thing is that my son talked to him, too."

The home run will likely be remembered as the greatest moment in St. Louis sports history. The Cardinals' 1926 World Series championship, the first in the franchise's history of more than 100 years, triggered a wild celebration in the streets of the city. There were other memorable world championships for the Cardinals, such as 1964 and 1982.

None of those moments and none of the city's most talented athletes ever created so much impact.

This season-long home run chase has been about more than sports for St. Louis. It will go down as one of the top defining moments for the city in this century, one that not only made St. Louis citizens feel a surge of self-esteem but carried the city onto a stage for all the world to admire.

There was the World's Fair of 1904. There was Charles Lindbergh's heroic flight across the Atlantic in "The Spirit of St. Louis" in 1927. There was the completion of the Gateway Arch.

And there is Mark McGwire toppling the most coveted mark in all of sports.

McGwire's summer of power went a long way toward reviving the national pastime, helping to erase bitter memories of the players strike of 1994 and the cancellation of that year's World Series. Fans who vowed to never again return to a major-league ballpark followed the game again.

"This put baseball back on the map," McGwire said. "It's the sport, America's pastime. Look at the people at the parks now, all the great players in the game.

"People say this has been bringing the country together. If it has, so be it. I'm happy to bring the country together."

All this from a superhero who has 20–500 vision and bad feet. "God doesn't give you everything," McGwire said recently.

He grew up in Claremont, Calif., a suburb of Los Angeles. One of his boyhood friends once described the neighborhood like something from *The Brady Bunch*. His dad was dentist and his little-league coach. His mom volunteered countless hours at the concession stand of the town's park while her five sons played a variety of sports.

It was the All-American childhood for the All-American boy. He was a star at Damien High in Claremont—as a pitcher, drafted in the eighth round by the Montreal Expos. With the signing bonus they offered less than flattering, McGwire chose instead to accept the only scholarship offered him, from the University of Southern California.

He played on the 1984 U.S. Olympic Team and was drafted that year by the Oakland Athletics with the 10th pick overall. Three years later, he spent his first full season in the big leagues and whacked 49 homers, a rookie record.

McGwire had a chance to hit a record-breaking 50th home run that season. Instead, he skipped the last game so he could be on hand for the birth of his son.

On July 31, 1997, with the Oakland Athletics struggling to make money and be competitive, they traded McGwire to St. Louis, where he could play for La Russa once more. He hit 24 home runs the final two months of the season.

In signing a long-term deal with the Cardinals, McGwire also said he would donate $1 million each year to help support facilities in St. Louis and Los Angeles that work with abused children.

Cardinals fans fell in love with McGwire, whose signing gave the Cardinals their greatest power hitter.

Now, he belongs to all of baseball.

"I just hope I didn't act foolish," McGwire said of his performance Tuesday night. "But this is history."

After winning their fifth division title under Tony La Russa in 2004, the Cardinals finally advanced to the World Series by defeating the Dodgers and the Astros in the National League postseason playoffs. It was the Cardinals' first World Series appearance since 1987 when they lost to the Minnesota Twins. After a 105-win season and an undefeated home record in the playoffs, the Cardinals looked like they were headed for their tenth world championship, especially since they were facing the Boston Red Sox, who hadn't won a World Series since they traded Babe Ruth to the Yankees. But this time the Curse of the Bambino was on the Cardinals, who lost to the Red Sox in four games. It was the worst World Series defeat for the Cardinals since they were swept by Babe Ruth's Yankees in 1928.

In his coverage in the St. Louis Post-Dispatch of the Cardinals' World Series loss to the Red Sox, Joe Strauss tries to sort out what went wrong with the Cardinals after such a successful year.

Over and Out
Joe Strauss

The Boston Red Sox are world champions, and the Cardinals can only wonder what happened to them.

Boston beat the Cardinals 3–0 in Game 4 of the World Series Wednesday night at Busch Stadium.

Derek Lowe's seven-inning start along with three early runs were enough to stand up against a Cardinals attack that disappeared after the eighth inning of its 11–9 loss in Game 1.

A team that terrified its opponents all summer ended its fall unable to cure a pandemic that claimed its unshakable core.

Long before the Red Sox celebrated on Busch Stadium's lacerated infield, the Cardinals had shown their frustration by repeatedly arguing with Chuck Meriwether about his strike zone and his judgment on what they believed was a fifth-inning foul tip.

After three losses the Cardinals finally received a quality World Series start, but struggling Jason Marquis's six innings weren't nearly enough.

After watching his team's first 32 innings pitched, closer Jason Isringhausen finally made an appearance, but inherited a 3–0 deficit with runners at second and third in the eighth.

The Red Sox didn't broadcast it, but they salivated at the pairing against a pitching staff that relied on command more than power. Patient early in counts with no one on base, they surprised the Cardinals with their aggressiveness with runners in scoring position.

Strikeouts were almost impossible to come by as the Sox hitters stretched at-bats by taking pitches and fouling off fastballs that rarely exceeded 90 miles per hour.

Their approach against the Cardinals' lineup reflected superior scouting. A team ready to pounce on fastballs was kept off-balance by split-finger pitches, change-ups, and sliders. The Cardinals managed eight RBIs in the Series and entered Wednesday with twice as many strikeouts (26) as their opponents.

The Red Sox began Game Four like all the others, jumping a Cardinals starting pitcher before he could shake the nerves from his first World Series appearance.

Four pitches into his start, Marquis fed center fielder Johnny Damon a 2–1 fastball that was driven to right-center field for a home run. It was the Red Sox's third first-inning home run of the Series and the eighth first-inning run allowed by Cardinals starting pitching. It also extended a maddening trend that saw the Cardinals stay even with the Sox for only two innings in four games.

Indeed, the Cardinals became only the fourth team in World Series history never to lead, joining an inglorious club including the 1963 New York Yankees, the 1966 Los Angeles Dodgers, and the 1989 San Francisco Giants. The Giants were vanquished during the earthquake-delayed Series by La Russa's dynamic Oakland A's.

Even given a favorable pitching matchup against the Cardinals, the Red Sox could not have expected this kind of dominance against a team that had won 105 regular-season games and entered the World Series 6–0 at home in the postseason.

But these weren't the same Cardinals. Instead of the disciplined, intelligent team that wore down opponents all summer, the Red Sox encountered a club that gave away outs on the bases, managed only 17 innings from its four starting pitchers and appeared to surrender at-bats after Jeff Suppan's Buckner moment in Game Three.

Damon's home run suggested a tough night for Marquis, who somehow allowed only three runs while slogging through six innings in 121 pitches, 70 in the first three frames.

Marquis stranded runners at second and third in the second inning before almost hitting a wall in the third. With one out, left fielder Manny Ramirez singled to left field. First baseman David Ortiz continued his menacing postseason by driving a double that left Ramirez at third and brought pitching coach Dave Duncan to the mound. Marquis received defensive help when Pujols threw out Ramirez at the plate attempting to score on Catcher Jason Varitek's grounder but immediately fell into a 13-pitch funk consisting of twelve balls.

Third baseman Bill Mueller walked to load the bases. Marquis then fell behind Trot Nixon, 3–0, before Nixon hammered a shoulder-high fastball to the base of the center-field wall for a two-run double.

Marquis escaped further damage by intentionally walking No. 8 hitter Mark Bellhorn, then striking out Lowe.

Able to last only 3 and 4 innings in his previous two playoff starts, Marquis became the only Cardinal starter to make it through 6 in the Series. He retired 9 of the last 11 batters he faced.

The Cardinals, however, were again overmatched by a Red Sox starting pitcher. Able to muster only one unearned run against Curt Schilling in Game Two and nothing in seven innings against Pedro Martinez in Game Three, they flailed for three hits in seven innings against Lowe.

Lowe retired 13 consecutive hitters after second baseman Tony Womack led off the first inning with a single. The Cardinals pushed their second runner into scoring position in the fifth when shortstop Edgar Renteria doubled and took third base on a one-out wild pitch. However, the opportunity only further enraged them when left fielder John Mabry struck out on a contested call and rookie catcher Yadier Molina bounced to shortstop.

The game nearly detonated in the eighth inning when Isringhausen inherited a mess left by Dan Haren, who had allowed Mueller a leadoff single, followed by Nixon's double into the right-field corner. With first base open, Isringhausen came on to walk pinch hitter Pokey Reese to load the bases with none out. Isringhausen then wriggled free from the jam by striking out Kevin Millar, getting Damon to bounce to Pujols, who made an acrobatic throw home to stop Mueller, and striking out Orlando Cabrera.

Millar's pinch hit meant the end of Lowe's night. Bronson Arroyo entered with six outs remaining, and the countdown began.

*The House That
Busch Built*

When August Busch purchased the Cardinals in 1953, he renovated Sports-man's Park and renamed it Busch Stadium. On May 8, 1966, the Cardinals ended their forty-seven-year stay at the old Sportsman's Park with a loss to the San Francisco Giants. Four days later, on May 12, they began play at the new Busch Stadium with an extra-inning win over the Atlanta Braves. "Busch II" was one of several unattractive multisports stadiums, dubbed "concrete donuts" by their critics, that were constructed in the 1960s, but the stadium became the House of Champions for Cardinal fans when the team defeated the Boston Red Sox in the 1967 World Series.

In his October 2, 2005, article in the St. Louis Post-Dispatch, *Tim O'Neil gives an account of the history of the old Busch Stadium on the eve of its final baseball game and the fan reaction to its pending demolition to make way for the opening of the new Busch Stadium for the 2006 season.*

A Toast to Busch
Tim O'Neil ————————————————————————

To the delight of Cardinal Nation, the ballyhooed "Farewell Weekend" in Busch Stadium is but a run-up to another dash for baseball glory.

So here's to Busch—may it be home to a long, prosperous October.

Sunday's chance to win a three-game set from the Cincinnati Reds will close the 40th and last regular season at Busch Stadium downtown. But fans are looking forward to as many as 10 more post-season games in the not-so-old ballyard: three in the first-round playoffs, four in the National League Championship Series and three in the World Series.

"It would be wonderful to get there for this special year," said Margaret Boes of St. Charles, who attended Saturday's 9–6 victory. "We could go out with a big, big bang. Make more good memories."

Of course, there could be as few as two more games. Boes, 37, spoke for the multitudes in preferring to hold a good thought.

Just next door, at the site of the next Busch Stadium, workers lift steel and mount bright red seats in preparation for their final assault upon the familiar arched-topped heights. Headache-ball cranes are to begin their work within three weeks of the last pitch.

The new brick-and-steel "retro" stadium will open next year and become the third graced with the name of Busch. The late Gussie Busch renamed old Sportsman's Park at Grand Boulevard and Dodier Avenue on the North Side, shortly after he bought the Cardinals in 1953 (he got the old park for an extra $1.1 million).

The second Busch, built for $26 million, opened as Civic Center Busch Memorial Stadium on May 12, 1966, when the Cardinals beat the Atlanta Braves 4–3 in 12 innings.

The estimated sticker on the latest is $398 million. Anheuser-Busch Cos. Inc. paid an undisclosed sum to preserve the name (more than $1.1 million, presumably).

It has been nearly 23 years since Bruce Sutter thumped a fastball into the glove of Darrell Porter, past the swinging Gorman Thomas of the Milwaukee Brewers (then of the American League), to win the Cardinals' ninth and last World Championship crown. The crowd of 53,723 rocked the sturdy concrete bowl with delirium. The time was 10:17 p.m. on October 20, 1982. Giddy fans elsewhere overwhelmed the local telephone system for 20 minutes.

Sutter returned to the mound with the other members of the Busch Stadium all-time team, who were announced to grateful cheers in a sold-out house. Scruffy as ever, Sutter's hair and beard have turned gray. But he also had the best line at the microphone.

Asked about striking out Thomas, he said, "The hair is gone. The black beard is gone. The arm is gone. But that memory will never die."

The roar of approval said this: Wouldn't another such moment be the perfect lights-out?

Cardinals fans already have paid suitable homage by gathering in record numbers this season at Busch II. Sunday's game will boost total attendance for 2005 past 3.5 million. That's nearly 200,000 better than the previous record, set in 2000.

Along the way, they have visited the old south concourse to rubberneck the work on Busch III. The surviving section of the wide concourse offers a foreman's view of the progress.

One of them was Alan Friesen of Lincoln, Neb., who bought tickets long ago for his Cardinals' "last games" at Busch. He surveyed the work Saturday on the new park and heartily approved.

"It's time for something like this," said Friesen, 57. "The truth is that Busch was built for too many purposes, the one-size-fits-all design of its day. The new one will feel much more like a ball park."

His son, Andrew, hopes to return in two weeks for a series. "I want many more last games at Busch," Andrew Friesen said.

Busch II has served its fans well. Since 1966, the Cardinals have been in six World Series (two of them victorious) and have reached at least the first round of the playoffs in four other years. Counting this season—and discounting 1994, when there was no World Series because of a player strike—that's a respectable post-season participation of 28.2 percent since 1966 (plenty of major leaguers don't hit .282).

Janet Frayne of Bridgeton wishes the Cardinals would have left well enough alone. "They shouldn't knock it over, " said Frayne, 43. "It looks pretty. It gives us all those wonderful memories. And it's not that old."

Frayne took part in KMOX radio's home-run derby contest Thursday at Busch. Among those pitching was Rick Horton, a Cardinal pitcher for six years and now a local broadcaster.

Horton, 46, said stepping onto the mound rekindled a sense of his time in the big show.

"I notice the way I stand, move and stretch my shoulders. I'm a young guy on the roster again, one who doesn't have sore knees," he said. "I was ambivalent about a new stadium at first. But I was sitting once in Camden Yards (in Baltimore) with my son, and I had an epiphany: Cardinals fans deserve something like this."

One batter who faced him Thursday was Tom Venverloh of St. Louis, who wore his red Cardinals T-shirt autographed by many of the players. Venverloh, 55, and his wife, Jill Woerhle, have tickets for all the home games in the first two rounds of the playoffs.

"The memories are the power of Busch," he said. "The new stadium looks beautiful, but I hate to see this one go."

Said Woerhle, "We said that about the arena, too. Now we love Savvis."

Venverloh: "Yeah, I'm sure I'll like it. It's still baseball. Cardinals baseball."

Venverloh tagged the generous Horton for a drive that hit the turf just shy of the track.

Acknowledgments

"Growing Up with the Game," from *Memories and Dreams,* published exclusively for Friends of the Hall of Fame (Winter 2004). By permission of John Grisham.

"Bob Costas Will Never Be As Young As He Looks Today," from *For Cardinal Fans Only* (Phoenix: Lone Wolfe Press). By permission of Rich Wolfe.

Jack Buck 1987 acceptance speech for the Ford C. Frick Award. Courtesy of the National Baseball Hall of Fame.

Harry Caray 1989 acceptance speech for the Ford C. Frick Award. Courtesy of the National Baseball Hall of Fame.

"The Gashouse Gang," from J. Roy Stockton's *The Gas House Gang and a Couple of Other Guys* (A. S. Barnes, 1945).

"The Mystery of Stan Musial," from *The Saturday Evening Post* (August 1954). By permission of Bob Broeg.

"Jeremiah Fruin," from Alfred H. Spink's *The National Game* (1911). Second edition.

"The First Baseball Games in St. Louis," a letter from Rufus W. Griswold, in Alfred H. Spink's *The National Game* (1911). Second edition.

"Alfred H. Spink," from the foreword to reprint of Alfred H. Spink's *The National Game,* (1911). Second edition. Published in the Southern Illinois University Press Writing Baseball Series (2000).

"A Charter Member," from Frederick J. Lieb's *The St. Louis Cardinals: The Story of a Great Baseball Club* (New York: G. P. Putnam's Sons, 1945).

"The St. Louis Browns Are Champions," from *The St. Louis Daily Globe-Democrat,* October 24, 1886.

"Farewell to Chris Von der Ahe, 1892–1899," from Jon David Cash's *Before They Were Cardinals: Major League Baseball in Nineteenth-Century St. Louis* (University of Missouri Press, 2002).

"Browns in American League since 1902," from Frederick J. Lieb's *The Baltimore Orioles: The History of a Colorful Team in Baltimore and St. Louis* (New York: G. P. Putnam's Sons, 1955).

"Jimmy Austin," from Lawrence S. Ritter's *The Glory of Their Times: The Story of the Early Days of Baseball Told by the Men Who Played It* (New York: William Morrow, 1984). By permission of the Lawrence S. Ritter estate.

"Rickey Tells How He'll Boss Browns," by Hunt Stromberg, the *Sporting News* (September 1913).

"The Dazzling Record of George Sisler," by F. C. Lane, *Baseball Magazine* (March 1921), George Sisler Number.

"Will George Sisler Equal Ty Cobb?" Interview with Hugh Jennings, *Baseball Magazine* (March 1921), George Sisler Number.

"The Rise of Baseball in St. Louis," in Steve Steinberg's *Baseball in St. Louis 1900–1925* (Chicago: Arcadia, 2004). Reprinted with permission from *Baseball in St. Louis 1900-1925,* Arcadia Publishing, 2005.

"From Rags to Riches: A Baseball Success Story," from J. Roy Stockton's *The Gashouse Gang and a Couple of Other Guys* (A. S. Barnes, 1945).

"Grover Cleveland Alexander," as told to Francis J. Powers, from *My Greatest Day in Baseball,* edited by John P. Carmichael, copyright 1945, 1950, 1951, 1963, 1968, by Grosset & Dunlap, Inc., renewed. Used by permission of Grosset & Dunlap, Inc., a division of Penguin Group (USA) Inc.

"Bob O'Farrell," from Lawrence S. Ritter's *The Glory of Their Times: The Story of the Early Days of Baseball Told by the Men Who Played It* (New York: William Morrow, 1984). By permission of the Lawrence S. Ritter estate.

"Country Boy," by Red Smith, in the *Dayton Daily News, February 11, 1970.*

"Fans on Rampage Nine Hours over Victory of Cards," in *St. Louis Post-Dispatch,* October 11, 1926. Reprinted with permission of the *St. Louis Post-Dispatch,* copyright 1926.

"'Me an Underminer? Not on Your Life,' Says Hornsby," by Rogers Hornsby as told to Dick Farrington, in the *Sporting News,* December 29, 1938. Courtesy of the *Sporting News.*

"The 1928 World's Series, from Frederick J. Lieb's *The St. Louis Cardinals: The Story of a Great Baseball Club* (New York: G. P. Putnam's Sons, 1945).

"The Cardinals' First Publicity Man," by Gene Karst, in *St. Louis's Favorite Sport, SABR 22,* June 1992. By permission of the Society for American Baseball Research.

"Bill Hallahan," from Donald Honig's *Baseball When the Grass Was Real:*

Baseball from the Twenties to the Forties by the Men Who Played It. Reprinted by permission of the University of Nebraska Press. Copyright by Donald Honig, 1975.

"Pepper Martin: Redbird Who Stole a World Series," from Ray Robinson's *Speed Kings of the Base Paths* (New York: Putnam, 1964). By permission of Ray Robinson.

"Admits He Would Like To Become a Manager," in Sid Keener's Column, from *St. Louis Star and Times,* September 1, 1932. Reprinted with permission of the *St. Louis Post-Dispatch,* copyright 1932.

"The Fordham Flash Becomes a Manager," by F. C. Lane, in *Baseball Magazine,* September 1933.

"Dizzy Dean," from *Super Stars of Baseball: Their Lives, Their Loves, Their Laughs, Their Laments (Sporting News,* 1971). By permission of Bob Broeg.

"Muscles and Me," from *The Gashouse Gang* (New York: Morrow, 1976). By permission of Robert E. Hood.

"Billy Southworth's St. Louis Swifties," by E. G. Fischer, in *St. Louis's Favorite Sport, SABR 22,* June 1992. By permission of the Society for American Baseball Research.

"A St. Louis Harbinger: The 1942 Browns," by Bill Borst, in *St. Louis's Favorite Sport, SABR 22,* June 1992. By permission of the Society for American Baseball Research.

"Marty Marion," as told to Lyall Smith, from *My Greatest Day in Baseball,* edited by John P. Carmichael, copyright 1945, 1950, 1951, 1963, 1968, by Grosset & Dunlap, Inc., a division of Penguin Group (USA) Inc.

"Branch Rickey Is Named President of the Brooklyn Dodgers," by J. Roy Stockton, in *St. Louis Post-Dispatch,* October 29, 1942. Reprinted with permission of the *St. Louis Post-Dispatch,* copyright 1942.

"Morton Cooper," as told to John P. Carmichael, from *My Greatest Day in Baseball,* edited by John P. Carmichael, copyright 1945, 1950, 1951, 1963, 1968, by Grosset & Dunlap, Inc., a division of Penguin Group (USA) Inc.

"World Series Review," by Sgts. Robert W. Broeg and Robert H. Meyers, in *Leatherneck Pacific Division,* November 16, 1944. With permission of Bob Broeg.

"Full House," by Tim Wiles, in *2004 World Series Official Program* (New York: Major League Baseball). With permission of Tim Wiles.

"Cards Champs for Sixth Time Because of Old Fight," by Frederick J. Lieb, in the *Sporting News,* October 23, 1946. Courtesy of the *Sporting News.*

"Enos' Dash to Destiny Revived," by Bob Broeg, in the *Sporting News,* December 21, 1974. With permission of Bob Broeg.

"A Troubling Year," in *Musial: From Stash to Stan the Man,* by James N. Giglio (University of Missouri Press, 2001).

"I'm From Missouri, Temporarily," in *Veeck—As in Wreck,* by Bill Veeck with Ed Linn (New York: G. P. Putnam's Sons, 1962). With permission of the Bill Veeck family, copyright 1962.

"Hail the Prodigal Rajah!" by Frank Graham, in *Sport,* March 1952. With permission of Frank Graham, Jr.

"The Day Veeck Played a Midget," from the Foreword by Bob Broeg to the reprint of Frederick J. Lieb's *The Baltimore Orioles: The History of a Colorful Team in Baltimore and St. Louis* (New York: G. P. Putnam's Sons, 1955).

From *Maybe I'll Pitch Forever,* by Le Roy (Satchel) Paige as told to David Lipman. Reprinted by permission of the University of Nebraska Press, copyright 1993.

"Distance," by Roger Angell, from the *New Yorker,* August, 1980. With permission of Roger Angell.

"Dick Groat," from *We Played the Game: 65 Players Remember Baseball's Greatest Era 1947–1964,* edited by Danny Peary (New York: Hyperion, 1994). With permission of Dick Groat.

From *October 1964,* by David Halberstam (New York: Random House, 1994).

"Redhead Cool Operator on Redbird Hot Seat," by Bob Burnes in the *Sporting News,* March 27, 1965. Courtesy of the *Sporting News.*

"Gibson Pitches Three-Hitter in 7–2 Finale," by Robert L. Burnes, in the *St. Louis-Globe Democrat,* October 13, 1967. With permission of the St. Louis Mercantile Library at UMSL.

"Tim Hails 'Vicious Desire' by Hoot," by Ed Wilks, in the *St. Louis Globe-Democrat,* October 13, 1967. With permission of the St. Louis Mercantile Library at UMSL.

"Untamed Tigers Savor Sweet, Sweet Victory," by Lowell Reidenbaugh, in the *Sporting News,* October 26, 1968. Reprinted with permission of the *Sporting News.*

"The 'Silly' Series: Heroes, Goats, Turning Points, Tears," by Bob Broeg, in the *St. Louis Post-Dispatch,* October 11, 1968. Reprinted with permission of the *St. Louis Post-Dispatch,* copyright 1968.

"Dred Scott in Spikes," in George F. Will's *Bunts* (New York: Simon & Schuster, 1999). Reprinted with permission of the *Washington Post,* copyright November, 1993.

"Cardinals Fire Schoendienst," by Bob Broeg, in the *St. Louis Post-Dispatch,* October 5, 1976. Reprinted with permission of the *St. Louis Post-Dispatch,* copyright 1976.

"Larcenous Lou Laughs Off Pressure," by Neal Russo, in the *Sporting News,* September 10, 1977. Courtesy of the *Sporting News.*

"World Champs: Cardinals Wrap It Up," by Rick Hummel, in the *St. Louis Post-Dispatch*, October 21, 1982. Reprinted with permission of the *St. Louis Post-Dispatch*, copyright 1982.

"Clutch Base Hits Came in Bunches," by Kevin Horrigan, in the *St. Louis Post-Dispatch*, October 21, 1982. Reprinted with permission of the *St. Louis Post-Dispatch*, copyright 1982.

"St. Louis' Wizard of Ozzie," by Jim Murray, in the *Los Angeles Times*, July 20, 1983. Reprinted with permission of TMS Reprints.

"Signatures," from *You're Missin' a Great Game*, by Whitey Herzog and Jonathan Pitts (New York: Simon & Schuster, 1999). By permission of Whitey Herzog.

"Twins Are Champs," by Rick Hummel, in the *St. Louis Post-Dispatch*, October 26, 1987. Reprinted with permission of the *St. Louis Post-Dispatch*, copyright 1987.

"Our Casey," in Thomas Boswell's *Cracking the Show* (New York: Doubleday, 1994). Reprinted with permission of the *Washington Post*, copyright 1990.

"The Manager," from George F. Will's *Men at Work: The Craft of Baseball* (New York: Macmillan, 1990). By permission of George F. Will.

"For Mark McGwire, It Was the Culmination of a Season-Long Quest," by Mike Eisenbath, in the *St. Louis Post-Dispatch*, September 9, 1998. Reprinted with permission of the *St. Louis Post-Dispatch*, copyright 1998.

"Over and Out," by Joe Strauss, in the *St. Louis Post-Dispatch*, October 28, 2004. Reprinted with permission of the *St. Louis Post-Dispatch*, copyright 2004.

"A Toast to Busch," by Tim O'Neil, in the *St. Louis Post-Dispatch*, October 2, 2005. Reprinted with permission of the *St. Louis Post-Dispatch*, copyright 2005.

I would like to thank several new and old friends for all their practical help and good counsel during my research and preparation of the manuscript. My deepest gratitude goes to Steve Gietschier, Director of Historical Records at the *Sporting News*, for making so many resources available to me and for his constant advice about the project. I am also grateful to Tim Wiles, Director of Research at the National Baseball Hall of Fame & Museum, for his help in providing important material and information. My thanks to Brian Finch, Assistant Curator at the St. Louis Cardinals Hall of Fame, and Erv Fischer, the Official Historian of the St. Louis Cardinals, for their generosity in providing important recommendations and contacts. I also owe a special debt of gratitude to the late Bob Broeg for his encouragement and support. I will miss his wise counsel and his wonderful stories about St. Louis baseball.

I am grateful to the editors and staff of the University of Missouri Press: to Bruce Clayton, editor of the Sports and American Culture Series for his early interest and support; to Beverley Jarrett, Director of the University of Missouri Press, for her constant encouragement and patience; and to Managing Editor Jane Lago and Editor John Brenner for their outstanding efforts in preparing the manuscript for publication.

I owe a world of gratitude to Eileen Glass. Without her remarkable skill and dedication in preparing the manuscript, I would have never finished the project. I also cherish her friendship and good cheer, especially at the times when I struggled with my frustration and self-doubt.

And, finally, I would like to express my loving gratitude to my wife, Anita. She has been the love of my life for over forty years and my companion on all the road trips to research this book. No one has ever had a more understanding audience for his baseball stories, a more helpful research assistant in gathering baseball materials, and a greater friend in sharing his passion for baseball. When I first met her in college, it was the luckiest day of my life.